A Beautiful, Cruel Country

Eva Antonia Wilbur-Cruce

A BEAUTIFUL,

The University of Arizona Press, Tucson

CRUEL COUNTRY

Wood Engravings by Michael McCurdy

THE UNIVERSITY OF ARIZONA PRESS

♾ This book is printed on acid-free, archival-quality paper.
Manufactured in the U.S.A.

05 04 03 02 01 00   9 8 7 6 5 4

Library of Congress Cataloging-in-Publication Data

Wilbur-Cruce, Eva Antonia.
  A beautiful, cruel country.

    1. Frontier and pioneer life—Arizona.   2. Arizona—
Social life and customs.   3. Indians of North America—
Arizona—Social life and customs.   4. Wilbur-Cruce,
Eva Antonia.   5. Arizona—Biography.   I. Title.
F811.W67   1987   979.1   87-10861
ISBN 0-8165-1194-2 (alkaline paper)

British Cataloguing-in-Publication Data
A catalogue record for this book is available from the British Library.

Contents

Prologue

OUR RANCHITO BASKS IN THE SUN, rather idle now, compared to the life of turmoil it lived at the turn of the century. It is still the home of a herd of horses that enjoys the creek with us. The strain of the Spanish horse—our "rock horses" that I have praised so highly in this book—still predominates.

In 1984, I decided to find better homes for these horses, a colorful remnant of the past, so that I could dedicate my time to other things.

My parents, my brother William, and my sister Mary, have all passed away. I now have my husband Marshall, my brother Henry, my sister Ruby, and a large number of nieces and nephews. Relatives visit us often when we stay at the ranch, but the greater part of the time the house sits empty.

I still spend some time there alone, though. When a cloud passes overhead, the tin roof contracts, groans, and pops, and a shower beating on the tin is a melody for me. The wind blows and groans and cries. But it also whistles and hums and sings, and I welcome it, too, as a friend of the old days. When I build a wood fire, the smell of the smoke is another of my old friends.

In my eighties now, I enjoy my aloneness as much as ever, for my isolation has always been only physical, not spiritual. I have never felt depressed or lonely when alone with the land. Something always happens that dazzles me and overwhelms me with amazement and wonder. Nevertheless, I would welcome an occasional chat with some old-timer. It would bring fresh memories of my parents' struggles and laughter, and of happier days.

I constantly thank God for the privilege I have had of having seen and ridden the open range, back in the days when the national forest was open country and not crisscrossed with barbed-wire fences and riders everywhere.

The hinterlands of the border were rugged—a turbulent sea of isolation. There were mole hills, jagged ridges, toothed mountains, buttes, mesas, washes, and gulches. There were cholla and mesquite thickets where some trees were enormous, old and gnarled. Some sported large, black fagot nests (cords of wood in their crowns) and huge clumps of mistletoe, bending down the branches of their mother trees.

Dusty burro trails wound down and across the arroyos, and not a living soul for miles. The purity of the atmosphere, the blue canopy above, the solitude, spiritual and beautiful, always made me feel the need for prayer. I threaded my way in and out of thickets, lost in thoughts only solitude of this kind can evoke. In this magnificent setting, thoughts came like dreams. Some are simple and fleeting, others worthy of holding and pondering in some more objective way. I was never in a hurry to leave that enchanted, eloquent solitude, and it plays itself out yet, as a vivid scenario in the back of my mind.

One reason I have finally written this book was to evoke that beautiful, cruel land of solitude for others in a form more accessible and permanent than it can take in my own memory. The first stimulus came several years ago when I decided to write formally what I had started so many years earlier.

My good friends, Linda Newell and Kathryn Murphy, whom I had not seen for many years, had arrived in Tucson to visit on their way to San Francisco.

Linda was the mother of two girls, Christine, who was then fourteen, and Nadine, twelve. When they found out that I still had the ranch, Linda suggested that a day there would be a wonderful outing for the girls. So, with an ice chest full of cold drinks and sandwiches, I headed south with my two young charges.

At the ranch I took them down to the creek, pointing out everything I thought of interest and telling them stories of ranch life, some amusing and some that were not so funny.

Back at the house we sat outside and I showed them old pictures that I thought would be interesting. I remember that one was of my brother William, thirteen years old, roping a bighorn. They were not at all impressed. A young boy astride a horse, with a bighorn at the end of his rope—so what? I told them of the Papago Indian tribe. They were not interested.

"Doesn't seem," said Christine, with barely concealed boredom, "that you'd have much work to do in a dead place like this."

"Back in the old days we did, though, Christine," I said. "Our little spread went clear to the Mexican border, fifteen miles south of here." I told her about bringing the horses up from the border ranch, and how the leaders would arrive here around ten in the morning, but those bringing up the rear would get here by sundown.

"Well, yes," said Nadine, "I suppose, one horse walking behind the other, it'd take them forever to get here."

"In the days of the open range, our horses ranged from New Mexico to the Mexican border," I told her grandly.

"You should have tied them, don't you think?" she asked.

"I guess we should have thought of that, Nadine." These girls were impossible!

I decided to fix lunch, eat, and start back to town early. The girls wanted jerky stew—"Indian stew," they called it—and nothing else would do.

I left them in the ramada and went to the kitchen to roast the jerky. Soon after, Nadine called me to see the beautiful "mini" bird. It was the same drab brown hummingbird that had lived in the yard so long, but I admired it for the children and told them of the beautiful multi-colored hummingbirds that used to come to our *milpita*. "We've seen them in books," said Nadine. They came back to the kitchen to watch me make the stew. Just as it was ready, there came a soft *"it, it, quit, quit,"* and then the loud call of *"los papagos."* I was so accustomed to hearing the call of quail coming to water, I had not paid attention, but both girls rushed to my side and whispered, "There is a man out there, Bonnie!"

"Don't worry," I said, "it must be one of the neighbors. Is he walking or riding?"

"We didn't see him, Bonnie, but he yelled, 'los papagos!'"

I laughed. "Oh, Nadine, that's only quail coming to water." I put my finger to my lips and tiptoed with them to the door to see the birds at the edge of the fountain. The yard teemed with quail of all sizes, and more were coming, followed by large groups of chicks. The girls were ecstatic. A large cock jumped up to the top rock and called again: *"los papagos, los papagos!"* Christine and Nadine giggled excitedly, and the quail suddenly lifted up with a whirr of wings, bringing dismayed exclamations and questions from the girls.

"You mustn't let them see you or hear you," I said. "That is the way the bighorns are too—you see them within a mile, but if they see you first, you won't see them at all."

Now the girls suddenly wanted the picture of William with the bighorn and they wanted to go down to the river again to take pictures. Luckily, we found some quail nests there that showed up well enough to be photographed. When we returned to the house this time there were some horses in the corral and the girls hurried to see them while I went on to the house to make us a cool drink. They came running, all excited, to tell me that there were some sick horses in the corral. . . . "Some are already dead, Bonnie!" I stood at the gate and counted twenty horses stretched out full-length, motionless. Christine, holding onto me, asked fearfully, "What made them die like that?"

"They're not dead, Christine. They are taking a nap."

"Horses, taking a nap, Bonnie? All of them? At the same time? Why?"

"Maybe the lion worried them last night, and they're catching up on their sleep. They knew we were here and they know we watch out for them."

"How did they know we were here?"

"They saw the truck."

This brought on questions of all kinds and they now wanted to see all the pictures of horses in action that they hadn't cared to look at in the morning. I asked them, "Why the sudden interest?"

"We didn't know it was like this, Bonnie," said Christine. "We've seen quail and horses and other animals in books, but live animals are different, aren't they? We were so lucky to see those quail and hear them! You know, if someone had told me that quail could say 'los papagos,' I never would have believed it!" It occurred to me then that my own nieces and nephews didn't appreciate the animals any more than these girls did, and that I could never get them to sit still long enough to tell them about the country life. I decided, then and there, to write them all a letter.

Back in town I told Kathryn and Linda about my idea and they said, "Sit down and write it now, before we go to California!" I did.

My friends stayed in Tucson ten days, and the day before they were to leave, I went to see them, taking with me a fifty-page letter. They found it so interesting that they suggested I write a little more and submit it to a publisher so that other children might read it too. The day they left I began writing. I wrote of many different things and writing soon became my chief pastime. I forgot about submitting anything for publication, as they had suggested, but writing for my own people was a great deal of fun, and I wrote on and on.

I wrote of the land, the animals, the rocks, the plants, of my parents and grandparents, the neighbors, the vaqueros, the Indians—of myself and my feelings. My memories of my childhood had always been sharp and clear, but as I wrote, more and more memory rushed to help me, from wherever it had been stored.

I do not think I had realized that my kind of clear, sensory memory was at all unusual until I was a young woman in my twenties. Until then I assumed that everyone remembered his or her past in great detail as I knew I did. But I have found over a lifetime that this is not so. The apparent ease with which I call up stories of words spoken, sounds heard, sights and smells of decades ago is apparently less common for most people than I supposed. I have become ever more grateful that I am endowed with this kind of recall as I have tried to record the joys and the sometimes bitter hurts of a past that exists now for me alone.

Or, perhaps, not quite for me alone. Once in a great while, a happy chance has let me see that my memories are shared, in part, by others from that long-ago time. One such chance occurred a few years ago, as I was working hard on this book.

The vaqueros I worked with are gone away or dead. I think of their names and faces and remember our experiences together so clearly, and I wonder what happened to them. I don't see them, and I don't look for them anymore.

One day, Marshall and Robert, one of my nephews, left early to spend the day at the ranch. I stayed in town to work on my writing. By sundown, I was exhausted and, pushing the typewriter away, I dressed and hurried to the market. Carrying my purchases back to the car, I was approached by an elderly man; black smudges on his face, hands, and clothing told me he had probably been working on cars.

"Dispense, Señora," he said, moving toward me. I hesitated, and he went on, "You got to be a Wilbur."

"Oh," I answered, "do you know the family? I am Eva—Bonnie."

"I am Federico Lara," said this stranger. I fell into his arms; my new white blouse suffered, but my heart sang. A whole clutch of memories came in a flash. My Grandmother Wilbur in the arms of Jesús Moraga, unshaven and dusty; my father rubbing liniment on the twisted hand of an old Indian woman (how *could* my father touch that, I had thought when I was five); and two lines of a poem I had read somewhere: "In the mud and scum of things, there always, always, something sings."

Federico spoke first: "I am stunned at such a delightful surprise. Are you in a hurry to go home?"

"Not at all, Fed. My husband and nephew are at the ranch and won't come back until sometime tomorrow."

"Follow me to my house. I want you to meet my wife, Panchita. I married a girl from Saric, you know, and we are getting ready to return to Mexico, finally, to make our home with our son in Sonora. We don't have anything here anymore. Our parents, friends—all gone or dead. We are surrounded by new people who don't understand us, and we don't understand them, Evita. Or perhaps you don't know what I mean?"

"I do know, Fed, I do know."

I followed Federico to his house where we found his Panchita standing over a stove. She didn't seem too surprised. She took both my hands and led me to the *sala*, saying warmly, "I was beginning to think I would never meet you."

We reminisced all evening of the way we used to work and the way we used to play, of the way we had agonized and the way we had laughed. And of the ways we had found to survive in that vast country of horrendous poverty, of pain, hunger, and hatred; in the vast country of illusory abundance, hidden like some precious metal in the heart of the bare rocks. And of how we had to blast it out and grind it and wash it, and how, finally, the "gold nuggets" had appeared, in the guise of hope, beauty, joy, love, and brotherhood, after which all things became more bearable.

Seeing one old friend, the past had come alive for me *outside* my own memory. Federico, too, remembered the names of all our horses, their bad habits and their good ones. "I used to tremble every time you got on Doradita. That was a mean and dangerous mare," he said.

"She was a good horse, Fed."

"There were others as good that you could have ridden. I was always sick with fear that a horse would kill one of you."

And so we continued until in a moment of quiet we heard a rooster crowing somewhere. What a gift for me! A whole long night, and a delightful breakfast, with an old, much-loved friend, at my age. I wondered again at the infinite expansion of memory—in our own minds and in what we give of them to others, in conversations, in our writing, our photographs, and our other keepsakes. That much-cherished night only deepened my determination to keep putting memories on paper as well and as fast as I could.

Ten years after the first visit of Linda, Kathryn, and Linda's two girls had prompted my "letter," Kathryn returned to Tucson. We talked about all the people we knew in Los Angeles and here, and finally came the old question:

"How about the letter you were writing, Bonnie? Did you ever go on with it?"

"Yes," I said proudly, and I brought out four two-inch-high stacks of paper, all tied up with jute. Kathryn laughed herself to tears and finally said, "Bonnie, you must have enough material there for four big books!" She took one stack of papers with her that evening, and three days later she told me she had separated some material. She suggested I write up to when the Indians left our creek country, the people, the animals, and the ranch work. It'll make an interesting book, Bonnie, but I warn you it will be a terrific job."

Not fully realizing what she meant by a "terrific job," I plunged ahead and rewrote my memories, up to the Indian exodus described in the last chapter of *A Beautiful, Cruel Country*.

I have written primarily to entertain, but also to share personal memories of that time with all who might care for them. I have made no real attempt at a formal recording of history, though I have falsified nothing that I am aware of. A certain amount of historical data that forms a necessary part of my own memories is, of course, included along with how I heard of it, what I and others thought of it, and how it affected us at the time.

But chiefly I have written of the country as I remember it at the turn of the century, and of our lives—rawhide-tough and lonely. Of the appalling racial hatred, so prevalent for so many decades—a poison with which we came in contact every day, its only antitoxins the scriptures quoted by my humble Grandfather Vilducea and the saint-like life he, but few others, lived.

Looking back, I wonder how I ever got this far with my "letter." And the answer is "one step at a time," and with the help and encouragement of my many friends, even from the time I was a child. Much help and a lot of hard work by teachers and editors I have sought out has also made A *Beautiful, Cruel Country* possible. And so, my warmest thanks to my many good friends and teachers: Leona Chipley, Kathryn Murphy, Sister Mary Antonia, Mrs. Florence Dubois, Jessie Belt, Nancy Williams, Florence Laughlin and, last but not least, I thank my great teacher and editor, Anna Norvelle. Without the help of this gracious lady, my friend, this book would not have been finished.

A Beautiful, Cruel Country

Grandfather Wilbur and His Friends

OUR HOUSE SAT AT THE FOOT OF PESQUEIRA HILL, which rises in a northwesterly direction from the banks of Arivaca Creek. The hill was named *Lomita de Pesqueira* for Don Ignacio Pesqueira, the man who had ruled the state of Sonora for twenty years as its governor.

In the days of my early childhood, the hill was smooth, cleared of brush except for one mesquite tree, under whose shade Hunga, a black female pup, and I often stopped to rest. From here I could see the Las Guijas Indian village and the Indian women going to and from the creek with *ollas* balanced on their heads. The men usually balanced *quijos* (baskets) on their own heads; and they were always stooping to add to their load the manure that they used to fire the ollas. The quijos looked like enormous inverted hats.

The rest of the lomita I always remember as being covered with a blanket of blue flax and large clumps of verbena. Above these small plants rose the dainty fairyduster with its orchid and white flowers, delicate little catkins, fresh each morning, or shimmering in the last light of the sunset. Horses, cattle, and the Indians usually stayed on the riverbanks, leaving the slope of the hill entirely to Hunga and me, and these morning and evening walks, always with Hunga for company, are some of my clearest recollections of my early life in the border country along the creek. Today, the mesquite has taken over, and the fairyduster is only a memory.

Most of the time, so that my mother would be able to keep an eye on me, I played in our patio, which was bordered by a five-foot-high wall that ran north and south just opposite the kitchen door.

Mother carried Ruby, my sister, on her left arm, and with her right hand she held the skirt of her black and white checkered dress, so that it wouldn't drag on the ground. The square-cut neck of the dress gave ample room to display her small, black onyx cross, which she wore more as a religious gesture than as an ornament. Mother was tall and slender, and her hair, done up in a pompadour, gave her more height and emphasized her bearing—serene and dignified. I can still see her in my memory, standing tall, as still as her little cross, her brown eyes scanning the distance.

Father, who was usually in the corral only a short distance away, would often call me, "Eva, get on the wall! I am going to let the cattle out." My name is Eva Antonia, and my father always called me Eva, but my mother and her family called me Toña, short for Antonia. At this warning, I would climb on a box and then crawl the rest of the way up to the top of the wall. Hunga would crouch on the ground and look up at the wall, gauging its height, and then suddenly bound up and sit beside me, as we watched the cattle run right under our feet on their way to the creek.

Father was light-complexioned and always clean-shaven, although in those days almost all Mexican vaqueros wore mustaches. One day I asked my Uncle Mike, who also wore a mustache, what made the Mejicanos want to look like that.

"Well," said Mike, "everybody doesn't like a naked face."

"Well," I countered, "all of you *Mustachinos*—my father's word for them—look like you want to scare people!"

"A mustache makes men look very dignified," said Mother.

"Ma, I hope Pa don't ever want to look like you say."

"Don't you worry," said Uncle Mike. "He never will. Your father, *Agustín—el Americano loco.*" Mother told him not to be so mean, but he just laughed at her, saying, "Ramona, you know how crazy your handsome husband is!"

What Mike meant as a criticism I was often to hear seemed to me then simply reassurance that my father would always look prettier than all the men in the big catalogue I looked at, who were also clean-shaven.

I don't remember Father's exact features clearly from those days now, but I do remember his smiling blue eyes. And so when Father came driving the cattle along the wall on his flea-bitten grey, wearing his· *chaparreras* with the dancing tassels, Hunga ran along the top of the wall barking, and I screamed with delight. The prettiest horse and the prettiest man in the whole world! That was my father!

My uncle's opinion (and that of others in the family) that Father was "el Americano loco" was not just because of his hairless face. His craziness was cried aloud many times in those days because of the way he allowed me to behave. In the family's opinion, he let me run wild and he set bad examples for me until they despaired of my ever learning "proper" behavior. And the family name! They despaired of that too. I adored my father above all else in my child's world, and I wanted nothing more than to be just like him. One day, I remember, some visitors arrived, and finding only me, one said to the other, "Oh, it's only that crazy girl of his." I shouted at them, in my best imitation of my father—I knew he didn't like them, "You son of a bitch! You're just trespassing here, don't you know that? Go away!"

So I was his crazy girl, and he was el Americano loco. Americano because of his father, my Grandfather Wilbur. It was because of Grandfather Wilbur that we lived here on our land by Arivaca Creek.

Grandfather Wilbur was a physician, a graduate of Harvard Medical College. He came to Arizona Territory sometime in the early 1860s with Charles Poston, who was a good friend of his. Within a year or two, Poston had become manager of the Cerro Colorado Mining Company, and Grandfather Wilbur had become the company physician.

Cerro Colorado had originally been called the Sonora Exploring Mining Company, and some years later it was called the Arizona Mining Company. The company mined for gold and silver, and great hopes were raised for its success because the ore assayed high. Eventually, however, Indian hostilities and mismanagement caused it to fail. I remember hearing Grandfather Vilducea, my mother's father, who used to haul freight for the mine, tell of the days of its decline: "There were pieces of machinery scattered like rosary beads, all the way between the mine and the Río Grande."

In the early days of its prosperity, General Samuel P. Heintzelman had obtained a furlough from the army and come out to superintend the mine, and the mill for processing the ore was known as Heintzelman Mill. The building which housed the mill had a pink tile roof that could be seen from any high point for miles, and five or six other houses sprawled down the hill toward Arivaca Creek. One of them was known as the White House, a large, two-story house where the machinery and other equipment were kept. The west side of the White House and all of its second floor were occupied by the mine personnel and housed their respective offices, and it was here that Colonel Poston and my Grandfather Wilbur lived.

By 1865, Grandfather R. A. Wilbur had decided to homestead on squatter's rights, to have a place of his own. You could get about 140 acres by homesteading, but you were required to build a habitable house and other improvements within a certain amount of time. My grandfather left the White House, moved down the creek about half a mile west of the mill, and began building, but lack of materials, time, and money forced him to build piecemeal, one room at a time. He planned the building as a doctor's office, hospital, drug store, and home, but finishing it within the allotted time was going to be a problem.

In the spring of 1865, the territorial governor, A. P. K. Safford, visited the White House to become acquainted with the mining needs of the Territory, and soon afterward, he and Dr. Wilbur traveled to Sonora to look at some mining properties. Don Ignacio Pesqueira, who had ruled Sonora for twenty years, was visiting the little town of Altar, where he met Governor Safford and Dr. Wilbur. Don Ignacio was known as *el Tigre de Mejico* and was widely feared as a merciless man, little better than a barbarian. He was invited to dinner with the visiting Americans one evening and surprised them both with his learning and gracious manners.

Upon learning that my grandfather was a practicing physician, Don Ignacio confided to them that he was ailing and was thinking of disbanding his men in order to come to the Territory. Governor Safford offered to help by alerting the army against the French, since Don Ignacio told him the French had sworn to capture him and his men before the winter was over.

In the fall of that same year, no longer governor of Sonora, Don Ignacio did come, with his family and the men who remained loyal to him, to Tubac, hoping to regain his health. His wife died soon after they arrived in Calabasas.

Although the officials in Tubac offered him protection, he remembered Dr. Wilbur, and taking his men with him, he went on to Arivaca to place himself under the doctor's care.

Of what was later to be the Wilbur Ranch—at one time in its history, some sixteen square miles—my grandfather had barely completed one small room and one large, mesquite corral. These he placed at the disposal of Don Ignacio, who accepted graciously and reciprocated by ordering his men to help in making adobes and bringing in rock for the foundation of another room, which the doctor needed urgently. They worked with great dispatch, and the room was soon finished. My grandfather put up shelves in it and loaded them with phials of all colors and sizes. Above the door he hung a picture of his alma mater, Harvard Medical College, and with that, although its only other furnishings were a small canvas cot and numerous suitcases containing medicines, bandages, cotton, disinfectants, liniments, and laxatives, the room became a going concern—my grandfather's office, hospital, drugstore, and home.

All that fall and winter, the original room was occupied by Don Ignacio, whose men camped along the creek. They spent most of their time on the crest of the hill that would become known by Pesqueira's name, making ammunition and keeping a constant look-out.

Forty-four years later, when I was nearly six years old, Barreplata told my mother and me about the winter of Don Ignacio Pesqueira. Barreplata was very old by then. He had lived on the ranch, coming and going, sometimes working, sometimes living off the land, ever since 1865, but that fall he had been a newcomer to the creek. His real name was Jesús Lopez, but he had early been nicknamed *Barre de Plata* (silver bar), which people had then run together and pronounced *Barre Plata* (silver sweeper). I could not remember a time I had not known him.

Barreplata sat at the kitchen table one afternoon, telling my mother and me how he and his two constant companions, Simon, a grey burro, and Fidel, a black and white pointer, had been going down the creek, looking for a good place to make a *juiqui*, a dugout where they could hole up for the winter. My mother worked about the kitchen, and he talked to both of us raising and lowering his voice.

"I noticed the Americans standing at the door of the small room, all looking at me, no doubt wondering, 'What is this *estropajo* (rag-amuffin) doing here?' They called to me, so I came right up here," he pointed to the very spot he had left Simon the burro, "and the doctor told me he was homesteading this place and he was a doctor for Cerro Colorado. I could see laid out and ready, rabbit stew, white rice, milk, and *pan vaquero* (cowboy bread), and the doctor invited me to join him and his friends for lunch.

"He introduced me to them all, and when he said that everybody knew Charles Poston, I thought surely not the Charles Poston of San Francisco! But it was he, and he put out his hand to shake mine. '¡Muy democratico, el Americano!' I thought to myself. And when he introduced me to Governor A.P.K. Safford of the Territory, I really knew they were dignitaries—but I didn't get scared, Ramoncita," he said to my mother, as he slurped his soup and paused for a moment. *"No, pero no me corte, Ramoncita."*

"Then . . .," Barreplata said to me, and stopped. He slurped up some more soup. "Th-e-en," slowly, "the doctor introduced me to the Mejicano, who had been eyeing me like the hawk. 'Don Ignacio Pesqueira, this is our new friend, Jesús Lopez.'

"*¡Ay, Madre de Dios!* When I heard 'Pesqueira,' my hair stood up on end, but still, I thought maybe, just maybe, it is some other Pesqueira. He shook hands and asked me, 'Are you from Mexico?' 'No, Señor,' I said, 'I am from California. Around San Juan Capistrano, I come from there.' I was shaking so bad, but I didn't let on."

"Why were you so afraid?" asked my mother. "Had you known him before somewhere?"

"No, no, Ramoncita, but I had heard of some of the people he had executed. Everyone knew he was a merciless, cruel man. I backed up to the door. I didn't want anything to do with this *sangrino*, and I was ready to leave.

"But the doctor handed me a plate of food and pushed a bench toward me. 'Sit down and eat!' he told me. But I ate standing up, and I pretended to be nervous because I had seen men camping down the river.

"'Oh, those are only *Pesqueiristas*,' said Don Ignacio. 'Don't worry about them.'

"'*¡Ay, Madre, esta es la fiera!*' I thought to myself, and if I know what's good for me, I'd better get going! I finished my food where I stood, I thanked them, and tried not to run as I left. But *el Mejicano diablo* followed me down the slope, slowly, and my knees were knocking together. He caught up.

"'Are you a good carpenter?' he asked me. I told him I was not, but I could nail boards together. He asked me to do a little work for him. He said, 'I want to make a *caballete* (easel), and I would like for you to go to the mill and get the lumber for me. You know, I can't let the señores furnish me with the lumber . . . and then have to bring it to me as well. But I am very ill, and the doctor doesn't want me to do any work.'

"I noticed then that he did look shakey and pale, and I told him I would bring the lumber. I did it the next day, and Cruz Cabo got here at the same time I did. He used to help the doctor with the chores around here. I cornered him in the corral, away from everybody, and asked him about this 'Don Ignacio.'"

"'*Si, seguro*', he told me, '*es Pesqueira, el Tigre de Mejico*. But don't be afraid of him, he is a good man. And besides, *está malo*—he is very sick.'

"What does he want to make a caballete for?"

"'To paint,' said Cruz. '*Es muy buen pintor.* Come, I'll show you.'

"He dragged me to Don Ignacio, who led the way to his room. Remember there was a layer of dirt on the thatched roof, and the gusts of wind kept blowing it down on anyone who came near the house. The only opening to Don Ignacio's room was a large square board place on the back, and as we came to it, Cruz picked up and moved the door, which was made of four two-by-fours with a cowhide nailed across. I stood behind them and laughed openly. I could not help it, Ramoncita. That thing looked so funny, and I had never seen a door like that before."

This tickled my mother and me, and we laughed too. Barreplata went on: "Don Ignacio was good-natured about it, but was I surprised when we walked inside! That ugly mud room was really nice! The wall was stuccoed and whitewashed, and the window shutters opened flat on top of the wall, letting the sunlight in. It had a fine ceiling made of hand-hewn beams and of *jarilla* (bamboo), evenly packed on top of them. In one corner was the saddle of Don Ignacio, and in the other, an iron bed, a high table, and a bench. That was all the furniture. But the wall! On the wall, Ramoncita, was a large painting of San Martin Caballero, on a white horse! He is my patron saint! I was stunned. The last thing I expected to see here was my patron saint. But there it was! The white horse seemed to be coming out of the white wall, and there was San Martin looking alive and warm. Just like the one my mother had in our home. It was as if San Martin had come to my rescue in this foreign place, and poured out a shower of memories—my mother, the rolling hills along the coast, the mission, the swallows flying in and out!

"Right then and there, I changed all my thoughts of Don Ignacio." Barreplata took out his blue handkerchief and blew his nose. "I thought, if he can make a thing like that, he can't be so fierce. No wonder the Americans like him. Yes, if he can make a picture come alive and speak and make you feel like a human being, then Don Ignacio is for me.

"On the way up to the mill, Cruz told me that Don Ignacio was well-educated, that he had been educated in France and in Spain. I was very surprised. I had thought, and many who did not know him thought, that he was just a bandit from the barrancas of Mexico. After that, I found he was warm and friendly, and we used to talk a lot. But once he made the caballete, he spent most of his time—many, many hours—painting. And, funny thing, Ramoncita, he was very *contra el clero* (anticlerical), and yet that man painted all saints. Nothing but saints! Hardly ever did he paint anything else.

"In the spring, Don Ignacio went back to Mexico. Charles Poston went to Phoenix, and Governor Safford didn't come back to the ranch again. But the doctor stayed here. Later he built this very house. He got married and became the Indian agent. You think, Ramoncita, there are lots of Indians here now? You should have seen them then! They came to the creek by the hundreds. There were Indian villages in every thicket. They used to sit against the wall there, waiting for the doctor." Barreplata pointed to the wall with his chin.

"I wonder what he built that big wall for. Did he ever tell you?" my mother asked. She had been wiping a large, carnival-glass bowl for a long time now, and I was getting bored and wanted to go outside.

"If he ever told me, I don't remember," answered the old man as he looked off toward the bowl she held, as though it might hold his memories. The colors of the carnival-glass gleamed, and the sharp cuts in the glass sparkled.

"Ma," I interrupted, "what are you doing that for?"

"Why not?" she answered. "This is the only nice dish I have. Why shouldn't I shine it?"

I left her shining the bowl and Barreplata talking about the Indians of long ago, and I went out to play on the wall. I climbed up and lay on my stomach, and wormed my way across to the end of the wall where the adobes had fallen, leaving a "stairway" on which I went up and down as I pleased. Hunga and I and my white angora goats spent whole days running up and down the crumbling wall that Grandfather Wilbur had built for some unknown reason. Unknown to my mother and Barreplata, maybe, but I knew why. He had built it so I could play on it. The kids would stay clean and white, but the dirt stuck to me until I looked grey and my eyelashes threatened to close up on me.

"It is getting late, Chiquitita, and I am going," called Barreplata from the kitchen doorway. He shook his head as he looked at me.

"Poor Dr. Wilbur, what would he think if he saw his granddaughter looking like a wild Apache and stinking like dirt?" Barreplata always talked like that—as if forty years ago were only yesterday. Nobody minded. He had been around forever, and he was like one of the family. He picked me up and held me with one arm and with the other picked up a dishwiper that was laid across the corner of the table. There, underneath it, was Mother's sparkling bowl, full of plump black figs.

"Ay, Tata," I cried happily, "why didn't you tell me you had brought them?"

"I wanted to surprise you, Chiquitita." He put me down, said his *hasta luegos,* and called Bull and Tobocito. His pointer, Fidel, who had been his companion when he came to our land so long ago, had long since died, but he always had dogs, and a burro named Simon for company. He mounted Simon now and left, followed by his two dogs. They went along the trail by the riverbank. "Poor old man," said Mother. "He is so lonely." Little puffs of dirt rose up as the burro walked slowly away. Barreplata waved to me just before they disappeared around the mesquite bend.

The Man with the Bible

BESIDES MY MOTHER, FATHER, MY BABY SISTER RUBY, me, and Barreplata, who oversaw the goat herd, milking them, feeding the motherless kids, and shearing the herd in early summer every year, there were many other members of our family living on the Wilbur Ranch when I was small.

My mother's father, Don Francisco Vilducea, had pensive blue eyes and a massive white beard. He was stooped and walked as though he was pushing against the wind, his Bible in one hand and his hoe in the other. Everybody said he was a God-fearing man, and they called him "the man with the Bible," yet no one could understand why he *had* a Bible—a Protestant Bible, the forbidden book of scriptures. Neither did any of them know why it was forbidden, or by whom, but it was forbidden, and Don Francisco Vilducea had that forbidden book. Some called him a hypocrite, but he ignored them all and went his way. He must have been religious, for he had snatched my mother, his daughter, back from my father after he had married her in 1901. They had been married at the Wilbur Ranch by Charles Poston, *El Cadi*, which meant one with the authority of a priest to perform the rites of marriage and other sacraments. But my Grandfather Vilducea soon found that, when the Jesuits had been run out of Tubac, Poston's authority had been lifted—before the marriage. He came and took his daughter and told my father that if he wanted her back, he must arrange to do it properly. My father waited until the spring, when he took my mother to Saric in Mexico. There, at the Dolores Mission, they were married again. Even that did not complete the process. My

parents had more trouble documenting their marriage than anyone
else I have ever heard of. But that came later.

My Grandmother Vilducea, Margarita, was a dark, petite, and high-
spirited woman who worked day and night and kept everyone on pins
and needles with her constant questions and demands.

My Uncle Nieves, the oldest of their six children, was tall and
slender, with very grey temples. He was a hard-working, mild, and
sober man who often worked away from home.

My Uncle Luis, their second son, was light-complexioned with
hazel eyes. He, too, appeared to be hard-working and able, but Uncle
Nieves often said that Luis was really lazy, and lived by his wits.

Uncle Miguel (Mike) was dark, stout, and quick with a quip. He
was truly a hard worker—a workaholic, as they call them now, but he
kept something of the spirit of a boy, too.

My Uncle José, or Joe, who could have been Luis's twin in appearance, had married. His wife had died in childbirth, leaving a baby boy
called José, or Che, in the care of her sister-in-law, my Aunt Rita. Aunt
Rita was a saintly woman who had once survived a siege of smallpox.
Her face was badly pockmarked, and this had obviously affected her
life until she absolutely buried herself in work, wherever she might
find it. No one ever *asked* Aunt Rita to work, but she was always on
the job. No one paid her, but sometimes one of her brothers would
bring her a pair of shoes. She was always pathetically grateful, and if
the shoes were too big, she would stuff paper in the toes. If they were
too small, she stretched them in a shoe-lathe. But she never complained. My mother sometimes bought her a few yards of calico, and
Aunt Rita would make herself a dress in the style of the "sack," buttons
down the front, high collar, and long sleeves. This, she said, was easy
to wash, easy to iron, and it wore well. Uncle Joe had married again,
and Aunt Rita had been allowed to keep his son, Che, and she did all
her work with him at her side. She never possessed a dollar of her own;
if she had one, as she did once in a while, she was keeping it for someone else. She worked from sunup to sundown so that she and Che
would feel she had earned something to eat and a place to call home.

Che was three or four years older than I, but he was a very timid
child. We played together sometimes, but as soon as some of the Indian
children came to play with me, he would be frightened and go in
search of Aunt Rita.

Che and I spent many hours with stacks of brown-bag paper that Mother had cut into small squares for me to write on. One day we sat trying to copy letters from a newspaper, while María Nieves stood laughing at us. When Uncle Mike had been sick, it was María Nieves who had searched the countryside for those medicinal herbs that Grandmother Vilducea didn't have in her garden. She had made the *remedios* and had stayed up nights with him, alongside my grandmother, until Mike got well. This had made María a member of my grandmother's family and she lived between both houses, ours and my grandparents'. She spent whole days in the *zaguán,* or central courtyard, and so on this day, she sat there watching us fold and unfold papers.

"You crazy like your father, Toña?" asked María.

"What makes you think that Pa is crazy, María?" I asked her.

"He is crazy—why he go to Arivaca, bring papers, then put in the stove? Tomorrow again, he go for horse, saddle, go to Arivaca, bring more papers, put in stove."

"That's the mail, María," Che told her.

"Mail! What mail? Papers, he brings. He no look, he no see. He put in stove. Tomorrow, he go for poor horse again, saddle, go to Arivaca, bring papers, put in stove. Why he no use wood? He loco!"

María Nieves obviously could not understand the idea of "junk mail." Che and I were young, but somehow we did understand it, so we ignored María and her one more reason for finding my father loco. Che and I went on tracing brands and letters. He looked up and said to me, "Your father don't like me, Toña, because I don't have a brand, but someday I will." I knew exactly what Che meant, even as young as I was.

In those days, cattle were the main industry of the West. Everyone had cattle, or a horse, a burro, or some other kind of animal that had to be identified. A brand was the only legal means of identification, and a registered brand was a must. If one did not have a brand, one did not exist. Families chose a name and a brand at the same time, long before the arrival of their first-born. If it was a boy, his name might be Charles McVey and his brand, CM, of course. Or a girl, her name would be, let's say, Vivian McVey and VM on an animal's hip would tell everyone—"Know all men by these presents. . . ." A brand was legal ownership.

And so, when I was born, Father, too, had had the $\frac{E}{W}$ registered in my name. I had been his first-born and my brand was the brand of our ranch, the brand which was on the ribs of all our cattle and on the thigh of each one of our horses.

A brand spoke loud and clear. When an animal crossed your path and flashed its brand before you, it was either comforting or annoying. If the brand belonged to someone you knew was antagonistic to your family, it sent you into turmoil; if it belonged to a friend, you would relax and feel secure again, safe in your knowledge of its owner's good will toward you and yours. A brand was a messenger, a reminder in passing. It was the owner himself. And so children knew the brand of every animal that crossed their paths. They were brand-conscious. Reading was not important to them yet, but brand-reading was a must.

But Che's mother had died, and Che had been given to Aunt Rita. One day I had heard my grandfather talking to our closest neighbor, Miguel Egurrola, whom we called Terrenate. A hard working ranchero whose ranch adjoined our own, he often visited my grandfather, always standing under some massive shade trees along the riverbanks. I overheard my grandfather say, "The pity is not that Che is an orphan. The sad thing is that he does not own a brand."

"You're right, Francisco, you're right!" cried Terrenate to my grandfather. "Get the boy a brand. José knew that he should have registered a brand for the boy, but he never did. A brand is *necessary*, Francisco! It is like the baptismal water. Without it, you are an errant."

"That's exactly what is the matter with poor Toña, Miguel," said Grandfather. "Five years old, and running up and down the creek like a wild Indian on that poor horse—and Agustín can't see it, Miguel. The man is a heretic!"

"She needs the baptismal water, Francisco. She does. And Che needs to know that he owns a brand."

So Che looked with longing at the brands all around us, for the *zaguán* walls were decorated with brands drawn in charcoal. I was sorry for him, but happy that I had a brand.

The *zaguán* (large passageway) divided our house. On the west side were a large storage room, the slaughter house, the dairy house, and the tackroom. Three other rooms in this west part were set apart—detached from the main house. On the east side were our living quarters. There were three bedrooms, but one my father had made into a kind of office. Here he kept Grandfather Wilbur's rolltop desk. Here also were the large picture of Grandfather Wilbur's alma mater, Harvard Medical College, a western saddle, a thirty-thirty rifle, Grandfather Wilbur's portrait, and another picture, a large print labeled "The Return of the Grand Army 1814." But the most important furnishing was a large, camelback trunk that contained what Mother called "very important papers."

One day when my mother and father went away for the day, Ruby and I decided to open the trunk and see just what important papers looked like. We took the papers out of large envelopes so we could see them, but they looked to us just as unimportant as the ones we burned in the stove every day. We scattered them on the floor and turned our attention to something else. There was a blue quill with a writing pen at one end, so we opened a bottle of ink and tried it on the important papers. It wasn't long before we had spilled the ink. We wiped it up with Mother's kimono.

Next, we found in the trunk a square can that looked like the empty syrup cans in the milkhouse. We shook it and heard the liquid splash inside—it had to be syrup. We tried to open the tightly sealed can. For this task we brought the forceps from Father's workbench, and while Ruby held the can, I gave it a twist and a pull with the forceps. It opened! Ruby fell backwards, dropped the can, and a black liquid oozed out filling the house with the familiar smell of creosote. It ran over the papers, over the quill, and over my mother's blouse, her shoes, and everything else we had scattered on the floor. Frightened now, we took the papers out and put them in the sun to dry. They crinkled up as they dried, and when we tried to pick them up to take them back inside, they simply disintegrated.

About this time, Aunt Rita discovered us, and she almost fainted when she saw the horrible mess we had created. The creosote had run all over the floor, and as we had moved about the room, we had stepped in it and then carried it all over the house in our trips back and forth with the papers. Rita closed the door and took us to her house to wash our feet, which were beginning to burn with the acid of the creosote.

When my parents came back, they took turns punishing us—they were so angry. They forbade us ever to mention to anyone that these papers had been destroyed, and in later years I often overheard them talking about the loss of the papers. Ruby and I did not know for many years that we had destroyed another kind of "brand," for among the papers had been the marriage certificate from Dolores Mission in Saric. Many people, some just spiteful, some greedy, could try to make trouble for a family with land. Some years later, my father and mother had to prove their marriage again—and years after that, still again. At one time my father had to pay seven years of back taxes because he could not produce his earlier tax receipts which had been destroyed by the creosote.

My grandparents' house was across the creek, just a stone's throw from ours. Their house consisted of three large rooms, the kitchen, the *sala* (living room), and my grandparents' bedroom.

The kitchen had a dirt floor, a wood stove, and a large window which was loaded with geraniums and cans that held mint, oregano, and winter onions. A long table sat in the middle of the room with wooden boxes pushed under it to be pulled out and used as seats.

The floor of the *sala* was carpeted with goat pelts and held a couch which made up into a bed for Rita and Che who used the *sala* as a bedroom at night.

The main feature of my grandparents' bedroom was the many prints of *santos* that covered all the walls. Sometimes a *santero*, a peddler of religious articles, would come by the ranch, and my Grandmother Vilducea would always buy the image of some saint from him that she did not yet have in her sacred collection. Room on the wall would somehow be made for it, usually by crowding the other images.

Under the window on the south side of their house was my grand-mother's *jardín de savila*. The *savila* (aloe) was the favorite healing herb. My grandmother called it the *protectora*. The furniture one had in the house was much less important to us in those days than the medicinal herbs that one grew in one's garden and the knowledge to use these effectively, for there were no doctors within a reasonable distance.

And so my grandmother took great care of her garden of medicinal herbs and plants. The leaves of the *savila* were cut, peeled, and applied to cuts, burns, or painful rheumatic joints. Then there was the true panacea of the Vilducea family garden—garlic. Garlic was used for everything. We chopped clubs of garlic into tiny little pieces and drank them down with a glass of warm water, both to thin the blood and to enrich the blood. We used it as a disinfectant for insect bites and stings. My mother used it often for scorpion stings. Grandfather chop-ped whole heads of garlic and put them in a jar of pure alcohol. He placed the jar in the sun until it took on an amber color. Then he divided the contents between two jars. One he used as an ingestive for internal troubles; the other as a liniment for massaging his joints and muscles. Grandfather never complained of muscular pains.

I can still remember my grandfather hurriedly cutting small branches or twigs from the *romero* (rosemary) plants, crushing them and dropping them into boiling water. He would cook them and let them simmer for awhile. Then he would seat whoever was having an asthmatic attack at the table and put a towel over his head until my grandmother could bring the steaming dish of romero tea and place it under the patient's nose so that he could breathe and inhale the steam. As the patient laboriously inhaled and exhaled, Grandfather and Grandmother would pound his back. I can still hear my grandfather saying to her, "Rhythm, Margarita, rhythm. Rhythm is important." I liked hearing the rhythmic, clapping sound of their hands as they moved them back and forth over the back of the asthmatic, who was gasping for breath. Then there would be the joyful announcement: "He is breathing! He is over the attack!" Grandmother would run and kneel before the picture of the Holy Trinity and thank the Lord for helping them to help the patient.

Grandmother's garden also boasted a big jojoba. Jojobas didn't usually grow at this altitude, so Grandmother took special care of hers, which was under the eaves on the north side of the house. It spent the winter under a tent of old burlap sacks and old quilts, but during the summer rains, it was always luscious and beautiful. We used the jojoba nuts to make poultices, and many times my mother would also use them to make "coffee." She didn't like the brew they made, but she would make it in desperation, when real coffee was not available.

My uncles had made a large bunk house that faced the kitchen of my grandparents' house, and they built their ramada so that it joined my grandparents' ramada. This made what we called a *ramadon*, a very spacious ramada with entrances at both ends, north and south. Here, my grandmother had more savila plants in cans hanging from the beams. These particular savila plants were supposed to keep the evil spirits away, and they may have done that, but they also kept the insects away from the other plants growing in the ramadon. From the beams on the north side of the ramadon hung a *filtro*, a specially made clay vessel, through which the water seeped and fell, one drop at a time, into an olla in which my grandmother had dropped a cupful of diced savila as a purifier. This was the drinking water for the day.

On the right-hand side of his own door to the ramadon, Grandfather had nailed a large cardboard on which he had copied some doggerel he had once seen on the main door of the great hacienda of Señor Calderon, in Mexico. Grandfather called it a *poesía,* and when some friend tried to enlighten him, he would become angry and say that it *was* a poesía, so great that one could gain 200 indulgences by reciting it—and that was something no poet would sneer at. So when he returned from a hard day's work in his truck garden, he would stand, wiping the sweat off his face, and read aloud these words written before him on his door:

> ¿Quién llena esta casa de luz? Jesús.
> ¿Quién la llena de alegría? María.
> ¿Quién la abraza en la fe? José.
> Luengo bien claro se ve
> Que siempre habra contrición,
> Tieniendo en el corazón,
> A Jesús, María, y José.

> (Who fills this house with light? Jesus.
> Who fills it with happiness? Mary.
> Who embraces it in faith? Joseph.
> Then we clearly see that there will
>   always be contrition,
> Having Jesus, Mary, and Joseph in our hearts.)

Indian Country

E̲L CERRO SITS DIRECTLY SOUTH OF OUR HOUSE. Some called it El
Wilbeño, the Wilburian, after my grandfather, who had home-
steaded here and had been so dominant a personality in his time. Many
called it El Papago, because our Arivaca Valley teemed with Indians,
some who lived there more or less permanently, and hordes of others
who came and went like ants. We called it El Cerro, as if it were the
only mountain in the world.

El Cerro is not a giant mountain, but it is a rugged one, and it dominated our thoughts in many ways, just as it dominated our landscape.
For one thing, its austerity often incited remarks from strangers who
were seeing it for the first time: "I'd sure hate to get lost up *that* damned
mountain!" or "That one would really be a devil of a mountain to
climb!" I remember always feeling angry at such remarks, as though
our El Cerro had been somehow desecrated by such ignorant and profane talk; and I think it angered the other members of my family, too,
for I remember one day hearing my Uncle Mike talking to a would-be
prospector, who was complaining of the rough time he had had in getting down the mountain. "It's not El Cerro," said Uncle Mike, dis-
gustedly. "It's you. You are a tenderfoot."

El Cerro was the landmark of our Indian country region. I often
heard people telling my father about the difficulty they had encountered
in finding their way home: "I saw El Wilbeño, Agustín, and I knew I
was getting home," or "I could hardly see El Cerro through the haze
of the blizzard, but I just pushed ahead toward it." And once I heard
a man telling Father, "I rubbed my eyes, Agustín, until I could make

out El Papago; then I made myself comfortable under the brush and went to sleep." Even then, as young as I was, I knew that this traveler had seen the mountain through a haze of drink, rather than the haze of a blizzard—but it was plain that El Cerro was a guidepost for all wayfarers in our region.

Our valley was littered with small ranchitos. Anyone was entitled to homestead a parcel of 140 acres, and nearly everyone did. The rancheros rode the range every day, seeing to their cattle. We saw them often along the creek and on the nearby hills, but sometimes they also had to ride far away from the home range, and El Cerro guided them back to their families, who stayed at home to do the unbelievable volume of work that needed to be done on a small ranch in those days.

The families of the rancheros stayed home, but the Indians, men and women together, were constantly on the move. Despite the flow of ranchers to the valley at the turn of the century, the Indian population predominated. The Indians milled in and out of our valley, occupied in traveling and newsbringing, in their "industrial" or "factory" activities, and in other, impenetrable "Indian," contemplative things. And in one more activity: they fought their constant battle against starvation.

The Indians who moved slowly, almost aimlessly, were our creek-dwellers. Others, large groups, came footing it up the creek in a businesslike manner, and these were only passing through. They were our travelers, or newsbringers. The people who were not accustomed to Indian ways could seldom tell the difference, however, for nothing the Parientes did made any sense to them. The Indians did not like to be called "Papagos," a name that had been foisted on them by the "Europeans" (Americans, Mexicans and others who had trickled into Indian country), and therefore they never used the name, calling themselves and all other Indians, instead, Parientes, a word which meant "kinsmen."

Our means of transportation then were slow and cumbersome. People who were settled, with work to do, were not, as now, constantly on the go. Trips were made only when absolute necessity called for them. But the Parientes, or most of them, were not "settled." Their centuries-old way of life had been disrupted gradually as European descendants settled the Southwest; most of them owned no land and had no "trades" or ways of making a living that were recognized by the newcomers to their region. So they traveled constantly, in search of a bare sustenance. When desert fruit was ripe in one place or another, they went to pick it. When news came of work they could do, they went away to do it. When possibilities of trade were heard of, they loaded their wares and went away. The houses of the rancheros were always surrounded by Indians, coming and going in search of mere existence. They would disappear suddenly, with no word of where or why they were going, and would be gone for months, or even years at a time. They would stay with other Parientes, working, trading, or traveling as they could, sometimes suddenly reappearing with news from the places where they had been. We had no telephones, radios, or television, as we do today. Letters and newspapers were slow to reach us. So when the Indians came with their news, we welcomed them and listened eagerly to their stories of the people they had seen and the places they had been.

One day, an Indian woman who had been gone for a long time approached the kitchen door, slowly, as the Indians always did, and began, "Comadre, Gondina no come back." She extended her arm to the east and went on. "New Mexico Lakes Apache killed Gondina." The news saddened us. Gondina had been a pesky old Mexican man who came up every year from Mexico, early in the spring, just ahead of the swallows, so that we had called him "Golondrina," which the Indians had shortened, making it easier to say. We never had seen Golondrina going back to Mexico, but he must have, for each following spring, he came again from the south, just before the swallows arrived from the same direction. The Indians all knew that he had always stopped at our house to rest and eat before hitting the trail north, so the Indian woman was eager to break the news of his death to us.

But she had been to many other places too, since we had last seen her. "Comadre," she went on, "I come from Yuma, from Finacas (their name for Phoenix), from Tucson—me and the other Parientes, and all places we hear, Chale Poston, he no here, he gono." Pointing west, she said, "Gono across sea, far away. Pobrecito! Maybe he no come back. Queen chop head off, maybe!"

Many isolated people in the Southwest believed that Queen Eliza-beth I was still on the throne of England. The Queen was the only European monarch of whom they had heard, in tales passed down to them through their families, so that, in their minds, if anyone were to be beheaded, it would be done by this Queen Elizabeth. To them, for Charles Poston, or anyone else actually known to them, to go across the sea to the lands where people's heads were chopped off was truly awesome news.

But the Indian news network had this particular item very mixed up, or six years out of date, or both. I had heard Grandfather Vilducea, many times, telling of a day late in September, two years before I had been born. In the fall of 1902, Azul, a Pima Indian from Florence, had arrived at the ranch, sent by a friend of Grandfather's to bring a message. Very weary, he had come immediately to stand before Grandfather, saying: "Francisco, *murió nuestro amigo, El Cadi.*" Grandfather Vilducea had been unable to speak for quite awhile, he had been so shocked. Then he asked, "When, Azul?" and Azul had raised three crooked fingers in answer: "San Juán, three months ago." On San Juán's Day, June 24, the day when, according to all who lived in our valley, the first big rain of the season came each year, Charles Poston, El Cadi, had died. Azul had walked all the way to bring Grandfather the message, and it had taken him the entire three months.

Now, however, we all looked at one another—and as quickly looked away. No one wanted to shut off the flow of news from the Indian woman, so we did not enlighten her just yet about Charles Poston's fate so many years ago. She continued to tell us of the people she had seen. My grandmother's brother, Don Ramón Lopez, was now living in Yuma, she reported; Grandmother was so excited to hear this that she jumped up and threw her arms around the visitor. "And did you *talk* to Ramón, Comadre?" she cried.

"I talk to him. And *el me dice a Magarita dice* (he tells me to tell Margarita) he will see her." Such news called for food, or even a drink of tesguin, in celebration. My grandparents were always delighted to share their beans and corn tortillas with such travelers, who broke our long, isolated months of boredom, bringing news we had no other way of receiving. We listened avidly to the Indian wanderers when they came, asking questions and more questions.

El Cerro loomed like the cone of a teeming anthill—the Indians always coming and going, in-out and around the Arivaca Valley. Clouds of smoke rose above the hill slopes—Indians were firing their ollas. Pottery was a big business. Long lines of ollas of all sizes circled the slopes where they had been made in this "outdoor" industry, and the mounds of manure and claysoil and piles of the small smooth stones used for polishing the ollas were close at hand.

The Indians made baskets as well as pottery and also spent much time dyeing the bleached cloth from flour sacks. They seemed to prefer the bright yellows and browns, perhaps because these dyes were the easiest to extract from the roots and sticks of barberry and from walnut hulls.

Groups of fifteen or twenty women often hurried up-country to gather the dye-plants, or to gather yucca leaves to make baskets, and bear grass to make *petates*, sleeping pads. While they combed the countryside for these materials, they kept their eyes open for prayer sticks, which they gathered as they moved along. They would tie these up in small bundles with yucca fiber or strands of horsehair and put them away for future use.

The Indian children who came to play with me taught me which branches made the best prayer sticks. All were cut into pieces about ten or twelve inches long, but there were a few very special branches that were much more powerful than the usual prayer sticks—they sent more powerful prayers. According to Wahyanita, an Indian girl older than I, not even my father's rifle had the great power carried by the good prayer sticks.

Wahyanita was stout, with a round face, and her hair, cut in a straight line above her eyebrows, made her head appear even more round. Her darting black eyes set her apart from the other Indian children, whose eyes were always dull and fixed on some distant prospect. It was said that Wahyanita was the daughter of an Apache—certainly she was different. In the years when she was my frequent companion, she taught me most of what I know about Indian beliefs. She showed me how to look for prayer sticks and how to pick out the sticks that had the most power. She told me all about the Indian creator-god, I'itoi, who will come again some day, the Indians believe, from his dwelling-place on the Baboquivari, the great mountain to the west of us. Wahyanita told me of the salt caravans the Indian boys made in the spring, and of how they had to fast for many days, running up and down the mountains, and throwing prayer sticks high up on the slopes and into the canyons.

Strangers to our Indian country did not understand the Indian attitude toward religion and saw many of their activities as senseless. Most of the Papago tribe had been converted to Catholicism. They spoke reverently of the God at the Mission and of the miraculous Saint Francis Xavier; but they clung to their own religion as well, simply adding the Christian theology.

One common sight of the time was of an Indian standing motionless for long hours, looking off into the distance, seemingly at nothing. An "Americano" who said he was looking for a little town of Arivaca came to our door one day. He told my Grandfather Vilducea that he had slept under the nearby trees, and Grandfather fixed him a quick lunch which he served the man outside the house. The man ate slowly, keeping his eyes on an Indian who had been standing on the crest of the Lomita since early morning, staring off toward the Baboquivari peak. The American turned to me and asked, "What is that Injun doing up there, girl?"

"Standing," I told him.

"Why?"

"Because 'him' wants to."

"Why does he want to?"

I told him that only an Indian could give him his own reason, and he put down his dishes and went up the hill to ask this one what he was doing. While he was gone, Grandfather scolded me for staying so close to the stranger. "Can't you see that he is eaten up with the white plague? It is a very contagious disease! When are you going to learn, *zonza?*" And he hurriedly picked up the dishes the man had used, broke them into small pieces, and rushed away to bury them.

When the man got back, he stood, emaciated and weak, in front of Grandfather and gasped out questions between his coughing spasms. He was speaking English and, given the language difference and the racking cough, Grandfather could not understand him and sent for my mother to interpret. When he finally understood that the stranger had been able to get no answer from either me or the Indian about his reason for standing silently on the hill for so many hours, Grandfather smiled and said, "Contemplation, Brother, contemplation!"

The stranger who had sought food and enlightenment from him angrily put his face right next to Grandfather's, saying, "Don't call *me* Brother! I'm not your brother! I'm not a Mexican and I'm not an Indian. I'm a *white* man!" Grandfather calmly picked up the sick man's hand and held it, looking at the two of them together. His own was much lighter. "In fact, you're a very *dark* man," he said, letting go of the other's hand.

When the man had gone, muttering threats to come back when he was well enough to fight, Grandfather sadly said to me, "That man will never understand contemplation!"

My mother and I had witnessed another, seemingly incomprehensi-

ble Indian "watch." An Indian woman had stood on the very edge of
the creek and watched the flood go by. She had not moved for many
hours, when Mother finally went to her and asked why she had stood
there so long. The woman pointed across the ditch. "Water take soil.
Tomorrow, more flood take more soil. I no like." She stood a moment
longer, then picked up a large, rusty ladle she had brought with her
and led Mother to the opposite side of the creek. She stooped down
and began to dig, quickly uncovering the bleached bones of a baby,
buried only two feet beneath the surface.

"My baby die. I sick. I no take to hill. I will take now. I no want
flood to take." I can still see her in my mind, walking away toward
the hill, holding the skeleton to her breast.

Many such incidents had taught us to respect the Indians' habit of
standing in silence for hours. Even such "contemplation" as the "white
man" had witnessed had a good reason behind it. Our Indian friends
lived on the edge of famine and often, as conditions worsened for
them, they stood looking toward the Baboquivari, seeking help or an
answer to their plight from the god, I'itoi.

Hordes of Indians constantly combed the hills in search of food.
In the spring, they hunted for cholla buds and the tender pads of
nopales. Enormous Santa Rita prickly pear plants grew on the edges
of canyons, their beautiful purple pads loaded with *tunas*. When these
ripened, they dropped on the white sand below, making easy picking.
The Indians could time to the hour when they were going to fall, and
they gathered them before the birds or squirrels could get to them.
They set snares, too, and caught quail, rabbits, skunks, or whatever
other unlucky animal fell into their traps.

My father told us of taking a friend up El Cerro one day, and of
meeting a group of Indians who were dislodging rocks and digging
away on the hard, rock-packed surface, their faces glistening with
sweat. They went on digging with their blunt tools, clawing the soil
out of the way with their broken nails, until finally, after a terrific
struggle, they brought out a carrot-like root—a *saya*.

"Those Indians are insane, Agustín!" said my father's friend, in
incredulous tones. "They have to be crazy to work like that for a little
root! What is that for, Agustín? Is it some sort of narcotic?"

"That," my father had told him, "is called eking out an existence
from bare rocks. More than we could do. The food supply is very
scarce, and they have to keep body and soul together."

It took newcomers to our desert some time to understand the Indians' plight in times of want. Even times of plenty left many hungry. They often traded and sold the sparse food supply they had gathered, and we learned to eat many things through this trade. Our house was always surrounded by Indians, selling their ollas and baskets. They brought us jojoba beans and bulky sacks of creosote twigs from which we brewed the strong tea called *hediondi,* or *governadora.* And always, they brought the flour and the bread made from mesquite beans. We liked this bread because it kept for a long time. These things were staples in our food supply. But I also remember being taught by an Indian to eat a dish that I have never had since.

One of the Indians who came to our house almost every day was an old man we called our "simple savage" because he was a truly primitive Indian and seemed happy to remain so. His name was José-José, and he always wore only a loin cloth and *quijo.* He went barefooted, picking up the cow chips and putting them in the *quijo* where he stored them to use for fuel.

One day, José-José appeared at Mother's door, accompanied by an Indian we did not know—his pariente, he told Mother. The stranger wanted a fresh goat hide that had been stretched and nailed to a board that was leaning against the barn. When Mother told them they could have the hide, they took it off the board, then immediately nailed it back, wool-side up, and the stranger began to scrape off the wool.

José-José, who was lazy and inclined to be sulky, left his kinsman working and came to stand in the corner of the wall. He looked toward the kitchen. This meant he was hungry; experience had taught us that he would not leave the spot until he had been fed. He seldom spoke, but today he was more talkative than usual, telling Mother that the Indians in his village were all very hungry.

Mother took the hint. She placed two tortillas on the stove, sprinkled them with crumbs of cheese, and topped each with a second tortilla. "Go get your pariente, José-José," she called to him. When the two Indians had returned from the corral, Mother handed them the tortilla sandwiches and some pieces of boiled squash, which they promptly devoured.

"What is your name?" Mother asked the strange Indian. He answered that he was Juán Pronto and that he was from the Pajio (Bajio). He spoke in the staccato manner of the Papago, but he was able to make himself understood quite well.

"Juán," said Mother. "Will you please tell me why you are scraping that *zalellita?*"

"To eat," he said simply. "Very good. Tonight we cook it near the river. All in Poso Verde very hungry. Food all gone." And the two returned to their task of scraping the hide.

I followed Mother back into the house. "Ma, did he say he is going to *eat* that thing?"

"That's what he said."

I was dismayed. The thought of eating a goat hide made me feel sick. When Father came home, I told him all about the strange Indian, and about how Juán Pronto and José-José were going to cook the hide and eat it. He was very interested, and that evening he took Ruby and me down to the river to watch the process. Mother, Uncle Mike, and Uncle Luis came along too.

The Indians had gathered enough wood to build a small fire and had cut the hide into two-inch strips. Seated on opposite sides of the fire, they tied strips of the hide to the ends of long sticks and held them over the coals. Grease dripped onto the fire, creating little clouds of acrid smoke that drifted up to us where we were sitting on the riverbank.

As each strip was cooked, it was spread out on a flat river rock to cool. Juán Pronto cut one of the cooled strips in half and presented it to Father for us to taste. Father cut it into several small pieces and gave us each one. Mother ate hers, saying it wasn't quite done. I chewed my piece over and over, but it seemed as though the more I chewed it, the bigger it got. "I don't like it, Ma."

"Hush," she told me. "You'd like it if you were hungry enough."

"Why didn't you fellows boil the hide, instead of roasting it?" Father asked the Indians.

"Oh, boil better," said Juán Pronto. "Make good soup. But no pot. No pot, no boil."

"I can lend you a pot," said Uncle Mike, jumping up. He went splashing across the stream to Grandfather's house and came back carrying a cast-iron pot, along with some salt, pepper, and onions.

Within minutes, the pot, half-filled with river water, along with the hide strips and seasoning, was propped on three rocks over the fire, simmering away. The Indians now planned to spend the night at the creek, guarding their goatskin stew. But before we went home, they made us promise to return in the morning so we could have a taste.

The following morning, Mother carried a bowl and spoon and an empty three-pound can, so that she could retrieve Grandmother's cooking pot and Juán Pronto could carry the remainder of the stew back to his village. Father and I came too, each carrying a bowl and spoon. The meat was now perfectly tender and I was able to eat it easily. But, thinking always of the way the goat hide had looked, I asked for a very small portion. The Indians declared the stew the best they had ever tasted, and they ate heartily. It was not the best I had ever tasted, but I ate it and said nothing.

Juán Pronto stood and spoke to Father: "I have good food, good rest, good friends, and now I go," he said, smiling at us. He turned and walked away, his baggy trousers flapping about his ankles, and he looked back and waved once more before disappearing into the thicket.

"Pa," I said. "He was happy, wasn't he, Pa?"

"Sure," said Father. "He is a good man. He fed lazy old José-José, he had a good dinner himself, and he taught us a lesson. Now we know how to eat hide."

"Oh, Pa, we're never going to have to eat hide, are we?"

"I hope not," said Father. "But if you ever do have to, Eva, eat it like Juán Pronto did—with a smile."

From the beginning the Indian children taught me many things that the older people would never have considered important. The adult Indian population were a self-sufficient people who knew how to survive. In time of want they extracted what substance they could from the land and went about patiently and serenely. They were difficult to arouse, but by the same token, they were never hysterical or violent.

By observing the Indians, we picked up courage and learned to bear whatever burden was thrust upon us.

In those days there was much waiting to be done. Waiting was not easy and sometimes it was painful and distracting but it was a basic for living at the turn of the century, and when it came to patience the Indians were experts.

The land of Mañana was real, but it was not created by the Hispanics any more than the desert was created by the Indians. It was an abstract entity of that time, for that time. And the time spent waiting for Mañana was a crucial time for each individual. Waiting was necessary because going along with the elements was easier than fighting them, and waiting was an important defense; for example, waiting for the cool of the evening. This may sound commonplace, but during the rainy season when the careless weeds grew six feet tall and the humidity was high, it was a matter of life and death. Waiting for cooler weather, waiting for the storm to pass, waiting for the tuna to ripen.

It was that period of waiting for Mañana that determined success or failure. Each used it according to his own needs and intelligence. The derelict lived an idle life and the waiting period was an ideal excuse for loafing away the hours, and Mañana never came. For responsible people Mañana sometimes was a godsend, a time to catch up with work that would otherwise have been forgotten.

In our house, under Father's supervision, we worked hard to catch up with work we had neglected. He would catch up with his correspondence and reading. Mike would take a last and hammer and repair everyone's shoes; Ruby and I worked at our lessons at Father's elbow.

I remember many years later, the day a big flood came spilling over the banks of the creek after a storm. We sat along the wall to work while we waited for the flood to run off. Papago Pio joined us at the wall, "Going Bajio," he said, pronouncing the *b* as a p, as the Indians did. "No cross, I wait." He sat working at his basket and telling Father of the people who lived at the Bajio.

Agustín Duran, El Negro, the mail carrier, who was on his way to Sasabe with the mail, stopped at the far end of the wall and called, "¿Me das posada, Tocayo (namesake)?" to Father in a booming voice. "Sure, I wouldn't like to see you drown," answered Father. "Unload your mailbags and Mike will show you where you can sleep." He tied up his horse and pack mule and joined us at the side of the wall, opening a large bag full of horse hair. He had busied himself weaving a bridle head while he waited for Mañana.

Jack Kinney, who had recently organized La Osa Livestock and Loan Company, the largest cattle outfit in Arizona at that time, situated east of the Baboquivari, had also arrived a little late to cross the surging creek. "On my way to Buenos Aires," he said, meaning one of the ranches comprising La Osa, "but I see the flood beat me to the crossing."

"Get down and join the mañaneños," said Father, "and you can sleep in that room across the way. Put your horse in the stable and come on in."

"Thank you, Agustín," and Jack put his horse away and returned with a bundle of letters and literature. He was very active in civic affairs and many years later ran for governor on the Republican ticket, lost the election to Dr. Moeur, and continued ranching. He brought beautiful Palomino horses and fine Hereford cattle. Father bought our first Palomino pinto stallion and a Hereford bull from him.

Jack now talked of the country and the people, the stock, and told us that he was trying to organize La Fiesta de Los Vaqueros, which he did (it became the famous Tucson Rodeo) and of which he was Rodeo Boss from 1925 until 1942. We were really excited and hoped that we could see the first cowboy parade the coming year.

A newcomer walked up to us with bouncing steps and darting blue eyes. "Hey you," he called. "How do I get across the creek?"

"You have to wait until the flood runs off," answered Father.

"Sure, sure," said the stranger, "but how long until it runs off?"

"Maybe by tomorrow noon," answered Father.

"Tomorrow?" boomed the stranger. "You people live in the land of Mañana. I want to go across. Now."

"You have to swim it, my friend," exclaimed Jack.

Pio the Indian grunted and said, "Wachum!" The Indian looked at Father and said, "He no know kiagani; he gewho."

"What's he talking about?" asked the newcomer.

"He says that you are going to drown, that you are wild and don't know how to wait."

"Why should I be wild? I just want to get across, now."

"Mañana, my friend," said Mike, "take it or leave it." The stranger went up and down the Pesqueira Hill looking at the flood, and he stopped in front of Jack saying, "It is not running off at all."

"It will," said Jack, "Mañana, and that will be good enough for me."

"You're Mexicanized, ain't you?" asked the stranger, and spitting close to our highly honored guest's boot, he turned and walked away.

Learning to wait for Mañana was not as easy as some people might think, but it was a healthy thing to do at the turn of the century.

Intruder in the Chicken Coop

THE INDIANS WE ALWAYS HAD WITH US. A few came almost every day, like María Nieves and José-José with his huge quijo. These regulars often began to seem like family members in some ways, even if we were not particularly fond of them as personalities. We became used to them, talked to them about their past lives, their families, and their customs, and we missed them when they did not return for long periods, or, as sometimes happened, not at all. Other, nameless Indians came, too, in large groups and sat along the wall or on the corral fences to watch the ranch activities. Occasionally, some of them worked or helped a little, but mostly they just got in the way, so that feisty old Barreplata had to drive them off.

One fall morning, I awoke to find the late morning sun shining in through the south window of my room. My father's good friend, Mateo, had come the night before, and they had all stayed up very late engrossed in conversation. Somehow, I had slipped their attention, carefully staying out of the way so I could listen. Mother had finally noticed my presence and scolded me off to bed, but in the morning she must have taken pity on me because no one had awakened me at the usual time.

The house was silent except for the twit-twit-twit sound of a sparrow that had found its way inside and was hopping back and forth along the window sill, anxiously looking for a way out. I got up and ran to the window, hoping it was a baby bird and I could catch it, but it flew up and disappeared somewhere among the reeds of the ceiling. I started to run in search of the bird, but the sudden appearance of a gigantic Indian woman, dressed in what was then my absolutely favorite color in all the world (bright purple), kept me rooted at the window. She was coming out of our chicken coop and proceeded to sit down on a patch of low, green weeds.

In those days, many Indians went each spring to Tucson to harvest the saguaro fruit from the hills there. They plucked the fruit from the cacti with long poles and made it into jelly, then brought it back to their villages, moving south along Avra (Abra) Valley to the Poso Verde Indian village, where they would wait for fall before starting their yearly circuit again—to Magdalena, to Tucson, and back again to Poso Verde. Many of the women went along but did not join the harvest, or they harvested only part-time. These women often found work in private homes in Tucson and were able to buy new clothes, or in some cases, were paid by being given their employers' old clothes. They would come back to our valley wearing brightly colored blouses and skirts—yellow, red, purple. I loved to see them. They reminded me of a flock of beautiful birds.

Some people laughed at them and called the bright skirts *naguas de jareta* (drawstring petticoats), cheap and ugly; flashy rags. This was beyond my understanding.

"The colors are so pretty," I told my mother. "Like a rainbow, Ma. A rainbow is pretty, even if an Indian is standing right on top of it!" Mother didn't know, but I had fully made up my mind to have one of those beautiful skirts, preferably a purple one.

The Indian woman now stood up and walked toward the house, and suddenly I recognized her. It was Zoquetosa, grown very fat. My heart stopped its singing at the beauty of her purple skirt, for I didn't like this particular Indian at all. She had made frightening faces at me, and she had pulled my pigtails hard whenever she found me alone. I ran to the kitchen, planning to lock the door to keep her out. But Mother, Ruby, and Aunt Rita were coming from the corral with arm-loads of wood and pails of fresh milk with Hunga leading them along a narrow trail that ended at the kitchen door. Mother and Zoquetosa reached the door at the same time.

"So you decided to stay, then, Zoquetosa?" asked Mother.

"Uh-huh," the Indian grunted, nodding her head and walking away to the shade of the nearby wall.

"Did you know she was here, Ma?"

"Sure, sleepyhead. I have already given her and María Nieves a good breakfast just after your father and Mateo left. María Nieves said

she expects Tula and her family and Wahyanita to come this afternoon."
Tula was Wahyanita's aunt, who lived in Poso Verde.

"But, Ma, what is Zoquetosa doing here?"

"She says she is going to stay here and rest. She doesn't think she
can go on to Magdalena this year. She is too tired, she says."

I decided to go find Barreplata—to tell him to run this mean Indian
woman off. But I couldn't find him, and the next thing I knew, I
heard him up by the wall, greeting her happily.

"¡*Quiubo pues*, Zoquetosa! I haven't seen you for a long time. Where
you been keeping yourself?"

She answered him in grunts and signs. They talked for a few minutes,
then Zoquetosa left the wall and walked away toward the Indian village.
But during the following days, she visited all the nooks and crannies
in the neighborhood. She went from chicken coop to corral, to the
barn, to the outbuildings at Grandfather's place across the creek, to
the eroded pits in the riverbank, and back to our own house.

The afternoon of Zoquetosa's arrival, just as Mother had said, Tula,
Wahyanita, and Tula's son, Tomás José arrived. They had rested only
one day and then left for Magdalena. Tula had been so proud of Tomás
José. She told us he had been chosen to go on the salt caravan for
that year. She was certain he would not be one of the boys weeded
out at the last, and that some day he would become a medicine man,
a very exalted calling. Tula had brought us news of other Indian ac-
quaintances. Coja, Zonza, and Chueca, she said, were resting at José-
José's hut before going on to Magdalena.

These names were not the given names of Indians, but nicknames
we had given them describing something about their personalities or
looks which had been particularly significant to us. *La Coja* meant
"the crippled one," *la Zonza* "the dull one," and *la Chueca* "the crooked
one." Often such nicknames (or, in many instances, the English or
Spanish baptismal names the priests had given them, or non-Indian
names they had simply heard and liked) became the only names by
which the Indians were known. They would adopt them and drop the
names they had been given in the Indian language.

Zoquetosa had been named in this way by Don Julián Molina, an
enterprising businessman who had equipped a large covered wagon
with a water barrel, and shelving which he had stocked with pots,
pans, and dishes, and a small stove. He also carried a couple of long
planks which could be propped up to serve as a table, and he had

named his setup *La Fonda en Ruedas*—the restaurant on wheels. He followed the *corridas* (roundups), catering to the vaqueros. Between corridas, Don Julián and his grandson Pepe prepared for the next one, gathering groceries off the land and buying or trading for what they couldn't locate free of charge. Don Julián had told us that two of his biggest moneymakers were the honey he and Pepe got from the wild beehives and the *bellotas* (acorns) they brought back each summer from the trees on our Cochis Ranch near the border.

Once, several days before the start of a corrida, Don Julián had hired Zoquetosa, then known by her Indian name of Chona, to make corn tortillas and to pound and roast a quantity of beef jerky so that he would not have to do all this while cooking at the roundup. She had been pleased and excited at the prospect of making some money and had immediately run down to the creek. She had parted her hair in the center and, laying the two halves of her long mane one on each shoulder, she had proceeded to plaster each hank of hair with thick handfuls of mud from the creek. Then she hurried back to her job of grinding the corn for the tortillas.

"¡Chona, *cochina!* You pig, you! Why did you get your hair full of mud?" Don Julián had shouted at her.

"I no pig one!" Chona answered indignantly. "I grind corn, hair get on corn. I put mud on hair, hair *no* get on corn. Hair on corn dirty. Mud on hair *not* dirty."

Don Julián had been very impressed with this logic. "The girls who wait tables in the fondas in Tucson could learn a lesson from you," he had told her. "Maybe they would at least pin those manes up, like I'm always telling them!"

From that time on, Chona was known by the name he gave her—*La Zoquetosa,* "the muddy one." She was very proud of it and used to tell people that Chona was only the name she had been given, but Zoquetosa was the name she had earned.

This year, while Zoquetosa was wandering mysteriously about the place, Father and Barreplata had their usual argument about repairing the roofs before the winter rains came. The roofs on the buildings of the old section that Grandfather Wilbur had built so many years ago leaked badly, and Father wanted to tear them all off and use the rafters for fence posts. Whenever this point was raised, Barreplata became incensed.

"I'll be damned if I let you do that! Those beams are hand-hewn,

young man," he would tell Father. This time he led the way inside
one building and pointed to the ceiling. "See how smooth they are,
Agustín! How well-squared! You don't know what the doctor went
through, making those rafters. He took great pride in his work, and
so would you, if you had ever made even one. No, no. That roof can
be fixed!"

"All right, Barra," said Father finally, throwing up his hands and
walking away. "You go ahead and do it then. I won't bother you."

Barra, small and wiry, still agile in spite of his years, quickly recruited
Grandfather Vilducea and two of the uncles, and they began the repair
job that same day, while Father began repairing the corral.

Grandmother came to the house just before noon with some fresh
tortillas and helped Mother get lunch for all the men. As she peeled
potatoes, she carried on endlessly with talk about the Indians, the
neighboring ranchers, the likelihood of finishing the roofs before the
rains came. Suddenly, though, as she was busy wiping out a bowl, she
stopped talking for a moment, a puzzled expression on her face, and
said, "Oye, Ramona, what has happened to all our dishwipers? I have
only this one left. I can't seem to find the others anywhere!"

"You'll find them, Ma," said Mother. "I wouldn't worry about it."

"I just don't know where to look anymore," said Grandmother,
shaking her head plaintively.

That day Don Julián Molina came by to see if Father would sell
him some horseshoes for the team that pulled his rolling restaurant.
When he learned that Zoquetosa was in the vicinity once again, he
went about trying to find her, hoping she would do some more cooking
for him. But somehow, Zoquetosa could not be found, so he finally
gave up and went on his way.

Late that afternoon, I saw Grandmother cross the creek from her
house to the part of ours where the men were working on the roofs.
Soon, however, she appeared at the kitchen door, calling excitedly
for Father who had just come in to wash for supper.

"Agustín! You must come and help! Zoquetosa has taken possession
of the hen house! The poor chickens are out, running around looking
for a place to roost."

"Just tell Barra to chase her away, Ma."

"No, No! He is the very one who sent me to tell you he needs
help!" cried Grandmother.

So we all went outside, only to find Barreplata running around in circles after the chickens, who were flapping about in mad confusion and trying to get back into their house. Zoquetosa was standing in the doorway of the chicken coop, a big rock in each hand. My two uncles, Mike and Luis, had left the roof-mending to try and help Barreplata, but had already been stoned away.

"Zoquetosa!" shouted Father, "I want you to get away from that chicken coop and go on home."

"Me no go!" yelled Zoquetosa.

Father whispered to the rest of us, "I'll get the Big Grey and drive her away."

"Oh, no, Agustín," said Grandmother anxiously. "Your horse might trample her!"

"Don't worry," Father soothed her. "You know very well I'd be the last one to hurt old 'Zoquete' (mud). I'll just come out on the horse with the rope ready in my hand, and you watch her take off!"

So we all retreated to the back door to watch Father get rid of Zoquetosa. We didn't have long to wait, for he came dashing out of the barn almost at once, riding Big Grey and twirling a *lazada*. Zoquetosa ran out and went behind the chicken coop. A moment later, we saw her running up the hill and, naturally, we thought she would just keep on going, so the show was all over. But she surprised us. She stopped at the working bench and picked up a slivered two-by-two that ended in a sharp point. As Father rode toward her, she turned and dashed headlong down the slope, aiming the two-by-two right at Big Grey's chest. Father turned the horse aside instantly and raced away from her, thinking that now she would drop back and give up the chase. But Zoquetosa came on, gaining fast, and apparently determined to stab the horse or Father himself, if she could. When he realized that she was actually chasing him, Father really took off.

To us, the whole scene was marvelously funny—Father, wearing his big Stetson hat, riding his big horse, and running away as fast as he could from the fat Indian woman who kept tripping over her wide purple skirt and viciously thrusting her wooden lance back and forth. When Father had finally put some distance between himself and Zoquetosa, she turned and went back toward the chicken coop, balancing her long weapon on her shoulder, comically mumbling to herself. But as she came close to us, it began to seem less funny, for we could all hear her, enunciating very clearly, "¡Americano *cabrón* (son-of-a-bitch)! I no play! I kill!"

Uncle Mike had been applauding her, and we were laughing uproariously at the wild chase they had put on for us. But to Mother, it had become no laughing matter. "She has become quite dangerous, Agustín," she said to Father as he came into the kitchen after putting the Big Grey back in the barn. "We are going to have to find some way to get rid of her."

We ate our supper, everyone talking about the problem of Zoquetosa, and everyone objecting to each plan brought up by someone else. Everyone was still arguing as Mother and Grandmother were clearing up the kitchen, until finally Grandmother said, "Zoquetosa isn't really bad, Ramona. We have always been great friends, you know. She likes me well enough. I'll just go talk to her and find out what was upsetting her so."

Again, everyone objected and tried to talk her out of this plan, warning her about how dangerous the Indian woman had seemed that afternoon. But Grandmother was insistent. She approached the chicken coop carrying a bowl of jerky stew. We watched her standing outside for a good while, talking to Zoquetosa, who apparently was refusing to open the door. Suddenly, though, it did open, and Grandmother vanished inside. Grandfather and the uncles immediately started toward the chicken coop, but Grandmother came to the door, motioning them to stay away, and then went back inside. She was in there so long, with no sounds of violence that we could hear, that we all finally got tired of standing there staring at the chicken coop and went back to the kitchen.

It seemed hours before she finally came back to the house with the empty bowl and a big smile on her face.

"Well, what's the matter with her, Margarita?" demanded Grandfather.

"Guess, Francisco, only guess!"

"Oh, for goodness sake, Margarita! *Estás loca?* What the devil is going on?"

"She has a baby girl, Francisco," answered Grandmother, laughing. "And, Ramona, she has her wrapped up in my dishwipers!"

All of a sudden the atmosphere of fear and uncertainty changed. Mother made rice pudding for Zoquetosa. Barreplata simply waited until it got dark to catch the chickens, which he put in a large box he had scavenged. He talked now about making a new shelter for them the next day, for it was quite obvious that Zoquetosa had appropriated the chicken coop for good.

When Barreplata had gone to his own little house and Grandfather and his family had walked back across the creek, Father and Mother sat for awhile at the kitchen table, drinking coffee and talking. Ruby and I had been sent to bed, of course, but I was still awake, listening. Finally, I called to Mother.

"What do you want?" she asked, as she appeared near my bed.

"Where did Zoquetosa get the baby?"

"Don Julián brought it for her in a satchel," said Mother. "Now you go right to sleep. I don't want you to call me again."

"Ma. Ma-a-a." She turned back reluctantly. "You know that purple skirt Zoquetosa has?"

"Yes, I know. I suppose you want me to take it away from her and make you a dress from it."

"Ma! How did you know? You always know before I tell you, Ma."

"You go to sleep, and I'll see what I can do about it tomorrow. But, Toña, that skirt is really a very dirty old thing. Maybe your father can find us some new material at the store, and I'll make you a dress from that."

"No, Ma. I want that purple skirt. I saw all the stuff they had at the store when Pa took me to Arivaca one day, and I didn't like it. Please, Ma."

So the next morning, Mother took some jerky and cheese to Zoquetosa and came back with the skirt in a paper bag she had carried just to the door of the chicken coop, for Zoquetosa was still letting no one come in, even after Grandmother had been allowed to see the baby the night before. Mother forbade me to touch the skirt, or even look at it, until she had washed it. When it was clean and spread out on the ironing board, she and Aunt Rita admired the material.

"She must have bought it when she worked in Tucson," said my aunt.

"I don't think so," said Mother. "It is such fine material, I don't think she could have afforded it. No, someone probably gave her a dress she was tired of, and Zoquetosa made the skirt from it."

The skirt was so huge that they were able to cut out not only a dress for me, but a bonnet and jacket for Ruby as well. My new purple dress was the first I had ever had that had not been made from flour sacks, and everyone admired it. People would ask mother or father where they had been able to come by such a beautiful piece of cloth, and I once heard Father answer, "Oh, I don't know. Ramona must have bought it from a peddler." Mother also evaded such questions, not wanting anyone to know my beautiful dress had come from an

Indian's "flashy rags," and no one but Mother, Aunt Rita, and I ever knew where it did come from. I wore it with great joy, and Zoquetosa liked to see me wearing it, so she and I finally became good friends.

Eventually, we all became very fond of her new baby. We were not allowed to see her for some time, though Grandmother went into the chicken coop once in a while. But after about a month, we became aware that Zoquetosa often left her alone and went roaming off, some-times being gone all day. Grandmother had chased the dog away from the chicken coop several times when Zoquetosa was gone, for we knew the dog could get in there through openings under the side. One day, as we drove off in the wagon to get mail, Rex, an Airedale, followed us. When we had gone part of the way, Grandmother looked back and noticed the dog was gone.

"Ramona, stop!" she cried. "We have to go back! I am sure that dog is going into the hen house, and Zoquetosa isn't there. She's been gone since early morning."

So Mother turned around and hurried back to the house, where we were all horrified to see Rex just slinking away from the chicken coop.

"She has hurt María! I know it!" cried Grandmother. We all ran toward the hen house, and Grandmother pulled open the door. We all followed her inside, our eyes taking a minute to adjust to the near darkness. But even when we could see, we looked all around the tiny space and saw no baby at all. As we stood there helplessly, looking around again, Grandmother whispered to my mother, "Ramona! Do you suppose the dog has . . . eaten her?"

Suddenly, Mother pointed. "Look there! No, up; look up!" Zoque-tosa had tied the baby girl in the sling she used to carry her whenever she took her out, and she had hoisted the sling up over a beam near the ceiling. The baby lay there peacefully, staring down at us with huge black eyes. We all laughed in relief.

"Is her name María?" asked Mother.

"Of course!" said Grandmother proudly. "I baptized her myself. Any-one can baptize a baby, you know; you don't have to be a priest. And she had to be baptized." She looked around disapprovingly at me, again upset at the heathen upbringing my mother and father were giving me.

"But," said Mother, "I asked Zoquetosa last week what she was going to name the baby, and she told me that she had already named her. She said the baby was Zoquetosita—the little muddy one."

"Her name is María," said Grandmother firmly, closing the hen house door behind us.

And María she remained to Grandmother for the next few years, though the Indian woman always called her Zoquetosita. My grandmother loved the baby as if she were her own, feeding her, playing with her, often caring for her for days at a time when Zoquetosa was off somewhere. María, or Zoquetosita, was sick many times with the usual sniffles babies seem to get, and Grandmother and Grandfather nursed her happily.

One day, some two years after Zoquetosa moved into our chicken coop, Grandmother came to our house to ask if we knew where Zoquetosa had gone. "She is not at the chicken coop, Ramona, and she took Marillita (María) with her this time. The baby's backsling and the little blanket are gone also.

"That, Ramona, could only mean that she has gone away," said Grandmother with a catch in her voice. "I'll go and try to track her to see which way she went."

We could hear Grandmother calling María's name from quite a distance and from different directions, the sound echoing throughout the valley, sometimes far away, other times closer. The forlorn sound went on, growing fainter all the time, as Grandmother roamed farther up the creek. Over several days she walked many miles from the house but could not find a trace of Zoquetosa and the baby, María.

On one of these days, Grandfather took my hand and said, "Let's go look for Grandma."

"Is she lost, Grandpa?" I asked.

"No, she is still looking for Marillita."

We followed the dusty trail along the riverbanks until we finally spotted Grandmother who was returning after being gone most of the day, but she was no longer calling María's name.

"You shouldn't waste your time looking for Zoquetosa, Margarita. One of these days she will appear at the kitchen door with María. You know how the Indians are."

"I am no longer looking for them, Francisco," Grandmother answered sadly. "I am only taking a walk to get away from the children. I'll get over this, Francisco, I know that, but right now I am fit for the *casa verde* (insane asylum)."

"I feel the same way, Madre, but there is work to be done, you know. Life is made up of rough beginnings and sharp, painful endings."

That expression, "rough beginnings and sharp, painful endings" remains in my thoughts even until today.

"I remember," reminisced Grandfather, "the day we left our home in Sonora. I was fixing the harness to plow the milpita. Beautiful white clouds were coming up and enormous flocks of *pitayeras* (whitewings) were arriving, all indications of good summer rains. I thought I would lay out a plot that afternoon for tilling in the morning. Just then Mike jumped over the wall and yelled, '*Los Federales, Pa!*' I hurried to the cluster of *nopales* (prickly pear), and squeezed myself through the thorny pads to the center of the thicket, dropping myself into a deep coyote den, and there I thought things out as I waited for the Federales to leave."

Grandfather was a victim of the Mexican Revolution at that time. He was an officer in the former government, and now the ones in power were hunting him.

"It was painful, Margarita. If I stayed, I would be caught and taken to Islas Marias, and," said Grandfather, looking off into the distance, "nobody ever came out sane from that prison. I decided to go north to the Territorio. And that's what I call a sharp and painful ending.

"And when you told me that you and the children were coming with me, I was as good as dead. I couldn't think, I couldn't talk, let alone object. That night we stood atop the big hill and took a last look at our home by the light of a pre-dawn moon, then we turned and walked toward the north . . . no trail, no plans, just the little food we were carrying. That was a rough, painful beginning! But here we are, happy as can be with our children and our grandchildren . . . and Marillita will come back to us, you wait and see.

"Every time we come to a painful ending we must let go of the past and get on with what lies ahead, with the work assigned to us by our Lord and God. Only then can he lead us on, Margarita."

"You are right, Francisco. How can He lead us on and help us if we balk like animals."

Walking back to the house together, I caught spurts of their conversation as I walked behind them. "I have to go up the creek and set snares to see if I can catch a couple of rabbits to feed these people up in the arroyo," Grandfather was saying as he pointed to the wash across the creek.

"I have a dozen *perdicitas* (Bobwhite quail); Mike brought them yesterday. We can cook them, Francisco, if you like." As always, Grandmother found ways by which she could lighten everyone's burden.

"Yes, Margarita, we have to work hard to feed the sick people."

At the turn of the century there was an influx of Anglo tuberculars searching for a warm, sunny climate in the hope of regaining their health. They came without ample resources to a rugged and strange country. Grandfather took it upon himself to feed and care for them.

"John Bogan told me yesterday up at the store that more people are coming and he said that all have the white plague, and not a penny to their names. We will have to feed them. No one else will, Margarita."

"The boys will help us, Francisco. *Nuestros hijos tienen compasion*" (our children are compassionate).

"We will have to teach these children to pray . . . very important, Margarita, very important." (I knew he meant me and my sister.)

"If only Igual would come back, Francisco. He would help us, you know." Igual (Ewell), Father told me back at the house, was one of the *tisicos* (tuberculars) that Grandfather had nursed back to health.

"Where is he now, Pa?" I asked.

"He went to live in Mexico, the country he hated so much."

"Pa, did he let go of the past?" Father wanted to know what I meant by this question and I had to explain what Grandfather had said about letting go of the past.

"I guess we all have to let go of the past some time or another," said Father.

I sat in the afternoon sun trying to piece together the puzzle that life had placed before us. We never saw Zoquetosa again, nor could any of the other Indians, who came bringing news of this one or that one, tell us anything more about her or her whereabouts.

And so another chapter in our lives came to a close.

My Earliest Recollections

My "MEMORY LANE" IS SPLOTCHED with recollections that have not dimmed or faded in the last seventy-five years. They stand out clear and sharp, but they are splotches just the same. They have no beginning, nor do they trail off to an ending. They are just there like ink splotches on a white wall.

I see horn tips glistening in the sun above a swirling of dust; I hear the bawling of calves being branded and smell burnt hair.

A high mound of moist, sifted soil. Swarms of red ants moving toward me. My belly and my chest already covered with them. My mother carrying me away from the anthill; my father back from the doctor; medicine bottles on the table; my mother crying and salving me up; Father carrying me out to see the quail going across the yard. . . . The crisis is past! All details are clear but disconnected.

Up on the crest of a neighboring hill I sit on the crook of my father's arm. I see the ugly, black rubber nipple of my milkbottle sticking out of the pocket of my father's Levi jacket. The horse reaches down to browse, and I cringe up into a ball. I put my hands around my father's neck, and I bring my knees up to my chest and scream in panic. I did not cry because the horse wanted to eat, as everyone seemed to think then, but because I was afraid of the terrific height in which I found myself when the horse reached down. I sat in my father's arm, a good twelve inches above the saddlehorn, and when the horse reached down I found myself sitting at the brink of a precipice. When the horse brought his head up, the back of his neck with its wide mane screened the height from me and I didn't feel in danger of falling. I stopped crying.

I am older now and riding on the saddle with my father. I no longer have to sit on his arms and he doesn't have to hold me. I sit just behind the saddlehorn and handle the reins and guide the horse. From the high hill slopes I see the surrounding countryside: our house, the little thatched-roof town of Arivaca. A big black V high up in the sky.

"Geese!" said Father, as he pointed to the Eastern sky.

"What is geese, Pa?"

"Birds, big birds," answered Father. Father got down. He adjusted the saddle and let the horse breathe. I stood on the ground and watched the bird formation fly overhead. When they had gone I sat on the ground and learned to make a V.

"It's like the 'A' for Arivaca, Pa."

"The geese are going to land. That's why they are flying so low, Eva."

"Land where?"

"At the Laguna de Aguirre (Aguirre Lake) just beyond the mountain."

"If there is a laguna there, Pa, why don't we go up to the top of the mountain and see it?"

"When you're a little older I'll take you up there. You're too little yet," said Father as he put me back on the saddle and headed for home.

The days that followed found me talking geese and making V's and feeling quite grown up, of course.

Now a new and very disturbing and confusing problem came into my life. I didn't know whether I was big or little, old or young. When I was around Ruby, I was a big girl, and no matter what blows I received at Ruby's hands I could endure them because I was a big girl. I could take care of myself and of Ruby, too. She had to be taken care of, and I was the one to do that. She was a baby. Now, taking care of my baby sister was a gruesome and dangerous job. Ruby beat up on me and did everything to me, short of killing me, and it was considered all right because she was a baby and, after all, I was a big girl now.

One day Mother asked me to take care of the baby. I walked outside to find Ruby lying down in a mud puddle. She had wet her diapers and then rolled on the wet ground. She had not only dabbed the mud over her face, but she was eating it too. I went to pick her up and take her into the house. Ruby threw her bottle aside and it went rolling down the hill. She brought up her knees, and when I bent down to pick her up she stretched her legs and kicked me in the stomach. I tried picking her up again. She grabbed my hair just above my forehead. I tried to pry her fingers open. No way. She used both her hands to pull me down and I screamed and yelled, and she pulled harder. I doubled my fists as my father had taught me to do whenever I had a punching bout with him. I punched Ruby on the back as hard as I could. Ruby didn't let out a whimper, she just pulled harder. I screamed like a steam engine and Mother came to pick up the "baby."

"She pulled my hair, Ma."

"She's just a baby and you're a big girl. Now stop crying."

"Spank her, Ma." Ma gave Ruby a pat on her muddy bottom.

"My head hurts." I howled as loud as I could, and howl I could.

Mother ignored me and walked away with Ruby. I ran to her side, and looked up at her. She was laughing. Now at the time, I thought I had been injured beyond repair, and my mother was laughing!

"What are you laughing for, Ma? My head hurts."

"No," said my mother. "Your head does not hurt you. Stop crying and stop it right now." She walked into the kitchen and sat Ruby on the highchair.

"Ma, that's my chair."

"No. That chair is the baby's chair. You sit on that box and take care of her."

As I sat on the box I noticed a bowl of roasted coffee beans. I knew my mother would soon go out to grind the coffee, as the coffee grinder was nailed to the branch of a mesquite tree about thirty feet from the kitchen. I would wait. Mother picked up the bowl of roasted coffee beans and walked out. Now I would yank Ruby off the chair and give her a good hard fall to even up the score. As soon as I heard the growl of the coffee grinder I walked up to Ruby, and as I reached for her foot she took the bottle by the nipple and conked me on the head with the bottom of the bottle. I saw stars and heard myself screaming. Mother picked me up and held me close to her.

"She gave you a good whack on the head," said Mother as she rubbed my head.

"Spank her, Ma."

"No, she's a baby and you were supposed to take care of her and to take care of yourself, too. Why didn't you?" I didn't know what to answer. I was not a tiny baby, but I was still very small and wanted at least to share the special attention of my mother.

When my father came, Mother explained to him in detail exactly what had happened. I heard Mother telling him how I had tried to pull Ruby down from the chair while she had been grinding the coffee. I stayed in bed and pretended to be asleep while I listened to my parents talk. It gave me quite a jolt to learn that my mother knew what I was about even when she did not see me.

Then there was the time Wahyanita, the Indian girl from across the creek, came over to play with me. I went with her to the creek as I usually did. No sooner had we made ourselves comfortable on the smooth white sand under the willow tree than Wahyanita began to speak, as she usually did, about I'itoi, the Indian god who lived in the Baboquivari Mountain. (The Papago Indians pronounce the B like a P.) So Wahyanita began in her sharp staccato style: "I'itoi, he lives in the Plue Papo Kipari. He is the God and Papo Kipari is his home. Do you pelieve me?"

"No, Wahyanita, I don't believe you. God does not live in that old mountain." Wahyanita stood up, reached for a willow whip and pulled all the leaves and small branches from it. She struck the ground with terrific force close to me. "I'itoi lives in the Papo Kipari. That is his home," she said, looking at me with a fierce look in her eyes. "Do you pelieve that?" she yelled at me.

"No-o!" I yelled back at her. Wahyanita applied the whip across my bare legs with a force I didn't believe possible. My legs felt as if they had been cut with a knife. She threw the whip away and ran into the tall cocklebur thicket, and just as suddenly I ran to the house. I looked down at my legs to see if they were bleeding. They were not. When I saw my mother I burst out crying and I showed her where Wahyanita had hit me—a big red welt across each leg.

"I have told you not to go with Wahyanita away from the house," said Mother. "She is too big. She is five years older than you. You are too little."

So, I had to endure the blows from Ruby because I was a big girl and the whippings from Wahyanita because I was too little, just a baby.

María Nieves, our best Indian friend, actually spent every day in our house. She must have weighed 300 pounds and had a round moon face, glistening white teeth, and had ghastly splayed feet which gave one the impression that her weight had flattened her feet out of shape. Her big toe and the toe next to it opened out like a V on both her feet. Everybody liked María Nieves. She was, they said, *muy Castellana* (very Castilian).

I for one did not like her. The distorted appearance of her feet made me sick. One day I asked Mother why María Nieves's feet were so ugly and she told me that maybe it was because she went barefooted all the time. This gave me something to think about. I, too, went barefooted all the time and I didn't want my feet to look like that, so I took a rag and wrapped them around the big toe and the second toe on each foot and I asked my mother to tie them, and tie them she did. I wouldn't have it any other way. When Father saw me dragging the long pieces of rag on both feet he told me that I would step on the ends of the rags and fall down. He asked why I had tied my toes up like that.

"They hurt me, Pa," I said. "My mother told me that María Nieves's toes spread out like the Geese V because she goes barefooted all the time, see? And I don't want my toes like that." I made the form of a V with my fingers.

"You don't figure things out right, Eva. You don't see when you look. Haven't you seen the other Indians going around barefooted too? And they don't have their toes like that. Doesn't that tell you that that is not the reason María Nieves's toes are opened like that?"

"Yes, Pa," I said. I didn't quite understand what he had said, but I proceeded to untie the rag. Father took out his pocket knife and cut the rags loose.

"You're too big a girl to do that. You should have known better by looking at the other Indians' feet," said Father.

And so the weeks and the months went by and I lived with the dilemma of being too little or too big. I couldn't do the things I wanted to do because I was too little and I had to do the things I didn't enjoy doing because I was too big. And I had better be learning to do the disagreeable chores because I was growing up—I was a "big" girl.

I decided that I had to determine when I was old enough to do certain things and when too young to attempt to undertake them. I engaged the help of my father. After all, I was his favorite daughter. He had told me so, and by that token I chose him as my favorite parent. But my favorite parent was not always the most understanding. My father was a hard man. When something had to be done it had to be done on the spot and one had to go about it the right way. Neither man nor beast was spared. How unpleasant, difficult, or painful the task might be was not to be considered. When one of such tasks was assigned to me I was expected to go in shoes and all just like anybody else. Neither my sex, my age, or my sensitivity was ever considered. Consequently, I grew up in emotional upheaval. The hard, unpleasant lessons on attention/observation snowballed day by day. "Pay attention—listen. See when you look." A favorite admonition—the same thing, but more of it every day.

"You see that cloud up in the sky? What does it mean?"

"I don't know, Pa."

"You're too *big* not to know. It's a mare tail. It doesn't mean anything. It will soon disappear. Remember that."

Suddenly Father would stop on the trail, then pointing at the tracks he would ask: "What kind of track is that, Eva?"

"I don't know, Pa."

"Well, study it and try to figure it out. You're too *big* not to know."

"It looks like Ruby's tracks, Pa."

"Do you think it is Ruby's track?"

"It could be, Papa." I always called Father "Papa" when I was nervous, afraid, or very happy.

"Was Ruby out this way last night?" asked Father, looking cross and disgusted.

"No, Papa."

"Well, then, those couldn't be her tracks. Think about it."

"All right, Papa," I said, looking at the tracks that looked like child's tracks.

"Those are coons' tracks. Look at them good and remember them."

"Papa, I want to go to Tucson with you next time you go," I said, trying to run away from the subject of the tracks.

"No, you're too *little*. When you grow up more, I'll take you with me to Tucson."

"Then take me to the peak of the Cerro. Why don't you? You promised me. Don't you remember you told me that you would take me up there when it was summer again. Well, now it is summer again. Isn't it?"

"Yes," answered Father, looking at me as if considering my age and my ability to withstand the trip up to the peak. "We'll talk it over with your mother tonight. See what she thinks."

That night after supper Father told Mother that he wanted to take me up to the peak of the Cerro before the rainy season started.

"No," said Mother with such finality that Father appeared disconcerted.

"She is much too young. She is a mere baby, and the Cerro is one of the worst mountains around here."

Mother left the table and returned with her book.

"Ma," I said before she began to read. "You told me that I was a *big girl* and now you say that I am *too little*. If I am big enough to be left with Ruby, I am big enough to go with Pa anywhere.

"See what I mean," said Father. "If she is big enough to talk like that she is big enough to go with her father anywhere."

We won! Father and I always did.

A Trip to the Mountain

THE FOLLOWING MORNING MOTHER DRESSED ME in the long overalls she had made me from Father's discarded levis. I didn't like to wear them.

"Wear them, wear them," said Father. "Those are your chaps and you'll need them to protect your legs against the brush and the catclaw." Well, I liked that. If they were chaps that was good enough for me.

Early the following morning, with a canteen of water and a bag full of well-pounded jerky, we left the house. Father put me behind the saddle. This was the first time that I was going to ride behind the saddle for a long stretch and I didn't like it, but Father promised to put me on the saddle with him when we left the flat country. We traveled along a small canyon that came from the south and emptied into the creek. Diamante walked on a hard-packed trail in the center of the arroyo. We must have been traveling for a couple of hours before I realized that we were climbing. The canyon narrowed and the trail went up the bank and down again, crossed to the south side of the canyon, and re-crossed several times until the canyon ended in a Y at the foot of a small hill. We climbed slowly to the top where my father stopped to adjust the saddle and to breathe the horse. He put me down and I noticed for the first time that we were fenced in by mountains. There were toothy ridges on all sides and small, but rugged little mountains all around us.

"Pa, where is the Cerro?"

"Right there. That's the Cerro," said Father as he pointed to an enormous pile of rocks and boulders. This horrible mound of rocks had no trees, no trails, and no shape.

"What is the matter with it? Is it falling?"

"No, Eva, what makes you think it is falling? You don't see it moving, do you?"

"No, Pa," I said, nonplussed and actually frightened at the appearance of the mountain. It had not dawned on me that the mountains were different on the opposite side.

"Do mountains have backs?" I asked.

"Mountains are not the same on all sides," explained Father as he put me on the saddle again. He didn't give me the reins as he usually did when we rode along the creek.

The painful shock I suffered when I saw the distorted appearance of El Cerro was soon displaced by the one that followed. We traveled along a well-worn, dusty trail past a mesquite thicket. Cattle that were bedded down got up and moved in a circle. Father reined Diamante and pointed out a very small calf.

"Eva, that calf is eaten up with screw worms and I am going to have to doctor it."

He put me down and left me close to a big mesquite tree behind whose big trunk I hid away from the cattle. I stood peeking from behind the gnarled trunk and saw Father making a big *lazada* (loop) and moving toward the cattle. The calf ran away from the cow, but Father headed it back to the same place where it was bedded down when we first saw it. He roped it easily enough, but Diamante stumbled and went plowing the hillside with his jaws, throwing Father over his head. Father got up and struggled with the calf. When he turned towards me I saw that his face was covered with blood.

"Papa!" I screamed. "You're hurt."

"No, I am all right. You just sit up there and don't worry. A drop of blood ran down to the end of my father's nose as he held his head down when he tied the calf's legs.

I ran to Father's side. "You have blood all over your face," I said as I felt my heart pounding against my chest.

"It is just a scratch," said Father. "Don't worry about it. Come over here and help me clean this wound."

I had seen maggots before, but not like these. The wound was packed full so that the maggots didn't move. They were just there.

"Oh, Pa, how did he get those straight pins?"

"You watch those straight pins drop out as soon as I pour the creosote in there."

Father uncorked the small glass bottle, and as he tipped it over, the black gruel ran out and into the wound, and the bedding ground was permeated by the pungent smell of the creosote. I was well acquainted with the noxious smell and it didn't bother me. The maggots disappeared. Father inserted his finger into the wound and the calf bawled.

"Eva, your finger is a lot smaller. See if you can put your finger in the wound and bring the screw worms out." I flinched and with a curled under index finger I approached the wound.

"Stretch your finger out and don't be afraid. It won't hurt him more than the worms do."

I put my finger inside the wound and felt the maggots moving against the tip of my finger. I felt sick, retched, and vomited over my father's hand. Vomit ran down the white coat of the calf.

"Don't be so delicate. Bring those screw worms out."

"I am sick in my stomach, Papa."

"Well, toughen up, toughen up," said Father. "You'll get over it."

I closed my eyes and tried it again. By now all the maggots were spilling out of the wound—fat white ones and small ones. I brought out gobs of them as I kept running my finger inside and around the bloody navel.

"Good girl. That's the way to do it," said Father. I guess I had toughened up. Good thing I did, for this was one task I had to do many, many times, month after month and year after year.

Father turned the calf loose. It joined the cow and both of them trotted down the slope.

"We're going to the water hole," said Father, "where we can wash up. Would you like that, Eva?"

"Yes, Pa."

I was silent. I felt sick inside. "Toughen up, toughen up," I thought.

Suddenly I remembered how Diamante had fallen. "Papa, why did Diamante fall down?"

"He stepped in a hole. I didn't see it. It was tunneled across the clearing. It is a wonder he didn't break his leg."

"What would you do, Pa, if Diamante broke a leg?" I asked.

"There is only one thing you can do," said Father. "Take off the saddle and shoot him and walk home."

"Oh, Pa, you wouldn't do that to Diamante. Would you?"

"Yes, I would. I would have to, and when you have to do something you do it."

I remained silent. This would have been worse than doctoring the calf. I would really have to toughen up then. We went between two trees, around the tall plants of desert mahogany, and suddenly we were at the water hole.

This was a beautiful spot and I soon forgot the incident of the sick calf and the thought of having to shoot poor Diamante. I was puzzled and fascinated by the water that trickled out of a big, dry boulder, ran down the slope, and spilled over a flat rock into a small gulch. Once Father put me down from the horse, I ran around examining every nook and crag. Inside of a hollow log were some speckled eggs. I called Father and showed them to him. He told me they were quail eggs.

"Now I want to show you something else, Eva," said Father as he led me down the incline. He stopped at the water hole and looked across the way and said, "Look at that cholla, Eva."

I looked up at the cholla with glistening white spines. A rattlesnake was working its way up the spiny trunk; it scaled up its main stem and very gracefully left one branch and reached for another until it arrived at a large fagot nest with a small entrance. The snake went inside the nest and went out the back way, then slithered down as businesslike as it had gone up. We stood still and watched the snake get into a hole under the rock.

"All right. You watch where you step."

"I will, I will," I answered. This had been even more breath-taking than the water oozing out of a dry rock.

"You see, Eva," continued Father, "You have heard Mike say that when he has to sleep in the open country he puts a hair rope around his bedroll so that a snake won't get to him. If a snake crawls all over the cholla spines, do you think a rope is going to keep it from going across it?"

"No, Pa. A snake won't care about a rope."

"All right," said Father. "I am going to clean the water hole and you better sit in the shade. I'll soon be through." I sat in the shade and watched Father reach under the clump of bear grass and bring out a shovel and a small bar and can.

He looked at me and said, "I hide my tools under there so that someone won't carry them off."

He shoveled aside the muck and with the bar he pried loose a big rock and the water gushed out and ran down the incline, carrying oak leaves and debris. Father took the can and dipped the water hole dry, throwing the water on the dry hot earth which sucked it up like a sponge. Hundreds of smoke-blue butterflies settled on the damp spot to sip the moisture. The place was teeming with bird life. Blue birds driveled ceaselessly. There was loose, moist soil under the big oak tree where I sat. Father said that a herd of *javelinas* had just left the *aguaje* (water hole).

"I see their tracks, right here, Pa."

"Yes, their tracks are here, all right, but the tracks you're looking at right now happen to be deer tracks and not javelina tracks."

"How can you tell," I asked. And Father pointed out the difference in the imprint. Education was hitting me in the face like a pelting rain.

Father put the tools away and went to the saddle to bring back the lunch sack and the can full of water from the aguaje.

"I think I like the water from the canteen," I said.

"This is better water," Father said as he pointed to the can. Father washed my hands in the little stream and wiped them with his jacket.

"Now have a little of that lunch, Eva."

I dropped by his side and sat devouring chunks of jerky and washing it down with cool water from the aguaje. As soon as I finished eating, Father brought Diamante back, bridled him, and adjusted the saddle.

"Let's get going, *mijita*." He put me back on the saddle and I took one last look at the surroundings. For the first time I noticed the different greens of the plants. The grayish-green leaves of some of the agave, the glistening green of the bear grass, the tender green of the desert mahogany, and the dark green of the mesquite leaves. The slope of the Cerro was across the way. Only a stone's throw from the water hole a display of tall yuccas in bloom made the Cerro appear a bit more friendly.

"The Cerro is a nice mountain, isn't it, Pa? Even if it is *chueco* (crooked)."

"Yes," said Father, "at least the antelope seem to be enjoying it. Do you see them, Eva?"

"No. I don't see anything," I answered, squinting my eyes.

I had trouble locating the herd, but with Father's help I finally saw them below a ledge of brown rocks, halfway up the Cerro.

"They are the color of burros, Pa." The antelope heard us talking and they bounded over the cliffs and vanished from sight.

We crossed the wash and walked on the trail along the bank. Clusters of yellow poppies peeked over the edge. The trail wended its way across the yucca thicket and we began to climb the Cerro. With my belly full of jerky and the hot sun beating down on my back, I soon began to get drowsy.

"Pa, this is a crazy saddle. Real crazy."

"Why do you say that, Eva?" asked Father as he climbed in a zig-zag manner.

"Can't you hear what the old saddle is saying, Pa?"

"No, what does it say? What does it say, Eva?"

"Wait, Pa," I said as I listened for the dry saddle leather to squeak out the word that had crept into the soul of the old lady of three. I started chanting in time and in tone with the saddle: "Tough-enup-pup-pup." I ended the last two "pups" in the staccato manner Wahyanita would have done.

"Wait a minute," said Father, "you are getting too tired. We better go to the path and follow the trail home."

"Oh, no Papa. We are almost at the peak. I can see it from here."

"Yes, Eva, but you are not there yet. We have quite a stretch and it is uphill and rough all the way."

"We are going up to the peak. You promised me, Pa."

"All right, Eva. Up we go."

And Diamante climbed one foot at a time. He stepped on a loose rock and it gave way and Diamante sank down, struggled, and finally got hold of solid ground, but some rocks went hurtling down the mountain. As they went down they gained momentum, and hit some other rocks which went down too. My heart was hammering against my chest. I was beginning to change my mind. The Cerro was not a nice mountain. It was a mean one. I didn't know the word "dangerous," but suddenly I felt afraid. We were at the rock ledge where I had seen the antelope.

"Pa, Diamante can't go over those rocks."

"Oh, yes he can. He has gone over them many times, so don't you worry."

"He can fall, Papa."

"No, he won't fall. He is a surefooted little horse."

"What is surefooted, Pa?"

"He is steady on his feet. He won't fall. We'll go slow and we'll get there pretty soon."

We went over the big boulders and I looked down the sharp precipice. The white patch of yuccas was far away. By now I was well convinced that climbing the Cerro was not only a serious business, but a pretty

risky one. There were no trails here. The climb was steep and high
and the rocks were loose; every time the horse took a step they would
slide and some would go down, bouncing and hitting other rocks as
they hurtled down the side of the mountain. I closed my eyes, got
close to my father, and held on. Somewhere along the way something
pulled my pigtail.

"Pa, stop, stop." My pigtail was tangled in a catclaw branch.

Father got down and broke off the twig which I carried at the end
of the pigtail. He promised to take it off when we reached the peak.

Higher up on the mountain now, the horse stopped to breathe; his
ribs moved in and out and his loud breathing worried me.

"Papa," I said, "this horse can fall down."

"No, he never has, and I have come up here many times. We'll
soon be up at those big rocks. We'll leave Diamante there and we'll
walk the rest of the way.

As the horse began to climb again I felt butterflies in my stomach.
"I am sick, Papa."

"Are you afraid?"

"No, I am not afraid. I am just sick."

"What are you shaking for if you're not afraid?" asked Father. "We're
up here now. This is where we are going to leave Diamante and we'll
walk up over those big boulders."

Father put me down and sat me on a smooth, large rock, and with
his pocket knife he worked the catclaw twig out of my braid.

"Does it hurt you, Eva?"

"No, Papa."

"Well, what are you crying for, them? You say you're not afraid."

"Well," I said, "This son of a bitch mountain . . ." and I stopped
abruptly. My father and mother had forbidden me to use profane
language. However, at this time I was beside myself with the fear of
falling, the fear of the height, and the fear of the mountain itself.
Besides all these terrifying things, my father's displeasure at my language
faded into something that was not worth considering.

"Papa, I don't think I can climb over those big rocks. Can't you
see that I am too little?"

"You are not going to climb any rocks, Eva. You just walk in the
trail between the rocks. That trail will take us clear up to the peak."

I didn't move. I just stood and looked at my Father.

"That horse could have fallen."

"But he didn't fall, Eva, so what are you worrying about?"

"He could have," I said, "and I could have gone down the mountain just like that big rock did. I would have been killed, and I wouldn't have seen Ruby again."

I suddenly woke up to the realization that I loved Ruby very much. "I would never have seen my mother again, or Barreplata either."

My father looked away and smiled and I was outraged. I assumed my mother's attitude and said, using her expression, too: "Sometimes I wonder at you, Papa."

"Well, now, Eva. I don't think I deserve to be treated like that. Both Diamante and I worked hard to bring you up here. We took good care of you. We didn't let you fall, did we?"

I put my head down on the rock and sobbed. My nerves were raw and in the back of my mind was the thought that we still had to get down from the Cerro. Father took me in his arms and dried my tears and talked to me about different things. He pointed at the water hole far down the mountain and across the gulch.

"See, Eva, how pretty the water is running down the mountain after I cleaned the water hole?"

"Yes, Pa. Will you have to clean it again?"

"Yes, I'll come back next week. Eva, look down there. See the antelope going to water?"

I saw the antelope munching their way along the trail toward the water hole. This put me at ease and in good spirits.

"All right, up to the peak we go!" exclaimed Father as he stood up and pointed out the trail. I walked ahead, climbing and weaving in and out of the rocks which I examined and admired as I went along. I stopped and gasped for breath. I felt dizzy in the hot stilling air of the rock compound.

"These hot rocks are smothering me, Pa."

"Well, come on out of there," urged Father. "A few more steps and you'll be on top of the world."

I made the last few steps on my hands and knees. The boulders stood high above me, and they exuded heat and blocked the air.

We had come over a drab and rough country except for that surrounding the water hole. The closeness of the mountains had obstructed the view. They had stood sharp, right before us, so that all we had seen were rocks, brush, boulders, gulches, and the mean catclaw that reached out and grabbed my legs and tangled my hair. Now I expected to see before me another mountain loaded with brambles.

I circled a rock and stood up. The thrill of going out of the rock compound, the gust of fresh air on my face, the sight of the desert mahogany swaying in the breeze, and the sensation of suddenly having my ears unplugged was like waking up on a fresh spring morning. The first thing I heard was the resounding blows of the ax on seasoned wood.

"Sounds like someone is chopping wood, Pa."

"That's just what it is, Eva. Mike at the woodpile."

"We can hear it this far, Pa?"

"Yes, and you can hear the guinea hens calling too, can't you?"

"Yes, Pa, and I can hear Hunga barking too, but I can't see them."

Our house nestled in a grove of willow trees so that I could see only the roof after Father pointed it out to me.

"It's very far away, isn't it?"

I looked around in all directions and finally realized that I stood before a breathtaking expanse! Before me was depth and distance and a riot of colors. The browns and the grays, the greens and mauves and blues.

The Cerro was high, but on this side it didn't have a sharp incline. It sloped down gradually and continued in small, smooth ridges that went all the way down to the banks of the creek. The countryside was teeming with cattle. Some were going down the ridges and others were coming up. Across the miles to the north stretched tier upon tier of clear blues, and lighter blues, and then the sky. A large mound of foamy white clouds rose against a blue sky over the misty Santa Rita Mountains on the east. The whole world lay shimmering at my feet; beside me, smiling and ruffling my hair, stood the most beautiful man in all the world. I felt giddy with a sense of pride and joy. I was proud of everything and everybody. I ran in circles as I had seen Hunga do when she was very happy.

"What's going on, Eva?"

"I love this place and I love you, Pa," I said as I wrapped my arms around my father's legs.

"Are you glad I brought you up here?" asked Father.

"Yes, Pa, and I am not afraid anymore."

This is one of the memories that I treasure the most. If someone were to tell me that all my memories would be blotted out except one, this is the one I would ask to keep.

I walked around the peak and I saw Diamante standing under a mesquite tree patiently waiting for us. Maybe the newness of the experience shocked me into seeing the hidden facts and not only the objects in plain sight. In any case, I was now seeing Diamante in a different light. He was no longer just a horse. He was a friend, our companion and helper. I didn't know how to tell my father what I felt or what I thought.

"Pa," I said, "Diamante is a good horse! Isn't he, Pa? He brought us up here on his back, on his back."

"Diamante is a good little horse, gentle and surefooted. He will be your saddle horse soon now, Eva. Come with me, Eva. I want to point out to you the different mountain ranges."

Far to the north where the little blue mountains touched the sky there was Tucson, Father told me, and my heart raised against my chest. So that was how far away Father went when he went to Tucson. To the northwest sat the Baboquivari Mountain with outstretched arms taking in the whole Abra (Avra) Valley.

"Pa," I began, "Wahyanita told me that I'itoi lives in the Baboquivari Peak, and she said that I'itoi is God."

"The Baboquivari is the cathedral of the Papagos and I'itoi is their God," said Father, as he pointed out the *Papaguería of the Poso Verde* (the Papago Indian village of the Poso Verde) where his good friend Martín Mariano lived.

Every fall the Indians came in large groups from Poso Verde on their way to Magdalena, Mexico, to visit San Francisco, whose feastday is the fourth of October. Wahyanita always came with her Aunt Tula, who usually stopped to rest two or three days with María Nieves in their village on the banks of the creek. In the meantime Wahyanita would visit with me and would tell me many stories about the Indians and I'itoi. On one occasion Wahyanita was left with María Nieves a whole year and I became quite able to understand and speak the Papago language. Now I could appreciate how far Wahyanita walked when she came from Poso Verde.

Father stood against a rock looking through the binoculars. "Do you see those black things on the road following that wagon?" asked Father.

I saw some black, round tent-like things moving along the road.

"Yes, Pa, what are they?"

"Comanches," answered Father.

"Comanches? How do you know, Pa?"

"Because only Comanche women ride horseback under an unbrella," answered Father. "They are passing by on their way to New Mexico."

I had heard my grandfather say that the only way one could come out ahead when trading with a Comanche was to trade him an umbrella. A Comanche would throw in all he could spare for an umbrella.

"Come," said Father, "and I'll show you the mountain ranges to the south."

As we moved around the peak, I stopped and asked him what the cattle were doing down there. The whole countryside was swarming with cattle. They looked like ants on the grassy hillside. "Where did that cattle come from, Pa?"

"They are there all the time," he answered.

"I never saw those cattle, Pa. Where was it?"

"They are there all the time. You see these cattle at the creek every day, Eva. They water there. Not all together, but they go in bunches."

"And are the bulls there, too?"

"Yes, the bulls are back already. You remember when they got back and scared Barreplata, don't you?"

"Oh, yes. I remember."

"Come," said Father. "Follow me and I'll show you the mountain ranges on this side of the Cerro." And he walked around the peak, showing me the different ranges and indicating how far the cattle travel. "You see, Eva, that body of water over there? That's the Laguna de Aguirre, and farther south is Sasabe."

"I thought that was the ocean."

"No, that's just a lake. All right, these cattle follow the creek clear over to the Abra, and then they turn west and go in a circle. They cross the Mexican line and then start going southeast. That black mountain over there, that is in Mexico."

"Pa! These cattle go to Mexico?"

"Yes," said Father, "and they stay over there until just before the spring. Then they go east and come back to the Cochis Ranch and follow the wash straight to Arivaca, and then down the creek they come. Do you see that square mountain over there, Eva?"

"Yes, Pa."

"That's the Cantizal. The Cochis Ranch is right at the bottom of that mountain."

"That's where you and Mother go sometimes, Pa?" I asked, as alarmed at the distance to the Cochis Ranch as I had been at the distance to Tucson.

At that time Father was trying to homestead the Cochis Ranch which was right on the Mexican border. He kept a family there part of the time as caretakers and had to make regular trips there to oversee the stock, fences, and water. I had seen my Grandfather Vilducea angry at my father for taking Mother to that "God-forsaken place" as he always said, and now I understood better why my grandfather got so upset when his daughter was taken to the Cochis Ranch. He had gone there many times and was well acquainted with the hardships of that area.

Father picked me up and sat me on a high rock. "Wait here, Eva. I am going down to get the water canteen and the rest of your lunch. We might just as well be chewing on that jerky while I show you the rest of the country."

I sat on the rock and watched Father walk toward Diamante. Looking in the distance, I remembered the day when Mother went to the Cochis Ranch the last time. She got up at dark and got ready while Father saddled the horses.

My grandfather came in grumbling and scolding my mother for letting my father take her to the *infiernos* (hell). "And," said Grandpa, "there isn't a thing for you to take for lunch. *Además, de eso vas en ayunas, muchacha."* (Besides that, you are going without breakfast, girl.)

Mother put on her hat and fastened it with a long pin with a large blue stone at the end. "All right, Toña. I am going and I want you to be good and take care of Ruby for me, and mind your grandmother and your aunt, and Juana, too. She is here to take care of you."

My parents walked over to the horses and Father lifted my mother up and sat her on the sidesaddle. Diamante moved to one side and showed my mother as she sat with her long, black skirt that reached down to the stirrup, a white dainty blouse, and the black straw hat. I thought she looked very pretty as she waved at me.

"Foolish," grunted my grandfather from behind me.

My father and mother were riding side by side; they crossed the stream and the flea-bitten gray that Father was riding took the lead as they disappeared around the bend of the bank.

As soon as the sun came up I hurried to the chicken coop to see if I could find an egg. All the nests were empty. Sitting inside a box, I watched the hens pecking the corn nubbins, and soon I heard Juana calling me. I ignored her and sat still thinking that they would not find me. Suddenly the chicken coop door flew open and there stood Juana!

"What are you doing in that box? You are going to get full of chicken lice." She picked me up by the back of my suspenders and in bucket fashion carried me to the house. After she questioned and scolded me, she gave me a bath and put me to bed.

When my mother came she was told how I had behaved and that there was nothing in me but bad.

"I was hungry, Ma, and I went to look for an egg."

"Of course," said Mother, "I know. I brought you some cheese and some cactus candy that Carmen made and we brought a good milk cow with a pretty little calf. You'll see her in the morning."

"You're spoiling her," said Juana. "We all told you how bad she was."

"I was not bad, Ma. They just don't know nothing. They are all dumb and mean."

"All right," said Mother. "Let's go to bed."

As soon as I found myself alone with Mother I said, "Ma, you know why I was in that nest box?"

"No, why?"

"I went to lay an egg for you, Ma."

"Oh, and did you?" asked Mother with a radiant smile on her face.

"No, Ma. I was afraid to cackle and I don't know what they would have done to me then. You and Pa were gone and they could hurt me, Ma."

Mother lay next to me until I fell asleep. The following day she explained to me that only chickens laid eggs.

I was a baby then. It seemed a very short time ago, but I wasn't a baby anymore. I was three years old and my self-awareness started at this point and at the peak of the Cerro. I can remember with utmost clarity that I was thinking very differently and I concluded once and for all that I was *big*—grown. Grown big enough to stand here on the rim of the Cerro. I was proud of myself and proud of my mother for having gone up that stretch of mountains, and I knew that my mother would be proud of me for having come up to the Cerro. I saw Father coming up the rocky trail as I stood looking down at the water hole and then far away to the Cantizal. How brave my mother had been to go so far and to come back at night, in the dark over the trail that my grandfather had often described as *la vereda del diablo* (the trail of the devil).

"What do you think, Eva?" asked Father as he handed me the sack of jerky and the canteen.

"I am wondering if my mother had any trouble going to the Cochis Ranch, Pa?"

"No, your mother enjoyed the outing and didn't seem to mind it at all. I guess she got tired. Everybody does. You got tired coming up here, but it was worth it. Don't you think?"

"Oh yes, Pa!" I said, "I love this place and I would like to come up here again."

"I know the climb was very difficult and unpleasant, but the experience makes up for it. Everything is like that, Eva. You have to reach and work for the things you want. Nothing that is worth having is easy to get. Remember," said Father as he picked up the water canteen, "no cross, no crown."

I had heard Father say that before, but now I wanted an explanation. I insisted on answers that I could understand. So Father spread the *chaparreras* on the ground and we sat down again and he smoothed the soil with his hand and I had him drawing crosses and crowns all over the ground.

"A cross," explained Father, "means a sacrifice, too."

"And what is a socofrice, Pa?"

Father did his best to explain what a sacrifice was, and what was meant by "no cross, no crown." Suddenly a whizzing sound ripped the air, and a black object went down like a thunderbolt. The suction of the air pulled my hair to the front of my face and left me trembling in my father's arms.

"What was that, Papa?"

"It is a hawk. It is hunting," answered Father. "It is down by those black rocks. It probably got a mouse, a rat, or maybe a rabbit. You'll see it come up in a few minutes."

Father stood with the chaps and the water canteen, waiting and trying to see the hawk. Far down the canyon, below the rocks, I saw the hawk rise up. It disappeared and reappeared and finally it flew straight up with a dark whip wriggling in the air.

"It got a snake, Eva. See it?" The hawk turned west and the white belly of the snake glistened against the pink sunset. "Pa, is it pretty or not?"

"What do you think, Eva?"

"I think everything is so pretty up here. I like it. I love it all and the socofrice, too."

We walked down the peak to the place where we had left Diamante. As the sun sank down the nocturnal wildlife began to make its appearance. Our trail home wasn't difficult at all. When we walked into the kitchen, the red light of the kerosene lamp woke me up. I remained awake long enough to hear Father say that I had fallen asleep and that he had to carry me and lead the horse.

Life Along the Creek

At the turn of the century Arivaca Creek was the life focus for the surrounding country. Thousands of burros grazed in the nearby hills and watered at the creek, as did enormous herds of strange cattle, all of which had horns that were different in size and shape. Their colors, too, were diverse, strange, and difficult to describe.

Hundreds of Papago Indians lived along the riparian banks of the creek. According to their own accounts: "Many grandmothers of grandmothers here born, here die. Much fish in the creek. Much tobacco in the banks, much corn, much elderberry. Much food. Much good. Now white man here, too." And they shrugged their shoulders as if they wondered whether things would be better or worse with the white man in their midst.

The Indians traveled every summer to Tucson to harvest the saguaro fruit and then returned to their home—the creek. The enormous cottonwoods and the musical stream were their paradise. And mine, too.

Abandoned Indian campsites, with their weathered bear-grass huts and their litter of broken pottery, made an intriguing playground for me. When Wahyanita came to play with me she always brought two or three of her Indian friends. Lupita, an obese little Indian girl of four whose only apparel was her coarse black hair, followed us everywhere we went. When she sat down her long hair fell between her chubby legs and covered her beautifully. She always brought her toys—tiny little ollas the size of my mother's thimble. Dreyah, maybe seven years old, also went about naked. She never smiled and seldom spoke. Her fun was in pinching Lupita and me. One day Father scolded me for not defending myself: "Next time she pinches you, you fight back. She might whip you but it won't hurt you as much as my *reata* will, and that's what I am going to use on you if you don't defend yourself." Father rubbed the coiled reata over the saddlehorn as he spoke.

It wasn't long until Dreyah again pinched my bare thigh. I screamed and then picked up a shank bone and hit her across her forehead. She dropped and lay still. I ran home, walked in the kitchen, and abruptly announced, "Ma! I killed Dreyah!" My mother and my grandparents ran to the ditch with blankets and smelling salts, crying their loud disapproval of the way my father was raising me.

Dreyah was sitting up, looking blank and groggy. "Next time, Dreyah," I warned, "you're not going to sit up." There wasn't a next time. Dreyah never pinched me again. We still had fights and threw rocks at each other, but at noon we stormed the kitchen together for whatever lunch Mother could dispense. Ruby and Che, still shy of strangers, played together at my grandfather's truck garden when my Indian friends came.

On many days, however, my Papago friends stayed away, busy with other concerns, and I would spend hours with my mother and Hunga, following the talkative stream as it snaked its way from one side of the bank to the other.

About a quarter of a mile east of the house was a wild grape arbor where the grapevines grew at the bottom of the west bank and then climbed up to the top of an ash tree. Somehow they managed to branch across to the east bank where they came together with the branches of another grapevine and went on to climb whatever trees they could. These vines formed a massive arch of green that reached up higher than the neighboring trees. At the bottom of the creek these grapevines grew and made a private, enclosed arbor with a hard-packed dirt floor, a delightful playground for me, and a cool resting place for my mother.

Sometimes the Indian children joined us, and when they did we played for hours, running up and down the banks and climbing the lower branches of the trees, or following killdeer, in hopes we would find their nests.

At one place up the creek erosion had terraced a stretch about a thousand feet wide and maybe twice as long. Here was sandy soil where river acacia, penstemon, and mariposa lilies grew. Desert willows, barberries, and many other shrubs thrived in the sandy soil of the terrace, making this place a haven for quail, killdeer, cottontails, and for the Indians who came daily to hunt them and to set their traps.

In the center of the terrace lay a dead cottonwood tree, long stripped of all its bark. Its thick, huge roots and its top branches held it two or three feet above the ground. I had named the log Pluma Blanca because of a white feather I found there.

Close to Pluma Blanca grew elderberry and other smaller trees whose branches hung low over the log. This shady resting place and the nearby surroundings for a little way upstream became one of our favorite spots.

Just up the stream a brush fence formed a foot bridge over the current. The stream came through the logs and brush and made a deep, narrow channel along the north bank where it gained speed and really outdid itself, wriggling and lashing against the bank. About three hundred yards ahead, a large ledge jutted out into the center of the creek bed. The stream dashed and splashed against it, and here Wahyanita and I threw small sticks for Hunga to retrieve. Sometimes the impact of the water against the rocks sent it flowing back and it would take Hunga along with it. The current would make a wide circle and come forward again, passing the rocks, and finally spreading out on a stretch of flat, level sand where Hunga could regain her feet. She never seemed to mind. She was having as much fun as we were.

Here the stream divided itself into two branches; one flowed against the banks of the terrace and the other flowed along the north bank, leaving an island of white sand in the center. My mother often watched us from this island, where she sat with my sister Ruby. She watched constantly for the cattle, which often came to water. When they were coming she would motion for us to move quickly over to the security of Pluma Blanca, while she herself hurried there with my sister. We would all get under the great log or climb up and sit on its smooth surface and wait until the cattle had drunk and wandered away from the creek.

Aimless play was all very well, but my mother soon began to feel that she had to teach me the basics of country life. One day when Mother and I were riding up the creek on Diamante, I pointed up to the branches of a cottonwood tree and said, "Ma, look at that bag up there. I think Barreplata left it up there." My mother reined Diamante, looked at me in exasperation, and said, "That is *not* a bag. That is an oriole's nest. Tomorrow," she said, suddenly deciding that I was much too big to mistake a nest for a bag, "we are going up the creek—and no Indians for company, please."

"Why, Ma?"

"Because I want to teach you a few things, and I can't teach you anything when the *Indiada* is following us." That night I overheard Mother telling Father about my mistaking the nest for a bag.

"Well," said Father, "she is nothing but a damned dreamer. Even Baby Lupita, the Indian, is smarter than Eva. Only a week ago she climbed upon the wood cord back of the corral and called me to see a black and red necklace. Couldn't she see that it had a head and that it coiled under the log? Eva just can't grow up to be that silly."

So the following day Mother fixed a beans and jerky lunch and we walked up the creek. As we walked along Mother pointed out birds, nests, tracks, different kinds of small animals, and every other thing of nature she could identify until finally we were atop Pluma Blanca. Pluma Blanca was to become my kindergarten classroom. Observation would be the main topic of the elementary course, and my mother, my teacher.

My first assignment consisted of only one thing: "Look where you step. There are a lot of cockleburs and cholla along the trail, so be careful." As I took longer walks by myself, I was told to look out for snakes and how to use a stick to feel my way along the trail where the weeds grew tall.

From the top of Pluma Blanca I also saw the smaller animals of the terrace—the birds, squirrels, moles, and skunks, and from them I learned many important lessons, not all at once, but one at a time, day by day. There was the time Mother held me up to look into a nest. I was actually frightened when I saw for the first time the tiny, featherless birds. When they felt my hand near them the four infant birds opened their beaks wide. Their mouths were much too big for such little birds. "They're yellow inside, Ma, and they are blind!" I cried excitedly.

"They are little martins," said Mother, "and they haven't opened their eyes yet. They will in a few days. They just hatched."

Here in my creek classroom I saw for the first time a black and yellow bird take a bath at the edge of the water hole. He came out, shook himself, and ruffled his feathers. He was all black and yellow like the mariposa lilies. "It's an oriole," said Mother. "That's the bird that makes the nest you mistook for a bag."

"But that one wasn't like the little martins' nest, Ma," I protested.

"No, different birds make different nests." And we walked to the opposite side of the bank where she pointed out to me the old abandoned swallows' nests left there since spring. Mother explained how the birds had built them, and to me these were even more wonderful than the oriole's bag nest. I stood watching the birds flying swiftly along the banks, dipping down into the water, and flying up again. There were so smart, I thought. I was jealous of their ability to carry water up where water was needed, but I didn't know how to explain this to my mother. I just stood there looking at her. "What's the matter?" asked Mother.

"I don't think I could do the things they do, Ma."

"Well," she said, smoothing my hair, "you are not a *golondrina*, you know."

Hunga and I loved to see the goats browse from our vantage point near Pluma Blanca. For one thing, the goats didn't run away here, as they did when we grazed them on the hill. Instead they went from one bank to the other and stayed right there in the terrace. The young members of the herd would run up the bank and suddenly jump up two or three feet higher, frolicking and twisting their little bodies, turning somersaults in mid-air, and making a perfect landing, all four feet on the ground and ready to go into even more intricate gymnastics. It was such fun to watch them. Strangers, upon seeing them, would ask wonderingly, "How is it possible that those little animals don't break their necks?" But they didn't. Kids no bigger than jackrabbits would run up a leaning tree to a tremendous height, turn, run down, and even while they were at full speed they would be able to judge just from what height it was safe to jump.

One day Mother allowed me to walk away from the immediate vicinity of Pluma Blanca. I went off happily with Hunga to explore the erosion holes along the banks, Mother's voice following: "Watch for animals in the brush and listen for pounding hoofbeats. It means that cattle or horses are coming, so get out of the way. Move close to a tree and wait."

I soon forgot Mother's warning, of course, and before I knew it a herd of burros coming to water ran over me. Hunga ran them down the creek and Mother came and picked me up from the mudhole. I was bruised and mud-spattered, but wiser for the experience. I was learning to listen and to get out of the way before animals came in sight.

But Pluma Blanca was not my only classroom. My father, too, became a stern teacher for this small girl of three who had so much to learn about the world she lived in. During the spring and summer, cattle grazed in the surrounding country, watered at the creek, and bedded down under the mesquite thickets above the banks of the creek, often in company of the Indians. Father made a ditch about five feet from the edge atop the bank and in it he would temporarily plant a line of leafy upstanding brush, usually thatch. When he wanted to look the cattle over he would walk along the bottom of the riverbanks and then very quietly climb up to sit close to the edge and look through the brush screen. In this manner he could see what cattle were watering at the creek and what calves needed doctoring or branding. Sometimes he had to wait until the cattle got up and moved about to see the particular animal he had in mind.

One day Father took me with him. With the help of the erosion-bared roots of a mesquite that was close to the thatch hide-out, he hauled me up the bank. We sat quietly, well hidden by the green, feathery fence of thatch.

A herd of cattle was bedded down right next to a group of Indians. A brindled cow lay under a mesquite tree chewing her cud. The brindled baby calf that slept at her side got up, moved a few feet away, urinated, went back, and playfully butted his mother on the head. Right across the way we saw an Indian woman chewing mesquite beans and somnolently looking into the distance. A naked Indian child slept at her side, half buried in the mesquite leaf mold. As I watched, fascinated, the child got up, rubbed his eyes, stretched, walked a few feet away, and urinated. The sweat of his body had rolled the leaf mold dust over and made black ridges across his back—a brindled child, unknowingly mimicking the brindled calf and playfully butting his mother on the head.

An Indian man got up and walked along the edge of the sleeping herd. Not one animal moved. They slept on.

Father told me to wait for him behind the thatch screen and then he turned and walked along the flank of the sleeping herd as the Indian had done. This way he could see the animals better and not have to wait for them to get up, which would be late in the afternoon. No sooner had he gone past the group of Indians than three or four animals stood up, raising their heads high. They trotted in a circle and came back to stand still, looking at Father, who continued to move slowly along the edge of the sleeping herd as he had seen the Indian do.

Suddenly, the whole herd stood up in unison, watched Father for one quick eyeblink of time, then stampeded up the hill. I could hear the thundering hooves and the rattling of horns. A cloud of dust rose above the thicket. Three or four Indian men stood up, looked at Father, then dropped back to the ground, laughing uproariously. One man stood up and yelled at Father. *"Jiawul."* When Father came back to our little hide-out he asked me what I thought the Indian had said.

"Pa," I said, "he called you a devil." Father laughed all the way back to the house.

My father and the thundering herd made me think of the time María Nieves took Mother and me down to the river to show us the place she had found to spend the winter.

"Good house," said María Nieves. "Warm. I'll show you." And we followed her down the river. As we came out of a clump of elderberries we saw a black bull coming up the trail. He stopped, raising his head and pawing the ground. "Come this way, María Nieves," yelled Mother, as she picked us up and ran up the slope.

"No," said María Nieves, "bull no hurt."

We stood directly above the bull and watched María Nieves go by within ten feet of him. He ignored her, still watching us and shaking his head. He was lean but in good condition. His satin black coat glistened in the morning sunlight; a startling white triangle on his forehead gave him a dangerous appearance.

I knew the bulls that watered at the creek: this was not one of them. There was Huaco (goggle-eyed); he had a white face with red circles around his eyes. There was Fajado (the belted one), a red bull with a white belt around his middle, the son of a jersey cow. He was chunky and had a set of small horns that grew forward. He won his fights without a struggle, simply jamming his little horns into his antagonist and pulling them out dripping with blood. Another was King Canelo, a strawberry roan with horns that grew outward with a snake twist. They could well have measured nine feet from tip to tip. King Canelo had a difficult time trying to hook his opponent; he would kneel on one knee, turn his head, and struggle to catch the other with his long horns. Limón (lemon) was another bull with an enormous set of horns, but his had an upward sweep. In a fight he butted with his forehead. But who was this?

"Where did he come from, Ma?"

"I can't see his brand, but he must be from Mexico."

"What's his name?"

"Azabache."

"What's that mean?"

"Black Onyx."

"Who told you his name, Ma?"

"I just named him myself," said Mother. So now I added Azabache to the list of outstanding bulls I knew. There were other bulls in the herd, but for some reason or other they didn't stand out for me. I looked down at the black bull and said, "Good-bye, Señor Azabache." I threw a rock at him. He didn't run; he came forward.

We left him pawing the ground and walked above the banks toward a huge cottonwood where we met María Nieves, who had squeezed herself through the big cottonwood roots. We followed her under the tree. The cavity underneath was large and round and high enough for us to stand. It was dank and murky and there was a musty smell, but it was warm. María Nieves was happy to have found such a warm place to spend the cold and rainy winter months.

We left María Nieves at her new house and started toward home. But once we were alone Mother told me never to go under the cottonwood alone, as there could be animals inside—skunks, or maybe even snakes.

I never forgot that María Nieves had gone fearlessly past the bull only a short distance from him, and the bull had completely ignored her. I still wonder at that phenomenon.

In the fall of the year the cattle went west toward Sasabe, a little thatch-roofed town along the Mexican border. They crossed the line and spent the winter months in the ravines south of the border, always traveling east, so that spring found them well on their way back to the Territory. They crossed the line into Arizona and came down the Oro Blanco wash, straight toward Arivaca, and then they turned west, always going down the creek.

It was from atop Pluma Blanca that we witnessed the arrival of the bulls one warm spring morning. I stood on top of the log, looking east. "What's coming over there, Ma?" Mother looked up the creek and said, "The bulls are coming."

"How do you know, Ma? You can't see them under the rainbow willows."

"I listened," said Mother. "When you can't make out what you see in the distance, listen, and you'll hear some noise that will tell you what it is. If you hear some nickering you'll know that it is a horse; if you hear someone talking you'll know that it is people. Learn to listen."

"Yes, Ma. Can we watch them now?"

"Yes, but I want you to hide under the branches and to hold Hunga real quiet. Teach her to stay quiet." Hunga tried to jump down, and Mother slapped her down.

"Ma! Poor Hunga."

"She has to learn and so do you. Or you'll get what Hunga got just now. When the bulls come to that big rock, you hide and be as still as you can. No squirming now, mind you."

"How still do you want me to be, anyway?"

"So still that if they see you they'll believe you are part of these dead roots."

"I don't think I can, Ma."

"Yes, you can. That's the only way you can see animals and people without being seen. And when the bulls go by here I want you to look at them good. Pay attention. See if they are cut, crippled, fat, or skinny." The bulls came out of the thatch and they walked down toward us, single file. "Ma, Azabache is leading them and Huaco is behind him. And there comes Fajado and King Canelo and Limón!" They were coming at a fast, steady walk. My heart was pounding against my chest. The bulls came close to the opposite bank, turned, and followed the trail that went right alongside the log. Azabache stood. He raised his head, testing the air. There was a scent he didn't like. He stood as still as the terra-cotta statue of an Astas bull that sat above the fireplace in the *sala*. Azabache's black coat was glossy and beautiful. The white triangle on his forehead matched the white tips of his slick, black horns. Mother put her finger to her lips. Everything was still. The bulls stood tense, looking in all directions. Huaco stepped ahead and put his nose to the ground. He must have smelled our tracks, for he immediately stampeded down the creek, followed at once by his peers.

"Now," said Mother, "what did you see?"

"I saw the bulls, Ma. They were fat."

"Is that all? Did you see Fajado? What was the matter with him?"

"Fajado was fat too, and big."

"Is that all you saw in Fajado?"

"Yes, he was big, too."

"Fajado," said mother, "had a piece of rope around his neck, which means that someone roped him and he broke the rope and got away. And it also means that you don't *see* when you look, and you will have to learn."

That day Mother took up my country education seriously. She didn't point things out to me anymore; instead she made me point things out to her, and explain them in detail. There were many difficult lessons that I had to learn before I was allowed to romp and run free, with only Hunga for company.

Guarding the Gap

ONE DAY I REMINDED FATHER THAT HE had promised to give me Diamante for my own saddle horse. I wanted to go farther along the creek and why couldn't I ride Diamante?

"All right," said Father. "I will leave Diamante in the stable and Mother will saddle him for you. You can ride him just to the top of Pesqueira Hill and back. Stay on the trail so your mother can keep an eye on you. I will be gone until tonight. Take care of Diamante. He is your own saddle horse now," he said as he swung in the saddle and left for the day.

I lifted my skinny hand and yelled, "Come early, Pa."

Later in the morning Mother saddled Diamante and put me on his back, sticking my bare feet into the stirrup leather. "Just go to the top of the hill and come right back," called Mother as I rode away.

Halfway up the hill I looked back to see if Mother was still watching me. At the door of the house stood my grandparents, my Aunt Rita, and Mike, plus Ruby and two or three Indians who usually came in the morning to ask for milk.

"They think I can't ride. We'll show them, Diamante."

I reached the crest of the hill and stopped to look over the surrounding country. I felt strong and confident. Below me at the foot of the hill on the west side was the Indian village of the *jacalitos* (little huts). I could see the place where María Ollas Coloradas lived. Mother had told me that when María burned her ollas they came out beautifully— clear, smooth, and red. The ollas made by other Indians had black spots and a dull film over them.

I looked back at the house. The audience at the door had grown. Barreplata with his dogs and Simon had arrived. I carefully gauged the distance—it was as far to where Mother stood at the door as it was to the jacalitos. Temptation was too great. I would ride down to the Indian village and let Wahyanita see me on Diamante, all by myself!

I followed the trail down the hill. The village appeared to be deserted, so I went past it for a few hundred yards, then I turned and rode back. Suddenly Wahyanita appeared beside the trail wearing her perpetual grin that always showed a row of white teeth. She stood poised with a rock in each hand. I reined my horse, my heart hammering. I turned Diamante about and rode west about a quarter of a mile, then came up the creek away from the village. To my dismay, as I came around a bend in the bank, there was Wahyanita again, standing in the center of the creek. Diamante pointed his ears and stopped. I sat frozen, not knowing what to do. The Indian girl lifted her arm, a big rock in her fist.

Just then someone shouted from the hill, "Stop! ¡*India cabrona!*"

I couldn't see him, but I knew Uncle Mike had come to my rescue. Wahyanita dropped the rock and ran across the riverbed. She scrambled up the steep bank and disappeared.

It seemed as though Mike had appeared out of nowhere, and now he stepped on the stirrup and swung himself up behind my saddle. Taking the reins from my hands, he headed home.

"¡*Muchacha loca!*" he said. "Crazy girl. That Indian could have hit you in the head with that rock."

"I know it, Mike."

"Then why don't you mind your mother?" He slapped my bare thigh with a heavy hand. I didn't cry, but my leg burned and turned red. When we arrived home Mother took me down from the horse and led me into the house.

"Let go of my hand, Ma."

"I will when I get through with you," answered Mother. In the bedroom she laid me across her lap and paddled me with the hairbrush. "You're not riding alone anymore," she said sternly.

When Father returned he scolded me, too, but when I told him how Wahyanita had threatened me, he immediately rode to the jacalitos to see María Nieves, with whom Wahyanita was staying at that time.

María Nieves adored my mother and was in our house every day, so Father could talk to her frankly.

He returned to tell me that Wahyanita would never bother me again. And she didn't. Soon they let me ride again.

I took to the trails at will, Diamante my faithful companion, my playmate. But he was also my protector. He would gallop joyfully down the creek with me on his back, but if there were any sign of trouble he would stop, point his ears, turn around, and head for home. Even if I pulled on the reins Diamante would take the bit in his teeth and never stop until he had arrived at the kitchen door.

One day Father asked me if I didn't think it would be fun to drive the goatherd up the hill across the creek, let them graze, and then drive them back to the riverbank. Yes, I thought that was a great idea. So, with the help of Hunga and Diamante I managed to shoo the herd up the hill. While the goats browsed I had time to explore every nook and cranny of the rocky ravine that circled the bottom of the hill.

I didn't dare to get down from the horse, for once on the ground I wouldn't be able to get into the saddle again. From Diamante's back I watched the squirrels jump from one boulder to another, disappearing into the trunk of a dead tree and reappearing on the branches above. I could see the nests in the trees. There were brown speckled eggs, blue eggs, and white eggs. In some of the nests I found ugly, naked little birds. Everything in nature held me fascinated.

Above me on the slope I suddenly spied a large stump with a smaller one right beside it. If I could get Diamante alongside these stumps, I thought, I could slip down and be free to run around. The same stumps would help me get my foot into the stirrup to mount again. Leaving Hunga digging furiously at the bottom of an old hollow tree, I hurried up the incline to try out the plan, but Diamante balked, refusing to go anywhere near the stumps.

The goats stood in a circle around us, ears pointed in my direction. They snorted, ran away, and came back.

"What's the matter with you, goats? Are you crazy? Haven't you seen me before?" Impatiently, I urged Diamante toward the stumps, but again he reared back, acting frightened. The big sawed-off stump was smooth on top, but the one beside it had two strange prongs sticking up from it. I looked at it again. I blinked, staring in horror. *It wasn't a stump.* It was a lynx cat, so still it might have been dead and perfectly camouflaged.

For one awful instant our gazes met. Then the cat jumped up and went slinking over the hill. I hurried home to tell Father what I had seen.

Father was shaken, though he tried to speak calmly. "*Attention, Eva,*" he said. "*See* when you look!"

As the months went by I became quite adept at driving the herd. I stopped it; I turned it back. I headed it in whatever direction I wanted it to go. I drove it slowly or at a brisk run. I was a real rider!

One day when I was amusing myself by watching the goats stand on their hind legs to reach for mesquite beans, Father appeared suddenly over the ridge. "Can you give me a hand, Eva?" he asked.

"Yes, Pa."

"Look, I'm going to drive those horses down to the corral, but as soon as they reach the river they'll head for the gap. If you ride down there and stand at the gap they'll go to the corral instead."

"All right, Pa." As I galloped down to the gap a sense of pride surged through me that I could help Father just like one of the men.

At the gap I stopped and waited for the horses. I heard the thunder of hoofbeats and saw a cloud of dust rising above the banks, then the splashing of water as they crossed the stream. Almost immediately I saw the herd coming straight at me.

I raised my hand and yelled at them. The horses swerved and headed toward the corral, only to turn and come straight for the gap again. I felt Diamante gear for the fight. He ran from one end of the gap to the other. Short as the distance was, he moved quickly and began to turn the herd back, but one old mare made a circle and returned to fight for the gap. Diamante rushed head-on to the west side and the mare shifted to the east side. Diamante shifted again and cut her off—on and on, whipping back and forth as I clung to his back.

Finally when Diamante moved again to the west I kept going east. I grabbed the saddlehorn, but I wasn't strong enough to regain the saddle and landed on the sandy embankment where I sat, unhurt, and watched Diamante perform by himself. He was soon driving the horses up the slope to the corral and Father hurried to close the gate.

As I limped up to the corral Father called, "What happened to you, Eva?"

"Diamante went crazy. He went this way and that way," I said, moving my hand to show how Diamante had moved from side to side.

"You're supposed to stay on the horse and *tell* him which way to go."

"I know, Pa, but he was bucking too fast."

"Eva, that horse was not bucking and you know it."

"Wasn't he bucking, Pa?"

"No, he was fighting off that old mare. You don't know how to balance yourself, that's all. But don't worry, I'll teach you."

That same afternoon Doña Tomaza Corea came to visit my mother. My new brother William was just a week old and she had come to meet the new arrival and to see how Mother was getting along.

Doña Tomaza made a striking figure when she got down from the buckboard. She always wore a man's white shirt and a long black alpaca skirt that reached almost to the toes of her boots. Her long green gloves had a fringe on the sides. She couldn't have been young when I knew her. She had lived and worked all her life on a cattle ranch, but she was still tall and straight, her hair still dark. She had an imperious air about her, for Doña Tomaza was known and respected by everyone. Grandfather Vilducea thought her a handsome woman. "*Muy hermosa*," he would say, shaking his head admiringly.

"I passed the doctor on the way," said Tomaza to Father as he greeted her. "I believe he is coming to see Ramona, is he not?"

Father told her that we expected him sometime today.

"Well," Tomaza laughed, "he'll be here before sundown. He is riding Black Nick—one step at a time."

"I was going to Arivaca myself," said Father, "but I spent all day getting the horses in." He went on to tell Tomaza all about my bad experience. "I must teach her to balance herself."

Doña Tomaza laughed again and patted me on the head. "She's very young, Agustín. Let her grow a little bit."

"She's almost four, and she's been riding all her life. Ruby is learning to ride by herself, too, and is showing signs of making a good rider."

"Well, I'll stay tonight and help you give Eva a lesson in the morning," said Tomaza in a matter-of-fact manner, moving toward the door. I followed her and Father inside where our guest was welcomed warmly by Grandfather and Grandmother. She was soon seated at the table, those wonderful gloves lying on her lap.

"I'm still a good rider myself, you know, Agustín," she continued. "When I was young I rode better than my two brothers. And I managed a few cattle drives in my time. We used to start the cattle at Abilene, and by the time we got to Río Colorado we'd be driving fifteen hundred to two thousand head. We hired hands as the herd grew, but I was trail boss all the way.

"We'd let the herds rest before reaching the river, then we'd hurry them more and more, and when we arrived at the riverbank, we'd rush them in. Not an easy job, Agustín! Those longhorns would try to break out of the herd, but once the leaders were in the water, with a lot of yelling and hollering, the rest would follow. When the last animal was in the water, I would jump down, tie a knot in my horse's tail, and grab onto it. I'd hang on until he swam across the river and not let go until I stood on California soil.

"On the way back we'd always have a lot of fun. We would waylay the payroll wagon and hold them up for water and food, Agustín." Tomaza winked at Father.

"How much money did you take back to Abilene, Tomaza?" Father asked.

"A quarter of a million dollars. Not bad, boy!" Tomaza emitted a loud laugh and slapped Father on the thigh.

"¿Más cafe, Tomazita?" Grandmother interrupted disapprovingly.

By now I was in the bedroom, watching through a crack in the door, and listening. I fervently hoped that Father would never tie a knot in Diamante's tail and tell me to hang on as he pushed the horse into the flood when the creek was roaring from bank to bank.

Mike arrived all out of breath. He had been up on Pesqueira Hill. "The doctor is coming," he announced. "I saw him from the hill."

"Well," said Tomaza, rising. "I'd better find some toloache (jimson weed). I promised the doctor I'd get some for him."

"I'll get it for you, Tomaza," offered Mike. "I know where there are a lot of plants." Mike ran out to search for toloache and Tomaza sat down again. Taking out half a pouch of dried leaves, she began to roll cigarettes.

"Don't tell me you smoke that weed, too, Tomaza," said Father.

"Seguro que no (of course not). I dried this little bit for the doctor, but I never got to give it to him, so now I'll have some cigarettes ready for him when he gets here. Poor man, his asthma is very bad now." Smoking toloache was supposed to be very good for asthma.

Mike came back with a bundle of leaves and Doña Tomaza asked Grandmother to dry them on the stove. "It's best to dry them in the sun, but the doctor will want to take some with him. I taught him this remedy, Agustín," she continued. "I visited him one day and found him almost choking to death. I sent for some toloache, then I pounded him on the chest and the back and talked to him. That's the way to treat someone who's having an asthma attack," she said, turning to Grandmother. "Talk, talk, talk, if you can get him to talk back to you he'll come out of it."

The doctor finally arrived. Grandfather went out to carry his satchel for him. Though he was still a good fifty yards from the house we could hear his wheezing.

Dr. Joseph Ball had been a doctor in the valley since he arrived at Oro Blanco, south of Arivaca, in the late 1800s. He was a handsome man in his forties, loved and respected by everyone. His black suit and black fedora hat, his slow, dignified manner inspired confidence in everyone. He often delivered babies to air and life while he fought and struggled for breath himself.

"*Caracho* (oh my), Tomaza," said the doctor as he stood at the door. "I smelled that toloache clear over to the gate."

"Sit down, Dr. Ball," said Father. "We are preparing some hot menudo for you." That was another thing Tomaza had recommended for the sick man.

"Ah, pepsin soup! I never refuse that. But first I'll see my patient."

Father led the way to the bedroom where Mother was lying in bed with her first male child in her arms. Ruby and I were shooed away, and we watched Tomaza and Grandmother set the table and place a pan of menudo on the stove to heat.

When the doctor came back, Tomaza remarked that he was blue in the face. She quickly took off his coat, sat him down, and pounded on his chest and back. Grandmother placed a bowl of soup before him and Tomaza began to talk. She talked and she talked until Ruby and I were getting very restless.

"Doña Tomaza," I said at last, "the doctor isn't blue anymore. He is white now."

"Yes, Tomaza, thanks to you. I'm going to finish my menudo, smoke a toloache and leave."

After Dr. Ball had gone, Doña Tomaza spent a long time visiting with Mother; again she talked ceaselessly, on and on, until even my curiosity failed and I stopped listening.

The following morning we hurried to the gap for my lesson. Father rode Diamante, and Doña Tomaza instructed me to watch him to see how he moved his body as the horse shifted from side to side, while Mike pretended to be another horse, fighting for the gap.

It was quite obvious that Mike didn't make a good horse. He seemed to be afraid that Father would take this opportunity to run him down, so he didn't put up a good fight. I laughed at the mock battle, so finally Doña Tomaza impatiently decided that *she* would be Canelita, the mare who had fought for the gap the day before, when I was thrown off.

"Keep your eyes on your father and his horse, Eva," she said. "They are a good team." Then she yelled at Father, "All right, Agustín, here comes the Old Canela Mare." And she ran full-speed for the gap.

Father headed her off, but she evaded him, now right, now left. Diamante moved quickly and turned fast, but the Old Canela Mare managed to squeeze herself between the fence post and Diamante's chest. She took the gap and ran free.

My grandfather, uncles, and Barreplata, who had all come down to watch, laughed and applauded. Doña Tomaza came back, laughing herself into spasms.

Next they decided to teach me how to drive stock. Uncle Mike was to be a calf, and I was to drive him. Tomaza got behind me on the saddle and told me how to head the calf back to the trail when he tried to run off. "If he comes this way, Eva, you move halfway to his flank. No, not too far ahead. He'll turn and run back on you. Wait! What have we here?"

She was looking down at the ground. I pulled in the reins.

"Hold the calf, Agustín," she yelled to Father. "I am going to give Eva a lesson in tracking." Mike and Father went to sit on a rock. "Every good range rider watches for tracks. What kind of tracks are those, Eva?"

"They are Mike's tracks, Doña Tomaza."

"I know, but if you were beyond the mountain and saw them what would you say?"

"Indian tracks."

"Well, let's say a man's tracks, a man afoot. Now, are they old or new? If they are blurred, they are old tracks." She pointed a few feet ahead. "What kind of tracks are those?"

"Horses' tracks," I said. "And those over there?" she asked.

"A colt's tracks."

"So what do they tell you?"

"Nothing, Doña Tomaza."

"They should tell you that a mare with a baby colt came to water. Now those tracks over there?"

"They are Diamante's," I said.

"They are a *shod* horse's tracks, and they tell you that a rider went by, don't you see?"

"But they are our own tracks, Doña Tomaza."

She finally gave up on her abstract lesson, since this four-year-old pupil insisted on taking it all literally. She shouted to Father, "All right, let's drive that calf into the corral." Mike got up and ran into the corral followed by Diamante. Father came to close the gate.

"She is going to be a great rider when she grows up, Agustín. But let her grow. She is just a baby."

"Oh sure, but she can be learning and helping while she's growing up, Tomaza."

Doña Tomaza and Father sat on the fence and talked for the rest of that morning, and after lunch they hitched her two *alazanes* (sorrels) to the buckboard. She left in a cloud of dust.

After the lessons from such an authority as Doña Tomaza I was expected not only to know how to drive stock, but to be a fully seasoned cowhand. The following day Father saddled Diamante and lifted me to the top of the wall.

"Do you see those horses, Eva, there on the side of the hill? That's the bellmare." He put me in the saddle. "Go bring them," he ordered. "I'll stand on the gap."

I hadn't really seen the horses, but I went in the direction they were supposed to be. I crossed the creek, and upon reaching the top of the hill I saw the Canela Mare. My spirits rose a little at this, but they fell just as quickly when the horses saw me approaching and took off at a dead run in the opposite direction.

Father appeared from nowhere, as he usually did when I was stymied in a task he had given me. "What's the matter with you, Eva? We spent half a day teaching you to drive stock and you don't know a thing? You have been driving the goat herd long enough to do better."

"The goat herd don't run away, Pa."

"Horses and cattle are driven in a different way." He looked up at the horses, now motionless on the crest of the hill. "Go down that arroyo and come up the slope. Move in a circle and come toward the horses from that side so they'll see you on the upper slope; they'll run down this way and on to the creek. Understand?"

"Yes, Pa."

"All right. I don't want to have to tell you that again."

I followed directions as well as I could. At first the terrain wasn't bad and I covered a lot of ground, but as I climbed, the hill became steeper and more rocky. The trail finally played out and Diamante slowed down, picking his way at will. I really had no choice, so I let him go at his own pace. We kept climbing and climbing, moving in a circle until Diamante finally stopped at the crest.

I let him rest while I looked in all directions. Father was nowhere in sight, but far down at the foot of the ridge the bellmare was running toward the creek. She disappeared into a mesquite thicket; then I saw dust rise above the trees just across from the ranch house. The horses were in the corral! My job was done.

I knew that I should go right home. I could see my trail about three hundred yards below me. Again, I let Diamante choose his pace, picking his way slowly and carefully over the loose rocks as we descended the hill.

We finally reached the trail and I pulled at the reins. I had heard voices on the path below and I went to investigate.

An Indian woman in a yellow blouse and a brown skirt was driving three little Indian boys along the trail. She had made a kind of whiskbroom from some burro weed and was slapping the bare bottoms of the children as she urged them on. "*Him! Him!* (Walk! Walk!)," she was crying to them. I heard one of the children say, pleading "*Tonk!*" He was thirsty and wanted to go to the creek. But she drove them on ahead of her.

I watched them for a long time, poking along behind. I loved the bright yellow blouse the woman wore. I knew that her clothes were made from flour sacks, colored with dyes she had made. The yellow was made from barberry sticks in a long process of soaking and boiling. The brown of the skirt came from the tint extracted from walnut hulls.

So I dawdled along, relaxed and satisfied with my stock-driving feat, dreaming in the saddle. All at once I had a sudden urgent desire to urinate. I couldn't get down, so I flicked the reins telling Diamante to hurry now. I couldn't wait. I had felt this urgency too late. Diamante's shoulder twitched as the hot urine ran down his side.

It got on the saddle, too, turning the leather dark brown. What would Father say? The hurry over, I now rode along more slowly than ever, hoping the saddle would dry before I reached home. But, of course, it didn't. When I finally arrived at the corral Father opened the gate for me without a word.

My grandfather was standing there looking at the urine-soaked saddle. "Agustín," he said, "you're the most inconsiderate man I ever met." Father didn't answer him.

He got me down, looking disgusted. The seat of the saddle was almost black. "Go in the house and eat your lunch, Eva," he said.

I walked to the house, hungry, thirsty, tired, and very dirty. I was sitting at the table waiting for Grandmother to warm my food, when Father came and stood at the door.

"Eva, did you have to stay out there till you peed? What were you doing all that time?"

"It was hard getting down from the mountain, Papa. Diamante didn't want to hurry."

"That excuse won't work, Eva. Next time I expect you to come in right behind the horses. Understand?"

"Yes, Papa."

The following day, Father put me in the saddle again.

"Go get the bellmare now and come back right away, not sometime tonight."

"Yes, Papa." I was lucky. The horses were just across the creek. I went around in a semicircle as Father had taught me to do. They ran down to the water, and I drove them into the corral at a gallop. My uncles and Barreplata, sitting on the fence, laughed and applauded me.

Thereafter, I drove both the goat herd and the bellmare, and I brought the milk cows in every day. But I could not relax in easy pride. There seemed always to be new and more difficult lessons to learn, and I was expected never to show any fear or signs of weakness.

As time went by, everyone took it for granted that I could help with the ranch chores as well as anybody. Ruby was learning, too. We often rode double and stayed out long hours working or playing. Sometimes Father took me with him to the little ranches in the vicinity and there everybody made over me. The old ladies scolded Father for making me ride so far. "Wait till she grows a little more, Agustín. She's no bigger than a flea."

One day Father went across the creek to bring in some cattle and left me alone guarding the gap. I was supposed to head off the herd and drive it into the corral as usual. It wasn't long until I heard hoofbeats and clattering horns. The herd appeared around the bend, and a mottled-faced steer ran straight toward the gap, the other cattle following him fast.

No matter what Diamante and I did the steer kept coming on and before I knew it he had taken the gap. I galloped through to head him back and the other steers followed me. When Father came up the creek driving an old cow, all the cattle had disappeared. He was angry.

"Do you know what guarding the gap means, Eva?"

"I couldn't help it, Papa. When I went to head the steer back all the others came through."

Father uncoiled his rawhide reata and whipped me across my arms and back. I rode fast up the wash, but he ran alongside Diamante, took hold of the reins, and pulled him close to his own horse. When Diamante stopped running I managed somehow to get off his back, slipping and sliding to the ground. I stumbled and ran down the wash.

Father ran after me and quickly caught me. I hadn't seen him get down from the horse, but when I looked back there were Diamante and Big Grey standing side by side.

"If you try to run away, I'm really going to whip you, Eva."

I screamed and got between his knees, but he pulled me out and somehow I found myself up on his shoulders. I looked down and saw that he no longer had the reata. Just then Hunga came running up, growling and baring her fangs at Father. Father picked up a stick and struck out with it. He actually threw me down to get rid of the dog.

"Come, Hunga," I said between sobs, starting off as fast as I could go for home.

"Come back here, Eva. I'll put you on your horse."

"I'm not going to help you anymore, Pa. Never."

Father was still in a rage at Hunga. "You'll do what I tell you or I'll get rid of that dog for you."

I had seen Father kill Chocolate, a dog that used to go after chickens and young goats. He found the dog one day in the goats' corral standing over a dead kid. Chocolate ran away and was gone all day, but he came back that evening. We saw him etched against the light on Pesqueira Hill.

Father got his rifle. He pulled back the lever and aimed the gun against that evening light. I remember the awful crack and the red sparks of fire, Chocolate standing still for one moment, then slumping forward onto his chest.

I couldn't stand to think of Hunga like that. I patted her and told her to go home, then I followed Father up the wash, my back and arms still burning from the lashing. I put my arms around Diamante's leg and cried heartbrokenly. What had happened to the beautiful man who had taken me to the peak of El Cerro?

When Father picked me up and put me in the saddle he held me for a moment, tightly. When he released me tears dropped from his eyes.

He mounted the Big Grey. "Come, Eva," he said.

I followed him up the arroyo to search for the cattle that had gotten away. We found them lying in the shade, but to my surprise Father ignored them and kept to the trail. At the top of a rise he stopped and looked back. "Eva, do you see that bunch of green trees down by the trail?" he asked, pointing.

"Yes."

"You go down there and wait for me. I'm going up the mountain to bring the team down. Stay right there, do you hear me?"

"Yes, Papa," I said.

Father rode up the rocky slope, and I went listlessly down the incline to the grove of trees. When I came near I saw that they were mulberry trees, heavy with the delicious black-purple fruit I liked so much. I dropped the tied reins over the saddlehorn and reached out to the branches. In spite of the scolding of a host of birds, I crammed my parched mouth full of the juicy, refreshing berries.

I ate and ate, enjoying myself so much I almost forgot the pain of the beating.

"Where are you, Eva?" My father's voice startled me.

I looked through the branches. "Here, Pa. See all these good berries I found."

"You were lucky," said Father. "By the looks of your face they are juicy and ripe." It was then I noticed my hands; they were purple. Father pretended to be surprised at seeing the ripe berries, but I know now that he had sent me there alone to pacify me, letting me have a joyful discovery before taking me home. He took his collapsible cup from his saddlebag so that I could fill it to take some home for Mother and Ruby.

"Pa," I said as we started for home, "I'm going to name this trail 'the trail of the mulberries'."

"All right. The trail of the mulberries it is."

The following day was Saturday and Saturday was bath day. Soon after breakfast Mother set a five-gallon can full of water on the back of the stove. Toward evening she brought in the old galvanized tub and set it between the stove and the dining table, filling it with hot water, tempering it with cold.

First she undressed Ruby and put her in the tub to play. She took off my flour-sack underwear, then held me for a moment before putting me gently in the water. "What's the matter with your back, Toña?"

"Pa whipped me, Ma. He hit me with the reata."

"He whipped you? What for?"

"Because the cattle took the gap from me and ran up the arroyo."

Mother had picked up the soap. Now she dropped it. Water splashed from the tub and across the floor. She stood still a moment, looking at it, then she hurried to the door and called Father to come in. "Please come quickly, I have something to show you."

Mother pointed to my back and said, "Why?"

"Well, she let the cattle go at the gap."

"You expect a four-year-old child to head off a herd of longhorn steers? You are insane." Mother's voice was clear, cold, and strong. I had never seen her look so tall.

An argument raged until dark. Father said at one point that if he was going to be tongue-lashed like this, he thought he should leave and never come back. "Never will be too soon," answered Mother, coldly.

Father went outside and stood by the wall.

I had already dressed myself and put Ruby's pants on backwards. Mother dragged the old tub outside and came back to put our supper on the table. Our evening meals were always scanty and that night it was spareribs, rice, and goat's milk.

Father didn't come in and Mother didn't ask him to. Neither Ruby nor I had spoken, but now I tried to get Mother's attention. "Hunga and I, we fought him, Ma. He was going to kill Hunga, Ma."

Mother put her finger to her lips, and we ate in silence.

The Bronco Busters

AS RUBY AND I GREW, SO DID THE LABORS for everyone on the ranch. There were more cows to be milked, more calves to be branded, more goats to be herded. The two eagles up at the peak of El Cerro had multiplied, too. They would swoop down on the goatherd and split it into three or four groups, then attack the group farthest from the sheep dogs.

We would leave the house at breakneck speed, hoping to rescue the victim—always the smallest member of the herd. More often than not we would arrive too late and the eagles would be high up in the air, flying toward the crags where they would eat their prey undisturbed.

The Mexican wolves at the Cochis Ranch along the border were becoming abundant and bold, too. They fed on the young calves, and the way they eluded our traps was uncanny.

With the work increasing by leaps and bounds, Father was always in a hurry and usually out of sorts. He would often ask me, "Have you seen the team, Eva?"

"Yes, Pa. They were up there." I would point vaguely upward.

"Up where?"

"By the trail, near the cottonwoods."

My inability to be explicit always exasperated Father beyond reason. One day he came to the house at a gallop. "Eva, did you see Midnight at the water hole?"

"Yes, Pa. He drank and went up the trail."

"What trail?"

"The trail of the mulberries."

Father jumped back on the saddle and disappeared across the creek. He came back within minutes leading Midnight. My description had worked beautifully. That was the way to answer Father. I decided then and there to name every rock, gate, hill, or hole in the ground, and it would be up to Father to remember just which place was Mockingbird Meadow or Lobo's Gulch, or Screech Owl's Hollow Tree.

In such ways I eventually learned to cope with Father's outlandish whims and unreasoning anger, and although he was exacting and severe, he was quick to praise Ruby and me when our work was good. Some of our most fulfilling experiences were when some hired man would announce that he was quitting and, asked why, would answer: "Because I don't like to be put to shame by those two puny little girls!"

One of Father's most difficult tasks was breaking the young horses to the saddle. It was dangerous work, and he struggled mightily with the broncs. He would rope one and get the saddle on, then he would tie a hundred-pound sack of sand to the saddle. The horses hated it and would buck savagely, trying to throw off the weight.

One day Father went to Arivaca to get the mail, and when he came back he told us that Doña Tomaza was coming to buy a milk goat. My heart hammered against my chest at the memory of my hard "lessons" from Doña Tomaza and Father's anger at me when I hadn't completely learned them. When Father left the kitchen I asked, "Ma, what does that old buzzard want to come here for?"

Mother laughed, "I have a hunch she was invited."

"What are you laughing at, Ma?"

"At your father," answered Mother. "I have an idea that he asked her to come to help him with the broncs."

Doña Tomaza came and sure enough, before we knew it she was on Diamante and I was with her behind the saddle. Father saddled one of the broncs in the creek bed, stepped into the stirrup, and swung himself into the saddle. He removed the blindfold from the bronc and the horse took off at a dead run.

Tomaza galloped alongside, heading the horse away from the creek slope and said, "Take hold of me, *hija,* and we'll keep him in the creek." Her calling me "daughter" reassured me a little and I held onto her as she asked.

The bronc ran close to the bank and stopped dead. Try as she might, Tomaza just couldn't get him to move one way or the other. She finally took the lead rope from Father, dallied it around the saddlehorn, and gradually pulled the young bronc away from the bank. The horse trotted, he sulked, and finally he walked. At last we were in the corral.

"Three more broncs to go," said Father. "Pay attention to Tomaza, Eva. Watch how she heads the horse away from the slopes. You're going to help me when she goes."

"When will she go, Pa?" I asked.

"As soon as we get through today."

"Doña Tomaza, can't you stay until tomorrow?" I asked.

"*Seguro que sí, hijita*—Sure little daughter."

My self-serving invitation was enough for Doña Tomaza. She got ready to stay. "Mike," she ordered my uncle, "you water the *alazanes* for me and put them in the little pasture for the night. I am going to sweep the floor of the buckboard and spread my bedroll."

"You're going to sleep in that room, Tomaza," said Father, indicating the bedroom next to the kitchen. "It gets cold in the early morning now."

"Oh, no, Agustín. Under the stars for me. It will bring back memories of the many nights I slept on the ground with the saddle for a pillow and my two young brothers for company."

"You need a good night's sleep, Tomazita," said my grandfather. "Working with those broncs is no joke."

"I enjoyed every minute of it. I love the way the horses handle themselves. Each one fights in a different way. And I have an idea this is probably the last time I'll be doing any tough riding. It makes me feel young again, Francisco! Work is good for me."

"Well, if work is good for you, I'll put you to work on my floor." Grandfather's project in the *sala* had been going on for months. "I am almost through with it, Tomaza."

"*Vamos a verlo*," and she turned to go in.

Grandfather led the way to the living room and Doña Tomaza stood in the doorway, admiring his new floor. "What a good old man you are," she said. "This brings me memories of other days—*pisos de barro*, clay floors in San Miguel de Allende! I was young then, Francisco, and I used to dance with the *charros*."

Grandfather took Doña Tomaza's arms and led her to the middle of the floor. They danced a waltz while Tomaza sang.

"Look at those two old fools," exclaimed Grandmother.

Father laughed. "They are in their second childhood, Margarita."

Tomaza and Grandfather, twirling around the room, didn't hear. Mike brought his guitar and played for them. I thought Doña Tomaza looked pretty. "When you hear this waltz, remember meeee." The song ended and she bowed.

"If the floor was finished we could dance all night, Tomazita."

"Don't worry," she said. "We'll work on it right now."

Making a clay floor in those days was a long and arduous task. First soil was brought into the room and was packed and tamped; then it was leveled, sprinkled with water, and allowed to dry. It was tamped again. This sprinkling and tamping went on for a week or so, and then the floor was allowed to dry for a week.

Meanwhile, red clay was brought to the yard and sifted into a cone of fine soil. A depression was dug in the flattened top of the cone and water was slowly poured into it while the clay was kneaded until all lumps were mashed. The result was a dark red batter. This was loaded onto a wheelbarrow and taken into the room where candles were lit and holy water was sprinkled upon the mixture.

The batter was dumped onto a two-foot strip of floor that ran the width of the room. When the batter became dry enough, pads or hides were placed before the strip and a worker would kneel down and begin to sand the floor with a fine, smooth rock. The fine powder that was rubbed off was poured into a can and saved for later use. At times, red-hot coals were scattered over the floor to harden the surface and take up moisture as they were moved back and forth. Each strip was rubbed and rerubbed, night after night, or whenever anyone had time to spare. If a crack appeared on the surface more batter was made from the fine powder that had been saved and this we poured into the crack to be reworked until the flaw was invisible.

When a strip was finally finished to everyone's satisfaction, it looked like a piece of red mahogany. The pads were moved so that the work could continue on a newly poured strip. It took ten to twelve months to finish the whole floor. During long winter nights the whole family helped.

Working on a clay floor gave everyone an opportunity to talk, to smoke, and to reminisce. Grandfather and Tomaza were soon on their knees facing the wall, running the smoothing stones over the dry, red clay. This was the last strip; the floor would soon be finished. My uncles and Barreplata decided to join in and the rhythmic sound filled the house. Roosh, roosh, roosh, roooosh.

In the kitchen Grandmother had begun her chocolate-making ritual. She had to have cinnamon sticks, milk, and flour for thickening the *champurro*. Aunt Rita and Mother were making *buñuelos*, similar to doughnuts, but with the dough flattened like a tortilla. They dropped them into hot grease and we watched them swell up into round balls. When they were a golden brown Mother took them out and sprinkled them with sugar.

Ruby and I threw a quilt on the middle of the floor and watched both the kitchen and *sala* operations, listening to the stories Doña Tomaza told. At ten o'clock everyone went to clean up, and then to the table to drink *champurro* and to smoke.

Grandfather was always very attentive to Doña Tomaza, lighting her cigarette, filling her cup with hot chocolate. "You shouldn't ride those wild horses, Tomazita. You must take care of yourself. What would we do without you?" But we knew that when she was not here Tomazita would become to him *la vieja sin verguenza*—the shameless old woman— because of the horrible things she and her brothers had done and the way she bragged about them when she found someone to listen to her. Holdups were her favorite subject. Ruby and I fell asleep, lulled by the sound of the smoothing stones on the new clay floor.

The following day everybody went to the corral, for the broncos had to be ridden before they would be really trained. Father saddled the Big Grey to wrangle the broncs and he put me up behind his saddle. Doña Tomaza decided to ride Bayo (Buckskin).

"I'm ready if you are, Agustín. Just don't let him leave the creek."

"We're ready," said Father. Tomaza leaned forward and lifted the blind from the bronc's eyes. He took off at a dead run, the Big Grey staying close to his flank. Whenever Bayo tried to get to the banked slopes Doña Tomaza slapped his jaw, turning him toward the center of the creek.

It wasn't at all difficult to head him off, so over the way back Father put me in the saddle and took the place behind me. Handing me the reins, he told me what to do all along the way: "Stay on his flank so he won't kick you. If you have to get behind Bayo, don't get so close that he can reach you with those hind feet."

When all four colts had been ridden Doña Tomaza began to get ready to leave. She sent Uncle Mike to the hills across the creek to get her some amole, the saponacious agave that produces suds when pounded on a rock. We used it for laundry soap, shampoo, and dishwashing.

When she was ready to go Doña Tomaza sat at the table drinking a last cup of coffee with Grandfather. She took scissors and carefully cut a corn husk down to the size of a cigarette paper. "Here, Tomaza," Grandfather said, pushing toward her a three-pound can full of corn husks already cut and stacked upright.

"Oh, Francisco, you are a rich man." She pulled a husk from the can and poured home-grown tobacco on it, expertly rolling and lighting it. She took one long puff, inhaling deeply, then threw back her head and emitted a cloud of smoke. "This ranch is a great place, Francisco," she said. "It's beautiful. And the Americano—he's kind of crazy, but a good-hearted man. I love Agustín."

My Grandmother Margarita brought out the little gifts she was giving Tomaza to thank her for always being ready to come and help. She put them on the end of the long table: a black silk *rebozo* (scarf), an old belt with a silver buckle, the old copper kettle, and, best of all, the portrait of Saint Thomas the Apostle, one that had been painted and framed by Don Ignacio Pesqueira in the winter of 1865. Just as the painting of San Martín moved Barreplata those many years ago, so Doña Tomaza had long loved this one, for Saint Thomas was her patron saint. She said she had wanted it for the longest time.

Grandmother sat at the table to drink her own coffee now while Grandfather went outside to load boxes of vegetables in Doña Tomaza's buckboard. Mike arrived with a burlap sack full of amole and this, too, went into the buckboard.

Father came in and poured himself a cup of coffee, and Tomaza thanked him for letting her help with the broncos.

"Next time you come they'll be gentle saddle horses and you can ride them again, Tomaza," he told her.

"God willing," she answered. "Every time I ride a horse I feel that it may be the last time." There were tears in her eyes; I was surprised. This fun-loving, daring old woman—crying?

Doña Tomaza told Father she would send a man she knew named Federico Lara to help him with the geldings. Federico was a good horseman, she told us. Then she took her leave, giving everyone a hug and much patting on the back.

Early the next morning Federico, a tall, muscular young man, arrived riding a chestnut sorrel. He met Father at the corral gate. "Federico Lara at your service," he said.

Father greeted him cordially and everything went smoothly until

Father roped a blazed-faced sorrel that had come in with the green-broke colts that morning. Father had decided to work the sorrel along with the others since he had Federico to help him.

Federico drove the rest of the broncos into the big corral, then hurried to help Father. Father gave him the lead rope and got down from his horse to tie up the bronc as soon as he fell. But the bronc kicked out at everything within reach. He pulled, reared, and put up a powerful fight, but he didn't fall as he was supposed to. Father finally took the end of the rope and tied it to Federico's saddlehorn.

"No, no, Don Agustín, don't play that way with me. I came here to help you, not to be killed."

"Nobody's going to kill you, Federico."

"I have had experience, Don Agustín. I take care of myself."

"All right, amigo," said Father. "Go get on your own horse and go back where you came from."

"*Siento mucho, Señor.* I am very sorry," said Federico, dismounting and walking away. He stopped at the corral fence to talk with my grandfather and uncles.

"Come over here, Eva," said Father.

My cowardly heart threatened to come out of my mouth as I walked slowly toward Father, amid loud objections from my grandfather and uncles. They were sharply told that they were no help and were ordered to leave the corral. They did not move. Mother had arrived by now and they all sat on the fence in a silence so tense it was almost audible.

Father put me on Diamante and tied the rope to the saddlehorn. He told me to let Diamante take one step forward. The bronc pulled, gasped for breath, and became wobbly. My saddle tipped foward with me until it stood up on the saddlehorn and the cantle touched the back of my neck. The bronc suddenly lunged forward.

"Back up, Eva. Back up!" Mother jumped down from the fence and came to hold Diamante while Father eared the bronc.

"I can't do this, Ma," I whispered.

"I am helping you," said Mother. "You keep this rope taut all the time and always face the animal you're holding."

"My saddle is falling, can't you see?"

"No. It just tips up because you are not heavy enough to hold it down."

Suddenly, without warning, the bronc fell and Father tied up his feet. "Loosen up," said Father. So Mother led Diamante a few feet forward and the bronc began to struggle again. He was almost up when Federico jumped down from the fence and sat on his head until Father could secure the rope around his feet.

"A nice horse, Agustín," said Federico.

"Well, are you going to ride him?" asked Father.

"*Seguro que sí.* That is what I came for. I'll get my own saddle."

He hurried to take the saddle from his chestnut sorrel and brought it to the bronc's side, putting the snaffle bit and the blind on the bronc while Father held him. They carefully let him up and Federico mounted him.

"Let him run along the creek, Agustín, *¿Está bueno?*"

"Sí, Federico. We'll keep him from going up the banks."

I rode along one side of the horse and Father on the Big Grey took the other. As soon as Federico lifted up the blind the bronc started to buck. Father took the lead rope and guided him along. Riding on the flank I tried my best to keep him from running up the slope. Father kept pulling him away, making the wrangling easier for me, and at last, I thought with surprise, great fun!

One by one Federico saddled and mounted the other broncs, Father and me riding along with him each time, helping to subdue them. Back at the corral as Federico stood patting and currying the last colt, Father asked him, "What do you think of my *vaquerita*, Federico?"

"She is great, Agustín! Nobody would believe it. How old is she?"

"She is five years old."

"*¡Dios mio!*" exclaimed Federico. "What a crime!"

And so the weeks turned into months and the seasons went by and we struggled with the endless work, taking what little pleasure we could from the company of those faithful companions, who, once broken, never hurt us or let us down—the scrawny little rock horses.

¡Ay! Caballito creollo que pasó y se fue!

The Spring Corrida

I
T WAS APRIL. EVERYONE WANTED TO LIE BACK and enjoy the beautiful weather, but the bustle of spring was upon us and work had to be done. Ruby and I did our share, taking orders from Father. We herded the goats and brought the horses down to the corral every day.

Father himself worked from early morning until after dark, riding the range and bringing in the mother cows with their newborn calves. He repaired the corral gates and made new fences. He shod the horses and worked at breaking the broncos.

Like the cows, the mother goats, too, were having their kids. This meant that our little herd had to be kept somewhere near the corral so that the kids could be born within easy carrying distance. Taking the kids to the corral after they were born was a delicate task, usually performed by Barreplata. They had to be picked up by their forefeet and held away to the side so their tails would not be touched. If the tail of a kid were rubbed or touched, the mother would refuse it and it would become a *lepe* (orphan) and we would have to feed it by hand. The mother goats that had somehow lost their kids had to be milked regularly so that they would not sicken with pain or have their udders ruined. All these jobs, along with bringing firewood to the house and keeping the curious Indians at bay kept Barreplata busy all day.

Grandfather, Mike, and Luis were getting ready to plant the *milpita*, the truck garden, on a small island in the middle of the river. It was actually a great clump of soil left by flood erosion; it started at a point and quickly widened to about thirty feet, stretching on to a length of about five hundred feet in the course of the stream.

While the uncles plowed around the trees, Grandfather dug up the compost that he had buried the previous year and worked it into the soil. They planted the seedlings he had started and piled old cottonwood leaves around them for protection. Work on the island garden would go on all day, every day, until the continued harvesting, planting, and harvesting again was over—usually until some time in October.

At the house Mother busied herself making the day's butter and cheese and curdling the milk in preparation for the next day's cheese. In the spaces in between these tasks she would place five or six flatirons on top of the stove. When they were hot she would pick up an iron, test its temperature with the tip of a wet finger, wipe it on a pad and apply it to a garment. Before one garment was half-finished, she would have to return the iron to the stove and pick up another one. She would walk to the stove and back to the ironing board countless times. The ironing was never completely finished.

Although Grandfather Vilducea and his family lived just across the river, they spent most of their daylight hours at our house, so that my gentle Aunt Rita came almost every day to help Mother with the cooking and cleaning. She always began by cleaning the water jugs. There were two ollas in the kitchen and two in the dining room. The fifty-gallon oak barrel in the zaguán was kept full of water for whatever needs there were. Aunt Rita would begin by emptying the ollas and barrel, sprinkling the old water on the earthen floor of the zaguán to pack it and to keep down the dust. Once the water containers were clean, she would refill them with fresh water she brought up from the creek.

That task completed, Aunt Rita would turn her attention to the kitchen, and while Mother ironed, she would take advantage of the hot oven to roast enough jerky for the week. When the meat was cool, she would pound and shred it and Ruby and I would feast on the crumbs that fell to the side.

It was on such an ordinary day as this that Don Manuel Oros, a friend of Father's, came to tell him that the spring *corrida* (roundup) would start in eight days. This was exciting news and it sent us headlong into the work of preparing for the day when Father would join the *remuda*—the boisterous parade of horses and riders on their way to a designated spot where they would begin the spring roundup of livestock that had strayed all over the range during the winter.

Barreplata worked long hours in the corral helping Father. We ignored the Indians in order to get the important jobs done and the Indians took advantage of the opportunity, coming to the ranch in

hordes. They sat along the wall or on the corral fence and looked toward the kitchen for hours at a time, signaling their hunger silently, as
always.

Father rode to the Cochis Ranch near the border and brought back
the four horses he usually took to the corrida. One was to carry his
bedroll and the others would be used to spell the Big Grey when he
was tired, since working at the roundup was as rugged for the horses
as for the vaqueros.

Some of the horses needed to be shod, so one day Father led Big
Grey to the work bench. He built a fire in the forge and brought out
the horseshoes and tools as I stood turning the handle of the blower
to keep the fire burning. Big shoes had to be made smaller and small
ones bigger. I loved to watch him pound the red-hot iron into shape
and then plunge it, sizzling, into the water tank.

Father tied on his apron and carefully lifted the Big Grey's foot to
his knee. The Grey reared back and headed down the hill. Father
hardly had time to wrap the end of his rope around the trunk of a
mesquite tree. The Big Grey choked and fell, fighting the rope, then
finally stood up gasping for breath. This struggle brought five or six
Indians out to the work bench, so old Barreplata came running after
them, brandishing a long stick over their heads to keep them away,
for they would crowd around until no work could be done. The Indians
picked up their bundles at the wall and went toward the creek. Father
brought the Big Grey back and Barreplata held the rope while Father
shod the horse.

He began on another. Once a man separated himself from the crowd
of Indians near the creek and came toward the work bench again, but
he stood to one side until Father finished his task.

Barreplata, standing beside me, looked up and tapped my shoulder.
"There will be no more shoeing today, little one," he said. "That
young Indio is one of the Marianos from Poso Verde and your father's
good friend."

I stared at the man. He didn't look like any Indian to me. His skin
was dark but he looked Castilian, dressed in fine clothes, unlike the
other Indians. He wore a jacket and trousers, a cowboy hat and good
boots. He was about the age of my Uncle Mike.

Now he stepped forward and spoke Father's name. Father looked
up, smiling with pleasure, then immediately cast aside his work apron
and held out his hand. "Mateo, my friend, how are you?"

"I am well, Agustín."

"And your father?"

"Oh, my *ugk* is doing fine, Agustín. He is busy just now preparing the boys for the salt caravan." The salt caravan was a periodic pilgrimage to the sea in Mexico to obtain salt for the tribe. It entailed a hazardous journey and complicated rituals, and it was considered a great honor for an Indian boy to be chosen to go.

"Then he always has the sick to care for," Mateo continued. "Many hungry, many sick now in the Papaguería."

"Your father is a fine medicine man, Mateo," said Father. "I'll never forget the time he saved my hand. He spent all night putting maguey poultices on it to draw out the infection from a thorn wound." He held up his hand to show that it was as good as new. Then he looked down at me.

"This is my daughter, Eva, Mateo. She is the best little cowgirl in the Territory. Run along in the house, Eva," he said. "Tell your Mother that we will have a guest for lunch."

The Indian smiled at me. "When I saw you last, Eva," he said, "you were riding a broomstick horse."

I ran into the house to ask Mother about this Indian whom I didn't remember at all. "If he is an Indian, how is it that he has boots and pants and everything?"

"The Mariano family has a ranch near Poso Verde," said Mother, already putting the coffeepot on the stove. "They are quite well off. Your father has known them all his life, and Mateo's grandfather was a friend to your own grandfather, Dr. Wilbur."

Mother sent me to check up on the baby to see if he was sleeping peacefully. He looked peaceful enough to me. I put my hand down and he curled his little hand around my finger, but he didn't wake up. When I came back to the kitchen, Father and Mateo were drinking coffee at the table. I slipped in beside Father, and he didn't even notice me.

The Indian was telling them about some trips he had taken. It seemed he had actually been raised by a man in Acaponeta, Mexico, whom Mateo called "Pa White." He had learned a lot from this man and had earned quite a lot of money. When he came back across the border, he gave his father half of it.

"Then," Mateo went on with a smile, "I took off with Pa White's son, Lonny, and we went to the northern part of New Mexico. We visited the Navajos there and they sure were good to us. We saw their ranches with huge herds of sheep and cattle. The Navajo Indians are more advanced than the Papago, Agustín. They are hard workers and they have stores and trading posts. And that is a beautiful country."

He paused while Mother came and poured him fresh coffee. "When I came back to the Papaguería I found my old man riding in a surrey. Would you believe it?"

Father laughed, "You're joking, Mateo."

"No, Agustín. That's what he bought with the money I gave him. You should see the old Papago driving it." Mateo sat up straight, imitating his father driving a buggy. When he called his father "the old Papago" I looked up at Father and felt just as I had felt when I was very little and Father used to throw me up in the air. Everything I thought I knew seemed to shift, for I had been warned *never* to say Papago, a name the Indians hated, in front of one of them. And this man called his own father "the old Papago!"

"You were gone from home a long time," Father said.

"Yes, and when I got back I didn't tell my parents about everything I saw in Navajo land. It would sadden them, our own people are so poor. And I don't wear these clothes at home either. I go half-naked like the other Parientes. My ugk taught me that I was born in the village because that is where God wanted me to be."

After lunch Father put Mateo on Big Grey and they rode double to the nearby Indian village where Mateo had left his own horse. Father spent much of the afternoon showing off the ranch to his old friend, who had not seen it since he was very young.

Mother began immediately to prepare a special supper. She cooked a big kettle of carne con chile and made beans, fresh tortillas, and *fruta de orno* (turnovers). When she brought the steaming bowls to the table that evening Father said, "Try some of Ramona's carne con chile, Mateo."

The Indian took a geneous bite. "The White family in Acaponeta always called this chile con carne," he said. "What is the difference?"

"Chile con carne is a lot of chile sauce with a little meat and carne con chile is a lot of meat with a little sauce," Father explained with a laugh.

"By any name, this is the best," said Mateo to Mother.

Mother was charmed by his good manners. When he left he thanked her and Father graciously.

"I will see you in a few days, Agustín," he said, meaning that he would join the remuda when it reached his father's ranch.

These few days before the corrida passed swiftly. Father finished preparing the corral to receive the animals he would bring back from the roundup. Barreplata cleaned and polished Father's saddle and groomed the Big Grey until he gleamed. He suggested that Father go to Arivaca and buy himself a decent saddle blanket.

Meanwhile, Mother was busy getting Father's clothes ready—washing, ironing, brushing. On the first day of the corrida all the vaqueros wore their finest riding apparel, although when the real work of round-up began they changed to well-worn, easy Levis.

"Your father may be gone two weeks or more," Mother told me. "He must look respectable."

Father got his bedroll and spread it on the floor. He dusted it and packed his shaving outfit, extra clothes, soap, a towel, and other odds and ends inside it. He rolled it up and placed it in a corner, ready to be picked up in the morning. Then he hitched up the buckboard and drove to Arivaca in search of a new saddle blanket. I begged to go with him, but Father was restless and wanted to be alone.

He brought back with him a very pretty blanket with an Indian design and the news that the remuda would come out of None Bernard's ranch near Arivaca early the next morning. By sunup the drive would be on its way west, toward Avra Valley, and on to Poso Verde. All along the way it would be joined by horses and riders from other outfits, and by the time the drive reached our ranch it would be sixty or seventy strong.

My grandparents were anxious for the remuda to arrive. They always met several of their good friends and so they dressed up for the occasion. They said their goodbyes early that evening and went home, fussing about what they would wear.

The tenth of April came at last, bringing a different atmosphere, a turbulent and almost unbearable tension. Even the animals seemed restless. The goats wanted out early; the young kids sensed it and began to mill around the corral. Finally, Barreplata let them out and herded them to a safe place to browse.

Father saddled the Big Grey and galloped up Pesqueira Hill to see if the remuda was in sight. After awhile he rushed back and dismounted to open the corral gate. "They are coming," he said, and mounted again and went to stand on the gap to watch the horses go past him.

They came down the hill in a rush, dust rising around them, and entered the corral. There were whickers of welcome and thundering kicks of rejection among the many horses.

When the horses were all safely in the corral and the gate closed, my grandparents, Mother, and I boosted ourselves to the corral fence to watch the vaqueros parade through the gap. I was so excited Mother had to grip my arm to keep me still.

None Bernard, the most important cattleman in the area, had sent ten men with their respective horses and bedrolls. They were led by his foreman, Ramón Ahumada, whose name in later years found its way into the Cowboy Hall of Fame. The cowboys all wore their best and their horses were fat, well shod, and well groomed.

Ahumada, always dignified and courteous, rode his chestnut sorrel, Lucero. His saddle, polished and silver-spangled, boasted long *tapaderas,* their points now and then touching the ground as the horse walked along.

"He's pretty, Ma. Isn't he pretty?" I jumped up and down in excitement.

One by one the riders came. When they reached the wall, most of them dismounted and squatted down to roll cigarettes and talk.

"They are waiting for the Norteños to come," said Grandfather. "Two or three small ranchers from the north are expected any minute."

A few of the riders did not stop at the wall but came on to visit with my grandparents. Don Porfirio, from the Tres Bellotas Ranch on the Mexican border, sat on his horse in a sidesaddle manner while he talked with my grandmother. He brought greetings from his wife, Francisca, and from others of Grandmother's old friends, for he often visited the little town of Saric, where my grandparents had friends whom they hadn't seen for many years and did not expect to see again.

Another old friend of Grandmother's, Don Nazario, also came to visit in the corral fence and greeted us with warm courtesy. Ramón Ahumada came last, my father riding at his side. He dismounted, took off his spurs, and came to offer his respects, inquiring after every member of the family, as was his custom.

"And how are you, Margarita?" he asked my grandmother, holding her hand.

"I am well, Ramón. But my son Miguel talks of going back to Mexico to live. If he ever does it will be the last of me, you know."

"Don't believe him, Margarita. Mike is not about to leave you."

Everyone admired my spirited little grandmother. People knew how she had left the town of Altar in Mexico one midnight, years before, and how she had followed my grandfather across the Apache-infested mountains with several children at her heels. It had taken them ninety days to reach the Arizona Territory.

"And how are you, Francisco?" Ramón asked, turning his attention to my grandfather. "Are you working too hard?"

"I am tired, Ramón," answered Grandfather. "I have been camping at my island garden for more than a month. It is just like being in prison. The irony of the thing, Ramón! I left Mexico because I was afraid of someday finding myself a political prisoner at Islas Marías and I came here to find myself a prisoner on an island on my own!" He was only half serious. He was very proud of his garden.

"But your garden is a very beautiful spot, Señor," said Ramón. "Remember, you showed it to me last summer. I'll never forget the delicious fruit we shared." He climbed on the fence and the conversation went on among the men and my grandparents.

"Here come the Norteños." Don Nazario, who had been relaxing in his saddle, suddenly broke into their talk. He pointed up the hill. The men from the three small ranches in the Guijas Range were coming in, each riding a saddle horse and driving three others which carried their respective bedrolls.

Ramón Ahumada slipped down from the fence, taking time to say goodbye to each of us in turn. Then he put on his spurs and mounted Lucero. All the men along the wall were now back in their saddles, moving slowly out onto the hillside, ready to resume the drive.

"Adiós," called Father. He waved to Mother and me. Then he and Ahumada rode away together to stand at the gap. Don Nazario and Porfirio rode inside the corral and drove the pack horses and spare horses out to join them.

"*Hasta leugo,*" they shouted back as they passed through the corral gate, and "*¡Vayan con Dios!*" called my grandparents in reply.

As the horses fought to run back through the gate, Ramón and Father ran down from the gap to head them off. The Big Grey looked very fine with the black martingale against his broad white chest, and Father in his fine Stetson could rival any rancher there.

Once the horses were out of the corral, there was no time for exchanging pleasantries. The men had to head them, drive them, and keep them together. There was no looking back. One by one the rest of the vaqueros joined the remuda until it moved as one body, all speed and commotion, with wild shouting and twirling ropes. The herd was all but obscured by the dust they raised.

"Almost sixty bedrolls!" exclaimed Grandfather. "It is a big parada." We stood up on the wide fence rail and followed the swirl of dust that rose above the mesquite thicket. The sound of hoofbeats reached us across the hillside, then slowly died away.

The remuda had come and gone. It left in its wake a heavy silence and a sense of letdown. Mother and my grandparents got down from the fence and went slowly back into the house, but I sat there, still swinging my feet. Thinking about Father.

I knew well what went on at the corrida. Father had told me about it. After the first day of merrymaking it would be nothing but hard work. The cowboys would be ranging for miles in every direction, into the far reaches of hills and canyons, to round up the cattle. The calves would be roped and branded and then castrated. After long weeks of this they would repeat the process to round up horses instead of cattle.

Father would be sleeping on the ground night after night and would eat chuck-wagon food. He might even buy some treat from old Don Julían whose restaurant on wheels would be stationed at the campsite.

I would miss Father. I longed to be riding at his side, yet I knew, too, that life would be much easier for Ruby and me with him gone. I had promised to help Barreplata, who had been left in charge of the corral, but he was always soft where I was concerned.

I dropped to the ground and went toward the kitchen. Aunt Rita was standing at the door with William in one arm. She pulled me toward her and pressed my head to her side. "Why do you look so sad, niñita?"

Grandfather and Grandmother were at the table drinking coffee, talking quietly. Mother had fixed Ruby a late breakfast of milk and tortillas and now she poured milk for me.

Barreplata came in, having asked one of the uncles to tend the goats while he came down for coffee.

"Come and sit down, Barreplata," said Grandfather. "Did you see the remuda?"

"How could I miss it! I was watching from the hill. It went past like a cyclone."

Grandfather nodded. "I was just asking Margarita how a diabolical uproar like that could end in such deathly silence."

"Like the aftermath of an Apache raid," said Barreplata. "I saw

Agustín and Ramón Ahumada racing each other up and down the slope earlier, riding like a couple of show-offs."

Everyone laughed except Grandmother. "Why shouldn't they show off?" she demanded. "They have beautiful, well-trained horses and they are proud of them."

Barreplata looked at her teasingly. "Oh, yes, Margarita, the horses are well-trained, but you must admit that these ranch horses are just a bunch of mixed-up little *criollos*. There were as many colors in that parada today as there were horses. I saw *canelos* (light strawberry roans), *rocios* (dark roans), *pintos* (paints), *moros* (blues), *tordillos* (greys), and *blancos* (whites). And," he continued with a grin, "I think I even saw a speckled *minorca* in the bunch."

He didn't mean just a speckled horse, but a horse as small as a chicken, and Grandmother was not amused.

"You are disgusting, Señor Barreplata," she said. "The grey that Agustín rides is certainly a big horse. And what about that big, beautiful sorrel Ramón rode today?"

"And what about Tostón?" asked Barreplata. Tostón was one of the horses Father had brought up from Cochis Ranch to pack the bedroll.

Grandfather spoke up haughtily. "Tostón is an exception, as you know, Barreplata—the only really small horse in the bunch. But make no mistake, Señor, he is a man's horse. When El Tejano was here two years ago he was always bragging about the big horses he rode in Texas. One day Agustín asked him to get on Tostón and to bring in the horses. Tex began to laugh and poke fun of the little horse, saying he was afraid he'd break the horse's back. Agustín told him, "Just so that Tostón doesn't break *your* back, Tex." So old Tex saddled the horse and got on, but Tostón didn't like him and he began bucking hard. He went all around the corral, got out, and started up the hill. He threw Tex off, then threw the saddle off, and was across the creek before Tex could even stand up. Tex couldn't ride for three days and he never again bragged about the giant horses he used to ride in Texas."

"Oh, there's nothing wrong with Tostón," Barreplata admitted. "I guess I've been thinking about the big bays I used to see when I lived in California. Those were real horses, well-bred animals. One size and one color."

"One size and one color don't make them one bit better than these horses, *viejo fastidioso* (obnoxious old man). And just where do you think these horses come from? For your information, Señor Barreplata, they were brought here from Rancho Dolores in Mexico, the headquarters of Father Kino, who had brought them from Spain—a fine breed of Barbs that were brought to Spain by the Moors, and they also brought their riding style which they called *La Jineta*. The Spaniards adopted it quickly, and it is the style the vaqueros use here today."

"Well," said Barreplata, "they call these small horses scrubs, you know."

"Anybody that calls these beautiful animals scrubs is an unintelligent, stupid bore."

"Margarita," said Grandfather, "Be careful. Such talk is very unkind."

"Well, Francisco," said Barreplata, "I never read the history of these animals."

"Well, read it, Barra," answered Grandfather. "Go to Las Guijas Canyon and visit Corona. He lives in that tunnel across from the Cozon's gulch. He has that tunnel full of books that he orders from Spain. Good books, too, Barra. That's where Ramona got all those books in the sala."

"I'll do that," promised Barreplata.

Six hundred head of horses were brought to the Territory in the late 1800s by Juán Zepulveda. He was taking them to the stockyards in Kansas City. While he was in Arizona every rancher bought some horses from him.

Grandfather Wilbur bought twenty-five mares and one stallion, and so did the neighbors in the Arivaca Valley. I often heard the old-timers say that Juán Zepulveda had sold all the horses before crossing New Mexico.

Grandfather Wilbur brought fine Morgan horses from Colorado, but they didn't survive. The Spanish horses thrived in the desert and were the horses of the day. They were our companions from sunup to sundown and sometimes deep into the night, year in and year out. They had speed, stamina, and intelligence, and, strange as it may seem, they had feelings. I have seen them die heartbroken. In all the sixty years that I spent in the saddle off and on, only once did my horse play out on me, and that was due to my own hard riding.

Riding twenty miles away from any habitation, approximately seven hours away from any help, usually made me nervous and tense, and this put my horse on the alert, so I watched him closely for any signal.

I knew if danger were near he would tell me. Years of close association had taught me his language.

We loved our voiceless co-workers dearly and were quick to take offense at any slight against them. Indeed, more so than at a slight against us.

In 1921 I saw an auction of horses in Nogales, Mexico, and I had the pleasure of seeing people fight for a small rock horse. People didn't even look at the "blooded horses." The small rock horse ran around the corral with his arched neck and distended nostrils. He stole the show. People were calling attention to his feet, his head, and the way he carried himself. The horse was sold to a prohibition officer, Frank Edgel.

The Spanish horse was made to build the West, and that he did. He was tough like the longhorns. I have since read where people complained that the longhorns were bony and meatless and no good. That may be so, but they made it to Kansas City. They were not left to die sore-footed on the trail. They fed the nation with their tough meat and shod it with their hides. They gave us all they had. They were good!

And so the Spanish horses were made for the country and were much like the country itself, rugged and beautiful. They carried themselves well and carried their riders with utmost care, placing their small feet on solid ground and balancing themselves as they reached out for better footing.

It was amusing to see an 800-pound horse under a 200-pound man with an enormous saddle and a 1000-pound bull at the end of a rope. They knew the danger they were under, but they worked with their riders with courage and outstanding intelligence. And none more beautiful! These were the horses that went to that spring corrida.

Visitors in the Milpita

During the days that followed, while Father was away at the roundup, life was quieter on the ranch. Grandfather often took Ruby and me to the *milpita* to play.

Grandfather's island was unique. It rose several feet above the creek and the sides were too steep for larger animals to climb. In fact, there was only one entrance, by way of a narrow strip of land, and that was guarded by a fence and gate that could be securely locked. A pomegranate fence along the edge of the north bank, and quince trees lined the edge of the south bank. Three peach trees and two apricot trees were staggered down the center of the island.

To me it was a magical place. In the spring it was filled with the tremulous green of newly growing things and the scent of flowering shrubs and trees. Swarms of beautiful hummingbirds visited the island. There would be a whirring of wings, and then suddenly the tiny birds, working on the peach blossoms. They hovered over our heads suspended in the air or going back and forth. They were never afraid of us. When we sat to eat our lunch under the willow tree where Grandfather had built an *hornilla* (mud stove) and had set up a long crude table, the hummingbirds would join us, sitting at the edge of a plate with sugar water that Grandfather prepared for them. When the plate was dry, they would sit on Grandfather's shoulders and look into his face. I remember a white hummingbird with a turquoise-blue collar; it would come streaking in and suddenly stop, only inches away from Grandfather's face, its wings twirling so fast they reminded me of a dancing top. We called it the white angel of the island.

Grandfather was not an authority on animals, but he made up little stories that not only taught us to observe the animals and plants, but whetted our interest in them and kept it alive. I remember the day I asked him if the mockingbirds were all alike and the whitewing doves and other birds were all alike, why then were the hummingbirds all different? Some were blue and some were red with black, some were blue-green.

"Well," said Grandfather, "the hummingbirds flew across a sunset like the beautiful one I showed you girls last week. Remember? That is where they were tinted blue-black, blue-green with red, and the other colors."

"And, why, Grandpa, does that hummingbird have such a curved beak? Did he get hurt coming across the clouds or something?"

"Oh, no, no. He is a *vacanuchi,* slang for Roman nose."

"Some are vacanuchis like some horses, Pa? But Grandpa, some of them also have the beak like a horseshoe nail and others like the roadrunner's beak."

"Oh well, maybe they take after their ma, like you take after me with your blue eyes."

And so I went around studying the birds. I came upon one hummingbird that seemed to be choking on a worm. "Grandpa!" I yelled, "Here is a hummingbird eating a worm! Come and see it!" Grandpa approached the old-fashioned lilac bush and looked: "Oh, no," he said, "that's his tongue. Can't you see? And, *mijita,* don't tell your father that you take after me. He may not like it."

"Yes, Grandpa, I see. He has two tongues."

"No, he's got a forked tongue like a snake." I stood unbelievingly and watched the hummingbird, and I was finally convinced that it did have a forked tongue, but it was certainly a long tongue. Even my grandfather's Minorca rooster didn't have such a long tongue.

In the summer the island would be just as tantalizing, for then the fruits would be ripe and the ground lush with vegetables ready for harvest—tomatoes, squash, peppers, and long rows of corn. Then Grandmother would roast the tender ears of corn for us and she would cook *quelites* (greens) and serve them in a big bowl that Grandfather had carved from mesquite wood.

Sometimes Grandfather would kill a cottontail and Grandmother would cook it and make biscuits in the hornilla Grandfather had built near the willow tree. Never since have I tasted the like of the biscuits that mud oven used to bake. The meal would end with slices of ripe, red watermelon sprinkled with black seeds.

Grandfather never forgot our springtime friends, the birds. We would place the leftover rind and melon on the ground for them beneath the high trees where they lived. I remember one time seeing several mockingbirds form a wall around a piece of melon. Suddenly a cardinal in brilliant red swooped down and crashed the blockade, soaring up again with the melon in its beak. Two of the other birds sped after him and there was a terrible tussle in the ash tree across the creek. Soon after the two "officers of the law" reappeared and dropped the melon at our feet.

"That's mockingbirds for you," declared Grandfather. "They are everything: polite, rude, mean, playful, greedy, and what birdsongs they steal and sing."

"Oh, Francisco!" exclaimed Grandmother. "They're a bunch of *sin verguenzas* (shameless ones). For me, the whitewinged doves—they are brave and humble at the same time. Beautiful to look at and what a pleasure to hear their call!"

Outside the fence at the bottom of the bank Grandfather had sunk a well. With a windlass he pulled up buckets of water to fill the tank from which he watered the plants. After the rains came, he would hang up the bucket and go to work, hoeing, weeding, and pruning. The long vines of the squash with its large leaves and trumpetlike yellow blossoms covered much of the ground, and he was forever reminding us: "Watch your step."

Near the bank, close to the well, was a large mesquite tree dresssed in gourd vines. The gourds dangled like bells from its branches. We gathered them and Grandfather cut holes in some and hung them in the trees for bird houses. Others he cut lengthwise and we used them for dippers. Indians who came by always took as many as he would give them.

Grandfather worked hard for all of us. During the spring and summer months, most of his life was spent in the gardens. When the plants were maturing and the harvest was near, he slept there to protect the produce from thieving Indians. So, when I remember him, even now, I usually think of him as there on the island, a thin, dignified man with a long white beard and serene blue eyes, wearing the familiar blue coveralls and a wide hat against the desert sun.

Grandfather had friends everywhere in the valley. When people visited the ranch more often than not they found an excuse to drop in on Grandfather on his island.

One morning, a few days after Father had left for spring corrida, Dr. Ball came by. He left his horse on the riverbank and Grandfather met him at the gate. My mother and grandmother were there, too, preparing our lunch.

After Dr. Ball greeted everyone and enjoyed a cup of coffee, Grandfather took him for a tour of the gardens. And, of course, I tagged along at their heels, always curious, always listening. I noticed at once that the doctor was in better health than before. He wasn't wheezing at all.

The doctor ambled about the island, admiring everything, but he suddenly stood stock-still upon coming face to face with one of Grandfather's *covachitas de San Ysidro* (niches of San Ysidro). Grandfather had spotted three of the little niches around the island, each containing a plaster figure of San Ysidro, the patron saint of farmers.

"*¡Caracho!*" said the doctor. "How this reminds me of my own country! You see lots of these little shrines in Alsace. They are everywhere on the farms of the French. But in Alsace," he added, "the *covachitas* are built to honor Santa Odilia, the patron saint of the blind.

"Do you know the story of Santa Odilia, Eva?" he asked. I shook my head. And so he went on to tell me this legend that I was never to forget. There was once a princess who had been born blind. Her father wanted to have her killed, but a nurse took the child away and raised her. When the little girl was old enough, she was baptized and at that time, miraculously, she received the gift of sight. She became a nun and her father, in his gratitude to God, gave her money to build a convent."

"Alsace is a long way from here," Grandfather told me. "Far across the sea."

"In many ways the people in Alsace, along the German-French border, remind me of the Mexican people here," Dr. Ball told Grandfather. "They fight hard to keep their own language and their way of life and Germans try just as hard to make Germans out of them."

We sat under a cottonwood tree while Dr. Ball told us about the life of farmers in his country. "Most of the houses," he said, "consist of just one large room. Living room, kitchen, and bedroom—all in one. The doors are always open and the dogs, ducks, and chickens go in and out at will.

"But they make everything beautiful, too." Dr. Ball went on to tell us how the beams of the houses were decorated with designs of flowers and how the headboards on the beds usually had large hearts burned into the wood, framing the names and dates of marriage of the owners.

The thought of those "burning hearts" worried me. After the doctor had partaken of lunch with us and enjoyed a dish of the wild purslane greens that Grandmother made especially for him, he went on his way. I asked Mother about what he had said.

"How could you burn a heart on the back of your bed, Ma?" I asked. Try as she would, Mother could not make me understand what he had been describing. That evening she actually took a running-branding iron, heated it in the stove, and burned a picture of a heart on a board for me.

"Did you think they were real hearts, Toña?" asked Mother, smiling. Yes I had and I was much relieved to see that it was not a real heart that was burned.

After the doctor had gone, Grandfather went back to work and Mother and Grandmother were still at the table, chatting, when Uncle Luis came from the far end of the island. "You can put down your hoe, Pa," he said. "I just saw 'The News' on the hill. They are coming this way."

Grandfather looked pleased. "The News" was an Indian couple— José and Cayeta Cipriano—who lived in the neighborhood. In the fall they moved from the south side of the creek to the north side where their bear-grass huts faced the afternoon sun during the winter. In the spring they moved back to the south side.

They spent their days roaming the countryside, visiting and talking with everyone they happened to meet. When people met "The News" they exchanged information and gossip, they sent messages, and sometimes letters and packages that were always carefully delivered for a small *propina.*

What they wanted to tell Grandfather this day was that there were a couple up at the Fraguita Wash. In those days all Anglos from the east were called *extranjeros* (foreigners). These particular foreigners had been in the area for just a short time, but already they were talking about homesteading, José told us.

"They are loaded with the white plague, coughing and spitting," José added. "And very unfriendly."

"You should have told them that the land up there is Dr. Ball's property," said Grandfather.

"You can't tell them anything," said Cayeta. "They are not nice. The woman has a long neck and a sneer on her face. She says nothing, just sits."

Meanwhile, Cayeta and José Cipriano kept up their endless recital of news and gossip about people and events in the valley. Early in the afternoon Barreplata came by to beg a cup of coffee, accompanied by Celso Vargas, one of the minor ranchers in the area.

When they had been properly greeted, Grandfather asked about the *extranjeros*, "Did you know, Celso, there are some people trying to settle at Fraguita Wash?"

"Yes, Francisco. I was up there. I did my damnedest to talk to the man, but no chance. He and his woman are very sick; they got watery eyes and flushed faces. And are they mean! The man met me halfway up the hill and told me dogs and Mexicans were not welcome.

"You should see the house he is making, Francisco. The poor *loco* is building one wall at a time without keying in the corners. The first breath of wind will blow it over on top of him."

Grandfather looked distressed. "And did you not tell him how to build the wall, Celso?"

"Oh Pa," said my Uncle Mike, who was standing near the table, "Celso is telling you how mean this man is, and you want him to help him?"

"Yes, Mike, I do. The man does not have to like Mexicans for us to give him aid, especially when he is sick. The Holy Scriptures don't admonish us to help only those who like us."

"Well," said Celso, "I don't care what the Scriptures say. I am not going to lift a hand for that *tísico chingado*." He had called the man a "tubercular son of a bitch" and Grandfather did not like such language or such sentiments.

"Celso," he yelled. "You are a barbarian!"

Now Celso was furious also. He declared that he had been insulted.

"Calm yourself, hombre," said Grandfather. "The Scriptures say to love your enemies. Bless them that curse you and do good to them that hate you. You are hurt and angry, Celso, but just because that *bruto* offends you is no reason for you to offend God. The man's likes and dislikes are his own problem, not yours."

"You are right, Francisco," said Celso meekly. "I talked like a loco myself."

"Do you remember Tom Ewell, the young man who stayed with us several years ago? He was really a mean one. He despised Mexicans, too, yet he considered himself to be a cultured, educated man."

We all knew Tom Ewell, or Igual as my grandparents called him. He was now a dear friend of the family and I never tired of hearing the story of how Grandfather had saved his life.

"I remember him," said Barreplata. "Francisco gave that white pig my *juiqui*." Everyone laughed, for Barreplata and Ewell were now the best of friends.

"How did he come to take over your dugout?" asked Celso.

"I dragged him into it myself," answered Grandfather. "I came down to get some water from the creek one day and I heard someone moaning. I went up the wash and found that young man right opposite the *juiqui*. He was nothing but bones. He was down and couldn't get up, so I dragged him into the little cave Barreplata had used. Then I went to the house and asked Margarita to fix a bowl of soup.

"What do you think he said to me when I brought the soup to him, Celso? He looked at it and said, 'I don't eat from the hands of Mexicans.' I just put the bowl down beside him and walked away. I went up the bank and around and came back right above him. Then I sneaked to the edge of the bank and looked down. He was eating fast and looking all around, frantic, just like a wild beast."

Grandfather told us how he had gone to the house and discussed the plight of the stranger with Grandmother. They agreed that they should get a message to Dr. Ball, so the next day the doctor visited the dugout. He found that the man had no place to go, no money, no friends. He was near death from tuberculosis. The doctor agreed to give him medicines and medical care if Grandfather would feed and look after him.

"One day," said Grandfather, "I was feeding the man when Dan Russel came by on his horse and stopped to see what was going on. Igual had not yet spoken a single word to me, but as soon as he saw this Anglo he sat up and said 'Hello, Pal.'" Grandfather shook his head slowly. "What he meant was, 'You and I are brothers. Let's get rid of this Mexican dog.'

"'I need help,' he told Dan. Dan said, 'You're in the best of hands.

What more do you want?' And he galloped away. I must confess that I laughed and told Igual that he sure knew how to pick his pals. He turned his face toward the mud wall and didn't answer.

"Another time when the doctor came, we walked together to the dugout to see our patient and Igual said 'good morning' to the doctor. Dr. Ball said, 'Aren't you going to greet the man who is keeping you alive, Ewell? This man has taken care of you for many days. You aren't paying him for his help, are you?'

"'You don't expect me to pay when I am in this condition, do you?'

"'I expect you to appreciate what he is doing, to show him some respect. If you don't, I won't bother to come back. Sit up now and eat every bit of the food he has brought you and say thank you to this man.'

"Igual began to eat. Then he put down his spoon and said, 'Thank you,' with his eyes on the ground.

"That evening when I came down the bank and past the dugout he looked up and saw me and he raised his hand in salute. When I got home I told Margarita that we had won. 'That man is going to get well,' I said. And he did, Celso, thanks to God."

"He was a lucky man," said Celso Vargas. "Thanks to you and the *juiqui*. I know it takes a long time to get over that terrible sickness. Some never do."

"Not in this case," said Grandfather. "This man was healed instantly. Instantly, Celso. The day I saw Igual raise his hand to me I went to him. I walked into the dugout and there was the warmest feeling. Igual was looking at me with the strangest expression. It scared me. I thought he was dying. He held out his hand and said, 'Pa.' I said, 'Hijo' (son)."

My uncles, who had just brought a load of wood to drop near the hornilla started to laugh. Grandfather became angry. "Why does everyone laugh, instead of praising God?" he demanded.

"I don't laugh, Pa," said Barreplata. "I believe it was a miracle. Tom Ewell talked with me about that experience many times. It changed his whole life."

"You are right, Barra. It took him time to build up his weight and to regain his confidence, but his healing was immediate. My own savage heart was healed there, too. At the entrance to the *juiqui* I felt a benediction and crossed myself. With the edge of this eye," said Grandfather, touching the outside corner of his right eye, "I saw the man cross himself and I thought, 'he is a Catholic. We will understand each other someday.'"

All this time José Cipriano and Cayeta had been listening attentively. Mother had gone to the house sometime before to help Aunt Rita with the chores. Grandmother, too, had been a part of the healing of Tom Ewell, but she watched Grandfather's face as if she had never heard the story before, with love in her eyes.

"Igual is as dear to us as our own sons," she said. "He stayed with us until he was entirely recovered. He learned the Spanish language and the Indian language. He is now living in Mexico and working there," she added wistfully. "We don't see him often enough."

"Sometimes he is more considerate of us than our own children," said Grandfather, watching the boys return to their watering at the other end of the island. "I don't know why I have so much trouble with my sons. When we came across those hills years ago," Grandfather pointed to the southern mountains, "without food and water, except what we could find along the way, the children saw how God answered our prayers. They actually lived through miracles, yet they are willful and disrespectful of God.

"One day, Celso," Grandfather went on, "we found ourselves in the middle of a *chollal* (a thicket of jumping cactus). We couldn't go forward or back. Margarita said to me 'Don't despair, Francisco. God is with us.' We prayed and soon saw our way through. We came across like the Israelites across the Red Sea, without a scratch. And one day we stood on that hill there, Celso," Grandfather pointed. "We saw this beautiful land, this shining creek, and this island. We knew we had come to our new home."

Grandfather shook his head sadly. "Our children lived through these experiences, yet they don't seem to see God in anything. Why, Celso, why?"

"I'm sure your way is best Francisco. Keep on praying."

"I do, Celso. And helping people is a prayer, too, you know. A great prayer. In a few days when we can leave the ranch, Barreplata and I must go to Fraguita Wash to see those poor foreigners there, to offer our hand to them."

"You know, Pa," said Barreplata, "I have been thinking of that old house across from the Doctor's place. It is abandoned and they might as well get themselves in there. Don't you think, Pa?"

"A good idea, Barra. We'll get up there before Agustín comes back from the corrida and takes the buckboard away from us."

Celso Vargas rose to go. He said a few gracious words of parting to my grandparents and rode away up the creek. José and Cayeta left in the opposite direction on foot.

A few days later Grandfather laid out tasks for the boys at the *milpita* that would keep them busy and Barreplata instructed Ruby and me to tend the goats and bring the milk cows. Then they harnessed the team to the buckboard and rode up the Fraguita Wash to meet the newcomers to the valley. When they returned late in the afternoon we were all waiting eagerly in the kitchen to learn more about the *extranjeros*.

The man's name was Mike Williams and his wife's name was Tina, Grandfather informed us.

"Were they hateful, Pa?" asked Mike.

"I don't know, Son," answered Grandfather. "I wasn't looking for hatred. We just went to help them and that's what we did. We stopped by the doctor's house and told him about them. He said he would look in on them soon. They are very sick with the fever."

"The poor things," said Mother, who had come in holding the baby.

"Yes, Ramona. It is very sad. We told them to make themselves as comfortable as they could in that old abandoned house and to put off building until they were better. They seemed to appreciate that very much. They began moving right away and we took some of the heavy things for them in the wagon."

"If Agustín knew you used the buckboard and team for that, Pa, he'd never let you have them again."

"He won't know about it unless you tell him, Mike," Grandfather retorted sharply. Uncle Mike went outside.

"The fellow gave me a brand-new 22 rifle, Margarita."

Grandmother looked at him with a disapproving frown. "You didn't take it, Francisco?"

"He wouldn't have it any other way, Margarita. But I'll make it up to him and someday I'll find a way to give it back."

We were all very busy the next few days trying to keep up the work without Father's help. Barreplata took advantage of having the buckboard to bring in a supply of mesquite wood for the kitchen stove which he put in the milkhouse. He also took a trip to Arivaca to get supplies for Mother. He learned that the corrida was already at the

Cerros Prietos, which meant that it would soon be in the neighborhood and then over until fall.

"So, Ramoncita," said Barreplata, "if you still want to go to the Indian villages you'd better make it the next day or two while we have the buckboard."

Mother had been promising us such an adventure for a long time. Now she nodded her head. "That's a splendid idea, Barreplata," she said. "We'll go tomorrow."

At the Indian Villages

ARLY THE NEXT MORNING BARREPLATA BROUGHT the buckboard around to the back door to take us to the Indian villages. We all climbed eagerly into the wagon—Mother, Grandmother, Ruby, and I. Aunt Rita stayed home to take care of William.

First we visited the Paul Indian Village down the creek where María Nieves lived. Beaming with pleasure, María Nieves met us at the entrance of her simple home and invited us inside.

I was puzzled to know how María Nieves herself, so enormously fat, could fit into such a small hut without adding Grandmother and the rest of us. But I was close behind as Grandmother bent to enter and was agreeably surprised to find the structure much more spacious inside than it had seemed from without.

The Indian huts were framed with willow wands and tied at the center of the roof and curved downward to the ground like the ribs of an umbrella. The ribs were laced together at even intervals from top to bottom and covered profusely with bear grass. They were so cleverly fashioned as to be almost totally waterproof.

María Nieves showed us a black-and-white basket she had been making from devil's claw fiber. Much work went into basket weaving, she told us, but she was proud of her art. She had *cajetes* (bowls), and ollas of all sizes for sale. There was one large olla, beautifully polished and fired to a smooth, even red with no black splotches. Grandmother immediately bought it and Barreplata put it in the wagon.

When we came outside I found my old friend and enemy, Wahyanita, standing near the hut. She was with her cousin, Tomás José, and her aunt. They had come from Poso Verde to stay with María Nieves for a few days while they waited to join the other Indians in their journey to Tucson to harvest the saguaro fruit.

Wahyanita had grown big and silly. When Mother tried to talk with her she giggled and squirmed, twisting her squat body and hanging her head as low as she could. When she saw me, she took hold of my arm and pulled. She wanted me to come and play, but I preferred to stay with Grandmother.

María Nieves took us around her village, showing us the pottery her friends had made. Every hut was surrounded by finished ollas on display. There were piles of wood, piles of manure, and piles of small round stones for polishing the wares. Indian children sat cracking nuts on rocks and picking out the nutmeats with mesquite thorns. At the entrance to every hut was an olla filled with water with a gourd dipper nearby.

On leaving the Paul Indian Village we next rode north to visit the Guijas Canyon Indians. Here we found huge piles of soil near the huts. We had to pick our way around them to find the pot-drying ground where the ollas were on display.

"What's all that dirt for, Ma?" I asked Mother.

"That's clay soil for making pottery. These Indians make lots of pottery. Sometimes people come to the village to buy from the Indians. But usually they trade what they make to the peddler for things they need."

José-José lived here. We found his quijo swinging from a branch of a mesquite tree and José-José himself standing mud-splashed and dirty, working a ball of mud. Long lines of ollas sat along the slope of the hill near his hut. He seemed to have more pottery and more working materials than any of the other Indians. When Mother remarked about it José-José told her that he worked harder than the others.

"They run here, run there, all the time. No work. No good. But some good workers." José-José held up three fingers as he named the women: "Trini, Zonza, and Belen, good workers all the time. Make ollas, baskets, saddle blankets, covers for winter—take care of house, take care of children. Belen good woman. But Pete Boylan, Belen's man, he no good. He sleep *kookooi* all the time."

Mother asked José-José what kookooi meant. He was trying hard to be a good host. He smiled and walked to the mesquite tree and touched it. "Kookooi," he said.

"Oh," said Mother, "he sleeps under the mesquite tree all the time?"

José-José nodded. "Pete Boylan no good," he repeated, shaking his head. "But Belen, his woman, she good worker."

Unfortunately, José-José's opinion of this Indian woman was not shared by most of the people in the valley, including the Indians themselves. She was thought to be a *bruja*—a witch. It was said that she had the power to cause those she disliked to get sick and even to die. María Nieves had once told Mother that she herself had been a victim of Belen's witchcraft.

When the woman wanted to get even with someone, she was said to make a rag doll, name it after that person, and then stick a pin in it. One day after quarreling with Belen, María Nieves experienced a terrible pain in her shoulder. She had to call Belen herself to treat the shoulder. The pain had vanished immediately.

"Belen is evil," María Nieves had declared. "God will punish her. You will see."

Now José-José was offering to take us to visit Belen. I was both apprehensive and curious. I wanted to see what this "witch" was like. To my relief she looked as ordinary as most of the other Indian women of the village, greeting Mother and Grandmother pleasantly, and calling her two daughters from the hut to meet us.

Lupita was quite a pretty girl with thick black hair that reached down to her ankles. With the aid of her fingers she told us that she was seventeen years old. Her sister Elena was fifteen.

Belen said, "Elena, she like her father—lazy. But Lupita work all the time. She make good wife someday. I will find good man for Lupita."

"You are a fine mother, Belen," said Barreplata.

"I try all the time," the woman answered. She turned to Grandmother. "How goes with old Señor?" referring to Grandfather. "He make *Velorio* soon, same as always?" She pointed to the crest of a hill nearby where a group of Indians had gathered. "Parientes come all time, every day, to wait for Velorio."

Grandmother nodded. "Francisco always remembers, Belen," she said. "Soon now, when Agustín comes back from the corrida they will begin to plan."

Everywhere we went among the Indians they spoke of Grandfather and of the coming celebration—the Velorio—the Feast of the Holy Cross. It was always held on May 3 and was eagerly awaited by everyone in the neighborhood—Indians, Mexicans, and Anglos. Grandfather Vilducea had brought the beautiful custom to our valley with him from Mexico years before, and so it was he who supervised the making of the willow cross that was carried to the top of Pesqueira Hill.

The celebration of the Holy Cross was a time of prayer and feasting. The Indians began to arrive about the middle of April and by May 3 there were hundreds pacing up and down the creek. After the celebration they would leave on their way to Tucson to be there for the harvest of the saguaro fruit.

José-José's black eyes glittered when the Velorio was mentioned. "Much food! Good eating," he said happily.

He showed us around the rest of the village. The bear-grass huts were built in a circle, entrances facing toward the center to form a large courtyard. There were big strings of devil's claw hanging from several of the mesquite trees. Some of the devil's claws were being worked by the Indian children. They would open the claws and extract the small black seeds which they liked to chew.

While we were at Guijas Canyon Village, a familiar covered wagon drove into the circular yard. Don Bernabe, the peddler.

At sight of him Barreplata struck his heel to the ground and swore. "That old robber," he said sourly. There was always contention between the two old men. Barreplata, who didn't care a thing about clothes, resented the fact that Don Bernabe was a natty dresser, always neat and clean.

At once the Indians began to bring out their wares and to place them in front of their respective huts. Each stood by his or her property while Don Bernabe made the rounds, the inquisitive Barreplata at his heels. The peddler would examine each lot of merchandise carefully, then make his offer—so much for the entire lot.

Some of the Indians, though, insisted upon selling each piece separately, whereupon Don Bernabe would begin to find cracks and other imperfections. In almost every case he ended the deal by taking everything offered at his own price.

The Indians actually emptied the wagon of almost everything the man had to trade. He replenished his load with their pottery, baskets, and metates, and even some ancient stone tomahawks that the Indians had picked up in the neighboring hills.

Mother noticed the beef he was cutting for the Indians and asked him to stop by our house before he left the area, as she wanted a beef quarter. While she talked with him, the Indian children stood expectantly around the wagon. Don Bernabe gave each one, including Ruby and me, some long sticks of sugar cane. Barreplata cut it at the joints for us and we chewed the pulp to extract the sweet juice.

Mother had bought some ollas and cajetas from the Indians. Now José-José took a basket and dipped it into water, holding it before my mother to show her that it did not leak.

"As good as an olla," said José-José.

Mother bought this basket, too, and we loaded everything into the buckboard and hurried home to wait for Don Bernabe.

When he finally came he climbed into the back of his wagon, opened an icebox and brought out a beef hindquarter. He carried it into the kitchen and laid it on the working table. Mother happily traded him some chickens and cheese for the fresh meat. But he was not quite ready to go.

"Wait," said Don Bernabe. "I have something to show you." He went back to his wagon and returned with something rolled up in paper. He tore the paper off and spread a bright piece of oilcloth out on the kitchen table. "You can have this for a dozen *quesadillas* (little cheesecakes) and a dozen eggs," he told Mother.

Ruby and I yelled with delight at the sight of the oilcloth with its bright blue morning glories on a white background. Mother would have traded at once but Barreplata interfered.

"One dozen quesadillas is enough for that, Bernabe," he said.

"All right, all right, nosy old man," said Don Bernabe angrily. The deal was closed, but then he turned back to Barreplata. "I didn't enjoy having you gawking at me when I was trying to trade with the Indians, either," he told him irritably.

"Well," said Barreplata, "I guess I wouldn't enjoy an audience either if I was robbing somebody." The two old men headed outside, still shouting at each other. Mother and Grandmother laughed hilariously.

Mother recovered first and stood. "I'm so glad to get the fresh meat," she said. "The corrida is almost over and Agustín will be coming and you know he always brings someone home with him."

"You're going to scare him with that table full of morning glories," said Barreplata who had just come back in. We could hear Bernabe's covered wagon rumbling away past the wall.

"Oh," said Mother with a smile. "Agustín likes pretty things, too."

"Yes," said Barreplata sarcastically, "that's why he keeps the roofs in such good repair." There was always an argument whenever the condition of the roofs was mentioned. "They were beautiful and they didn't leak when Dr. Wilbur put them up." That was Barreplata's never-ending song.

"You were like a gazelle, too, a hundred years ago," said Mother sharply, "But look at you now."

Sometimes this old argument ended in laughter, at other times in real anger. And in spite of constant makeshift repairs, the roof popped on louder, day by day.

On the last day of April, just before dark, Mateo Mariano drove in five horses—Tim, Father's Big Grey, and three others, carrying their owners' bedrolls. From a distance it appeared to us that the Big Grey was wearing a red apron, but as they came closer we could see that he had been slashed across the chest. Shocked, we could see the blood splashing out and running down to his hooves. As he dismounted, Mateo told us the horse had been gored by a bull.

"Where is Agustín?" asked Mother anxiously.

"He is not hurt. He has gone over to the hill to get some *pipichagui.*" This was a small desert shrub whose roots were used by the Indians to staunch bleeding.

"He is riding Vaquerito," Mateo added, trying to reassure Mother, who was having a great deal of trouble pretending that she had not been shocked and frightened at the sight of the injured horse.

The whole family, including Barreplata, stood near the corral fence looking on. Grandfather lifted me gently to the top of the fence, keeping his arm about me.

"Can you give me a hand, Barra?" Mateo asked.

"Sure, Mateo. Tell me what the hell I can do and I'll do it." He, too, appeared shaken.

"Get me a big rag and a bucket of water while I unload those bedrolls and let those poor horses out."

"*Ahorita.* Right away," Barreplata grabbed a bucket and went toward the creek.

Mateo unloaded the bedrolls and laid them along the corral fence. Uncle Mike drove the horses out of the corral and came back to hold the Big Grey for Mateo. Barreplata returned with the bucket of water, and Father arrived at the same time.

He jumped down from his horse and reached into one of the saddlebags, taking out a handful of small, brown tubers. Nobody greeted anybody. Everyone rushed to lend a hand where help was needed.

Mother held a small pan while Father split the tubers with his pocketknife, extracting some dingy cotton-like fiber that expanded as it was released.

"Let's have some of that stuff quick, Agustín. This poor animal is bleeding like a stabbed pig," said Mateo.

"I'm all thumbs, Mateo," said Father. "Why don't you do this for me?"

So, Mateo took the tubers from Father, expertly breaking them open and peeling them with his fingernails. "Don't tell me a little accident like that has unmanned you, Agustín?"

"No," answered Father, "not when I have one of the Marianos to rely on." But his voice sounded strange to my ears and I called out: "Papa! Papa!"

"What's the matter, daughter? Do you want to help me?"

"Yes, Papa," I said, trying not to cry.

"All right," said Father. "You just sit there real quiet. That's the only way you can help me now. After we're through here, I'll talk to you."

It was dark now. A third horseman rode in and slid from his saddle. He led his horse to the big corral, unsaddled him, and came to stand beside Mateo. No one took much notice of him.

"We'll have to take care of one wound at a time," said Mateo. "The flow of blood is pushing this cotton out. If you could bring me a big piece of cloth maybe I can bandage it somehow, Agustín."

Father took me from the fence and carried me into the house, with Mother and my grandparents following along with Barreplata and Luis.

"How have you been, Ma?" asked Father, as he walked into the dim light of the kerosene lamp. "And you, Pa, have you been working yourself to death while I've been away?" He put me down, but I clung to his side.

"Not that bad, Agustín," said Grandfather. "But it's good to have you home."

Mother brought an old sheet and Father split it down the center lengthwise and handed it to Uncle Luis to take to Mateo. He looked at the table. "Where did we get so many morning glories?" he asked, his arm around Mother.

"I did some trading with Don Bernabe," answered Mother.

"Will you be able to fix something to feed those poor fellows out there?"

"I was lucky to get some good fresh meat, too, Agustín. I'll ask Mother to cook up some steaks for you."

"Fine. That takes care of my worries for the night. I thought we'd have to go begging from you, Ma," said Father, turning to my grandmother.

"We went to the Indian villages while you were gone, Agustín," Grandmother said. "The Indians are all excited about El Velorio."

Father lifted his hands in a gesture of acknowledgment. "I saw them gathering along the creek when I rode in," he said. "I suppose that's the next thing we have to worry about."

"But what about you, Agustín? How did the corrida go? And what happened to your horse?"

"The corrida went fine, Ma, until this very day when the Big Grey got tangled up with a bull. It was just a little accident. I'm going out to check up on him now. While I'm gone you get those steaks ready for us. Then I'm going to bring a friend of yours in to visit you."

He turned to Barreplata. "And you, Barra, please open the side door to the washroom so that the men can come in and clean up."

"Everything is ready *para su majestad*," answered Barreplata, giving him an ironic little bow.

As Father left the kitchen with the old lantern my little dark-haired grandmother immediately began to give orders. "Francisco, you peel the potatoes. You, Rita, roast the chiles. And you, Ramona, you set the table."

Grandfather shook his head. "And you, Margarita, what are you going to do?"

"I am going to go and freshen up. I don't know who it is Agustín has brought to see me. It might be Porfirio, Francisco."

"Oh, Margarita, you're not a fifteen-year-old girl. Why do you care who it is?"

"I care, Francisco," she said with a toss of her head. She went into the washroom. In a few minutes she came out, beaming and ready to receive her mysterious guest. While she waited, she put on an apron and set about preparing the steaks.

It was some time before we heard the men go into the washroom. Soon Father came into the kitchen. "You look very pretty, Ma," he said. "You're the spirit of this place."

"*Gracias, hijo.*" Grandmother began to take the food to the table for the men. In those days when we had guests the men always ate first; the women and children ate later, only after the men had finished.

Mateo Mariano opened the kitchen door, then moved aside to let someone else into the room. Grandmother turned from the table, staring, too surprised to speak.

A stranger stepped in. He reminded me of the cattle inspector, but Father had said he was a friend of Grandmother Margarita, and where could she get a friend like this?

A lanky, light-complexioned man with a lot of gray on his temples. His face was deeply clefted, and a dimple on his chin. I had never seen a dimple and I thought, "He got into a fight and took it on the chin." His hooded, piercing blue eyes were glued on my grandmother. The cattle inspectors always look like that. Mother had told me that it was bad manners to look at people in such a manner. Maybe he thought Grandmother had been stolen. The next thing I knew Grandmother was in the stranger's arms exclaiming, "*¡Igual, hijo!*" Grandmother began to cry. I hated to see Grandmother cry, and so I was glad when Grandfather got up and led both of them into the sala where they could exchange greetings. They returned before long, looking like children on Christmas morning.

"Barreplata," scolded Grandmother, "Why didn't you tell me that Igual was out there?"

"Agustín wanted to surprise you and Pa."

"It was cruel not to tell us," said Grandfather. But he was smiling, and his eyes, too, were wet with emotion.

"Please welcome Mateo, too," said Father. "If it had not been for his quick thinking the Big Grey might have been killed. And I might not be here myself," he added.

"You should have seen this man in action, Pa," said Ewell, tapping Mateo on the shoulder. "Everyone at the corrida was scared out of his wits when that wild bull charged. Mateo was farther away than anyone else, but in one split second he had his rope flying and was dragging the bull back from the horse."

"But not before the horse was gored," said Father's Indian friend, regretfully.

"Well," said Father, "the wounds were shallow. The Big Grey will be scarred, but he will recover."

"You should have been more alert, Agustín," said Mother.

"You know, Ramona, accidents do happen," shot back Father stiffly.

"That was no accident, Agustín," Mateo said. "Felipe Riesgo was in a perfect position to rope that animal before it charged. He could at least have warned you. He *acted* guilty, too. Didn't you notice that he was the only man who did not go to see how badly injured your horse was?"

"Mateo," protested Grandmother, shocked. "Felipe is not able. He's just a poor simple-minded man."

"Yes, Ma," answered Mateo, "but there is a lot of hatred there, too. He envies Agustín."

"It was my own damned fault," said Father at last. "Now let's have some supper." He led the way to the table and the other men joined him, including Grandfather and the uncles.

Barreplata changed the subject. As Grandmother came to the table with a plate of tortillas, he looked up at her teasingly. "Are you happy to see Igual again, Margarita?"

"Of course I am! You don't have to ask that."

"She cries as much when that man comes as when he goes."

"That's enough, Barra," said Grandfather.

"My parents don't cry when I leave the village," remarked Mateo. "At least they don't let me see them do it. But once when I came back to the *koksh* (nest) after being away a whole year at school, my ugk scolded me for not waving goodbye to my mother when I left. He said she had been deeply grieved. So I know they love me, though it is hard for them to show it."

Mateo folded a tortilla. "With my other family in Mexico it is totally different. Grandma White begins to cry two days before I take leave of her. I can hear her now: 'Our little Indian is leaving us.' She is very emotional." Mateo laughed sheepishly. "I remember when I was a little kid. If she thought Pa White wanted to discipline me she'd put a cloth around my head and put me in her bed and pretend that I was sick. And when I was fourteen and getting ready to return to the Territory she wanted to hold me on her lap!"

Mike and my parents began to laugh. Grandmother, who was standing near the stove, spoke up sternly. "It is no laughing matter. When someone you love goes away it is like a funeral. You never know if you will see them again. It was that way with us when Ewell left that first time five years ago."

"Well, he is back now," said Father, looking across the table at Ewell. "I hope you are going to stay a few days. Velorio will be upon us in a few days and we could use your help."

"I wouldn't miss it, Agustín. I remember my first experience with the Feast of the Holy Cross after Pa had let me out of the juqui and had taken me home. I never saw anything so beautiful as that cross on the hill, with the lights all around it. And what a feast we enjoyed!"

"And you, Mateo? Won't you stay? You could help me handle the Indians. It looks as though the ranch will be overrun with them. There'll be plenty of work for everyone to do. Barra and I plan to butcher a steer for the barbecue."

"I'll be here," said Mateo. "In fact, Agustín, if you'll let me have the buckboard, I'll go up to the Guijas and bring back a load of mescal plants to roast for the *biguata*. It's good food and free for the taking."

"Fine," said Father. The men went on out to the corral to see how the Big Grey was faring and Mother cleared the table and set it again so that the rest of us could eat.

It had been both an exciting and a frightening day for me. But the corrida was over and Father had returned unharmed. We now looked forward eagerly to the next big event on the ranch—the Feast of the Holy Cross.

Feast of the Holy Cross

ᴇᴀʀʟʏ ɪɴ ᴛʜᴇ ᴍᴏʀɴɪɴɢ ᴏɴ ᴛʜᴇ sᴇᴄᴏɴᴅ ᴏꜰ ᴍᴀʏ, three Indians arrived at the ranch and sat on the wall, waiting. They were José-José, Pete Boylan, and Carmelo Tosco. They had come to help Grandfather gather the green willow branches for the construction of the Holy Cross.

Perhaps in honor of the occasion, José-José had substituted a pair of tattered coveralls for his loin cloth. Pete Boylan was more vain about his dress. He was slender and that day he wore a pair of faded Levis and a clean shirt. His hair showed signs of having been shorn at some time and on his feet were his familiar handmade moccasins protecting his store-bought shoes. Pete made these overshoes from fresh cowhide. He cut pieces of the rawhide somewhat bigger than the soles of his shoes, made holes in the edges and laced the hides around the shoes with wire. When the hide dried he could slip the molds on and off at will. When he went to Arivaca he hid the molds in the bushes and proudly entered the town well-shod.

Pete was an exceptional Indian. He spoke Spanish quite well and was willing to talk. The Parientes feared him as a *brujo* (witch), and respected him as their spokesman.

Carmelo was another story. He came without shoes, without shirt, and without a hat. His baggy, ankle-length pants were held up with baling wire. His front hair was chopped off above his eyebrows; the rest hung straight down the sides of his face to his shoulders. It was a common sight to see Carmelo sitting in the sun munching devil-horn seeds. You'd see him suddenly cast aside the seed pod and sit very still, listening. A black louse would crawl down from his hairline and he would seize it, pop it in his mouth, and chew it with the same gusto he gave to the devil-horn seeds.

"Carmelo, *puerco*," Uncle Mike asked him one day, "how can you eat lice?"

Carmelo was not without logic. "You eat rabbit? You eat squirrel? Lice all the same good to eat. You hungry like me, you eat lice."

It was Father, just risen from the breakfast table, who saw the men waiting patiently on the wall. "You'd better bring those men in," he said to Mateo, "I know they are hungry."

"No, Agustín," said Father's Indian friend. "They are *muy broncos* (very wild). They'll feel more comfortable out there. I'll take them something in these plates."

"Give them some of that roast mutton, Mateo. They'll like that."

Mateo walked outside with three loaded tin plates, returning almost immediately with the plates empty.

"What happened?" asked Father in surprise.

"Nothing, Agustín. They just wolfed it down." Mateo laughed. "Carmelo said they hadn't had anything to eat since the last Feast of the Holy Cross a year ago. Pa, they asked me to tell you that they are ready to go to work," Mateo told Grandfather.

"Tell them to wait a few minutes, Mateo," said Grandfather. "I have to go to my place for an ax. I'll be right back." He left through the back door.

"I'll tell them," said Father. He told Mateo and Mike who were still at the table, "You boys had better get the buckboard hitched up and be on your way if you're going to bring back enough *nopales* (prickly-pear pads) for tomorrow's feast."

"We're ready," said Mateo, pushing aside his plate. They both stood up and walked outside with Father, going toward the corral, while Father stopped to talk with the Indians. I was at his side.

After giving them Grandfather's message he spoke to Pete Boylan. "I heard at the corrida that the Parientes in the villages around here are going to move to the reservation," he said. "Will you go in the fall, Pete?"

"Yes, Parientes all go to Poso Verde. After Feast of St. Francis, all go. Won't be here no more." He shook his head solemnly.

"First go Tucson, pick fruit," said José-José. "Then walk, walk, to Magdalena for St. Francis Day. Then go reservation." Poor José-José sounded as though the very thought of the long journeys to come wearied him. It was an annual custom of the tribe after spending much of the summer in Tucson harvesting cactus fruit, to make the pilgrimage to Magdalena in Mexico. Many, many weary miles, all on foot.

Carmelo Tosco seldom spoke unless spoken to, but this morning he suddenly burst forth, a wild look in his eyes. "Carmelo no go Tucson, no do woman's work," he declared. "Go last year. Work, work, work. Pick saguaro fruit." He held up his arms, mimicking how the fruit was plucked from the top of the saguaros with long poles. "All day work. Bones hurt. I put pole down. María Nieves, she come. She grab by neck, kick hard. She say, 'Go fruit down.' Cayeta come with stick. I go fruit down. Much work. Much tired." He turned and pointed to the south. "This time Carmelo go there, pick *bellotas*." He would rather harvest acorns than be at the mercy of his women again.

Grandfather arrived with the ax, a pair of pliers, and some wire, and the three Indians slipped down from the wall. It wasn't long until we saw them following Grandfather up the riverbank, single file, and very businesslike, going toward the willow thicket.

"You'd better go inside if you want any breakfast, Eva," Father called to me. "This is going to be a busy day." He put on his chaparreras and went to the corral where Vaquerito had been impatiently pawing the ground. Father was going to bring down a steer for butchering. I got on the wall and watched him until he disappeared over the southern ridge, then I went into the kitchen.

Preparations for the big event had already started. In fact, they had started weeks ago. On April 24 my grandmother filled three ten-gallon crocks with corn mash and other ingredients. This was the ninth day of fermentation and it was time to strain the product, *tesguin*, which was a delicious but mild intoxicant—a lady's drink, but enjoyed by the men as well.

This morning, as large kettles of frijoles simmered behind them on the stove, my grandmother and mother tested the *tesguin* that would be served this evening on the *vispera* of the Holy Cross. They found it excellent—better than last year's, they said happily.

Meanwhile, María Nieves had arrived at the ranch to help. She and Aunt Rita set about pounding amole to make suds for washing the big pieces of mosquito netting. The clean netting would then be left in a tub of clear water until needed for the barbecue.

When Mike and Mateo returned around noon with a wagonload of mescal heads and nopales, preparations for the feast were well underway. Grandfather's Indian crew had gathered the willow boughs for the cross and taken them to the foot of Pesqueira Hill. He had instructed José-José to dig two pits. These were lined with rocks and the mesquite fires laid in them were already burning hotly.

Father had set up a butcher's block and with the help of Tom Ewell, who had stayed the night at Grandfather's house, he had already dressed the beef he had butchered. Mateo and Mike went to help them cut it into manageable pieces.

As the men cut up the meat, Mike pierced each chunk in several places with a sharp knife, making small pockets. In these he would insert herbs and spices—pieces of garlic, onions, cilantro, cloves, and other good things. The chunk would then be seasoned with salt and pepper and wrapped in a piece of mosquito netting, over which vinegar would be poured.

As a final step, when the rocks in the pits were red-hot and the coals had been brushed aside, each piece would be wrapped once again, in wet burlap this time, and placed directly on the rocks. The packets would be covered with pieces of corrugated iron and a thick layer of soil shoveled over the top. The meat cooked on the hot rocks for many hours and would come out tender and delicious.

Mateo prepared the mescal he had brought in the same fashion, lining the heads up on top of the red-hot rocks in a narrow pit, and covering them with corrugated iron and earth.

All this time the hungry Indians were gathering. Grandfather appointed Barreplata, Carmelo, and Pete Boylan to keep them away from the work. Barreplata shouted and threatened them with a club, and they would leave for a time, only to return again, more numerous than ever. It was plain that a guard would have to be kept near the barbecue pits at all times, so my uncles Mike and Luis agreed to take turns during the night.

Toward evening other guests began to arrive at the ranch to join in celebrating the Velorio. The first to come with a whirr of wind and the strangest rain-like noise made by surrey wheels, were my great uncle, Don Ramón Lopez, and his wife Juanita.

Tío Ramón, my grandmother's brother, was an independent man who didn't believe in imposing on anyone. Within minutes, having greeted the family briskly, he had his tent set up in the yard near the spot where the meat was cooking. It was all very neat. He spread newspapers on the ground inside the tent and proceeded to unload his surrey. Pots, boxes, and folding chairs were taken inside and a 100-pound sack of lentils, his contribution to the feast, was taken over by Barreplata and carted to the kitchen in a wheelbarrow.

Tío Ramón then built a fire in front of his tent and set a pot of coffee over it, and was at home. The men gathered around, squatting on the ground as they listened to him talk and enjoyed his coffee and *buñuelos*. Tío Ramón always had a story or two to tell.

"Have you seen your friend, Prudencio Escobar, lately, Tío?" asked Father, prompting him.

Tío Ramón shook his head sadly. "Poor Prudencio, he never got over what happened. I hear that he is quite out of his head."

"What did happen, Don Ramón?" asked Mateo.

"Well, it was some time ago, when Juanita and I were coming out of Mexico. We met Prudencio and his little family near a water-hole and agreed that we should travel together. It was a cruel journey. We had almost nothing to eat along the way. Five days later we arrived at the foot of the Sombretillo, across from Saric. The *bledo* (a stand of weeds) was tall, but some plants were still tender enough for cooking, so we stopped the wagons there.

"While the women built a fire and cooked a kettle of greens, Prudencio took his gun to the arroyo and brought back a brace of partridges. We all pitched in and cleaned and cooked the birds while the four children played out in the tall weeds.

"I remember what Prudencio said when we had spread a piece of canvas on the ground and set out the food. He said to me, 'It looks like I am going to feed my poor hungry children, Ramón. I am happy.'

"Inez, his wife, turned toward the *bledo* and called her children. Beto, Luis, and Rosario came running and laughing through the weeds. But Antonio did not come.

"The children sat down and we began to tear the birds apart, as people who are starving do. And Inez called again, 'Antonio! Toneeeee!' But Antonio did not come. Then the dog came, creeping and whimpering from the weeds. We all stood up. Everything was silent except for the call of a whitewing far off and the moaning of the dog.

"Frightened now, we began to search for Antonio, backtracking the children through the crushed weeds. Twenty feet away we came to a gaping hole—a deep well, partly filled with water. The boy's tracks ended there. It was all I could do to keep Inez from jumping into that well."

Shivering, I moved close to Father's side.

"What did you do?" asked Mateo.

"We gathered the hysterical children and put them into the wagon. Prudencio took his frenzied wife and wept with her. I dumped the food into a paper bag and loaded everything; we came on north to the Territorio. I drove Prudencio's wagon and Juanita followed in ours. There was nothing else to do, Mateo."

When I went to the house, I told Mother about poor Antonio. She had already heard the story, but, as usual, she turned the old tragedy into an object lesson for me. "Antonio was eight years old," she said. "He should have watched his step. Alertness is the key to survival, Eva."

Barreplata came in just then to tell us that Celso Vargas had arrived and my grandmother quickly put another plate on the table.

After supper was over Aunt Juanita took Ruby and me to her tent to give us two pretty dresses she had made for us to wear to the Velorio. She also gave us pictures of the Virgin Mary and rosaries—pink beads for Ruby, blue ones for me.

"Who is your patron saint, Vita?" she asked me.

"I don't know," I answered.

"What saint do you pray to when you ask for help?" she persisted.

"I don't ask for no help."

"Don't you pray?"

"No," I told her, "we didn't."

"¡Ay! *Jesús libramos de todo mal,*" she said, crossing herself. "Jesus, deliver us from all evil." She took us back to the house and asked Grandfather if it were true that our family did not pray.

"Yes," said Grandfather sorrowfully. "They are raising them like animals. The children know nothing about prayer."

Juanita was truly shocked. "The nieces of Father Suastigui do not pray, Francisco?" One of our uncles was a priest.

"You'd better not let Agustín hear you speak of this either," Grandfather said in a whisper. "Margarita will tell you about it when you come to our house tomorrow."

Mother came in and took Ruby and me to bed, and I did not get to hear anymore about our animalistic upbringing. Ruby and I kept the pictures and pretty rosaries, and our parents neither approved nor objected.

When we awoke early the following morning, the ranch was already bustling with activity. Besides the usual chores—milking the cows and goats and tending to the horses—there were a hundred things to do to get ready for the huge celebration.

Celso Vargas was helping Uncle Luis rake up the yard. Some of the men were putting together long plank tables from which the food would be served that evening. Grandfather was supervising the making of the Holy Cross at the foot of Pesqueira Hill. I ran to watch.

The cross was already put together and was lying on the ground. Now the Indians were covering it with fresh willow, twining and folding it around until every inch of its eight-foot length was covered. After it was finished Grandfather set them to making dozens of *luminarias*— crude lamps made by half-filling paper bags with sand and placing candles inside. The luminarias would be placed along the wall around the house and around the cross on the hill.

As the day unfolded, wonderful aromas filled the air. Cooking for the feast went on all day and into the night. In the kitchen Grandmother and Aunt Rita were making tamales and baking apple turnovers. Tío Ramón built a fire in the *bodega*, surrounding it with rocks and setting up a ten-gallon vat to cook the lentils.

I told him the lentils looked exactly like fat ticks. "You won't say that when I fry them up with red chili and onions, little Miss Nosey," he said.

Mateo Mariano, between chasing Indians away and tasting the *tesguin* with Father, had found time to take the first steps toward cooking the nopales he and Mike had brought in. This was a long and complicated process. Mateo was using the stove in the milkhouse and had enlisted the help of some of the Indians, including Belen, the "witch" we had met the day we traveled to the Indian villages, and her two daughters, Lupita and Elena.

One Indian would singe the prickly-pear pads over an open flame to remove the stickers. He would hand them to a second man, who scraped off the skin. Then the women put the pads on a board, chopped them into small pieces, and tossed them into a large iron pot where the nopalitos boiled furiously.

Two strange Indian men came in with an iron pipe. They stood a moment at the door of the milkhouse looking toward the hornilla. They neither spoke nor smiled. They walked to the hornilla and stuck the pipe under the bail. Each one took one end of the pipe, lifted the pot of boiling water, and carried it outside where they turned it over on the slope of the hills. The water ran down the incline, leaving a stream of white-greenish foam and a cloud of steam above it. "Pa," I cried, "it looks like horse pee." Juanita gave me a mean look. No doubt, this was what came of no prayer or rosaries in my life. Father merely said, "Yes, Eva. We have to get rid of all that slime and acid. But I can hardly wait to taste those nopalitos."

All this time we had mouth-watering thoughts of the meat that was growing tender under the ground in the firepits. The Indians must have been thinking of it, too, for they swarmed everywhere along the creek and on the hillsides. I could feel their hunger.

Other guests, friends of the family, kept arriving during the day and evening. Cipriano Gallego came from the Cochis Ranch with his wife, Carmen, and two of their children, Chanito, eight, and Carmelita, who was three. They brought quince preserves, cactus candy, and prickly pear jelly.

John Bogan came with his wife, Phoebe. Don Jesús Manzanares brought his family, and Ramón Ahumada arrived with his beautiful wife, Virginia, in their shining surrey with the yellow fringe. Late in the afternoon, as the sun wheeled toward the west, Doña Tomaza drove in with her two daughters and some friends in her buckboard.

After she had exchanged boisterous greetings with everyone in the *sala*, Tomaza hurried with Grandmother and Aunt Rita to the prayer room. Every year Mother set aside one room of our house to be used for thé Velorio. Boxes were placed at one end to make an altar. A white tablecloth was draped over them and a crucifix centered on it. Chairs were arranged for worshipers.

Grandfather brought a box of candles, and I watched Tomaza place two of them in a can half-filled with gravel. She lit them and put the can in front of the crucifix. There were many more candles, and while we were there, the Indian women brought in their own *candiles*, presenting them to Tomaza, who had taken charge. *Candiles* were simple devices made by the Indians for this occasion. They placed small bags of salt or pieces of twisted and coiled rag in cans of melted tallow. When the wicks were lit the candles gave off excellent light.

The prayer room would be tended and vigil kept all during the night. Anyone who wished might come to pray and light candles.

Grandfather soon left the room and when I followed him outside I saw the three Indians—Pete, José-José, and Carmelo—taking the cross up Pesqueira Hill with Grandfather leading them. When the cross was in place and securely anchored, women and girls came with baskets of flowers—wild larkspur, penstemon, and desert verbena. They climbed onto boxes and began fastening the flowers to the cross. It was very impressive, standing out against the pale blue sky with the late afternoon sun shining upon it. Excitement was growing. People seemed to be everywhere, all looking up to the cross, for it would soon be time for Grandfather to lead the procession up the hill.

I went back in to find that more visitors had arrived. Among them were Dr. Ball, his nephew, and El Prieto Murrieta and his wife. Murrieta was a close friend of my grandparents. He was a tall, black-skinned man, the only real musician in our area. He owned two guitars, a violin, and an old accordion and he was always the first to be invited to a fiesta. He would come well supplied with *tesguin,* some for himself, and some which he sold to other guests.

Doña Tomaza, the old "outlaw," had now taken charge, not only of the prayer room, but of the entire celebration. She sought out El Prieto Murrieta, and I heard her order him to play his violin for the ceremonies, but not to start the music until he had reached the top of the hill.

Grandmother came out to greet Dr. Ball and take him to the prayer room, while Uncle Mike took Old Nick, Dr. Ball's horse, to the corral. The good doctor wanted to walk to the crest of the hill, but was afraid he might get an asthma attack, so Grandfather had Mike hitch up the buggy and drive him, circling around the slope to reach the crest.

The Indians who had gathered in the yard were becoming quite restless. Mateo spoke to them, asking them to wait until Grandfather and his close friends—"the people of Pa"—had started up the hill before they moved. Then, he explained, my father would give them the signal to follow by shooting his rifle.

Tomaza wasn't satisfied with this. She was afraid that some of the itinerant Indians would get out of hand and raid the food supply while the ceremonies were taking place. She suggested that Father should round up several men with guns to stand on the wall beside him and show authority.

Doña Tomaza was known as a shrewd trouble-shooter and a born gunfighter, so Father listened to her.

The moment finally came. Grandfather lifted his arm and started up Pesqueira Hill, followed by "the people of Pa." In the afternoon Aunt Juanita had found time to comb our hair and clothe Ruby and me in the pretty dresses she had made for us; now I held Ruby's hand and walked just behind Mother in the procession.

When we were halfway up the hill, I heard Father's rifle go off. The detonations of six guns followed in rapid succession and the Indians dashed up the hill behind us like a herd of cattle, pushing many people aside in their eagerness.

When the crowd was finally positioned on the hillside near the cross, Grandfather invited Dr. Ball to begin the prayers.

Everyone in the valley knew and loved the doctor, and the crowd was respectfully silent now.

"If I knew more Spanish," he began, "I would say many good things I'd like to share with you. As it is, I shall start the prayers and let "Pa," as you affectionately call Señor Vilducea, carry on.

"For whenever two or more are gathered in my name, there I am amongst them," he quoted. "Certianly we are gathered in His name and we have come in great numbers. So we know that he is with us in this beautiful and peaceful country."

A shaft of sunlight shot through a rift in the clouds above the jagged peaks to the west, bathing the flower-decked cross in a pink glow. "This ray of sunlight," said the doctor, "is significant of His blessings. We praise Thee and we glorify Thee forever . . . Holy, Holy, Lord God of Hosts. Heaven and earth are full of Thy Glory. Blessed is He who comes in the name of the Lord. Hosanna in the Highest. Amen."

A soft murmur ran through the crowd as the doctor lifted his head and moved aside to let Grandfather take his place beneath the cross.

Grandfather began by saying a few words to the Indians. He praised the three Parientes who had made the willow cross. He reminded all present that, even though times were hard, God was always with us. Before long, he said, the harvest would be upon us, and we should all go diligently in search of the natural desert produce.

He started to pray the rosary, as was the custom, and those who could or wished to, responded. All this time El Prieto Murrieta was playing his music sweetly in the background. Between the rosary chapters the ladies sang beautiful hymns. The devotions went on for some time until the sun had entirely disappeared and the shadows lay darkly across the hill.

We came down the hill in reverse order, the Indians first, "the people of Pa" right behind them. No one lingered, for our way was lighted by the *luminarias* all the way along the walls, and the tantalizing and delectable smell of the cooking food assailed us. Father, Tom Ewell, and Great-uncle Ramón stayed below to open the barbecue pits and prepare the other food for the Indians. They were now cutting up the barbecued beef. Dotted across the yard were several little cooking fires where big pots of coffee were brewing.

At the house Aunt Rita and Aunt Juanita had been busy setting the long tables in the *sala,* heaping them with steaming platters of good things to eat. Crocks of *tesguin* were ready for dipping. Grandmother had wisely kept them at the house or there would have been little left by now.

Mateo had designated several of his Parientes to help keep the alien Indians in line while they waited for their food. The Indians who lived in our neighborhood were docile and patient, but those who were passing through on their way to the saguaro harvest were demanding and aggressive. All were hungry.

Feeding two hundred Indians is no small feat. Some of them had brought their own bowls, but most of the food was handed to them in corn husks. A generous serving of lentils, a tortilla, a slice of the beef. When the food ran low, Mateo hurried to the milkhouse to scramble the dozens of eggs which he had sent the uncles to steal from a neighbor's hen house. The neighbors, after all, were here too, eating away. He mixed the eggs with onions and chile and the nopalitos he had prepared to make enough food to feed all the Indians.

Doña Tomaza was trying to be everywhere at once. She made introductions. She appointed some of the ladies to serve other guests in the *sala* and some to help in the kitchen. She kept the glasses filled with *tesguin* and ate her own supper while running from kitchen to prayer room, where she kept the prayers going.

There were a number of children at the fiesta—cousins and children of family friends. I was fed in the kitchen with them, but I didn't waste time playing with them. I wanted to be on my own so I wouldn't miss anything. For a long time I watched the Indians moving about the yard in the light of the bonfires. I watched Grandmother at the stove as she dished out tamales and made applesauce for the apple hotcakes that would be served for breakfast in the morning. And I listened outside the door of the *sala,* clapping my hands to the music of El Prieto Murrieta's accordion.

That's where Aunt Juanita finally caught up with me and tried her best to drag me off to bed. "Ruby is already asleep," she scolded me.

She had a battle on her hands. When our first fight was over she gave me an unpleasant look of total disgust. "Little girls do *not* stay up this late," she shouted. "The Velorio is for grownups."

"I'm not a little girl! I'm a big girl. I can stay up late in my own house if I want to. I'll tell Father," I yelled back at her.

Father, as he had a habit of doing, appeared out of nowhere. "I'll take care of her, Juanita," he said. He took my hand and we walked to the milkhouse where all kinds of interesting activities were taking place. This was fun!

Uncle Mike was there playing his guitar. Some of the older girls were singing and dancing. Carmen and Cipriano Gallego were making *buñuelos*. Father put one on a plate and handed it to me.

I noticed with satisfaction that Chanito, Carmen's son, was there. He was eight years old and he was still up. I was only five.

At the hornilla Mateo Mariano was frying ground meat and onions in a two-foot frying pan, getting ready to mix up more nopalitos for the Indians. When he saw me he left the chore to his Indian helpers and came to talk with Father. "Mateo," Father told him, "they are serving the *biguata* (barbecued agave) out there. If you want to taste it you'd better get some now."

"Follow me," said Mateo. He led us to a table, then went outside. He returned in a moment with a big platter of biguata, and a pitcher of *tesguin* for him and Father.

"I hope you're not going to get drunk on me, Mateo," said Father.

"You never saw me drunk, Testiní," Mateo bragged loudly. I noticed, though, how he was acting sort of tipsy and pronounced Father's name in such a funny, slurred way.

I felt happy and important, sitting beside Father. But while we were eating, something unpleasant happened—something that was not unusual in those days. Ben Russel, Jr., a boy around Chanito's age, came into the milkhouse. As he passed our table he looked distastefully down his nose at us.

Chanito noticed and instantly came toward us, accosting the Russel boy. "What's the matter with you? Did you eat a rattlesnake or a toad? What do you want?"

"My father sent me to get something to eat, Mr. Mexican," Ben sneered.

"Well, have you got any money? If you don't have money you'd better put on a pleasant face or you'll go hungry."

"I don't have to," said Ben. "I am a white boy."

"In that case, go over to the foot of that tree there," said Chanito, pointing through the open door to a mesquite tree in the corner of the yard. "There is a big hole at the foot of that tree and inside is a white pig with blue eyes just like yours. You get in that hole with your white brother and we'll throw you some scraps."

Ben kicked Chanito in the shin and Chanito grabbed his foot and threw him down. Chanito's father sprang toward his son and held him while Chanito yelled, "That Ozarki is looking for a fight, Pa. He's going to get his head knocked off!"

"You don't talk like that, Chanito. You understand?" Cipriano was pulling the belt from the loops of his trousers.

"That's the way he talks, Pa."

"You are a Gallego. He doesn't know better, but you do. And if you don't, then I'll have to teach you." He slashed the belt across the boy's back and Chanito yelled and threw himself to the floor.

"Come, Mr. Ben," said Cipriano politely, taking the boy's hand. "I will get you something to eat."

Ben yanked his hand away and stood glaring at Cipriano.

"Then follow me," said Cipriano.

"I don't follow no Mexicans," said Ben.

"In that case, my friend, I bid you goodbye," said Cipriano. And he walked away, leaving Ben standing in the middle of the yard.

Father said, "You wait here, Eva. I'll take that boy to the kitchen and get him something to eat. He has made himself unwelcome here." He led the boy away and Chanito got up from the floor and came to sit by me. He was having a hard time hiding his pain.

"Chanito, why did you call Ben an Ozarki? What does that mean?" I asked.

"My father told me about the white Anglos who lived in the Ozark Mountains. He saw them when he went on a horse drive to Kansas with Don Agustín."

"He didn't go with my father, Chanito."

"Yes he did. He helped your father take a drive of horses to Kansas a long time ago. Before I was born."

"We'll just ask him when he comes back," I said, sure I was right. But when Father returned a little later with John Bogan and Señor Moyza, I found that I was wrong. He had gone on such a drive and when I asked if Chanito's father had gone with them Father said

Chanito was right. And now their talk turned, as usual, to horses and memories of that drive.

"That was quite an adventure, Eva," Father said. "Kansas is a long way from home. I had four hundred horses and three men and myself to look after."

"Didn't you deal with a man named Juán Zepulveda there, Agustín?" asked John Bogan.

"Sure, John," answered Father. "Juán Zepulveda was a horse trader from way back. My father bought fifty head of horses from him when he brought the big horse drive from Rancho Dolores in Mexico in the 1800s. I think every rancher in southern Arizona did the same."

"Sure," said Señor Moyza, "I know I did. That's where I got my *tordillos* (greys)."

"Then Cipriano and I met him in Kansas," my father went on. "He had five hundred horses in the stockyards. I observed how he worked and the first chance I got I lent him a hand. He appreciated my help and gave me good advice about selling my own stock. I sold the last bronc I had and was sure glad to hit the trail for home."

"Would you do it again, Agustín?" asked John Bogan.

"No, John," said Father. "It was a good experience for Cipriano and me, but for so little money it wasn't worth the effort."

Chanito had a sparkle in his eyes and swaggered when he got up from the table. Even so young, boys needed to win arguments, I was learning.

Doña Tomaza was still at it. She came into the milkhouse looking for Father. It was past twelve o'clock, she informed him, time for midnight supper to be served. She thought it would be a good idea if the people who were praying would replace the people who were working and vice-versa.

Father looked weary. Fortunately, Tío Ramón appeared just in time to overhear her suggestion. "Tomazita," he advised, "let the people who want to pray, pray, and let those who are willing to work, work. You don't expect Dr. Ball to wash all those dishes, do you?"

Father finally told me that it was time for me to be in bed and ordered me to go to the house and find Mother. Chanito's mother came along and ordered him to go, too. As we walked toward the house, Chanito told me what he had seen earlier in the evening.

"You know what, Toña? Doña Tomaza and Doña Mercedes had a fight in the *sala*. Tomaza rammed Doña Mercedes against the wall and

Doña Mercedes kicked her in the stomach. Doña Mercedes cried and then Dr. Ball made them shake hands. People said that Tomaza really is a *bandida,* you know. Everybody thinks she will kill someone again someday."

"I like her," I said. "She's my friend."

We found Mother in the kitchen, filling a pitcher with *tesguin.* In spite of the hour her dark eyes were sparkling. But she was surprised to see us.

"I thought you were in bed long ago!"

She put down the pitcher and hustled us out the door. In answer to my pleading, she let us make one last visit to the prayer room to see what was going on there.

The room was almost full of worshipers; light from the tallow candles flickered over their faces. The candles were escalated from the floor up to the altar and around and down to the floor again.

Virginia Ahumada was sitting in the front row of seats, very pretty in her long black skirt and white lace blouse. Her hat resembled a basket full of red roses. María Nieves was in the center on the aisle holding her rosary like the others.

Mother, Chanito, and I stood in the seat beside Grandmother. Aunt Juanita got up and went to extinguish a candle that had burned low and was smoking. As she approached the altar, she knelt for a few seconds beside María Nieves and made the sign of the cross. When she came back she was smiling.

She whispered something to Grandmother, who got up and went to sit behind María Nieves. When she returned, there was an expression of dismay on her face. Grandmother had spent many hours teaching María Nieves her prayers and she believed María knew them well, but the truth was that while the others were saying their Hail Marys, changing the beads as they changed prayers, María Nieves was saying: "*Pasa bolita. Pasa bolita. Pasa, bolon.* Pass, little ball. Pass little ball. Pass, big ball."

Mother was still smiling at this as she led Chanito and me to the bedroom. She gave Chanito a blanket and told him where to sleep and helped me out of my fiesta clothes. "Go to bed now, with Ruby," she whispered, as she went out and closed the door.

As soon as my eyes became accustomed to the darkness I saw that the room was filled with sleeping children. There were pads and pillows everywhere. The four children of Jesús Manzanares were sprawled on a *petate* (straw mat) on the far side of the room. Carmelita was sharing the big bed with Ruby and me, and others lay all around the floor.

I was still keyed up and excited at all I had seen and heard that night. Before I slipped into the bed beside Ruby and Carmelita I went to the window and had one last look at the fiesta. Men were still in the yard sitting around their fires, gesturing and laughing as the smoke rose above them and finally disappeared into the darkness.

The Desert Harvest

JUANITA WAS STANDING AT THE FOOT OF MY BED. "Aren't you going to get up today, Vita?" I sat up, startled to find everyone gone from the room. The big petate had been picked up from the floor. The goat pelts and blanket Chanito had used were gone, and so was Chanito.

"Where is everybody, Juanita?"

"Everyone is gone except the Bogans. Your father and Mateo have been chasing Indians. I don't know what good it does."

"It does good, Juanita," I said. I jumped out of bed and ran to the kitchen. "Where is everybody, Ma?" I asked again.

"They went home a long time ago. It is midday, sleepyhead."

"I know it." I stepped outside. The cross was still standing atop Pesqueira Hill. I stood looking up at it and thinking that by that evening Grandfather would have taken it down. It would be a whole year before there would be another cross there—if Grandfather were still living, that is. That's what he always said when asked if he intended to have another fiesta.

I saw Phoebe Bogan leaning on the wall talking with Father.

"I think it is outrageous for you to hit a poor Indian like that, Agustín," she was saying. I saw the Indian who had just experienced the sting of Father's rope trotting across the ditch toward the thicket.

"Shut up, Phoebe," said John as he walked toward his wife. "I want to thank you, Agustín, for putting us up in your *sala*. I had a good sleep while all that praying was going on. Did you sleep well, Phoebe?"

"I didn't die like you."

"It was a great celebration, Agustín," said John Bogan. "It went very smoothly—with so many cultures involved. I compliment you."

"It's really Pa's fiesta," said Father. "Ramona's father has lots of patience and everyone loves the old man, you know."

"It must have cost you a good bit of money."

"Oh no—mostly just the steer we barbecued. It's mostly Indian labor and wild produce and what the old man raises in his truck garden. And everybody who comes contributes something. You yourself brought enough candles to last a year."

Phoebe spoke up: "It is a Mexican custom that I wouldn't have missed for anything. The assembly on the hill was beautiful. I can't wait to tell Carlota all about it."

John shook his head. "And I imagine you'll spoil it all by telling her how Agustín applied his rope to that Indian's back."

"John," said Phoebe sternly, "you must admit that it is outrageous for Agustín to treat the Indians the way he does."

"No, I don't. This is Agustín's property. When the Indians are told to go they had better go."

"What do they do wrong, John, just standing around?"

"Nothing, Phoebe. But did you ever think about this? If they were left to do as they please you'd sink to your ankles in human feces."

"Oh, John!" exclaimed Phoebe in horror. "It never dawned on me."

"Yes," said Father, "we could easily have an epidemic of typhoid fever. I couldn't afford that, Phoebe."

"Do you see those three Indians over there, digging a hole?" John went on. "And that group over there? They are cleaning up after last night's fiesta. Raking and burying human excrement."

"And how do you know so much, John?"

"*Por observación,*" he told her teasingly.

Phoebe Bogan was a student of Spanish. My Great Aunt Carlota, my Grandmother Wilbur's sister, was her Spanish teacher and close friend. At that time Phoebe was collecting material for a book about the Yaqui Indians. John Bogan was always laughing at his young wife's ambitions, but she eventually became an important translator from the Spanish and published many poems and several books.

That May morning, after taking leave of my grandparents, John hitched his dark bays to the surrey, helped Phoebe to her seat, and drove away, looking the picture of citified elegance, just as he always did, in contrast to our dusty, ranch-bound selves.

With all our fascinating visitors gone, life on the ranch settled back to normal. Most of the Indians who had stayed for the Feast of the

Holy Cross now went to the Guijas Village to rest up for the long trip to Tucson. Every day I saw fewer and fewer Indians around the ranch and by the middle of June almost all were gone. Mateo and Tomás José were the last to go, promising to come back for the fall *corrida*.

José-José came down to the creek every day. He was always declaring his aversion to picking saguaro fruit, so he had been left by the others in charge of the *jacales* (Indian huts).

Big cumulous clouds had begun to gather above the Santa Rita Mountains. Little dust twisters picked up the leaves and danced them across the yard. Big whirlwinds were constantly forming at the foot of the Baboquivari and then rising up above its peak. At night we frequently saw sheet lightning in the sky.

One day toward the middle of June Grandfather looked at the sky and said, "Mike, tomorrow you'd better bring the burros down so that we can get started on the *pizca*. We must begin the harvest or the rains are going to be upon us before we know it."

The following morning Mike threw a rope over his shoulder and left. He was back before noon, riding Pancho and leading Pardo. Father brought Diamante to the corral also, and on a Monday morning they hitched up both the buckboard and the buggy for our annual foray along the river to gather the desert harvest.

Mother loaded burlap sacks, boxes, a piece of big canvas, and our lunchbox in the back of the buggy under the seat. She put Ruby in the middle of the buggy seat and me on the outside. She drove with William seated on her lap, and Hunga followed behind us. Diamante took off at a steady trot, following the road that ran alongside the riverbank. My grandparents, with Mike and Luis, came along behind us in the buckboard.

Grandfather had left my Uncle Nieves, who had come to spend the summer, behind to guard the *milpita* from birds and other intruders. Uncle Nieves had been away for so long that I scarcely remembered him, but my grandparents were overjoyed to have him with us that summer.

Mother drove through thickets of sunflowers. Diamante stepped on them, laid them low, and the wheels of the buggy went over them, cutting them in two. We saw lots of baby quail scuttling along the roadside, urged on by their parents.

We soon came to a grove of *nogales* (walnut trees) and Mother pulled up for a moment to look the ground over. When the walnuts were sparse on the ground we moved on until we found a tree under which the ground was literally covered with fallen nuts. Here we would climb down and while I brought down the buckets and sacks Mother would unhitch Diamante and let him browse, the harness hanging at his sides. She would spread the big canvas under a shade tree and sit William in the center, surrounding him with his "toys"—clean, well-bleached bones. The small knucklebones were his "baby calves," larger ones were "mother cows," and the long shank bones were his "bulls."

These were the toys Ruby and I had grown up with, too, and it never dawned on us that there was anything better to play with. The beautiful dolls that Juanita had given us were now hanging by their necks on the wall of the *sala*. We considered them *recuerdos*, souvenirs, and souvenirs were not to be played with. As long as we had plenty of mother cows, plenty of offspring at their flanks, and enough bulls and steers, our cattle "industry" was healthy and safe, and we knew it would grow by leaps and bounds since we could always find more bones to add to our herds.

Now Ruby sat with William on the canvas and made a large corral with pebbles. She filled it with bone cattle, while Mother and I were gathering walnuts into big mounds.

My grandparents were busy in the nearby trees. Mother and I moved farther away, piling up more walnuts and marking the mesquite trees that looked heaviest with the fat, sweet mesquite beans. We left Ruby and William in Grandmother's care. She kept an eye on them while she picked buckets of elderberry fruit from nearby trees.

During these annual harvest rambles I remember always the feeling of being virtually surrounded by the great variety of birds that lived along the banks of our creek. Mother and my uncles considered them a great nuisance, but I loved the birds and often neglected the harvest to watch them.

They had many guises, and we had a different name for each role. Take the blackbirds, for instance. They have brown feathers, *chanates* we call them. When they ride around on the backs of cattle, feeding on lice, they are cowbirds. They are called *intrusos* when they lay their eggs in the nests of other birds. When they perch high in the trees and shriek their raucous warning to intruders they are *centineles negros* (black sentinels).

One time a surveyor and his wife came to our house to buy a team of mules. As they waited for Father to bring the mules they stood around admiring the scenery. "That's an interesting mountain there, Bill," the woman said to her husband, pointing to the north. "The hillside actually glistens!"

"That's black volcanic rock," the man told her, full of knowledge.

I touched his sleeve to get his attention. "That isn't rock, Mr. Olson," I said. "That black stuff is birds—ravens and cowbirds."

He ruffled my hair, condescendingly, and went right on. "The volcano must have erupted thousands of years ago," he told Mrs. Olson and me.

Just then, as if by magic, the shining black coverlet lifted from the side of the mountain, breaking up and flying away in all directions. I felt vindicated and Mr. and Mrs. Olson stood still, transfixed.

"Never have I seen anything more beautiful," said the woman, finally. She put her palms together in a gesture of prayer. "Holy is the Lord of Hosts, the earth is full of His glory." She reminded me then of the statue of the Blessed Virgin that Grandmother had in her room and I have always remembered her awed reactions.

Mother and I had just such an experience that first morning of the *pizca* (harvest) after our festival, except that our vision was in reverse.

We were resting for a moment on the hillside when Mother said suddenly, "Listen, Eva."

I heard the rustling whir of thousands of wings in the air above. Then a dusty-blue cloud settled onto the sandbar just beneath us. The blue mass did not lift up again; it slowly dissolved before our eyes as each bluejay moved away in turns, some to the edge of the stream, some to the brush along the banks.

Mother stared at them for a long time. "Tell me what they are doing, Eva," she said.

"I don't know, Ma. They aren't doing nothing."

"Most of them are drinking water, Zonza! They are thirsty. That means that they have come a long way."

"Oh, yes! I see now. Some of them are drinking from the *charquitos.*" The *charquitos* were deep cow tracks full of water.

Mother and I had already raked most of the fallen walnuts in the immediate area into piles for the boys to sack. Mother handed me a little pail now, and we moved on up the hill to pick some mulberries. I stood on a rock to reach the fruit, putting as many in my mouth as I did in the container. The overripe fruit burst in my fingers and the juice ran down my arms.

"You are a mess!" scolded Mother, putting down her pail. "Don't squeeze the berries, just snip them off." She showed me how to pick the fruit properly, and we filled our pails while some birds scolded both of us from the top of their tree.

"That's enough," Mother said, at last. "It is almost lunchtime and Pa is calling us."

"I don't hear him Ma."

"You hear with ears only? You don't hear because you aren't looking. He is signaling to us from over there."

I could now see Grandfather some distance away. He took off his hat, lifted it high and brought it down toward his chest.

We started back down the slope, leaving the mulberry tree to the chattering birds. Halfway down we stopped and looked back. The tree was now in the complete possession of the bluejays.

"They're beautiful, but mean like hawks," said Mother. "They have chased all the smaller birds away."

At the walnut grove we found Mike getting the lunch box from the buggy and Luis sacking the walnuts. Mother picked up William. Ruby and I gathered up the bone hunks and the canvas, and we all followed Mike to Grandfather's campfire where Mother began to make coffee and warm the *carne machacada* for our lunch.

When we had eaten and had thrown the meat scraps to some road-runners, Grandfather suggested that we leave the walnuts for another day and concentrate now on picking fruit. "If we don't pick fruit today and tomorrow there will be none. Flocks of birds are coming in from every direction."

We spent the afternoon picking fruit and sacking what was left of the walnuts until we ran out of containers. Finally we hitched up the buckboard and buggy again and started for home.

The next day we went to harvest elderberries on the south side of the creek and here, too, birds abounded. Some were friendly, others were wary. The ravens, roadrunners, and quail became pets after one feeding. The mockingbirds sang their purloined songs fearlessly; blue-jays scolded incessantly.

I asked Mother if she thought a bluejay might learn to sing if he could be raised next to my grandmother's mockingbird, Cantador.

"No," said Mother. "Jays are nothing but crows. They eat baby birds and they cannot sing or be pets. Perhaps we can get you a little bluebird for a pet. There are some beautiful ones near the Cochis Ranch. I'll ask Carmen to find one and raise it for you."

On the third day of the harvest I got bored trying to pick berries from trees too high for my reach. I wanted to visit my old haunts along the creek, and when Mother said I could go, I took off with Hunga at my heels.

Delfina, the squirrel who lived in a hollow tree above the bank, greeted us with much chattering. Hunga raced around playing hide-and-seek with her. We had met the squirrel in the spring when we caught her out sunning her babies. I taught Hunga not to hurt them and the squirrel had accepted us as her friends.

We left her now and walked on down the river looking for wild-flowers. I saw a nest in a branch of a tall hackberry tree, and several bluejays flying near it. I started on, but I noticed a baby jay half buried in last year's leaves. Thinking that it must have fallen from the nest, I picked it up and cradled it gently in both my hands. I couldn't restore it to the high nest so I decided to take it with me. In spite of Mother's prejudice, I would doctor it and feed it. Perhaps it would learn to sing from Cantador.

As I retraced my steps one of the jays flew along above my head, screeching. Something suddenly struck me and I stumbled, accidentally lifting my hands and flinging the little bird to the rear. I straightened up and looked for it, but the jays were making such a fuss that I went on without my prize. At a little distance I stopped and looked back. The bluejays were acting very strangely.

They flapped their wings along the ground, circling around some object. Others flew in and joined the little circle, emitting a cry I had never heard jays make: *ta-wee, ta-wee*. They doubled the vowels with the "A" soft and long, *Taa-wee, taa-wee*, over and over. It was a mournful tremolo, ending in a short staccato note. Somehow I knew the little bird lay among them, and I knew that it was dead. Had they come to pay respects to their dead? I knew the cattle sometimes did this. I remembered a time when Mother and I hid under Pluma Blanca and watched a sad and frightening ritual. A calf lay dead and Azabachi, the big black bull, came running. He stopped before the carcass, slowly bent one knee and then the other. He bowed his head and rested it on the dead calf and cried pitifully. I cried too.

"He's only an animal," Mother said, trying to comfort me. "For all we know, he is having fun." But I knew he was not, and I was not comforted.

"Come, Hunga," I said now. "Let's go back to the *tapiros*." I went straight back to the elderberry trees where I had left Mother. "Ma," I said, "a little bird is dead and the other birds are crying! Come and see."

"That's silly," Mother said impatiently. "We have to get as much done here as possible and leave early. Your grandfather is getting very tired."

"Please, Ma." I took her hand and led her along the river and up the bank to a spot above the hackberry tree where we could see the tiny bird lying on a flat rock. The circle of bluejays had increased two-fold. They were hunched down, still crying their *taa-wee, taa-wee.*

"How pitiful," said Mother. "The little bird must have fallen."

"I killed it," I said, "but I didn't mean to, Ma. I was carrying it and something hit my head and I threw it."

Mother examined my head. "One of the jays nipped your scalp, but it isn't bad."

Mother told my grandparents about the birds, and Mike and Grand-father ran to the spot to check. When they finally came back Mike told us that there were only a few birds left mourning the tiny bird. "But it certainly did sound like they were crying," he admitted. "It's very strange."

"I never saw birds act like that before," remarked Grandfather.

"Live and learn, Francisco," said my grandmother.

When we returned home from the *pizca* that day a surprise was waiting for us. Aunt Rita had made a big elderberry pudding, and we all sat at the kitchen table and enjoyed it. It was delicious.

"How is everything going at the *milpita*, Rita?" he asked. "Is Nieves getting along all right?"

Rita nodded. "He's doing fine except for the birds. They are giving him a hard time. Juana and I went to the island this morning to help Nieves cover some of the fruit trees with netting to keep them off. And he has poor Che running his feet off going from one end of the island to the other, shooing birds away from the plants."

"I don't like having to make Nieves work so hard when he has just come home," said Grandfather. "Mike, you had better go to the *milpita* and replace your brother. I want to talk with him about going to the oak country to mark some trees."

"Sure, Pa." Mike replenished his bowl with more pudding and went off, carrying it with him.

Marking oak trees was another annual custom. It meant a long trek to the oak groves to the south to mark our usual trees and to search out and mark new acorn-bearing trees that had not already been claimed by other people. If our trees were not freshly marked they could be taken over by new owners.

There were several ways to claim a tree. Some people burned their brands or initials on the trunk. Then the brands had to be renewed each year so that they would appear fresh, indicating that the owner intended to return to harvest the *bellotas*. Other people swept beneath their trees and encircled them with rocks. Still others burned off the vegetation under their trees, at once claiming ownership and killing the larvae of the worms that would bore into the acorns and ruin them. As a further protection against insects and worms most of us stored acorns in ashes after harvesting them.

My Uncle Nieves arrived at the kitchen, mopping his face with a red bandana handkerchief. "Pa, the world is burning up," he said. "I have never seen it so hot." He had brought a sack of *elotes*—ears of fresh green corn—from the milpita. He handed the sack to Aunt Rita who would roast them for our supper.

Grandfather smiled fondly at him. "You are not used to the heat, *hijo*. You have been living in the cool country." Nieves had been working on a mountain ranch in New Mexico. "The rains are coming soon. Someone must go to the oak country to mark our trees and claim some new ones, if possible. I'd like to harvest three or four hundred pounds of acorns to see us through the winter with some left over to sell."

Grandfather was always looking for ways to make a little cash to buy the things the land did not produce, such things as sugar and spices, shoes, blankets, and medicines.

"I'll be glad to go, Pa." Nieves said. "I can take Luis with me to identify your trees and keep me company. Right now I'm going down to the creek to wash up and then I'm going to hike over to Arivaca. Old Tomaza came by to see me today, Pa." He grinned at Grandfather. "She's just as brassy and know-it-all as ever, and just as generous.

"She talked the soldiers at Fort Huachuca into giving her a bundle of mosquito netting. Now she says she will give it to us to cover the rest of the fruit trees. When you pick the fruit along the riverbanks as you're doing now, the birds come in droves to your island seeking whatever fruit they can find there, Pa. If we don't protect those trees, there won't be a peach left to ripen."

"That's true, *hijo*." Grandfather lowered his voice and looked somewhat embarrassed. "Now, Nieves," he said, "when you bring the netting back, don't carry it over your back like a *mochila* (backpack). Some of the Sajones may see you."

"Oh, Pa. I wouldn't worry about the Americanos. They have their way of coping with their problems and we have ours. And believe me, their ways are not always the best. Just to show you what I mean, Pa, I saw Fred Lyon leaving the store the other day, on his way to the Jarillas Ranch. He had a large bag in each hand, three or four books under his arm, a piece of canvas over his shoulder, and a pair of shoes dangling from his belt. He dropped the books three times before he finally got away. Now if he had made himself a mochila with the canvas and thrown it over his back he would have been a lot more comfortable and looked a lot more intelligent. I suggested it to him, and he was so insulted you wouldn't believe it. 'I want you to know that I am *not* a *mochilero*,' he shouted at me."

I often think of my uncle's story now when I see the men and women, too, for that matter, with their backpacks. If I give them a chance they go to great lengths to tell me how comfortable these backpacks really are and how much you can carry this way. We have come a long way. Or maybe we have just slipped back. There were many people then, both Sajones and Latinos, who thought it beneath them to harvest acorns (though most of them did it anyway on the sly); those who were too proud to do this were apt to be the very ones who would later come to Grandfather's door in the middle of winter to beg a little sack of *bellotas* to feed their hungry children. Grandfather never refused them.

Activities relating to the *pizca* used to run for many days. Uncle Luis and Nieves departed for the border ranch where they would first mark our oak trees and later harvest the *bellotas*. Mother and Grandmother worked long hours along the riverbanks continuing to harvest wild fruit and to bring in more walnuts and what ripe mesquite beans they could find. Meanwhile, in the kitchen, Grandmother, Aunt Rita, and Juana worked long hours every day, preserving and storing all this food for later use. The different varieties of beans were placed in different piles so we could thresh them and then sack them. The little white tepary beans were difficult to handle and were usually left for my grandmother to clean. Prickly pear pods had been processed earlier in the spring and were already in jars on the shelves. Tender Chinese squash from the milpita had been cut and dried, sacked, and put away. Careless weeds were next in line. After the first two or three rains of the summer they would sprout up all over and in three days they had to be cut, cooked, and dried so we could store them. The weeds matured fast, and once they became tough their harvest was over.

All day long now wonderful smells were coming from the kitchen, the aromas of jams and jellies simmering. That's where I would have liked to linger, but Ruby and I were not allowed to be idle. After our regular chores were done, we were sent to work on the island garden.

From sunrise to sundown work never ceased at the milpita. The produce was ripening so fast Mike had to work constantly picking fruits and vegetables and carting them to the kitchen. Now it was not the birds that worried Grandfather so much as the Indians. After working at the *pizca* most of the day he would come to his garden and work some more, eating and sleeping at the milpita, making his bed on the crude table near the hornilla. One time he was awakened by Carmelo, the Indian, who was in the garden picking the fresh corn and throwing the ears down the riverbank. "Carmelo!" yelled Grandfather. "¡*Indio tosco, sinverguenza* (clumsy, shameless Indian)!" Carmelo fled through the gate and ran away, but not before picking up the armload of elotes he had thrown down the bank.

About a week later Father went to the huts to pay Carmelo for a few days' work he had done for us. He gave him a chit. "You take this paper to John Bogan at the store and he will give you your money," said Father, writing rapidly. "Now, your name is Carmelo Milomah."

"No," said Carmelo, "my name is Carmelo Tosco."

"I thought your name was Carmelo Milomah."

"My father, Carmelo Milomah," said the Indian. "Milomah good name. Tosco better, more strong. Very strong, so I Carmelo Tosco."

"Where did you get that name?" asked Father, surprised.

"Him," said Carmelo, pointing at Grandfather.

Carmelo took the chit out of its envelope and left, waving it in his hand like a white flag.

Grandfather explained to Father the incident in the garden which prompted him to call Carmelo, "Indio Tosco," ill-bred, stupid Indian. The Indian had liked the sound of the word and quickly took it for his name, not caring what the word meant, but only what its sound suggested to him. The Indians did this very often.

My father, too, spent as much time as he could on the island, helping with the heavy labor of hoeing and irrigating, and keeping the water tank filled. Old Barreplata came every day, too, but he was ailing now and starting to have rheumatic pains in his back. He rested a lot.

Father put Ruby and me to work carrying small buckets of water to the plants that were inaccessible to the main ditches. We worked very hard, but one day when we were left alone on the island for awhile, I came up with a smart idea which I was sure would please Father. He had so often said to us, "Plan your work ahead and you'll get more done."

I now noticed the big bucket that hung from a rope above the well, and it occurred to me that Ruby and I could finish our watering much sooner if we were to use this instead of our little pails.

I pulled the big bucket toward me and, with some effort, managed to untie the rope. Then I saw that there was a rock, wrapped in chicken wire, tied to the edge of the pail. I decided that this must come off. I left Ruby alone and went out the gate and to the workbench to get Father's nippers, the ones he used to snip off the ends of horseshoe nails.

The nippers were too big for my hands, but with some difficulty I cut the chicken wire, and the rock fell away from the pail. We filled the bucket to the rim by dipping it into the tank and stuck a pole through the bail. Carrying the pail between us, we proceeded to water the plants. In this way we were able to water several plants at one time. Our work went very fast and the water tank was soon empty.

When I set the bucket back on the edge of the well I heard a splash, but I paid no attention to it. Ruby and I were just about to go to the hornilla to make ourselves a burrito when Father appeared.

"Is the tank empty already?" he asked.

"Yes, Pa." I proudly told him how we had used Grandfather's big pail to water the plants.

Father took a look at the pail and frowned. "All right. We'll refill the tank now, Eva." He tied the pail to the rope and told me to drop it into the well. "You let it fill with water and I'll pull it up."

I walked nervously onto the platform that covered part of the well and dropped the bucket into the water. I shook the rope. The pail floated.

"What's the matter, Eva?"

"It won't sink, Pa. The pail just stays on the water."

Father turned the windlass till the bucket was near the top of the well. "Now you get down there and bring the pail toward you," he said, handing me the discarded rock and some wire he had taken from Grandfather's tool shed. "Put this rock back on the pail where it belongs."

Tying the rock onto the bucket proved to be much more difficult than snipping it off, but I did my best. Father finally took up the pail and tightened the wire with pliers. He gave it back to me, and I climbed back onto the platform and again dropped the pail into the well. This time it tipped to one side with the weight of the rock and disappeared below the surface.

"Now, Eva, do you know what that rock was for?"

"Yes, Papa."

"Come along, then. Your mother wants you at the house. I'll send Mike along to guard the *milpita* until your grandfather comes." Barre-plata had already gone for the day, leading old Simon toward his *casita* beyond the hill.

Father took Ruby's hand and I followed them to the house where he immediately confronted Mother with the tale of my latest stupidity.

Mother looked at me with despair. "Eva, you have been watching your grandfather draw water from that well all your life. Am I to believe that you did not know what that rock was for?"

"Yes, Ma. I mean no, Ma, I didn't know."

Mother had just taken a pan of apricot turnovers from the oven. Mike helped himself to a few and departed to guard the island. Father started to follow him out the door, but returned almost at once.

"Eva, what happened to my nippers?" he asked.

My heart bolted as I remembered that splash at the well. "I don't know, Pa," I lied.

"Why don't you? You used them to cut the wire from the rock, didn't you?"

"No, Pa."

"I'm going to Arivaca to get the mail," he said. "You have those nippers on the bench where you got them by the time I get back. Do you understand?"

"Yes, Papa." I watched him go out the door, then turned around. "Ma!"

"Yes."

"Do you know where the nippers are?"

To my utter astonishment Mother answered yes. This positive reply silenced me for a minute. Then I said meekly, "Where, Ma?"

"In the bottom of the well, where you dropped them."

It was frightening. It was awesome that your parents knew what you had done without having seen you do it. "Can you get them out of the well for me?"

"No."

"Please, Ma."

Mother relented a little. "You could go back to the island and ask Mike," she suggested. "He might take pity on you."

Uncle Mike went down into the shallow well and brought the nippers out for me. "You'd better tell your father that you dropped them in the well," he said. "You don't have to keep on lying, you know."

"Yes, Uncle Mike. I will."

When Father came back in the late afternoon, he rode the Big Grey to the stable, then came into the kitchen to put a newspaper and some mail on the table. "I see you found my nippers, Eva."

"Yes, Papa."

"Where were they?"

"In the well, Papa."

"Why didn't you tell me?" he asked sternly.

"I was scared you'd get mad at me, Papa."

"Scared or not scared, right or wrong, you must learn to face up to the consequences of your actions. Do you understand?" Father launched into one of his tirades. He talked about lying and being sneaky. He talked of cowardice and how I must be strong and squeeze the fear right out of myself. He said something about taking the bull by the horns and looking at the bull, eyeball to eyeball. And he ended the lecture by telling me that if he had to go over this lesson with me again he would use his reata.

"Yes, Papa," I said, as fast as I could. "I will take the bull by the horns. I will look him straight in the eye and lie to him, eyeball to eyeball."

"Never lie," roared Father.

Grandfather had come in just in time to hear the last of this lecture. "Agustín," he chided, "you talk so much you have her confused. After all, she is just a little child."

"Are you just a little child?"

"No, Papa, I went to the Cerro with you when I was only three."

"Never mind the damned Cerro!"

My mother and grandmother laughed, and I didn't know whether they were laughing at me or my father.

"Ay, *mijita*," exclaimed Grandfather. "That mountain is just a *picachito*—a little lomita compared to the mountains you will have to climb during your life."

"And she'd better be preparing for them," said Father, getting the last word.

The next day Grandfather began his preparations for the impending rains. He dug ditches and made large saucers around the trees. He mixed cement and chinked the cracks on the garden *covachitas* so that water would not enter and ruin the *santos* he had placed in their niches. I loved the colorful pictures of San Ysidro, especially the one where an angel was pulling a plow. Grandfather also made a cross out of two boards and placed it in the center of the *milpita*.

"My father won't like that," I told Grandfather. Father had little patience with religious symbols. Except for his annual contribution to the Feast of the Holy Cross, which he made mainly for Grandfather's sake, he wasted little time on prayers and such.

"Agustín likes to eat the food we raise here, doesn't he?" Grandfather retorted. He looked at the cross and touched his forehead. "The *milpita* has flourished and the desert *pizca* has been most successful. We should be thankful to God for a bountiful harvest."

It was true. There would be fresh produce from Grandfather's island garden far into the fall. The uncles were yet to return from Cochis Ranch with their loads of acorns, but for the most part the *pizca* was over. The shelves in the milkhouse were stacked with numberless jars of preserved fruits and vegetables; there were quantities of nuts and corn and beans and sacks of dried herbs stored away.

Besides all that, there would be much milk and cheese. And I had heard Grandmother boast of having two or three dozen roasting hens. The family would eat well for many months, but whether all this bounty was due to the blessings of God and San Ysidro or to the labor of our hands I did not know. I asked Grandfather what he thought about it.

"Of course it is God's blessings. Without his blessings our hands would be paralyzed. He gives us the strength and intelligence to do our work, *Zonza.*"

When the Rains Came

EACH YEAR, JUST BEFORE THE SUMMER RAINS BEGAN, two matters of crisis inevitably arose at the Wilbur Ranch. The first involved a frantic effort to repair the roof of the milkhouse where the fruits of the *pizca* were stored. Grandfather constantly fretted about the condition of the roof and begged Father to replace it with a new one, but the repairs were always temporary and always a race against time. The second crisis was that both Father and Barreplata were stricken with agonizing bouts of rheumatism, not to be alleviated until the rains fell.

This year, it was Barreplata who succumbed first. When he hadn't appeared at the kitchen door for two whole days both Mother and Grandmother became anxious. They called Mike down from the roof and asked him to go and check up on the old man. Mother prepared a pail of hot food, and Grandfather sent tobacco, even taking time to roll some cigarettes. Grandmother added a jar of *unto de zorillo* (skunk grease) to rub on his aching back.

Mike returned an hour later with woeful news. "Barra's flat on his back and hasn't eaten for a whole day. He was glad to get the food and tobacco, Pa. I fed the animals and tried to rub his back, but he's in too much pain."

"*¡Pobrecito!*" said Grandmother. "He is an old man and he works too hard."

When Father came in later that day and learned of his old friend's plight he was much concerned. "Poor old fellow. I know how he is suffering." He looked at me. "Would you like to go with me to see him, Eva?"

"Yes, Pa."

The Big Grey was waiting by the wall and Father lifted me onto his back. Then he called to Uncle Mike who was again working on the milkhouse roof, "Will you please hitch up the buckboard, Mike, and follow us? We'll probably have to bring Barra back here to look after him."

I rode on the saddle behind Father as Big Grey galloped along the creek. We climbed a couple of hills and came finally to Barreplata's front yard. Father dismounted, wrapping the reins around the pommel, and lifted me to the ground. I followed him into the one-room adobe house.

"¿Como estás, Barra?" he called.

"¿Vinistes, hijo? You came?" A feeble voice answered from a dark corner. Barreplata was lying on a bed next to the adobe wall. He had a dirty canvas for a sheet and his pillow had no slip. Dirty dishes lay on a box next to his bed. On the other side of the room a grey cat perched on top of a cold wood stove, so still I looked at it twice to make sure it was alive.

"You came to see your Tata, *Chiquita.*"

"Yes, Tata, I came." I felt shy and sad. It is frightening to see someone you depend upon lying helpless and in pain.

"Would you see what you can find to feed me, Agustín, before you go?" asked Barra.

"No," said Father. "I am going to take you home with me. You need care and I can't come every hour to look after you. Especially if I get down myself, as you know I will."

"But, *hijo,* I can't move from this bed," Barra complained. "I can't even sit up."

"I know all about it, Barra. It hurts like hell."

"And there are the animals. Simon hasn't had water for two days."

"Yes, he has. Mike fed and watered all of them this morning. He is on his way now with the buckboard. Don't worry about Simon."

Moving Barreplata was not easy for he really could not sit up. He moaned and he yelled as they tried to move him. "He sounds just like you, Agustín," declared Uncle Mike.

"Rheumatism is no joking matter, Mike," said Father grimly.

They finally improvised a stretcher from the sheet of canvas and two mesquite poles. They placed it across a box and a chair next to the bed and rolled the sick man onto it as gently as possible. Barreplata cried out and begged not to be touched, but Father was firm.

Mike had brought blankets and had already made a pad in the back of the wagon. They carried Barreplata from his little house and maneuvered the stretcher onto the pad.

Father drove slowly as we returned to the ranch house. I looked back from my seat beside him in the wagon and saw Uncle Mike on Father's horse, Simon and the dogs trotting along behind him. The old burro looked thin and very sad with his head down and his long ears flopping.

They carried Barreplata straight to Don Ignacio Pesqueira's room in the old part of the house. I tried to follow them, but Mother grabbed my arm. "Stay right where you are."

Father soon came back, saying, "He's in bed now, comfortable and quiet."

"Can I go see him, Pa?"

"When your grandmother takes him something to eat, you can go with her then."

Mike turned Simon loose in the small pasture and fed Barreplata's dogs, then he went back on the roof. Great cumulus clouds were rising over the southern mountains, and distant thunder sounded in our ears.

Only two days later Father was stricken.

Grandfather suddenly appeared before Mother to tell her, "*Oyes*, Ramona, Agustín is coming and I think he must be sick because he's riding at a snail's pace. He's been coming down the *minita* hill for a good hour now."

Mother looked resigned. "He shouldn't have gone out this morning, Pa. He was complaining of pains during the night." She poured my grandfather a cup of hot coffee, then turned to Juana Gallego. "Juana, will you please bring some fresh sheets? We'll have to make up his bed."

Juana lifted her brown eyes in a quick questioning look. She had been playing with the baby, but she lowered him to the floor, her thick, shining braids swinging, and then ran quickly from the kitchen in obedience to Mother's request.

Father eventually arrived, riding slowly past the wall to the kitchen door. He seemed frozen to the saddle, his face a picture of agony. We were all waiting for him.

"Have you thought how you are going to get down from there, Son?" asked Grandfather.

"Yes, Pa," answered Father. "I . . . I've been thinking about it." He spoke between spasms of pain. "Mike, go bring the *tapojo*. It's hanging on the saddle rack." Mike ran to the stable and returned with the blindfold, putting it on the horse quickly so that the Big Grey couldn't see what was about to happen. "Now go get that workbench from the barn and put it right there."

The bench was brought and placed beside Father's right stirrup. With great effort Father was able to plant his right foot on the bench, but he was unable to bring his other foot over the saddle. By now the Big Grey was moving nervously, stomping his hooves, and Mother and Grandfather had moved up, with some danger to themselves, to support Father on the left.

"Lift yourself, *hombre*," ordered Grandfather.

With a great show of courage Father managed to lift himself a few inches above the saddle and Uncle Mike led the Big Grey out from under his rider, leaving Father for a perilous instant standing on one foot with the other awkwardly raised in mid-air. Mother and Grandfather hoisted him toward the bench and he sprawled on top of it.

From there he flatly refused to budge. Mike ran to fetch the makeshift stretcher which they held online with the bench. Father rolled onto it. At last they were able to cart him away to his bed.

The ridiculous scene would have been amusing had it not been so painful to everyone. I sniffed hard as I ran after the procession.

Now we had two patients to pamper. Grandfather offered to give Father a rubdown with the skunk grease, but Father disdainfully refused such treatment, so Grandfather went to Arivaca to summon the doctor. However, Dr. Ball, too, was sick with another asthma attack and could not come. He promised to visit Father the next day.

He arrived before noon with liniments, ointments, and pills, none of which did any good, according to Father. Dr. Ball diagnosed the ailment as bursitis, as he always did, and said that the atmospheric change wasn't helping.

No sooner had he left than Doña Tomaza arrived—our outlaw with the saintly hands. She strode into Father's room, oozing self confidence. "*Como estás*, Agustín? I met Francisco in town yesterday and he told me you were down with arthritis."

"Arthritis, bursitis, rheumatism, Tomaza. Whatever it is, I can hardly move. It is killing me."

Tomaza took a bottle of Sloan's liniment out of her bag. "I'm going to rub you with some of this, Agustín. I know it will make you feel better. Now I know it's hard, but you'll have to turn on your stomach."

Father groaned and moaned, but he finally rolled over to expose his back. Tomaza opened the bottle of liniment and poured a few drops on the back of her hand so that Father could smell it. Then she set the bottle down and out of his line of vision she picked up the jar of skunk grease which she began to rub across Father's lower back.

I opened my mouth, but Mother silenced me with her hand and pushed me out through the door. As I left I heard Tomaza say, "This is the best damned liniment in the world. The only thing is, it smells like hell."

"You're right about that," I heard Father say in a strange muffled voice.

I heard her in the washroom a little later, vigorously washing her hands. When she came into the kitchen she whispered to Grandfather, "That skunk grease will help him, Francisco. It's better than all the damned junk the doctor left."

After paying a visit to Barreplata, Tomaza went with my grandparents to the *milpita*. They loaded her buckboard with fruits and vegetables, and she left in a hurry as she always did, stirring up a great cloud of dust.

With both Father and Barreplata down, Ruby and I had to do more than our share of chores. After breakfast we followed Mother to the corral to help with the milking. That done, we moved to the goats' corral to feed the *lepes* (the young animals who had no mother), separate the kids from their mothers, and finally to let the herd out.

Ruby and I drove the herd up and over the slope of the hill. On our return we let the kids out, too. It was fun to watch them run and play along the creek banks. When we got home we usually found Mother curdling the milk and making cheese, while Aunt Rita and Juana prepared fruit to dry in the sun.

"Go gather the eggs," Mother would say. Feed the dogs and sweep the zaguán. Run and see if your papa needs anything. Father was still lying in his bed, angry and frustrated, "toughing it out," and waiting for the rains to fall. The traffic and activity in the kitchen was so noisy that we often could not hear him when he called for help.

The day of June 23 dawned hot and clear. I knew early that morning that something important was in the wind, because Grandfather had brought his burros, Pardo and Pancho, down from the hill and penned them in the little pasture near the house. He had built some shelves and boxes along the sides of the buckboard. Late that afternoon he and Grandmother began to stock the wagon with produce, mostly fresh fruits and vegetables. Green beans were abundant, and she had put them in bags. She filled the wheelbarrow with elotes from the early Indian corn and wheeled it to the wagon to join a pile of ripe *sandias* (watermelons).

Mother was just as busy in the kitchen. She put a number of cheeses in a box along with a lot of quesadillas. She packed eggs and cactus candy. She put a large box of things she had gathered into the cooler to be loaded in Grandfather's wagon the next morning.

"Where is he going to take all that stuff, Ma?" I asked.

"To Arivaca," answered Mother. "Tomorrow is San Juan's Day and there will be a fiesta in town and horse races. Pa is going to peddle his produce and some things for me, too."

There is a legend in the Southwest that there is always rain on San Juan's Day, June 24. In that part of the country it always did rain, and the celebration was a prelude to the rainy season.

"Can Ruby and me go along, Ma?" I asked.

"It will be a hot day and Grandfather may not want to be bothered with you girls. We'll talk about it tomorrow," said Mother.

The sun was just coming up when I was awakened the next morning by a commotion outside. I jumped out of bed and ran to the window, amazed to see a band of beautiful young people near the house.

The girls sat sidesaddle on their horses, their long skirts reaching below the stirrups. Their hats looked like baskets full of flowers, their ribbons flying on the soft morning air. Red ribbons were tied to the horses' bridles and the young men wore tall Stetsons and colorful ties. One of them rode toward the door, strumming his guitar, leading the group in singing *Las Mañanitas*. His white horse chomped the bridle and pawed the ground as they sang a little love song:

> Que bonitas mañanitas
> Como que quiere llover.
> Parecen las mañanitas
> En que yo te empece
> A querer.

Their song ended, they galloped away toward the road, and I flew to the kitchen. "Ma, they ran away, Ma!"

Mother smiled. "That's the way it is supposed to happen when a young lady is serenaded. They sang for Juana because this is her feast day. Now they are on their way to Arivaca where they will have the horse races."

Juana turned from the open kitchen door to face us. She had a shawl over her head and a dazed look on her face. Her eyes were shining.

"Mother," I demanded. "Why did you name me Eva Antonia? Why? Didn't you know any better?"

Mother stared at me in surprise. "What has come over you? You have always been happy with those names."

Not knowing what to say about my resentment, I quickly changed the subject. "Ruby and I are going with Grandfather to Arivaca," I stated.

"Your grandfather left a long time ago," Mother said.

I dropped on the floor and cried.

Mother wasted no sympathy. "Get up and get dressed," she ordered. "You can go out later and watch the people pass by on the road as they go to the festival."

When I went to the edge of the bank where I could see the road to town, a big wagon passed by, loaded with happy children. It was followed by buggies and surreys and many single riders, all dressed in festive clothes.

After breakfast I sought out old Barreplata, to share with him my unhappiness. He was sitting in the shade, whittling on a stick, the two dusty dogs at his feet. He assured me that, had he been well enough, he would have taken Ruby and me to the celebration.

Grandfather returned to the ranch soon after lunch carrying a canvas bag full of silver coins. He and Grandmother sat at the table, happily counting the money. He handed Mother her share of the coins and told her that the cactus candy had sold better than anything except the watermelons.

"I could have sold a lot more," he said. "But I felt that the rain was coming so I hurried home."

Grandfather was wise, as usual. Great rain-swollen clouds had already begun to gather over the Santa Rita Mountains. They piled up toward the center of the sky and spread toward the western horizon. By two o'clock in the afternoon the wind had begun to blow, its strength increasing gradually until the big willow trees bowed to the ground, and the cottonwood branches, not so pliable, broke off and were blown in piles all across the yard. All the while the wind was picking up tons of blinding dust that rose in a massive cloud and tore across the land.

Cattle left the creek and streamed up the ridges toward the highlands, lowing as they trotted along the dusty trails. Some straggling Indians ran toward their village. And Grandfather hurried to Don

Ignacio's room to bring Barreplata to the house so that he wouldn't be alone during the storm. Barreplata walked slowly with the aid of a cane and Grandfather's arm. They stopped in the open doorway to view the approaching storm. Suddenly El Cerro, the dark mountain to the south, was completely obscured by a sheet of falling rain. The wonderful smell of it striking the parched earth was perfume to our nostrils.

The wind blew so hard now that we could hear the boards rattling in the barn. A streak of lightning split the sky. Then came a loud clap of thunder and Barreplata and Grandfather were actually blown into the house. The rain came to us at last, so generously it seemed as though a million buckets were being emptied from the sky.

Grandfather pulled the door shut, but we could still hear the rain pounding on the roof, its repairs just finished, fortunately, even if only temporarily.

Barreplata limped into the bedroom to see Father, who was now sitting up and talking rather cheerfully. By the time the rain subsided both Father and Barreplata were sitting in the kitchen drinking coffee and laughing as though they had never had a pain.

"I hope Nieves and Luis are keeping dry," remarked Father.

"Don't worry," said Grandfather. "Carmen and Cipriano will see that they have shelter."

The rains passed; the sky cleared and the cottonwood leaves gleamed metallic in the sun. The atmosphere was pure and clean, colors sharper. Everyone felt lighthearted.

My grandfather was still elated because of his successful sale. It was not only that people had bought the wares he had offered; they had been kind and friendly and had begged him to bring more sandias and elotes to town for the Fourth of July. Father and Barreplata were happy that they were finally able to move around. As for Ruby and me, we were overjoyed because we could splash in the cool puddles left by the rain.

At the same time, even while everyone was enjoying this fresh new world in his own way, we felt a certain ominous stillness in the air. We all listened intently for the aftermath of the storm, the roar of the flood that we knew was sure to follow.

Che came running from the creek. "I see it coming, Pa," he shouted. *"De orilla a orilla!"* From bank to bank.

We ran to the banks of the creek, and stood at a safe distance to watch the flash flood. By this time the wall of water had struck and rushed on. The island garden was now only a couple of feet above the churning waters.

"Francisco," called Barreplata above the roar, "it will be a miracle if it doesn't take the whole island."

"No, Barra," said Grandfather. "That cottonwood there"—he pointed to a large tree that stood at the point of the *milpita*—"that's what breaks the flood."

The force of the flood was awesome. Posts and sections of fence went sailing by. Entire trees appeared, spinning and bumping against the banks. Then caught by the main current, they went on, bobbing up and down like matchsticks. We heard the rumble of falling earth as the turgid stream took great bites from the sides of the channel. The dust from the dry interior released, dust rose above the mesquite.

Strangest of all, a saddle rack came riding the crest of the flood with a perfectly good saddle upon it. "Wouldn't you like to get your hands on that, Agustín?" said Barra, who was standing beside Father.

"A nice saddle, Barra," answered Father. "Some poor hombre will miss it."

We watched the rack sweep to the curve of the bank and pause for an instant upright against the big cottonwood. The saddle slipped off the rack and fell into the water with a splash. It sank halfway, but then the fenders and stirrups spread out, and the saddle bobbed up again, riding in a circle until it was caught by the main current. It faced west and went swiftly down the muddy stream. The power of the water pushed the front of the saddle down and the cantle back, so that it went rocking merrily along, giving us the impression that it was galloping away by itself.

Ruby and I laughed hysterically. Grandfather laughed with us. "That must be the spirit of a vaquero riding there," he said.

"Yes," said Grandmother, joining the fun, "there is surely an invisible rider on that saddle."

After watching the water for some time we walked around the slope of the *lomita* enjoying the fresh, cool air and looking out over the desert. The land that had been parched and dusty only an hour before was now dotted with ponds, gleaming in the late afternoon sun. Father and Barreplata, beginning to feel the chill of the damp air, decided to go back in. Ruby and I brought the goat herd down from the slope.

My grandparents and Mike, Rita, and Che also spent the night at our house, as they could not get across the swollen creek. Toads seemed to have sprouted everywhere, and they kept up a steady loud croaking. Mother was afraid that Hunga would bite a toad, so she brought the dog inside, too. When toads are bitten they excrete adrenalin, and the dog absorbs the secretion, causing its heartbeat to increase until sometimes it dies.

The night was cool, wet, and noisy. The roar of the flood, the rumble of the chunks of earth being carried away, the rustling leaves of the trees and the distant thunder continued through the night.

Don't Be a Zonza

THAT SUMMER FATHER RODE THE RANGE regularly to bring in sick animals that needed care and had to be doctored. My job was to be on the lookout for him so that I could open the corral gate, and to build fires when fires were needed. So I spent many days gathering wood and piling it in the stable to keep it dry.

One day Father brought down the mule team, Tula and Pancha. Pancha was a big gentle animal, smart and dependable, and, of course, Father was upset when he found her dragging a hind leg. Undoubtedly, she had caught it in barbed wire and it was cut and swollen. We usually treated such infections by washing the wound with *yerba del pasmo*, an herb tea that we often made in the corral over an open fire.

Now Father walked to the center of the corral, swept a spot on the ground, and placed on it three large rocks. "You can build a fire for me, Eva, between these rocks."

"Yes, Papa." I had seen how such open fires were made, and I confidently made my preparations. But when I finally struck a match to the wood it just smoked and smouldered and finally went out.

"All right," said Father. "I will build a fire foundation and you watch carefully and see how it is done. Here on the side away from the wind you build a small Indian tepee of very small kindling. Leave an opening where the air can get through. Now cover the tepee with one just like it, made of larger sticks, and, finally, put good-sized wood on top. When you strike your match always protect the flame from the wind. And always pretend that you have only one match. That will make you careful."

Now what could be easier than that, I thought. But it wasn't easy at all. After three tries and three smoldering failures, Father kicked the sticks to one side and had me make a new foundation under his supervision. This time the fire burned beautifully.

After that Mother had me make fires in the kitchen stove in the mornings using the same method. Ruby learned along with me, and we took turns making fires, sometimes drawing matchsticks to see which one would get to do it. Having mastered this simple art, I was often amused to find that many grown men could not build a proper fire. They would light match after match, fanning a nonexistent flame, and then curse and blame the wind.

One day Father brought in a couple of young calves to be branded. While he sharpened his knife to earmark and castrate the calves, I got an armload of wood, built a little dome, and placed the branding irons on it in a circle, burying the handles as Father had taught me. I struck a match, and the little fire roared with hardly any smoking.

"Good work!" said Uncle Nieves from the corral fence. "You should be proud of yourself for making a fire like that."

"*¡Que hubo!* Hello, Uncle Nieves." I looked past him at Cipriano's wagon that was standing across the yard. "Did you just get here?" I asked. "It's funny I didn't hear the wagon drive up."

"You were too busy building that fire." He came inside to stand beside me and ruffle my hair.

"Did you bring lots of *bellotas* from the oak country?"

"A whole wagonload," he answered. "Cipriano had to lend us his wagon to bring them." He and Uncle Luis walked over to talk with Father.

They told him where the fences were down at the Cochis Ranch and how packs of wolves were now coming clear down to the corral. "After the first big rain most of the *belloteros* left," said Uncle Luis. "We had the acorn harvest all to ourselves, except for Carmelo Tosco. But he was a big help to us. He gathered wood and helped clean out Cipriano's well. The flood had filled it with debris."

"Cipriano returned the favor by taking us all into his house when it rained," said Uncle Nieves. "And he made his *chamacos* help us pick the acorns. We brought the Indian back with us," he added.

By now, Carmelo Tosco was down from the wagon and coming across the yard to join the others. He told Father that he had picked "pig sacks of acorns," and that he was happy to have worked for "Los Tíos." Now the uncles would take him to his own village.

Carmelo stood tall and declared loudly, "No country nowhere is so fine as Wilbur country. Everything good. Good people. Good *perdices* to eat. Good water running down big rocks make pretty noises. Birds sing. Wolves howl. Your country, good. Saguaro country, no good." Then, his speech of praise concluded, the Indian jumped into the air, letting out one of his loud savage screams.

"Los Tíos" broke into loud laughter. And, indeed, Carmelo's pleasure made us all feel good.

After lunch that day Mike took Carmelo and his 200 pounds of acorns in the buckboard to Las Guijas Village. After they had gone, Father told Mother that he would like to take advantage of the dry spell we were having to ride out and inspect fences and locate stock that had wandered too far.

"I'll take Eva with me. She's a big help to me. We'll start out early," he said, and he kept Diamante and Vaquerito in the small pasture overnight.

Mother got out my Levis, made from Father's castoffs. These were not like the coveralls that I wore every day, but were exact copies of Father's Levis, except for the rivets. The mini-Levis were a product of my mother's clever hands, for in those days Levi Strauss did not manufacture pants for women, much less for children. Cowgirls wore divided skirts, and not without criticism. Such ugly comments as "I'd like to stone her to death" were not uncommon.

When people saw me dressed in the small Levis they made remarks, too, some kind and some unkind: "You'd better get her a dress, Señor. She thinks she is a boy. Don't you see, she is going to grow up like a boy!" As for me, I walked like my father, I sat as he did, and struck the very same poses. Strangers stared, and if they thought my parents weren't looking, they sometimes scowled at me. I didn't care.

Father and I left the corral before sunup, taking the trail south toward the ridge. We were going up El Cerro again, but I was on my own horse, Diamante, this time. We followed the trail toward the ridge. The desert creatures were early risers, too. A family of quail strutted along beside the trail, emitting their amusing call. We heard it as, *"los papagos! los papagos!"* At one time a killdeer walked in front of our horses, flapping its wings against the ground and pretending to be hurt.

"It's leading us away from its nest, isn't it, Pa?" I said.

"That's just what it's doing, Eva." Father rode back in a circle and I followed him. He stopped suddenly: "See the nest?"

"No, Pa."

"Right there in the grass. Don't you see the speckled eggs?"

"Oh, yes, Pa. They look like pebbles."

And the killdeer flew anxiously around over our heads until we turned away.

At the top of the ridge we stopped to breathe our horses and to take a look at the surrounding countryside. The creek was well hidden by a stand of green cottonwoods. Pesqueira Hill was dressed in pink *huajillo* (dwarf fairyduster); from a distance it seemed a solid pink coverlet. The sloping hills we had traveled wore tender green, splashed with lavender verbena and spears of red ocotillo.

Ahead, the scene was different. The dry arroyo that we had crossed on our way to the peak two years before was now a crystalline stream. Along its white clay banks grew Arizona coral with its large green leaves and showy red flowers. The dry green pods we had seen on the earlier trip were now open and lined with a satiny white fiber which cushioned clinging red beans, the ground underneath littered with beans that had already fallen.

Father pointed upward. "What do you think of the *cerro* now, Eva?"

"It is beautiful, Pa," I said, tipping back my head to look. The slopes of our mountain were now covered with Arizona jasmine from the banks of the arroyo clear up to the peak. The air was so heavy with perfume it made me sneeze. The yellow jasmine blossoms smelled as sweet as *azucenas,* the Madonna lilies which my grandmother called *florecitas de Jesús.*

We finally arrived at the water hole. "Pa, when I was here before this place was bare. Now there are flowers everywhere, and the birds are crazy with singing."

"This is the rainy season, Eva. The rain makes everything come alive."

Alive, indeed! The clump of fairyduster around the water hole had grown enormously. The water hole itself was now a running stream and wildlife was all around us. A herd of *javelinas* went across the wash. Squirrels chirped from every rock, and antelope, deer, burros, coyotes, and foxes trotted by.

Many of our cattle were at the watering place, and as our horses arrived, the cattle rose and ran down the wash. Father threw down his branding irons, saying, "Make a fire, Eva, and get those irons hot. I am going to bring Dormidita's calf in to brand and doctor him."

Dormidita was one of our good milk cows, and Father had been looking for her since the beginning of spring. I soon heard the calf bawling and knew that Father had roped him. I built the fire, setting the branding irons around it, then I stood on a rock and reached into the saddle bag for a bottle of black-walnut liquid. Whenever we ran out of creosote, we substituted the black extract of walnut shells. It was slower than the creosote in killing worms, but it finally brought them out where they would slowly die.

Father flanked the calf and tied it, and from there on, he and I worked as a team. He sharpened his knife while I cleaned the maggots out of the calf's wound. Gobs of them came out, and when the wound finally appeared to be clean, I poked it full of horse manure to suffocate whatever worms may have been left.

"A good job, Eva. I couldn't have done it better myself."

I got a rag out of the saddlebag so I could hold the hot irons, then I picked up the running iron and branded the calf on one side. Father turned him over, and I quickly branded him on the other side. Then Father castrated and earmarked him, handing me the *señal*, the tip of the ear he had cut off. We used to thread them on a baling wire, and at the end of the season we counted them to see how many calves we had branded.

By now castrating the baby goats was fairly easy for me, but cutting through the tough hide of a calf was quite another thing. Father didn't think there was much difference; nevertheless he continued castrating the calves himself this time, always reminding me, "Next year you will have to do it yourself."

I had made quick work of burning the Wilbur brand—my own initial "E" over a "W"—on Dormidita's calf that day at the water hole. But it had taken me six long months to learn to make a proper E. I practiced that letter on the ground, on paper, and on all the corral posts, yet when I was made to brand my first calf I got it backwards, and Father was totally exasperated with me, declaring that only an idiot would make a mistake like that.

Mother had been just as angry, but with him: "Only an imbecile would expect a child of five to brand cattle like a seasoned cowhand!"

When my father first got the idea that I would soon be old enough to handle the branding irons he began to show me how to draw the "E" for the EW. It looked easy enough, but first, he said, I must know right from left.

"But, Pa," I argued, "I already know how to make an E." Ruby and I had been learning our alphabet and numbers at the kitchen table.

"You will have to learn more about it to do the branding," said

Father. "Put your hands on the table. Now this is your right," (he tapped my right hand), "and this is your left. Your right hand is the one you will draw the E with. Understand?"

"Yes, Pa."

"Now the letter E has three little points," said Father. He drew an E, making tiny arrows at the end of each bar. "If these arrows point toward your right hand, the letter is an E, but if the arrows point to your left hand the figure is like a number three. Do you understand?"

"No, Papa."

"No, Papa? What do you mean? Don't you hear what I'm saying? Don't be a *zonza* (so stupid)!"

In the mornings, as soon as Father left for the day, Mother would start again, trying to teach me my right from my left and the difference between an E and a three. After supper, my father would again take up the devastating lesson, which I always finished in tears.

One night when I had drawn an E upon being asked to draw a three, Father was furious. He said he had never known a child who had taken three months to learn one letter. "Get up and go to bed," he ordered.

"I will!" I cried. "And I hope I don't ever wake up!"

The following evening Father told me that he was going to make the lesson easy and fun for me. He drew a calf facing to the left and showed the E facing to the rear of the calf. He drew another calf facing right. Branded on this side, the E should be facing toward the calf's front shoulder.

This was even more confusing. I began to cry, whereupon my mother demanded to know what in hell the rear of the calf had to do with my drawing an E.

"You interfere," said Father. "That's why she can't get anything straight. Besides, she is stupid, like you."

"We'll find out right now who the stupid one is," said Mother. "It is the right and the left that determines whether the letter is to be an E or a number three, not which way the head of the calf is pointing!"

"It matters," said Father, "if the head of the calf points to that gate."

"All right. If the head of the calf points to that gate, or west, you, the brander, will be standing at the side of the calf, with your back to the creek, to the south. You will make an E that points to the rear end of the calf. When you get through you'll pick the calf up by the feet and flip it over. Now, the head of the calf will *still* be pointing toward the gate. But *you* will have to go around to the north side of the calf and make an E that points toward the head.

"The head of the calf will still be pointing to the gate," she continued. "So what determines which way the bars of the E are facing? Your right hand or the head of the calf? Answer me, Agustín! Don't stand there looking like an idiot."

Mother took a pencil and drew a calf on the paper. She handed me the pencil and said, "Brand it. And forget the rear end of the calf and the head of the calf. Think only of your right hand and see that the bars of the E point to that hand."

That did it. Suddenly it was completely clear to me and I couldn't understand why I had been such a *zonza*.

My grandparents and my uncles laughed as my Mother went on drawing calves for me to brand. I branded each swiftly and correctly, with my pencil. She ended by drawing a calf on its back with its feet up. I branded that one, too, and my grandparents applauded.

"There!" said Mother, looking Father straight in the eye. "You couldn't have done better yourself. You confuse the child just to have an excuse to chew her up!"

"You're turning her against me," roared Father.

I don't remember having another lesson as difficult for me as that E was until years later when I was thirteen. That year Father walked into my room one day and handed me a sheet of paper and a pencil. He ordered me to draw a map of Pima County and show exactly where I sat in relation to the range, section, quarter-section, and so forth. When I walked out of the room my head swam with unidentified squares. I didn't see, I didn't hear, I didn't feel. Father dropped that lesson for the time being, but not without telling me that I had rocks in my head.

At the water hole, Father and I ate our lunch in perfect harmony, then he repaired a fence and checked the other cattle.

We left the water hole to follow the Cieneguita Wash westward, passing a large rock corral and two small rock houses.

We continued westward for some time, then circled back toward the creek. We stopped on a ridge to rest, and to pass time we counted the burros going up from the creek. There were 1,002! We saw a herd of antelope munching their way up the hill. We finally rode on toward the sloping hills covered with pink *huajillo* through grass that came above our stirrups.

Back at the ranch Father began to fret and worry about making a trip to his other ranch along the border. Since Uncle Nieves's report about the fences being down and the flood damage, he had been anxious to check for himself and to see Cipriano Gallego.

"Am I going with you to the Cochis Ranch, Pa?" I asked.

"Sure, Eva. You're the best helper I have."

I was thrilled. His praise always wiped out the anger and insults that came when I was a *zonza*. This would be the first time ever for me to see the other ranch and to take such a long trip from home.

The Cochis Ranch

IT WAS ALMOST A MONTH BEFORE FATHER was able to get away to make our trip to the Cochis Ranch. "We'll be gone for three days, Eva. That will give you a full day to rest up before we come back."

Mother began to get my things ready and to tell me how to behave and how not to behave when I visited the Gallego home. We left early on a Saturday morning. Father wanted to get to the Cochis by early afternoon because the rains usually came around two o'clock.

We were now in blue country. In the thirty days since we had gone to the water hole, the land had changed again. The red *huajillo* was dead and had turned brown. From the path the hills beyond us appeared bluish-pink. Morning-glory vines were everywhere, and even the tops of the oak trees were splashed with their blue, the vines festooned from tree to tree. They entwined themselves along the barbed-wire fences, blue flowers clinging to the strands of wire; they strung themselves on the trees that followed the slopes of the hills like strings of beads. Blue flowers climbed to the end of every ocotillo branch. And most of the birds that flew around us, it seemed to me, were also blue—bluejays against a blue sky.

All at once, ahead of us on the trail, we saw a herd of deer led by a five-point buck. The buck had a garland of morning glories wrapped around his antlers, trailing down his back. He must have acquired them while browsing in the brush.

We stopped, enchanted by this spectacle. The buck stopped, too, and looked at us for one brief instant. Then, followed by the rest of the herd, he took off at a gallop into the trees.

We finally left the path and began to climb over some very rugged

terrain. We rode for a long time, and when we reached the crest of
the hill the sun was very high in the sky and beat down on us with
scorching rays.

Father pointed to a spiral of smoke that rose above the trees in
front of us.

"Oh, Pa, the smoke is blue, too! Is that where Chanito's house is?"

"That's it. We have only a little way to go now."

"I'm glad, Pa." I had enjoyed the blue scenery so much I hadn't felt
the hot sun. Now I realized that I was both very hot and very thirsty.

Father got down and adjusted our saddles. "You are lucky to be
taking this trip when the desert is so beautiful."

I reached out and patted my horse's neck. "Do you think Diamante
likes coming here, Pa?"

"He loves it," said Father. "This is his birthplace and his *querencia*—
his favorite place."

"No wonder he has been walking faster, Pa."

"Yes, he is telling you in horse language that he is happy to be home."

Father stood on a boulder and pointed to a black mountain in the
distance. "That is Cerro Prieto, Eva. And over there, where you see
that crown of rocks," he indicated a peak to the southwest, "that is
El Cantizal. And this one right here is the Alesna."

"I knew that it was the Alesna, Pa, because it is pointed like an awl."

"On the other side of the Alesna is the Alesnal Indian village."

"Pa, I can hear the cattle bawling."

"Yes. The boys must be milking and separating the calves from their
mothers. Let's go." He led the way down to the arroyo. We followed it
around a curve, coming out just below the corral of the Cochis Ranch.

The corral was filled with cattle, some that I recognized. "Pa, there
is Tomasina with a baby calf. And there is Black Chapa, too! I thought
you had sold those cows."

"No, Eva, they have been here all the time."

Cipriano came running up. "¡*Bienvenido*, Agustín!" he shouted,
shaking hands with Father and lifting me down from my horse. "I am
so glad to see you both! Roberto," he called to one of his sons, who
had come to the gate, "take care of their horses."

He led us to the house where his wife, Carmen, served us a second
breakfast. Carmen was very fat and very kind. She wore her black hair
in a pompadour with a chignon on top of her head. She set me on a
high box and wiped my face and hands with a wet washcloth. "She
is too hot, Agustín. *Pobrecita!*"

We sat at the table across from a crude sign printed on a piece of cardboard: "KEEP THE LOVE, PEACE, AND HARMONY. THESE ARE THE GOLD NUGGETS: THE REST IS SAND."

Father smiled. "Where did you get the big philosophy, Cipriano?" he asked.

"It comes from your own father-in-law, Agustín. Do you remember when old Bizco, the cross-eyed one, came to Francisco begging for vegetables? What made me mad was that only two months before I had heard Bizco belittling Francisco in front of a lot of people in the store at Arivaca. He called the old man a low-down acorn picker. I reminded Señor Vilducea of that, but he gave the man the vegetables that day anyway.

"'Cipriano,' he said to me, 'always keep the love, the peace, and the harmony. These are the gold nuggets; the rest is sand, *hijo*. Sand to be blown away.' Those words rang in my mind all the way home and that sign has helped me, Agustín. Sometimes I run in here so mad I want to kill my Carmen. Then I see those words and stop in my tracks. And soon we are drinking coffee together and laughing."

Cipriano went on talking to Father, telling him about the cattle and the state of the fences. But mostly he talked about the *belloteros* who had invaded the land to pick acorns, and then, at the first hard rain, had scuttled away.

"They took more than acorns," he said in disgust. "While they were around here our milk cows came to the corral already milked. There were no eggs in the nests, and they were killing a calf every time they needed one.

"And now we have the Mexican revolutionaries. They cross the line, kill the calves, and steal the saddle horses. It would have been a terrible summer if it hadn't been for the Vilducea boys and that Papago, Carmelo Tosco. They were all a big help to me during the floods."

Carmen asked me if I had become tired during the long ride.

"No, Señora," I answered politely, remembering my manners for once. "The country is so pretty. We saw a big buck dressed in *trompios.*"

"The weirdest damned thing you ever saw," said Father. "His head was wrapped in the vines and he was dragging a trail of flowers twenty feet long. Eva thought it was something out of fairyland, didn't you, Eva?"

"Yes, Pa. I did."

"There was a mass of them in our yard, too," remarked Carmen. "A great wall of blue flowers! I said an 'Ave María' every morning in thanks. And the other day the devil got into Cipriano and he tore it down."

"Agustín," said Cipriano, "the vine was so big and thick the calves would stand behind it, bawling and dying for water because they couldn't cross through it. Carmen wouldn't talk to me for two days after I cut that vine down, so I promised I'd buy her two ollas for *tesguin.* I was getting ready to go to the Indian village today for them. Would you like to come along?"

"Sure, Cipriano. I'll look over the range as we go."

"I want to go, too, Pa. Can I?"

Father agreed that I could go, but before we went back to the corral he called me aside and told me where the outhouse was. The tiny building was made of red corrugated iron, and when I closed the door I felt as though I had walked into an oven. I sat down quickly and jumped up just as fast. The boards burned my buttocks.

I ran outside and went behind the privy and squatted down. At home Grandfather had made a privy inside the tool shed, so that it was both private and cool.

I went back to Father and told him, "The seat burned me, Pa. So I went outside and made a Mississippi near a big *trompio.* "

Our horses were resting, and Cipriano saddled two of the ranch horses for us. Father rode the big *grullo* with the roman nose—ugly, but a good cow pony—and I rode Cilantro, a blaze-faced bay that spooked at everything.

"Be careful," said Father. "That horse is not like Diamante."

"He really is very gentle," said Cipriano. "Chanito rides him most of the time."

We watched Chanito cut some calves and drive them to pasture on the slopes of the mountain. "He is a good vaquero," remarked Father. To be a good vaquero one must be quick in thought as well as action, for his life and the lives of other riders depend on his intelligence and speed. Eight-year-old Chanito managed himself and the stock like an old hand.

The Indians at the Alesnal village had the whole hillside strewn with ollas. Paloma, a pretty Indian girl who was the belle of these villages, came out of a bear-grass hut. She was dressed in the traditional flour-sack dress. She took my hand and led me to the display of ollas where she invited me to choose one. I picked up a small red olla marked with black dollar-sized circles.

Paloma talked to me shyly. "Carmelo Tosco was here," she said. "He pick acorns. He friend of your papa. He good man—funny." She began to laugh as if he were there now being funny, her whole body shaking. And I couldn't keep from laughing, too. We walked about together, not saying much, but in perfect accord, while Father and Cipriano sat under the ramada in the center of the circle of *jacales* (huts). They drank *pulque* and talked with the Indians who groaned, shook their heads, and pointed to make themselves understood.

When we rode back down the arroyo to the Gallego house we had a cargo of ollas, a bottle of pulque, and a jar of prickly-pear jam.

Carmen's house smelled fresh and inviting. The dirt floor had been swept, sprinkled, and well-tamped. The large table in the middle of the room was covered with a flour-sack cloth and was neatly set. Big earthen bowls were steaming with *cazuela* (jerky stew), *calabacitas* (zucchini), and nopalitos, cooked with eggs and red chili.

Cipriano put the ollas on the floor and said, "I'll go call the children, Carmen."

"*Sí*, Cipriano, *sí*. But go quickly. The food is getting cold."

The younger members of the family were soon at the table: Roberto, the oldest; Damián, who was fifteen; Chanito, Carmelita; and the youngest, the one on the way. This was the one that baffled me. Whenever the children spoke of Lupita I looked for her everywhere. She was silent! She was invisible! Yet everyone spoke of Lupita. Even the Indian women at the village had sent Carmen some washed flour sacks for Lupita.

That afternoon when Chanito, Carmelita, and I went to play in the water trough I asked Chanito where Lupita was. Chanito just looked at me. "Don't you know? She is not here yet. She's on the way, you know."

"No, I don't know, Chanito! Tell me. On the way from where?"

"Well, my brother Damián told me where she is. She is inside my mother's belly. That's where."

I pondered that strange information. "My brother William was brought to my mother by Dr. Ball. He brought him in his satchel one day when it was very cold."

"You're a *tonta* (fool). Let's go in the house and I'll show you."

The three of us ran up the slope. Carmen was washing dishes as Chanito went up to her and said, "Ma, let this *tontona* feel Lupita."

Carmen placed my hand on her mountainous belly. Something moved and I jumped back.

"It's the baby," she said.

"How did she get in there? How does she breathe? How does she eat?"

"Well," said Carmen, "she does eat and she stays warm in there." This was horrifying, and I must have shown my dismay because Chanito and Carmelita laughed.

"Someday when you are grown you will have a baby, too," said Carmen.

"If I do I'll have it brought in a satchel by Dr. Ball or by Doña Tomaza if she wants to bring me one," I told them. I have often wondered since how strange that as a child who had witnessed the birth of a hundred baby goats, I had missed the obvious connection with the birth of human babies.

The rest of that afternoon was spent clipping the manes and the tails of horses that Roberto and Damián had brought in from the range that morning. The horses belonged to other ranches; some were from Mexico. The Mexican boundary was not fenced at that time and stock went back and forth at will. One could be prosecuted for clipping somebody else's horses, but Cipriano wanted horsehair to make *bosalillos* (head-bridles), hat bands, quirt handles, and tying ropes.

He sent Damián to the top of Cerro Prieto as a lookout. If a rider appeared, Damián was to signal. One flag, a yucca stalk with a white rag tied to it, meant that a rider was approaching from the south. Two flags hoisted indicated danger from the north.

Cipriano brought to the corral three burlap sacks in which he would put the *cerda* (horsehair). We separated the hair by color: white, black, and sorrel. Some of the animals were wild and had to be roped and thrown. Roberto and Father did the roping and tying, Cipriano did the clipping, and Chanito and I picked up the hair and put it into the sacks.

They clipped the *sonoreño*, a big white stallion from Mexico with an enormous tail and a long, massive mane. His *cerda* filled a whole sack and I was told to take it to the house and to bring back another sack.

Carmen met me at the door. "What in the world are they doing?" she asked with a frown.

"*Tusando*," I answered. Clipping.

"That's bad," said Carmen fearfully. "They can end up in Yuma." Although the penitentiary had already been moved to Florence, the horrible word "Yuma" remained a symbol of the dreaded *calabozo* of an earlier time.

"Your Father," said Carmen angrily, "should forbid Cipriano to do this. Instead he is helping him. ¡*Madre de Dios! ¿Donde vamos a acabar?* Where will we end up?"

I walked back to the corral with an empty sack. The weather was hot and sultry, and clouds were gathering in the sky. The horses were running in a circle and Roberto was roping a chestnut sorrel with a white star on his forehead. Immediately I recognized the horse as Lucero, Ramón Ahumada's favorite saddle horse.

Father approached the animal with open shears. I ran to him. "Don't shear him, Papa! Carmen says it is bad."

Just then we both looked up to the mountain and saw two white flags held high. "Turn him loose, Cipriano!" shouted Father. "Someone is coming."

Cipriano turned the horse loose and Roberto opened the gate and stampeded the *caballada* down the arroyo. His father opened the gate of the large pen and let the cattle back into the corral.

Chanito and I quickly gathered the remaining *cerda* and packed it into the burlap bags. Cipriano and Father picked them up and carried them to the house, Carmen and I following them quickly with the shears and ropes.

The wind began to blow very hard and big drops of rain pelted us just before we reached the door. Damián arrived at a gallop, pulling off his saddle and dragging it into the kitchen. "They're coming here," said Damián. "I think one of them is a ranger."

The two riders reached the house, soaked from the downpour. "Come in. Come in." Cipriano greeted them cordially. The visitors were Ramón Ahumada himself and Paton, the ranger.

Ramón greeted Father and me affectionately.

"What are you doing out in the storm, Ramón?" asked Father.

"I'm showing this poor man the country, Agustín," said Ramón in Spanish. His companion looked left out, not knowing the language. "He's a most incompetent man for the job, but he has a wife and two children. We must be compassionate, Agustín."

"The government could give him a job doing something else," countered Father curtly. "To hire an incompetent man as a ranger is a disgrace."

The men all sat down. I stood, waiting to get a word in, but Father took one look at my face and said, "Eva, go play with Carmelita."

When I didn't move at once, Damián took my hand and led me to the ramada where Carmelita was watching Chanito spin a top.

Damián told me, "Don't you tell Don Ramón that we were *tusando*. People don't like to have their horses clipped and they could have my father arrested."

"But I wasn't going to tell him that, Damián. I was just going to tell him we saw his horse, Lucero, in the corral."

"*Tontona!*" said Chanito, "You think he won't know if you tell him that? My horse Cilantro is not only going to throw you off, he is going to kick you. He doesn't want such a *zonza* on his back!"

The storm passed. Ramón and the ranger drove off toward Arivaca and we all went down to the arroyo to watch the flash flood roar past. For me it was more spectacular than the flood I had watched at the Wilbur Ranch. The wild water tore over big boulders; it fell and splashed onto other boulders; it turned around rocky curves with a crest of white foam. The stream narrowed some twenty feet below us, and fell, finally, onto a flat slate rock where it splashed high above the trees and sent a mist higher yet. The rays of the late sun touched the mist, forming a rainbow across the canyon.

Damián and Roberto teased us by pushing huge rocks into the ravine so that the water splashed us and we younger children ran, laughing, away from the bank. A flock of birds flew across the abyss and lit on a hackberry tree where they burst into song.

No wonder Carmelo Tosco had let out his joyous and barbaric yell when he described for us the Wilbur country.

That evening the men sat in the ramada, disentangling the horsehair so it would be ready in the morning to twist into strands for matching *cinchos*.

The last night at Cochis Ranch I heard Cipriano telling Father about a friend of his who had clipped the *cerda* from all the horses belonging to some Indians and how, three days later, all this man's bulls had come in to water castrated. Father laughed, but I thought now how lucky he was that Ramón Ahumada had not arrived to find him clipping Lucero, and that they had kept me from saying something foolish to him.

Roberto and Damián carried the long kitchen table into the patio and we ate our supper there. We slept outside, too, on a variety of cots and beds brought from the house. By the time we went to bed the clouds had vanished, and we pulled off our boots and went to bed lying on top of the covers, the sky brilliant with stars above us.

I slept with Carmelita in an old brass-trimmed bed. Cipriano told my father that this bed had been brought from San Miguel Allende by Moraga, the last of the Spanish conquistadors, related to my Grandmother Wilbur through the Suastigi line. Someone had put the headboard out to use as part of a fence on the ranch, and Cipriano once had found the footboard half-buried in the goat corral. Cleaned up and put back together, the bed was a valuable heirloom.

"It rightfully belongs to you, Agustín," Cipriano said. "When a wagon goes in your direction, I will send it to you." Father was much pleased.

The talking finally stopped. I was just drifting off to sleep when the silence was broken by the lonely wail of a wolf from somewhere in the Cantizal. Silence again, but not for long. The wild call was returned by a prolonged howl that erupted from our very midst.

I jumped out of bed. Cipriano was running to get his rifle, and Roberto and Damián, who had been sleeping near the corral, were running toward us with a shotgun. Just then a black form streaked across the bed-strewn patio and disappeared. Chanito came running to tell us that he had just come out of the privy and had barely escaped meeting the wolf face-to-face.

The following morning Cipriano and Father took the sacks of *cerda* to the shade of an elderberry tree and began preparations for making horsehair rope. While Father separated the strands Cipriano filled a large bucket with stones and selected the appropriate *taravillas* or twirlers for the job. The *taravillas* were devices for twisting and pulling the strands while continually adding new material. Cipriano decided to use short black hairs to make two cinches and poor Chanito was chosen to do the hard work.

Damián first tied some strands of hair to the *taravilla* and Chanito began to twirl it as he pulled back. "Keep it taut," said his brother as he added more strands of hair. "Now move back. Don't let it twist up on you. Keep moving!"

I sat on the corral fence, watching. As Chanito moved back the twisted strands of horsehair grew longer and longer. Carmen went past me loaded with milk buckets and followed by little Carmelita, who was weaving her way between the calves' legs and the cows' horns like some small animal, ever alert to keep from being trampled to death. I was dreamily half-conscious of the calves' bawling, the laughter, the cuss words, the cloud of dust, when I was suddenly snapped to attention by Father's voice.

"Eva, get over here!"

I was now given a *taravilla* and instructed in the art of twirling. "Keep pulling back so as to keep the strands of hair taut. See how Chanito does it. Move back, Eva."

Obediently, I looked over my shoulder at Chanito. Just then a rock zoomed past me and hit Chanito in the leg. His face twisted in pain, but he kept twirling furiously, limping backward. Tears ran down his brown cheeks.

"What's that all about, hombre?" Father asked, surprised.

"I don't beg them to keep moving, Agustín," answered Cipriano. "I stone them back. It works every time."

Learning to twirl the *taravilla* was not too difficult, but the sun was beating down on me, my hair was in my eyes, and flies buzzed around my face. I began to slow down. "Move back!" I jumped and came to a stop, confused.

"Keep that *taravilla* going," Father shouted.

To my great relief Roberto appeared and took the thing from my hands. Damián came up to take Chanito's place, while my father fed them the *cerda*. By noon Cipriano had two fine horsehair cinches and had attached the buckles to them.

By two o'clock black clouds were piling up once more over the Cantizal. A gust of wind tore through the corral and big drops began to fall. With a crack of thunder the deluge was on. Chanito, Carmelita, and I were playing in the water trough, and we ran to the house where Carmelita's mother took her and me into the bedroom and dressed us in dry clothing.

When the rain stopped Father and Cipriano decided to brand a few calves that had been penned up for that purpose. The boys went to the tack house, brought out armloads of wood to the corral, and built a fire. Chanito mounted his horse, Cilantro, sticking his bare feet into the stirrup leather and beginning to uncoil his reata.

He easily roped a big calf and dragged him toward the branding area where Damián flanked and tied the calf for him. Chanito jumped down, took up the iron, and quickly branded the calf with the Wilbur mark.

"Don't let him get up with a reversed E," warned his father.

The calf struggled to his feet, perfectly branded, and ran off. The boys threw down another animal. "This one is for you, Eva," said Father.

I ran, picked up the running iron and I branded the calf on the side. They turned him over, and as I started to make the second mark I felt the eyes of the Gallego boys on me. When I had finished and looked up, they were all smiling and staring at me with admiration.

"She's a good vaquerita, Pa, isn't she?" asked Chanito.

"She's good, Chanito, but she is too little for such work," answered his father, patting my head.

When I went to brand the last calf Damián came and took the branding iron from me. "I'll brand him," he offered, adding, "You might burn your *manitas*—your little hands." Such talk was what my grandmother called a *caricia*, a caress, as when my grandfather would take Ruby's hands and say, "Your *manitas* are cold." There at Cochis Ranch that day I tucked this *caricia*—my first from a much-admired older boy—in the back of my mind to build up *recuerdos* (memories), I suppose.

When all the branding has been done and the calves turned out, Roberto went up to Cerro Prieto and brought Diamante, Vaquerito, and Pimienta down, penning them up for the night in the corral along with Chanito's horse. Father and I would leave for home before dawn the next morning, and Chanito was to go with us, leading a horse for his sister Juana. Carmen wanted her daughter to come home and be with her when the baby was born.

That evening, our last at Cochis Ranch, I have always remembered as one of the happiest of my life. Before dinner Carmen took me into the bedroom where she removed my muddy shoes and Levis. She sponged me off, combed my hair and made two braids, tying the ends with pink ribbons, in place of the chamois strings I usually wore. Then, to my great delight, she slipped over my head the first underslip I was ever to own and a blue-flowered voile dress that she had just finished sewing.

"The blue flowers match your eyes," said Carmen as I stared happily in the mirror. My eyes, inherited from my Grandfather Vilducea as well as my father, remained blue until I was nine years old when they suddenly began to turn brown, causing me no end of distress.

Carmen let me remain barefooted and led me to the table. My father was delighted and when the boys came to the table they were all smiles and fought over who would sit next to me. Damián won out.

"Thank you, Carmen, for being so kind to my poor little daughter," said Father.

"She is not poor," declared Damián. "She is a princess." To my surprise he proceeded to fill my plate with food and then began to cut up my meat.

"Take that knife and cut the meat yourself, Eva," said Father sharply. I knew that Father was annoyed by the attention I was receiving, but I didn't understand why. Carmen was amused by his reaction.

"Agustín," she said, "if you are jealous now, when Evita is only a baby, how will you act when she is fifteen?" Cipriano here was really put out when he learned that Juana had been serenaded by the young men on San Juan's Day. Jealousy never brings happiness to anybody!"

"Oh, Carmen!" protested Father. "I am not jealous. I just want Eva to learn proper behavior." I looked at Damián, who bent his head over his plate and ate very fast.

His father said, "When you are through eating, Damián, go to the saddle rack and shorten the stirrups for Eva. I let them down when I used her saddle this afternoon, and I forgot to put them back up."

"I'll go now," said Damián, putting down his fork. He seemed glad of an excuse to leave the table.

"Go with him, Eva," said Father, "and get on the saddle so that he will know how much to shorten the stirrups. And come right back."

"Yes, Pa." I left my dinner and hurried to the *sillero* that was opposite the kitchen door, feeling Father's eyes on me all the time.

Damián lifted me into the saddle. "Your father is a jealous man," he said, "but I don't care. When you are fifteen years old, Evita, I am going to marry you."

"Will we live here when we get married?" I asked.

"No. My father is a mean man. We will go to live with my grandfather in Mexico. He has a beautiful ranchito far away across from the Baja." Damián went on to tell me all about his ranchito and he said it would be mine some day. It was called the Gallego Ranch and was near the Pinacate Mountain and beautiful Quitobaquito, near the sea.

I had never seen the ocean, but I had seen pictures of it in one of Father's books, and the idea of living near the water was very appealing. I knew that Damián loved his grandfather very much for I had heard Cipriano tell my father that Damián had been raised by that grandfather. When Cipriano finally went to bring him to the Cochis, Damián hid out for three days to avoid leaving his grandfather.

"Let me tell you something, Damián," I said. "I seem to grow up very slow."

He smiled at me. "That's all right. I make money very slow. I am going to get a job with the Noneños when the fall corrida starts. I'll make money for us while you are growing up. But don't tell anybody that we are going to get married."

"I won't, Damián."

"Promise."

"I promise."

He bent his head then and began busily adjusting the stirrup leather. I looked down and saw a red harmonica in his pocket. "Damián, you have a *musica* in your pocket."

"I know. It is for you. I am going to give it to my mother to give to you so that you won't have to tell your father that it is from me."

"Why, Damián?"

"Because he'll take it away from you. *¿Cierto?*"

"*Cierto,* Damián."

"Put that girl down and let her come and finish her supper," yelled Cipriano from the kitchen door. Father was standing beside him.

"In a minute," said Damián, moving around to adjust the other stirrup. He lifted me down, and we went into the house together. It wasn't long until Carmen hustled Carmelita and me off to bed.

I was still half asleep the next morning when by the light of a kerosene lantern we had a hurried breakfast while Father and Cipriano talked about the corrida.

"Talk to Ramón, Agustín. Give a good word for Damián. He is a good vaquero."

"Don't worry, Cipriano. I'll get him the job," said Father.

We hurried to the corral. Chanito, Damián, and Roberto were waiting with the horses, saddled and ready for our journey home. Damián lifted me onto Diamante's back and tied the small bundles that Carmen was sending to Mother below the saddlehorn. "*No me olvides, Chiquita,*" he said.

"I won't forget you, Damián." Carmen had already given me the red harmonica, and it was safe in the pocket of my Levis.

We started off in the dark, Chanito leading the way and leading the extra horse for Juana. Chanito was familiar with every step of the trail.

I felt a little sadness. I had so much enjoyed my first visit to Cochis Ranch that I was reluctant to leave. But a few hours later when the

sun was well up in the sky and I was looking down into the valley to
see smoke rising above our house, I knew that Mother was there working in the kitchen and I found myself eager to get home.

Later that day when Father went to Arivaca to get the mail, I told
Mother and my grandparents that Carmen was going to have a baby
and that I had felt it jump inside her stomach. Grandfather was horrified
that she had been so frank about it. Poor Carmen. She was criticized,
censured, and ridiculed.

"That woman has a lot of nerve telling the child that!" said Grandfather.

"But Chanito told me, not Carmen," I said, puzzled at their reaction.
"He said Damián told him about the new baby."

"There you are!" declared Grandfather. "Damián is only fifteen. How
does he know such things?"

Ruby came in just then wearing the blue-flowered dress that Carmen
had sent for her, just like mine, but a little smaller. She stood in front
of Grandfather, but he paid no attention to her for he was still looking
at me in despair, I suppose at my new grown-up appearance and
knowledge.

"That is the one who is going to drive us out of our minds, Ramona,"
he said to Mother.

Mister McTavish

RUBY AND I WERE TOO DIFFERENT IN NATURE to play well together, and I much preferred to be by myself most of the time. When I was old enough to get on and off my horse at will I could escape. I often herded the goats to a favorite spot just below the top of El Cerrito, a small mountain next to El Cerro. There I discovered a gnarled old mesquite tree that became my own retreat.

The old tree was shaped somewhat like a tripod. The bark had long since fallen and the branches were clean and grey-white. Where the huge limbs joined there was a comfortable seat from which I could watch the goats and observe the countryside for miles around. I watched the Indians wander back and forth over the many trails. I could see Dr. Ball's house and watch him ride away in his buggy to Arivaca and on to Oro Blanco.

From my place of vantage I could see the great Baboquivari, the dark landmark that dominated the entire region. I often contemplated its mysteries. Father had told me that the famous mountain could be seen from California, Colorado, New Mexico, and Old Mexico. Grandfather Vilducea and Barreplata both remembered when the sacred peak had caught fire.

This happened on July 14, 1898 at sunset, when the *picacho* was dark against a reddened sky. Grandfather remembered that a light appeared at the top of the mountain, and as darkness fell the light became a blazing fire leaping skyward. In the valley consternation spread. People watched anxiously from their patios and from the tops of trees. Some thought a meteor had fallen. Visitors to the area brought by Colonel Charles Poston to inspect some mining property said that the fire was of volcanic origin—the mountain was erupting.

To keep the Indians from panic the priest in Arivaca rang the church bell, but he managed only to increase their agitation. Many of the Indians had got hold of horses, borrowed or stolen, and had galloped wildly from place to place. Others had run along the creek, breaking branches from the trees to use as prayer sticks, and planting them upright in the ground to propitiate their powerful god, I'itoi.

Not until two days later was the mystery solved. News reached Arivaca that the great mountain had been conquered. Dr. Robert H. Forbes, a professor at the University of Arizona, Tucson, succeeded in climbing to the peak, and in celebration he built a big bonfire to show the world that he was the first man ever to reach the top of Baboquivari.

Old Gnarled, as I called my mesquite tree, was for me a place of fantasy and dreaming. It was where I practiced my reading and writing. Ruby and I did our lessons at the kitchen table or at a long table under the trees in the yard.

It was there in the branches of Old Gnarled that I made my first real attempts to make friends with wildlife. It wasn't easy, for I wasn't readily accepted by the animals. The birds certainly didn't think I had any business being in their haunts. When I talked to them, they scolded me.

The cactus wren, perched on a cholla twenty feet away, showed in many ways that my presence was disturbing to her. A small sparrow hawk flew in a circle above my tree, then lit on a nearby hackberry, screaming a loud *"Peeeeeee, peeeeeee!"* determined to scare me away from its domain.

The roadrunner was the first to accept me. I would throw scraps of food down to her and warn Hunga, who usually lay at the base of the mesquite, to remain still. The big bird would grab the food, fly to the top of some high rocks, eat, and return for more. I named the roadrunner Chihuihui, or Cheeweewee, if you will, and in time we became real friends. She built a nest of fagots nearby where I sat, and she filled it with eggs. When the baby birds had hatched she brought them to feed on the scraps I threw down.

One day she did a strange and touching thing. She flew from the tree to the ground and attacked some tiny creature in the dust, shaking her big round head as she killed her prey. She flitted back into the tree and jumped across my legs, depositing a mutilated praying mantis in my lap. I threw it to the ground, and again she went after it, bringing it back to me. When I finally understood and pretended to eat the unsavory fare she rewarded me with her fluttering cuckoo call. I longed to hold her and stroke her, but she was not to be restrained. Like Shelley's famous lark she was a blithe spirit: she ran, she floated, she disappeared and reappeared, and finally she became even so bold as to perch on Diamante's saddle, much to his disgust.

In time, some of the other birds responded favorably to my presence. The little finches eyed me curiously and ceased to scold. When I whistled softly, they answered with song. The cactus wren sang to me too from the spiny branches of the cholla. When I threw food scraps for Chihuihui, the wren raced the roadrunner to snatch them.

One day while I waited for our two sheep dogs to bring the goat herd down the hillside, I saw a mother skunk followed by five babies making her way down the ridge and hurrying to get out of the herd's way. She managed to push three of her babies under the edge of a rock. Then she ran back to rescue two runts who had dawdled behind. The dogs were barking from above and the mother skunk had a decision to make. I saw her nuzzle the babies to the ground side by side. With her dainty hands she smoothed their long bushy tails over their seemingly dead bodies, then backed herself under the rock. All I could see were her two beady black eyes.

Fearfully, I watched part of the herd walk right over the pile of black and white skunk fur. When the goats had passed, the mother skunk came to uncover her babies. They seemed no worse for their experience, and the little mother gathered her family and took them on to the rocky knoll atop the Cerrito.

Before I rode home that day I threw some leftover food near her hideaway. The next day I brought an old pan which I placed securely between two boulders. I emptied half the water from my canteen into it and the other half I sprinkled around near the pan. The smell of water on the dry earth brought the mother skunk running. From a safe distance I watched her drink.

From that day on the skunk, too, was my friend. I named her Valentina and ordered Hunga never to bark at her or chase her babies. Hunga wasn't hard to convince, for she had already had one bad experience with a skunk she met at the chicken coop. I would have liked to have taken one of Valentina's babies home for a pet, but I, too, had had a smelly encounter with a mother skunk, so I was satisfied just to watch them in the wild, and pleased when they sometimes followed me about.

When the lower hills were cleared of feed the goat herd moved farther up toward the crest of the Cerrito, and I had to leave my tree and move higher, too, to guard the path and keep the dogs on the job.

Here in the crags I discovered other animals. There were chuckwallas, horned toads, and chattering ground squirrels that learned to come right up to my hand to eat. Around the rocks were piles of fagots where huge rats went in and out of their dens.

Here I had to sit on the ground to watch the goats so I brought a piece of canvas with me and spread it out. On it I placed my tablet, my books, and a stub of pencil I used to practice the spelling lessons Father assigned to me, or to write my fanciful stories using the "big words" I learned from Mr. McTavish.

Mr. McTavish was a very special person who had a profound influence on my whole life. He was the editor of *The Tucson Daily Citizen.* During my early childhood he spent part of every summer camping near the creek at the Wilbur Ranch. He would arrive with his tent and his dutch oven and his beautiful books and magazines and would spend most of his time riding or wandering over the desert hills. I often accompanied him and we learned from each other.

One time, for instance, he found a round rock on the hillside. He struck it with another rock and, to my amazement, it broke open like a book. On either half of the flat surfaces was the imprint of what looked like a little tree.

"Those are dendrites," said Mr. McTavish. "Ages ago they were living plants. The elements turned them into fossils and encased them in stone."

Another time Mr. McTavish rode out with Ruby and me to herd the goats. The goats headed straight for the salt licks along the creek bed, and when we caught up with them they were happily at work. Mr. McTavish got down from his horse and stood looking at the long line of smooth round depressions along the bottom of the clay banks. Ruby and I shooed the goats away and Mr. McTavish examined these holes with his hand.

"Interesting!" he said. "These holes are a good two feet deep and smooth as glass. Work done by geophysts."

"No, Mr. McTavish," I told him. "Those holes were made by the goats with their tongues."

He got to his feet and patted my head. "Goats, or any other animals that lick the ground in search of salt, are known as geophysts, Bonnie," he said. He got out his small box camera and took some pictures of the holes as though they were something very special.

It was always fun for me when Mr. McTavish came to the ranch. He liked me and I liked him. He was an old man, but he was never in a hurry and never impatient with me as Father often was. And best of all he called me Bonnie. That was the name of his own little girl who died many years before of typhoid fever. He said that I looked like her. When he learned that I, too, had once had typhoid fever and had come close to dying we felt drawn together.

One day when I was riding home just before sundown, I saw a white tent set up just across the ravine. Mr. McTavish usually came in May and it was now just mid-April. But there beside the tent stood his pretty green buckboard with the yellow wheels, and I eagerly turned Diamante in that direction.

Both Father and I arrived at the camp at the same time, Father coming from the opposite direction.

Mr. McTavish was delighted. "Hello, Bonnie!" he shouted. "How are you?" Before I could answer he had turned to greet my father. He said that he had seen Father's horse, Vaquerito, tied at the hitching post in front of the store in Arivaca. "I hurried to get here and set up camp so that I could have something cooked before you got home. So get down, both of you. I have rabbit stew and hot biscuits, as you can see."

The dutch oven was covered with coals and a kettle of stew steamed at one side. I sat on a box watching as Mr. McTavish dished up the food. He handed me a blue enameled plate loaded with rabbit, potatoes, biscuits, and jam. I ate hungrily.

Father and the newspaper man sat on the ground talking as they ate. I heard Mr. McTavish tell Father that he had taken an early vacation because he wanted to attend the spring corrida. I saw the pained expression that crossed Father's face. I knew that he considered our visitor something of a greenhorn.

Mr. McTavish was smiling at me. "I really admire the vaqueros, Wilbur," he said. "From what I heard your little Bonnie can ride with the best of them."

Father turned suddenly to me and asked if I had finished eating.

He sounded irritated but I didn't know why. "Go get one of the boys to help you unsaddle that poor horse, will you, Eva?"

I gave my plate to Mr. McTavish and led Diamante to the corral where Uncle Mike helped me tend to him. Soon after I had gone into the kitchen Father appeared. "Eva," he said at once, "I want you to tell that old man that your name is *not* Bonnie."

"I can't tell him that, Pa. I like Mr. McTavish and I like the name Bonnie better than Eva."

"I named you Eva and that's your name. Do you understand?"

"Pa, you told me to tell the truth. The truth is, I like the name Bonnie. Why did you name me Eva, Pa?"

"You silly girl," he said angrily. "You don't see your sister Ruby trying to change her name, do you?"

"I am not Ruby, Pa," I said to him.

I went outside to the corral to get my books and tablet from the saddlebags and when I came back I found Father now talking to Mother about a story I had written. It was about a white horse named El Blanco, who had stomped Mrs. Noneña to death. The horse had fled to the Cantizal, where he married a Mexican who gave him a chestnut colt with a white mane and tail. We called such horses *jilotes*, and we loved them. The *jilotes* and the *grullos* were the true iron horses—descendants of the Tarpans that people said were so ugly they had to be descended from the horses of Attila the Hun. The colt was long-legged and fast, but he was a "night horse"—he would never go to bed at night and gave his parents no end of trouble. I called him a "noctambulist" in the story, a word I was most proud of.

I don't remember how my story ended, but I do remember that when I read it to the family my uncles went into spasms of laughter.

"Do you know where she keeps it, Ramona?" my father asked. "I told McTavish about Eva's story and he wants to read it." Mother asked me to get the story of *El Blanco*.

I went to my bed, reached under the mattress, and removed a sack of shabby papers. I found the story of *El Blanco* and gave it to Father.

I followed him at a distance when he went to take the story to Mr. McTavish and stopped before I reached the tent. It was dark now, but I could see Mr. McTavish silhouetted against the bonfire. Slender and a bit stooped foward, he was reading my story with the aid of his flashlight. I pressed anxiously against a willow tree, but Hunga gave me away. Father called me over to them.

When I walked across the ditch to the fire Mr. McTavish met me with an extended hand. "You're a real writer, Bonnie," he told me. "I enjoyed your story about *El Blanco*. Tomorrow I'll teach you how to make it even better."

His breath smelled strongly of liquor and when we sat down he refilled his own glass and my father's. As a rule Father didn't drink, except a little *tesguin* when we had huge groups of friends visit and this was a rare occasion. Now both men were acting quite tipsy. "As I told you, Agustín," Mr. McTavish said, "I lost my little girl a long time ago. She was talented in writing, too, and your child reminds me so much of her."

He sat staring into the fire for a long time as they both drank. Father must have told Mr. McTavish how he felt about his calling me Bonnie, for suddenly the newspaperman looked at Father and shook his finger at him. "I don't see how any decent man could 'oject' to my calling this little girl Bonnie. You don't really oject, Agustín, do you?" he demanded, his speech becoming more slurred.

Father didn't answer right away. When he finally did his voice, too, was fuzzy. "No, McTavish, I don't oject."

Mr. McTavish got unsteadily to his feet. He went into his tent and brought out a large box with a tulip-shaped horn. He turned a handle around and around and placed a black cylinder on it. I thought he was going to light a lamp. I did not even know there was such a thing as a phonograph. The cylinder gyrated and music filled the air. A voice sang, "My Bonnie lies over the ocean; my Bonnie lies over the sea . . ." I was enthralled by the song and by my new name.

My nickname was one of the nicest things that ever came into my life. It wasn't long until our friends and relatives adopted it, to my delight. Heretofore, people had called me Eva at first, then, sensing perhaps that the name did not suit me, they substituted a variety of other names. I had been called Eve, Evita, Evangeline, Toña, Antonia, Niña, Niñita, and others. Even my mother quickly accepted the new name and called me Bonnie thereafter. But my father continued to call me Eva all his life.

The day after his talk with Father, Mr. McTavish saddled Tim, one of his team horses, and went with Ruby and me to drive the herd up the back trails of El Cerro. Father promised to catch up with us later. When we left the creek Hunga was following me, and Chihuihui, the roadrunner, came out of the bushes and got behind Hunga. Cafecita, one of the milk goats, walked along behind Chihuihui. And even Valentina was bold enough to join the parade.

By now Ruby and I had made this trip many times, but it was a fascinating adventure to our city friend. No sooner had we left the creek than Mr. McTavish yelled, "Wait, Bonnie!" Jumping down from his horse, he picked up a rock and started after the skunk.

I quickly slid down from Diamante's back and ran to pull at his jacket. "Don't, Mr. McTavish!" I yelled. "That's Valentina! She's a tame skunk. She won't hurt you. She's one of my friends."

He look down at me in amazement, then dropped the rock. "A skunk is nobody's friend," he said. "She'll stink us all up."

"No she won't. One time she sprayed on Chihuihui, but that's because she thought the roadrunner was a chicken, see, and she wanted to eat her. But Chihuihui fought her, and whipped her, too."

Ruby and the animals had stopped halfway up the hill while I defended Valentina. "You see," I insisted, "you don't kill skunks just because they smell bad. That's the way they are. All of *us* smell bad sometimes, too."

Mr. McTavish sat down on a rock. He rested his chin on the palms of his hands, his fingers covering his eyes, and put his head down. He was making a funny noise and I thought he was crying. "Are you all right?" I asked.

"Everything is terrific," he said when he finally stopped laughing. He got out his camera and told us to start moving again so that the animals could string out behind us as we traveled up the slope. He snapped a picture of the whole menagerie, including Ruby and me and our horses.

"You girls go ahead," said Mr. McTavish. "I want to write a few notes while I have this scene in my mind. I may stay here and wait for your father."

By noon Ruby and I were in the west basin. The herd was grazing peacefully and we took a nap at the foot of the cliff. Later we saw Father and Mr. McTavish on a high ridge up the trail. They waved to us as they disappeared over the mountain.

That evening Father told me that the newspaper man wanted to visit the Cantizal. Father was looking dubious. He didn't have much use for writers in general, and perhaps less for Mr. McTavish in particular. I had often heard him say that writers were no damned good.

"There is McTavish," he said now, "who can hardly get a bucket of drinking water for himself! And I had to almost carry him down from El Cerro today. Now he wants to go camping alone in the Cantizal!"

"You musn't permit it, Agustín," said Grandfather. "That country is entirely too dangerous."

Father laughed. "Well, he insists upon going to the corrida. He'll get his belly full of adventure there, I'm sure." Father turned to me. "He was very much interested in your pets, Eva—the roadrunner and the skunk. He thinks you have quite a way with animals."

Mr. McTavish did go to the corrida. He slept one night among the vaqueros or at least he tried to. However, early on the second morning he loaded his bedding on his pack horse, telling Father he would go back to the ranch and would return to the rodeo on the final day.

He arrived at the ranch bewildered, dirty, and hungry. From then on he stayed close to his camp and spent long hours visiting with my grandfather. Grandfather took him around the island garden and showed him the rooms where we stored the harvest. Mr. McTavish wanted to examine and taste everything.

Grandmother made him some mesquite-bean pudding. We called it *atole*, but sometimes the Sajones were offended by the native term, though they enjoyed the pudding itself. Not Mr. McTavish. He enjoyed learning the Spanish and Indian terms; he was out to learn as well as to teach, to write, and to make friends.

He made sketches and wrote long descriptions of mesquite beans in his notebook. He copied down the recipes for *atole de pechita,* and *melcocha de granada.* The latter is pomegranate juice, boiled with sugar until it forms a caramel. It is kept for coloring drinks. One drops small chunks of the caramel into a glass and pours the drink over them. The caramel gives *tesguin* a beautiful dark pink color and Grandfather used to say that it made the drinks look not only more appetizing, but more civilized.

Mr. McTavish wanted to know about everything. He wrote long passages in his notebook about the acorns—how we gathered and stored the nuts and how we prepared them to make cookies and mush. As they rummaged through the various sacks of native foods and herbs Grandfather would call out the names and describe the products and our visitor would make notes. Mr. McTavish wanted to buy samples of the items, but of course Grandfather simply filled paper bags and gave them to him. I remembered how I was always asking Grandfather for some *pinole de pechita*, and he would dole it out to me by the teaspoonful. And here he was giving Mr. McTavish a whole pound, and the recipe with it!

One day Mr. McTavish came into the kitchen while Doña Tomaza was visiting us and surprised everyone by saying: "*Yo estoy aprendiendo la lengua hispana* (I am learning to speak Spanish)." Then he opened a shoe box he was carrying and named all the items inside in Spanish: *pechitas, bellotas, jojobas,* and so forth.

Tomaza said, "You already speak very good Spanish, Mr. McTavish." When he had gone, she turned to Grandfather. "*Bueno*, Francisco. You have always hated to see that man come here, and now you seem happy to have him at your elbow all the time! How is that, hombre?"

"Well, Tomaza, that's the way it is . . . if you knew me and I knew you, we wouldn't disagree," he said, though he quoted the proverb in his own Spanish, of course.

I spent all my spare time with Mr. McTavish whenever he came and Father would let me. Mr. McTavish taught me how to spell big new words and how to use little words in my writing. He told me that simple words were better to use than big words, when one wrote for the public. Sometimes he told me stories. One day Grandfather took him into our sala, and he saw the picture of "The Return of the Grand Army" above the fireplace. The next day he told me all about the great French general who had met his Waterloo. When Mr. McTavish told me the Napoleonic story I could actually see the horses stampeding from the battlefield with empty saddles and stirrups flapping.

On the last day of the corrida Father took Mr. McTavish to the final roundup, and this time the editor returned exhilarated, but still somewhat shocked by the behavior of the vaqueros. The next day he packed up his tent and left. "Goodbye, Bonnie," he called to me. "I'll see you all next year." He raised his left hand in a goodbye salute and flicked the reins with his right hand. The little team began to move and the pretty green buckboard rolled away. We had learned from him and he had learned from us, or so he said.

I, for one, remember quite clearly the Spanish words I had taught Mr. McTavish in exchange for the vocabulary he taught me. Some of these words were: *cabrón, pendejo, lengón, hablador, mala, raza,* all words of personal insult I thought he should be able to recognize.

Long after my friend had gone away I showed Mother the list of words I had taught him. She laughed and warned me not to tell Grandfather. "Why, Ma?" I asked.

"I am afraid he would take a switch to you."

"I think that if someone calls Mr. McTavish a *cabrón* he should know what it means, don't you, Ma?"

"Yes, but in teaching him those words you showed how terribly you yourself can talk."

"Wahyanita and I can do worse than that, Ma."

"I know, I know," said Mother, sighing, as she often did, and looking off into the distance.

Start of the Fall Corrida

I T WAS SEPTEMBER AND THE CICADAS were flying everywhere. I was fascinated by their pretty light green, transparent wings, and their loud, shrill mating call. At night the fireflies flicked their little lights just for me. The whitewings were already gathering in big flocks.

"They are thinking and talking things over before leaving," said Grandfather. "We'll have an early winter, *hijita.*"

A few Indians were already going up the creek. The fourth of October would find them in Magdalena, celebrating the feast of San Francisco Xavier. At this time of the year the Indians were on the move. They went from one place to another. Even if they didn't go on the long journey, they stopped along the way, visited, and returned to the *reserva* (the strip something like thirty miles below the Mexican border, given the Indians by the Mexican government before the Gadsden Purchase). Here they settled down for the winter. Such was the case this morning when Emilia Rosa made her appearance over the riverbanks gasping for breath and suffering from the humid heat of September. She hurried to the corral where we were doing the morning chores and was soon holding the milk pail for Mother. She wasn't going anywhere. She was just visiting, she said.

Emilia Rosa had lived and done housework in Tucson for five or six years. She had become a good cook, prompt and efficient in her work. She had learned to talk, and according to her, this accomplishment had pulled her out of many straits. And now she was talking as only Emilia Rosa could talk.

"Let's go to the house. It is getting too hot here," said Mother as she led the way out of the corral.

"Yes, I go and help. I always help. I don't beg for food. I earn food."
And she followed us talking ceaselessly. Her daughter Sofía Ana had
married and gone to live at Poso Verde, and Emilia Rosa and her son,
Julio Juán moved to Poso Verde to be near Sofía Ana. Now she stood
gulping draughts of air as she excitedly told us how the Indian boys
were already preparing and training to go on a *caravana a la sal* (salt
pilgrimage) in the spring.

Julio Juán had been weeded out. "My boy not well," Emilia Rosa
told us. "He no run like Tomás José. Tomás José good boy. He kill
eagle when he was only fourteen. He will be medicine man someday.
He training now to go with boys. He fasts. No eat, no drink. He run
up mountains and throw prayer sticks, on washes, up ridges, all over.
My boy good boy, too, but maybe sick. Not strong." She placed a
bowl of *cazuela* (jerky stew) before me. I picked up a spoon and began
to eat.

"Say thank you, *malcriada* (ill-bred girl). I teach children to say
thank you. I work for good people." She washed the dishes for mother
amid a ceaseless chatter. Mother tried to get up to stoke the stove.
Emilia Rosa pushed her down on the chair. "I help, you rest. I talk,
you listen."

"Mmmmmmmmy God!" exclaimed Mother.

"Yes, I know God, mine too. Now where is coffee? Oh, here. God
is my God, too." She served Mother her lunch and then sat down to
eat. After she had eaten and made sure that helping Mother was going
to be her job, she went to the Guijas Village, to visit her Parientes.
She would be back to help.

October came in with its smoke-blue mist that cloaked the land. Grandfather and my uncles were hauling in some of the late *cosecha* from
the gardens. Mother, with the help of Emilia Rosa, was packing away
the dried mesquite beans in burlap sacks loosely woven so that air
could get to the beans. The acorns we had brought from the Cochis
Ranch were packed in layers of ashes to discourage weevil larvae, and
the dried outer skin of the walnuts was rubbed off and the clean nuts
sacked and placed above the ground on two-by-four boards. The
cooked, dried *bledos* (careless weeds) and the elderberry fruit Mother
stored in cheesecloth sacks and hung from the beams.

Doña Tomaza came one day to tell Father that Ramón Ahumada

planned to begin the fall corrida around the twelfth of the month and she warned him ominously, "By that time the Indians will be back from Magdalena, Agustín."

"I know," said Father, "and I won't be here to give poor Barreplata a hand. He'll be swamped, keeping them in line."

"I used to go to the fiesta in Magdalena every year, too," said Tomaza, "but I am tied down now." For some time she had owned and operated a general store in Arivaca. "You just can't leave a store, you know," she would say. "A store is a cash register. You either have to close it or take care of it."

"Incidentally, Tomaza," Grandfather asked, "have you seen Damián in Arivaca recently?"

"Yes, Francisco, I saw him the other day. He was going into the cantina."

"What the devil was he doing in the cantina?" Grandfather was fretting about Damián Gallego's welfare.

"You know he is going to the corrida, don't you, Francisco? He has to show those vaqueros that he is a man, doesn't he? Let him grow up, Pa. The boy can't be a *monigote* (a rag doll or sissy) all his life."

Grandfather stood and silently stalked out of the kitchen. Tomaza and Father laughed. "When I was Damián's age I was a better man than he is," Tomaza said.

"He has been raised like a baby," said Father.

I felt angry at them for calling my friend a *monigote,* but I felt help-less to defend him, so I walked out, too. As I left I heard Tomaza's coarse laugh again. "He'll be a full-fledged vaquero by the time the corrida ends," she stated.

The days that followed found Father finishing repairs on the old corral. He always saw that gates and fences were secure before he went to a corrida so as to have a safe place to put the stock when he returned. We all worked hard to have everything ready, and the days fled by. Early one evening Ramón Ahumada came out of the mesquite *bosque* and followed the trail to our house. Father met him at the wall.

"That's a beautiful animal you're riding, Ramón."

Lucero champed at the bit and pawed the ground impatiently, and Father became visibly anxious, thinking, of course, that I might still tell Ramón how I had saved Lucero from being clipped at Cochis Ranch.

"Eva," he said quickly to me, "go take care of William."

"How is the boy, Agustín?"

"He's growing big and mean." Father looked at me. "Right now, Eva!"

I went but I watched them from the bedroom window. I saw Ramón take off his spurs and walk to the door with Father. Ramón visited with my grandparents, as he usually did, and I heard Grandmother tell him to take good care of niño Damián at the roundup. Ramón laughed. "That character takes care of himself." He went on, "I have just told Agustín that we are not going to bring the remuda here this time. We are going straight through."

"Then we'll have to go up on the hill just to see you go by, Ramón, and I will not get to see my friend from Saric."

"Maybe in the spring we'll stop here, Margarita, so that you can get news of your friends from the vaqueros."

So, immediately after Father drove his horses out to the road the next morning, we all hurried to the top of Pesqueira Hill to watch him joining the remuda and to see it go by. It was one thing to see it leave our own corral, as we had done in the spring, but quite another to see it coming toward us from the distance. We saw the horse-drive as it was leaving Arivaca—just a cloud of dust that rose high and moved down the road, the animals lost from sight. As the cloud approached we heard the hoofbeats like the rumble of distant thunder.

Suddenly, the herd burst out of the *mesquital* preceded by three riders, and we saw Father run his horses up the road to join the remuda. The stream of horses seemed endless. Some of them broke away from the herd and ran up the slope, only to be followed by an alert vaquero who ran at their flank until the strays turned back.

Four or five vaqueros were riding flank at each side of the herd, one riding behind another at distances of about a hundred yards. In this way they kept the speeding herd on the road. It rolled by our eyes like a flood high against the rising sun.

"Those three horsemen leading the herd are riding point, Margarita." Grandfather had to shout as the *cavallada* passed us, for the clatter of hoofbeats had become deafening.

We were all looking for Damián, the youngest man at this; it was to be his "coming of age." *"Adónde fue a dar el muchacho?"* called Barre-plata. "What has happened to the boy?"

"I haven't been able to pick him out," answered Grandfather, looking somewhat anxious now. But just then Damián appeared over the north-ern ridge following three horses that had broken away from the remuda.

Two vaqueros broke away from the drive and galloped up the hill to help Damián bring the horses into line.

"See, Margarita, the vaqueros are helping the boy. They all seem very friendly."

"I am glad for him, Francisco. God knows, the work at the corrida will be hard enough without mischief-making."

The remuda disappeared down the creek and all we could see was the dust cloud as it drifted slowly off to the west.

We returned to the house where we had a second breakfast and sat at the table talking about the corrida, the vaqueros, the cattle, and the Indians. Barreplata scratched his grey head and said, "All this—the horses, the corrida, too—those things are dying. All you will see there on that road will be the machines—those new automobiles like the one Robles has, you know."

"Where will the cowboys be, Tata?" I asked him, puzzled.

"They will be ghosts. Dead."

"My father, too, Tata?"

"Yes. Your father, your mother, grandparents, myself, even Damián. Maybe you will live to see it, Chiquita. If you do you must tell the world how beautiful this country was, for even the land will be dead, too, in a way—like us and like the remuda, the corrida. I do not think it will live for long."

By noon everyone was hard at work performing some chore that must be done before the end of the corrida. Emilia Rosa went in and out of the house, lending a helping hand here and there, still talking ceaselessly. Barra and the uncles made more repairs on the roofs. Wood had to be brought in for Grandfather's house and for ours, so the buckboard went back and forth from the houses to the mesquite thickets.

Grandfather brought in the last of the *cosecha* from the *milpita* to the milkhouse, then immediately started to get his soil ready for planting in the spring. He dug deep holes and filled them with layers of cottonwood leaves, soil, and goat manure, then finally covered them with more soil and leaves.

Whenever my chores were done, I was now free to spend hours riding up and down the creek on Diamante. One day I rode halfway up the Cerro to drive the bellmare and her small herd of geldings down. Canelita, the bellmare, led the horses down the trail at a dead run, trying her best to beat me to the gap. I ran at the flank of the stampeding herd, as I had seen Father do. Diamante jumped over some high rocks, cleared a deep ditch, and beat Canelita to the gap by a horse's length. The horses turned, circled, and dashed up the slope to the corral, amid rising dust, kicks, and whickers.

My grandparents and mother were at the *milpita* loading Tomaza's buckboard with squash and other late produce. They stood on the bank and watched me beat the horses to the gap. My uncles said I was crazy and Mother threatened to punish me. But Doña Tomaza said it was a beautiful performance.

"She's just like her Father. Why punish her? She has been taught to handle the horses and now she is trying her wings. Right, amigo?" she said to me. (She jokingly used the masculine noun, implying that I was as good as a man.)

"Right, Doña Tomaza. This is my first time to bring in the horses all by myself. I didn't need any help at the gap either," I boasted. "When I was coming down the hill Diamante jumped clear over a great pile of rocks! You wouldn't believe it!"

"You bet I believe it. Rock horses are not called *berrenditos* (antelope) for nothing. That was fast and beautiful work over at the gap. Scared the hell out of me!"

I was so proud, and I told Tomaza now that Father always had to have someone stand at the gap for him, but *I* didn't need anyone to help me.

"I noticed that," Tomaza said gravely.

The following day I promised Mother that I wouldn't drive the horses, I would just go up the hill and back. Mother helped me saddle Diamante and I put my foot in my make-shift rope stirrup, laid myself across the saddle, and kicked and squirmed until I could straddle the leather and sit upright. Then I folded the rope stirrup and tied it to the saddlehorn. I rode clear up to the path at the side of El Cerro. From there I could see in back of the mountain to the south. If I turned and looked down I could see our house and Dr. Ball's place, and beyond that, clear to Arivaca.

I slipped down from my horse, tied him to a mesquite branch, and began to explore. There were so many things to examine. The lichen on the rocks delighted me. It grew around one big rock in spots like light green leaves. In other places it formed dark red splotches like red roses.

I looked at many things near and far that morning, and I found myself happy to be alone for a change. From the mountains to the east I saw a black "V" coming toward me, and lying back I watched a bird formation cut through the blue sky above me and disappear over the Cerro. Looking to the north once, I happened to see a string of burros silhouetted above a ridge, walking slowly in a seemingly endless line, one after the other.

By then I had learned to count to a thousand. Father taught me to draw an upright bar to mark every hundred. Four upright bars with one drawn diagonally across was five hundred. I called this symbol a *cuerdita* because it reminded me of a cord of wood. In this manner I now counted the burros as they disappeared down the canyon, and when the last burro had left the ridge I had made two *cuerditas* and two extra bars. Twelve hundred animals!

After I had gazed my fill, I went back to Diamante and sat near him under the mesquite tree to do some daydreaming. Like most young children who play alone, I spent much of my time in a world of fantasy, thinking about how life would be when I grew up. For one thing, I dreamed of making my own dresses, not like the ones in the mail-order catalog, but prettier. My dresses would have lace and pretty buttons like the clothes Virginia Ahumada wore. I might even make dresses for other people! I began picturing how my imaginary ladies would look in my creations. Some of them looked beautiful in my mind, but some of them looked like Papagas, and there was nothing I could do with them, as hard as I tried to imagine. They didn't even know how to comb their hair, but wore it parted in the center and down on the sides like broomtail mares. They put their heads down and the hair hid their faces. This ruined the idea of the dresses. I took one lady by the hair and gave her a good slapping. "Pin up that hair. You are not a mare! What do you want a pretty dress for if you're going to act like a Papaga?" The lady pinned up her hair like Mrs. Bernard and she looked better.

When I got hungry I found my way home.

"Where were you?" asked Mother. "You've been gone all morning."

"Riding the range, Ma."

"No more of that. You are not to go riding by yourself again until your father returns from the corrida." But the following days, almost every day found Diamante and me again galloping down the creek and up into the hills.

About ten days or so after the start of the roundup, Father and Mateo returned to the ranch. The corrida had reached Las Guijas and would be at the creek in a day or so and then Father would go to bring home the strays. In the meantime Uncle Luis and Tom Ewell were staying with the corrida to watch over whatever cattle with the Wilbur brand came to the creek in the drive.

"And how did it go with Damián, Agustín?" asked Grandfather.

"Oh, he's fine, Pa. But the other vaqueros didn't fare so well at the hands of young Damián."

"What do you mean, Agustín?"

"Well, the boy took care of himself. The first night El Babucha, a cowboy from the Sopori Ranch, sneaked up to Damián's saddle and tried to untie the reata from the saddle horse. Damián came up behind him and hit him with his quirt, cutting his face and his eye. Then he picked him up and threw him down the hill. That same night Mateo here tried to steal the boy's boots, but he couldn't find them."

"Lucky for me," said Mateo. "The second night out some of the boys tried to steal Damián's rope, but the boy reacted like a *toro de astas*, and he scared them off good! Ramón got up that night and talked with the vaqueros, trying to get them to stop their foolishness. But that didn't stop the tricks or make Damián any less cautious. When some smart vaquero picked up his saddle and ran away with it, Damián followed him and attacked him with the quirt, too."

"Who do you think that was, Ma?" asked Father.

"I don't know, *hijo*."

"It was your friend, Jesús Manzanares."

"*¡Madre de Dios!* Why would Jesús do such a silly thing?"

Mateo laughed uproariously and Father said, "I don't know, but I bet he won't try it again. The third night of the corrida Damián was still prepared. He spread his bedroll near the corral fence and put his saddle on it for a pillow. Then he moved his canvas a safe distance away and lay down in the shadow of the corral to wait. It wasn't long until he heard a noise in the brush, and suddenly a rock was hurled straight at the head of the bedroll. Well, Damián jumped that hombre from behind. It was stupid Babucha again, trying to get even. When that fight was over Babucha saddled up and left for good."

"Can you imagine the nerve of that boy!" exclaimed Grandmother.

"I don't blame him, Ma," said Mother. "Do you remember when brother Joe first took part in a corrida? The first night somebody hid his shoes and he spent all the next day looking for them, and only the *next* morning did he find them beside his bedroll. So he worked all that day, but the third day he was barefooted again and his horse was gone, too, and nowhere to be found. The fourth day his horse came in with the remuda. That's the way he spent the two weeks—working every other day. What makes the vaqueros so cruel, anyway? They deserve to be hit with a quirt when they are so vicious with the beginners."

"The same thing would have happened to our Damián if he had let the men run over him," said Mateo, laughing. "I mean if he had allowed *us* to do it, Agustín."

"Well," said Father, "the boy is a polite young fellow and a hard worker, and he is one tough hombre. He takes after old man Gallego, the grandfather who raised him. The old man didn't do a bad job of it, either!"

"And, you know, Agustín, I think Ramón plans to keep him on at the big ranch," said Mateo.

"He told me so, too, Mat," Father agreed.

And that was how niño Damián fared at his first corrida. It made me feel good to hear Father and Mateo tell the story.

Father looked down at me now. "In a few days, Eva, the rodeo will be at the *vaceran*—down at the spring. I think I will saddle Diamante for you and take you with me for the last day of the roundup. Would you like that?"

"Oh, yes, Papa. *Please* take me!"

Everyone laughed. It was probably the first time they had ever heard me say that magic word. I was so excited at the prospect of going with Father to the corrida, even if only for a few hours, and on the last day, that I hardly knew what words I had used.

The Last Day of Corrida

ECAUSE I HAD STAYED AWAKE, TOSSING AND TURNING until the early hours of the morning, I slept late on the last day of corrida. I had a hurried breakfast, after which Mother began the difficult job of bathing me. I fussed and fumed as usual. While she was brushing my hair I heard cattle lowing and calves bawling on the northern hill above the creek.

Father came into the house and said that Diamante was saddled and ready. Moments later we were riding along the creek on the way to the place of roundup. Mateo Mariano was waiting for us at a spot in the middle of the riverbed where the bank sloped upward to a huge clearing. We joined him, and now, facing south, I could see a number of vaqueros on horseback standing in a circle at the far end of the clearing. "Pa, what are those men doing up there?"

"They are standing guard to keep the cattle from escaping up the hill."

"Oh," I said, "they are man posts."

"That's right, Eva. They make a human fence."

Soon cattle began to come down from the north side of the creek in large droves single file, attended by the vaqueros. When they saw us standing there in the creek, they plodded straight across, up the south slope, and found themselves inside the human fence. On and on they came, in ever larger groups. We could hear the continual thundering hoofbeats and clattering horns back in the cover of the mesquite thicket; then the cattle would burst from the trees and splash through the water to join the others. The human fence expanded, and the cattle milled about within it in a circle. Lost calves bawled and ran in search of their mothers, who answered and hurried to locate their young. Some of the steers moved to the edge of the circle and faced the cowboy guards. When one of the steers saw an opening he would dash through and take to the hills. One of the riders usually went after him to turn him back.

Down the creek and across from where we waited was a group of Indians bathing in the water holes along the side of the bank. I saw Tula and Wahyanita and Tomás José. Mateo rode over and talked with them and came back to tell us that they had just returned from the fiesta of San Francisco in Magdalena.

I wanted to go over also and talk with my Indian friends, but at the moment I was too fascinated by what was going on before me on the hill. I had seen cattle come down to water every day at the ranch, but never in my life had I seen so many in one spot, or so much variety.

There were spotted cattle, or pintos; there were white-faced cattle, goggled-eyed ones, some that were belted, blacks, blues, greys, strawberry roans, and others with solid red hides. Their horns were varied too, some spreading out to the sides, others with an upward sweep, horns pointing straight forward, horns with a snake-like twist.

When all the cattle were in, I followed Father and Mateo up the hill to a better vantage point. Mateo left us now, galloping away to join the vaqueros. By now some of the men had moved out of the places in the "fence" and were dragging in mesquite wood with which to build several branding fires. The fires were soon blazing away, twenty or thirty running irons placed on the ground around each, branding ends in the flame, to be kept red-hot for immediate use. Three men worked at the fires; one kept the woodpile replenished, another chopped wood and stoked the fires, and a third took care of the branding irons.

Each branding crew had a *lazador* (roper), flankers—men who picked up the calves by the flanks, throwing them down and tying them—cutters, who castrated and earmarked the calves, and a medicine man, who stood by with a jar of salve for dabbing the animal's wounds. The most important member of the crew was the *herrador*, the brander himself, who applied the red-hot irons to each calf and drew the permanent mark of its owner.

If the brand consisted of two or three letters, it usually took two or three *tabos* (irons) to do the job. When the running irons got cold, the *herrador* would yell, "*Tabo!*" and another cowboy, called the *corre tabos,* would run to put a hot branding iron in his hand. This process would go on for three or four hours, depending on the number of calves to be marked.

I had seen Father brand calves, two or three at a time, but the branding of a hundred calves or more was a totally different matter. At first the whirlwind of activity, as the skilled cowhands worked their trade, was confusing to me. I was mainly conscious of masses of smoke and clouds of dust rising as the animals were being roped and tied. From that dark, clouded center there came the smell of burning hair, the bawling of calves, and the yelling, cursing, and loud laughter of the vaqueros. Fortunately, Father was beside me to explain what was going on, and soon the spectacle began to make sense.

When a *lazador* delivered a calf to the flanker, he would hurriedly call out the brand needed and immediately rush away to bring up another calf. I saw that a mother cow would usually stay near the fire waiting for her calf to be turned loose. Sometimes, though, the mother cow would not come and at these times the *herrador* would often yell, "What brand did you say?" If the *lazador* had meanwhile forgotten the correct brand, the calf would have to be turned loose to join its mother again, and the *lazador* would send loud curses in the direction of the *herrador* and his helpers.

The *herradores* often got tired, and always seemed willing to let some volunteer replace them for the few minutes it took to roll a cigarette and take a few puffs. At one such time, Tom Ewell came up to Father and asked him if he could try his hand at branding.

"No, Ewell," Father said. "You haven't had enough experience. You have to be fast around here."

"I know how to use a running iron."

"But you don't know the different brands, Ewell."

The man would not give up. He took his case to Ramón Ahumada, the rodeo boss, and asked him if he could help brand.

"*Si, seguro,*" said Ramón indifferently, turning away to another chore. At once Ewell found himself with a hot running iron in his hand, a calf dragged in and thrown for him, and the *lazador* called out, "A-cero!"

"Acero," Tom Ewell echoed. He said later that he had wanted to ask about that brand, but that nobody had time for questions and answers. Another calf was already being dragged to the fire so he quickly burned the letters A C E R O across the calf's ribs. Then, just as he reached down to untie the animal, the owner arrived.

"What in hell did you do to that calf!" Without waiting for an answer the man pushed Ewell aside yelling "*¡Tabo!*" A hot running iron was brought to him immediately and below the bold letters Ewell had made the calf's owner burned the correct brand—*ℛ*. Ewell tried to apologize for not having been familiar with the mark.

"Well, you can see the mother cow right there in front of you, begging for her calf. Can't you see the brand on her side?" demanded the owner, still angry.

Ewell got on his horse and came back to the spot where Father and I were standing. Mateo had joined us again, too, and just as Ewell came up the calf with the botched brand ran right past us.

"What kind of branding is that, hombre?" Mateo asked, laughing. The story soon got around and the vaqueros began to shout, "Where is that great *herrador* of the *acero?*" Tom Ewell began to look as though he wished there were some place to hide.

"What will happen to that calf, Agustín?" he finally said.

Before Father could answer Mateo spoke up. "They'll just have to name him after you, Ewell."

Ramón Ahumada came by. "The men want you over there at the branding site, Tom," he said with a big smile.

"I'm sorry I made a mess of that brand, Ramón."

"Don't worry amigo. You'll know better next time."

While all this was going on, other interesting activities were taking place around the working area. About two hundred yards distant Don Julián had set up his *fonda en ruedas*—the restaurant on wheels. He had unhitched his horses, putting them to graze nearby, and I saw Don Julián himself and his grandson Pepe carrying boxes toward a cottonwood tree where they had placed their long plank table.

It was the custom in those days for wives and children of the ranchers to attend the last day of corrida in celebration for work well done. Now I saw Virginia, Ramón Ahumada's wife, and Phoebe Bogan driving toward us in a shiny black buggy. Ramón left us and went to lead them to a shady mesquite tree.

"Come, Eva," said Father, "let's go say hello to Virigina and Phoebe."

I followed him to the side of the buggy. Phoebe was cool and ignored me entirely. Virginia was merely polite. I had never liked either of those ladies, and now I turned Diamante's back to them and faced the rodeo while my father chatted. When we left them a few minutes later, None Bernard and his wife, the owners of the Arivaca Cattle Company, were coming up the bank. Mrs. Bernard wore a long black skirt and a black, flat-rimmed hat; she had black hair, very white skin and blue eyes. She rode sidesaddle, and she was aloof and arrogant. She and her husband rode in slow state around the cattle inspecting their own stock. Ramón, who was their foreman, then joined them, and I could see from a distance that Mrs. Bernard remained distant and haughty with him, too. There was no smile for him or anyone else she saw.

People were arriving all the time now. A group of Mexican girls came on horseback. They rode around for awhile until they, too, found a shady place to sit and watch the rodeo. They seemed to be having a good time. Damián Gallego came with some of his friends. He saw Father and me sitting on the bank and got down and came to join us.

"*Hola*, Damián," said Father. "Where have you been, hombre?"

"I took part of the remuda to the big ranch, then I stayed to saddle horses for the Noneños. La Señora had trouble with the black horse, so I saddled the bay she's riding." He looked at me. "The niña here can ride better than she does."

"I hope so, Damián," said Father.

I was on my feet now, tugging at Damián's jacket. "When you were at the corrida I brought the bellmare to the corral all by myself," I told him.

"Do you think I haven't heard? Doña Tomaza told everyone in the valley about that. I am proud of you, Evita," said Damián.

Damián had changed. He looked different from the last time we had seen him. He no longer dropped his lower jaw and stared into the distance. He had acquired a sharp, searching look and the sweet boyish smile on his face had been replaced by a slight frown. I noticed a splash of dried blood across one leg of his chaps and dried manure on the lower part of his boots. Even his new hat was worn out of shape.

"Agustín, let me take the niña to the fonda. Maybe I can find something for her to eat."

"Sure, Damián. But Don Julián hasn't rung the *cencerro*. You know how angry he gets if anyone comes around the chuckwagon before he rings that cowbell."

"Well, he is only waiting for this sack of sugar I brought for him. But he had better feed us, or he won't get it. Come along, niña." He took me by the hand and we walked toward the cottonwood tree.

"Damián, call me Bonnie, will you?" I pleaded. "I am a big girl now, you know."

Damián laughed. "You are growing fast, Bonnie. Sometimes you act more like a fifteen-year-old señorita than a little girl."

I was delighted. Mother told me that when I became fifteen years old I would be a señorita, and I could hardly wait for that time to come.

Don Julián had a stack of tin plates and cups laid out along the plank table under the cottonwood. "Here's the sugar you ordered," said Damián. "Make us some burritos or something, please."

"Sure. Take the little girl over to the table."

Father had come up behind us and we all sat down together on some old boxes. Before long Don Julián brought a large tray with burritos and green chile salsa, and coffee for the men. He gave me a burrito on a tin plate and a dish of rice pudding with raisins. When Damián picked up his burrito I saw that he had rope burns and nicks on his hands.

"Don't I rate any of that pudding, Julián?" asked Father.

"Sorry, amigo. That was a special order for Ahumada. I have already packed it in a box for him. I saved out just a little for the niña here."

"Thank you, Julián, for your kindness," said Father.

I was supposed to be grateful, but I pouted in silence. There was no way out of it. No matter what I did, how well I rode, I was just a niña to everyone—a little girl.

Don Julián now rang his *cencerro* and vaqueros came to sit on the ground and eat their lunches hurriedly. Others came on horseback and were handed food which they ate in the saddle. Then they dashed away so that other men could leave their posts.

Ramón Ahumada came to pick up the lunch box Don Julián had prepared for him. He took it to a mesquite tree where his wife was sitting with some other ladies. The ladies spread a canvas and sat down to enjoy their lunch. Ramón returned to work.

Father told us that he had heard Mrs. Bernard was angry with Ramón. She didn't like the way things were going with the Noneños ranch. She had threatened to replace him with a "white man." Grandfather's friend, Señor Manzanares, had been heard to say that he hoped she would replace Ramón, "so that she would lose her pants." (Eventually, the Noneños did oust Ramón and Manzanares got his wish.)

When all the branding was finished each ranch owner began to cut his own cattle from the main herd and drive them to a selected spot to form his small herd, or *partida*. A couple of cowboys would keep each owner's animals together until all were rounded up. Then, with a wave of his hand and a final farewell, each rancher would drive his stock off to his own ranchito. Not until all the small ranchers had cut their stock and driven them away would the Noneños move the remainder of the herd to the big ranch at Arivaca.

Father had enlisted Tom Ewell and Mateo to help Uncle Luis cut out the animals he intended to take back to the Wilbur Ranch: all the cattle bearing the brands $\overset{E}{\underset{W}{}}$, LH, and ℛ. When his *partida* began to get out of hand, Father called to me to get my horse and come help Uncle Luis guard the herd.

I had been longing to take part in this, the last day of corrida. Happily, I trotted off to take up my post. As I approached the herd, a cow with the Wilbur brand escaped and passed in front of me at a dead run. Mateo was after her in an instant, but every time he managed to get in front of her to head her back the cow would charge him, and he would have to move quickly to one side to keep his horse from being gored.

I tried to go to Mateo's aid, but Tom Ewell held me back. "No, Bonnie. That cow is dangerous. You stay with Luis. I'll go."

Ewell was soon joined by Father and Ramón and they all chased the cow up the hill. Father finally managed to rope her and lead her back toward the herd, Ramón and Ewell behind her, prodding her whenever she balked.

Ramón suggested that Father have this cow dehorned, before she had another chance to injure someone or to gore a horse. He sent Ewell to the branding site to bring back a saw.

The man cut out the cow and threw her to the ground. I left Uncle Luis to guard the *partida* and went to watch the dehorning. None Bernard and his wife on their horses stood beside me, and a number of vaqueros, including Damián, formed a circle around the animal. "What horrible sabers she has," said Mrs. Bernard.

"If it were your animal you would probably call them beautiful specimens," someone said, laughing. The mood was light, for the rodeo was almost over, and there was a lot of bantering as Mateo picked up the saw. But the jokes had come too early. Suddenly the cow lurched to her feet, moved her head from side to side, and, finding my father the closest target for her sabers, she charged him.

I felt Diamante jump, almost spilling me to the ground. In a split second Diamante had thrown himself between Father and the cow, striking the charging animal's shoulder and shoving her forward. The cow stumbled to her feet again and took off, dragging two ropes, while two horsemen went after her.

Hearing the shouts, more vaqueros gathered around us, wanting to know if anyone had been hurt. "No one—thanks to that niña," I heard one of the men say, describing the incident. "A niña again," I thought.

But all at once I was the object of admiration and praise. None Bernard hurried to my side to take me down from the saddle. But Damián grabbed me first. He raised me to his shoulder, not wanting anyone else to touch me, even Father. People kept coming up to us to exclaim and ask questions. "What a brave little girl! How did you think so fast, muchachita?" "Weren't you afraid?" My father leaned against a tree trunk, a smile on his face, enjoying the show.

But poor Diamante. My horse stood with his head down, still laboring for breath. No one praised my little rock horse. Only I knew that he was the real hero, and that I stole his credit.

Don Julián came now and asked father to let me go back to the fonda. He had some little gifts for me. "She can go," said Father, calling to Damián, "Take care of her, hijo."

Damián carried me to the fonda and Don Julián opened a box of things that someone had ordered and then refused to pay for. It held little sweaters and knitted caps. I chose a red sweater and he gave me one for my sister, too. I also got some trinkets from a smaller box, and Don Julián added to these a package of cookies.

I was sitting on a box, and Damián bent down and pretended to be tying my shoelaces. I saw that his hand was shaking. "I was scared for you, Chiquita," he told me.

"It's all right, Damián. I wasn't hurt. And that cow didn't get a chance to gore my father. But I want to tell you something, before we go back where everybody is."

"All right, go ahead and tell me."

"I didn't really save Father, you know. Diamante did it all by himself, and even I was scared." Damián and I both knew all about the intelligence and ability of the little Spanish horses. We sometimes called them rock horses because they were surefooted on rocky surfaces, and the Indians called them doghorses because of the doglike devotion they had for their masters. Diamante had proved his today.

Damián straightened up. "Don't tell that to anyone else, Bonnie. You deserve a lot of credit, too. You and Diamante are a team working together." He picked me up again and started back toward Father. "I'll see you at the ranch tomorrow," he said in my ear. "I heard your father tell the Indio that they would be going to Palo Alto to bring back some strays."

He put me down at Father's side. Virginia Ahumada and Phoebe were waiting in their black buggy. They wanted to get a picture of me on Diamante. So Father lifted me into the saddle and Ramón took the picture and then handed the little camera back to his wife.

"Now to get on to the business at hand," he said, "and get that animal dehorned."

The cow had been brought back and was lying on the ground safely tied this time. Mateo took the sharp saw and put one foot on her neck. Then, holding the tip of one horn with his left hand, he sawed the horn off. The cow bawled and struggled to get loose. Blood spurted from the wound and ran down the slope. The man flipped the animal over and Mateo removed the other horn. She lay panting with her hornless head resting in a pool of blood.

"Leave her there till we finish the cutting," said Father. He ordered me to join Uncle Luis and Ewell in guarding the animals already in the small *partida,* and he and Mateo went back to separating Wilbur cattle from the big herd.

I could see that Mateo was having trouble with the greenbroke colt he was riding. Soon he and Father came to borrow my horse for him. "Diamante is a good cutting horse," said Mateo, "and the vaqueros are tired. They want to finish the job and get home, Bonnie. We'll bring your horse right back."

"All right, Mateo." I slid down from the saddle and stood watching Mateo exchange it for the saddle on the colt. He tied the colt some distance away, then came back and picked me up. He placed me on the dry branch of an old elderberry tree. "You stay here out of harm's way," he said.

As he and Father rode off, a group of Indians came up the bank and joined me under the tree. Carmelo Tosco was with them, and my old friend-and-enemy Wahyanita. Wahyanita had brought a couple of tin pails of mud up from the river. She wanted me to sit down and play "mud" with her. I was glad to see her and we were talking so fast we couldn't hear each other when Father suddenly came back.

"Eva, take that stick there and stand on the bajada and don't let any strays get past you," he said.

Obediently, I picked up the stick and walked to the center of the twelve-foot-wide slope. There was a drop of about six feet on either side. With this club in my "powerful" hands, I was expected to keep the herd at bay. True, there was a man on a black mule a short distance from the bajada, and if things got out of hand he would come to my aid, I thought.

Wahyanita followed me up the slope, buckets in hand. "We can play here," she said.

"No, Wahyanita. I have to do what he said."

She knocked the pole from my hand and thrust the pail of mud at me. I took it automatically, not thinking. Just then I looked up and saw Mateo and Diamante chasing Old Mora, a blue cow with a crumpled horn and a calf at her side. She ran back into the big herd, winding her way in and out among the cattle, then came out on the side facing the bajada.

Mother had warned me about Old Mora and told me to stay clear of her. But I was so busy trying to pick up my stick and trying to make Wahyanita take back the pail that I didn't see the cow coming in my direction until I heard a shout from the man on the mule. I looked up to find Old Mora not four feet from me. There was not time to run. Instinctively, I raised the bucket of mud against her. She collided with it full force, knocking it from my hand and knocking me to the ground.

The rim of the pail cut her across the nose, and blood splattered all around. She turned back, dazed and shaking her head, and ran toward the herd. Wahyanita was now nowhere to be seen, but other people came running from all directions. Carmelo Tosco was the first to reach my side. He picked me up and carried me back to the branch of the elderberry tree and set me on it. I was not to move, he said.

Ramón and Damián came. When Ramón saw the blood on my shirt he rode off to bring Father. Father turned pale as a ghost at all the blood. He got down and felt me all over. "Are you hurt, Eva?"

"No, Pa." I sat up. "I wasn't afraid of Old Mora. I cut her nose with the bucket Wahyanita gave me."

"So I heard," said Father. "You're my brave girl. I want you to stay here with Damián now until we get through with your horse. We're going up the hill to bring back a few strays, and then our work will be done and we can go home. All right?"

"Yes, Pa."

Damián sat down beside me, a troubled frown on his face. He patted my head and said, "You're too little, Bonnie, to do the work of a forty-year-old man."

"Don't you worry about me, Damián," I said. I unbuttoned the collar of my shirt and pulled out a small medal on a string. "See, Damián, my grandmother put this around my neck. She said he is my guardian angel, and nothing can happen to me because he takes care of me."

Virginia Ahumada got down from her buggy and came over to us. Without any preliminaries she said angrily, "Damián, you seem to have some influence with these people. Why don't you tell your friend Agustín to take better care of this little girl?"

Damián stood up politely. "No, Señora, I have no influence. I am just a poor *jornalero* (day worker). Right now I am as distressed as you are." Virginia went back to her buggy.

"Damián," I said. "I love you as much as I love my father."

"I love you more than I love my father. And this corrida is making an old man of me." He looked away. Finally, he said, "Bonnie, I want you to stay right here. I am going down to the river to get you a drink." He walked away.

The man on the black mule had come to stand at the bajada. But first he came over to offer me some advice. "Muchachita," he said, "never stand in front of moving cattle. You could have been killed. That *Americano chingado*—that son of a bitch—he had no business putting you on the bajada." He probably did not know that the Americano was my father. He wiped his eyes with a red handkerchief and rode off.

Damián brought me a drink in a collapsible cup. He told me that I could keep it, so I drank the water and put the cup in my pocket. He had washed his face and hair, and his eyebrows looked very black. He finally looked like the neat, fair-complexioned boy whom we had last seen at the Cochis Ranch.

We sat together now, watching the final activities of the roundup. The huge herd had gradually diminished until only Noneños cattle were left. Now the vaqueros were tidying up loose ends, putting out fires, gathering up tools. Meanwhile, a number of people had moved to our vicinity. They stood in groups discussing some matter in heated voices. But it was some time before I realized that they were talking about me.

The Bernards were there, and Phoebe Bogan, and the cattle inspector. There were a couple of rangers, too, and some cowboys who had finished their work. When Father finally arrived with Mateo and dismounted, the group turned on him with angry questions and accusations. They frightened me much more than had my encounter with the cow. Mrs. Bernard raised her voice and I heard her say something about the mistreatment of children and about the law.

"Are you telling me, Señora, that you are going to press charges against me because I let my daughter take part in the corrida?" demanded Father.

"No, no, Agustín," her husband intervened. "It's just that none of us likes to see a child get hurt."

"She didn't get hurt," said Father coldly. At that Bernard took his wife's arm and led her away. But Ramón Ahumada came over and he, too, was critical of Father.

"It was a horrible experience, Agustín, to see that little girl just inches away from the horns of a vicious animal. That she was able to save herself was a miracle. You saw how people reacted. You had half the vaqueros here sniffling over the affair. What a shame."

"I appreciate their concern," said Father. "I guess I would have been that upset myself if I had actually seen the cow so close to Eva."

Don Julián had been standing nearby listening, and now he had his say. "I tell you, Agustín, my grandson Pepe is fourteen and I take good care of him."

"You'd better take care of him if that's the way you treat him," replied Father, angry again. "I teach *my* children to take care of themselves, and they do."

"She seems to have done a good enough job of it," said Mateo. "Just take a look at the cow." Some distance away Old Mora was still shaking her muddy head and spraying blood around her. I realized, somewhat sadly, that she, too, would have to be dehorned. It was an unwritten law of the range that a cow that had endangered or injured a horse or a human must sacrifice her horns.

Don Julián went back to his kitchen on wheels, the cattle inspector rode off, and one by one most of the onlookers drifted away. But not

Phoebe Bogan. She came and shook her fist in Father's face, ranting on and on. "You endangered that child more than once today. She had *two* bad escapes from dangerous cows. You are a selfish, inconsiderate man, Agustín Wilbur. Attila the Hun is a piker compared to you!" With that final insult she turned and marched back to the black buggy where Virginia sat reciting her rosary beads.

John Bogan remarked to Father that he never had approved of women and children attending the rodeo.

While all this was going on Damián brought Diamante to me and put me on his back. "Take good care of yourself," he whispered. "Now I have to go back to work." He waved to Father, "*Hasta luego,* Agustín."

"*Que te vaya bien,* Damián, *y un millón de gracias,*" answered Father. "Good luck and a million thanks."

Ramón was talking to Father. "In spite of everything, Agustín, the corrida was successful. The cattle are fat and all the boys came back hale and happy."

"Thanks to your good management, Ramón."

Ramón moved to Diamante's side. He embraced me and said, "God bless you, niñita, and keep you in his care always." Father gave me a warning glance and I looked up at Ramón and said, "Gracias." I was finally beginning to learn manners from Emilia Rosa, who had once bragged to mother that the hardest job she had was to teach the Wilbur family to say "thank you." As we stood waiting for Mateo to come back from the creek, Pa put me down, unsaddled Diamante, and adjusted the saddle blankets that were slipping from under the saddle. I walked around stretching my aching legs and looking at the different groups of people who were forming and shifting in preparation to leave, and telling one another, "*Hasta luego!*" and "*Hasta la otra vista.*"

At the trunk of the cottonwood trees where the fonda had been was a group of vaqueros. One vaquero was strumming a guitar, and their laughing and talking gave the place a carnival air. Here where only a few minutes before there had been nothing but cursing and anger amidst the sweat and hard work, there was nothing but an air of friendship and happiness now after a job done well. Ramón came by to talk to Father again, so I moved about, enjoying the sight of the rodeo grounds now turned into an amusement park. There was Don Julián shaking hands and thanking the boys for patronizing the fonda.

I heard Ramón telling Father something about a serenade. The boys were composing something, he said. They would probably serenade

Phoebe for scolding Father, I thought. And I remembered the day I talked to my grandmother about the man who had serenaded Juana on San Juan Day, and how she explained to me that someday a young man would serenade me, too, but not before I was fifteen years old, a señorita.

Ramón went back toward the cottonwood where the boys were composing their song. Maybe for Virginia. She was the sweetest lady, people often said. Father called me, "Come quick, Eva." He put me back on Diamante and told me to head the cattle back toward the partida. I rode south away from the vaqueros, avoiding them as much as I could. They had not talked to me. I was a niña. Only Damián and Ramón had been good to me. Well, to hell with them all, I thought, rebelliously. I with my little hand had beaten back a 700-pound vicious cow—they had not done that.

I could see a line of men standing along the bank, and as the cattle began to move in that direction I was forced to face them. All the vaqueros suddenly waved at me with both hands. Ah! Maybe they did like me. "Stop now, Eva," said Father. "Face the vaqueros and raise your hand. But don't wave. Just hold your hand high." I didn't like this greeting; it was the Indian way. But I looked questioningly toward him and held my scrawny hand up. They all began to sing to the accompaniment of two guitars. All I could hear of my first serenade was "Adiós, Evita," and the pounding of my own heart against my chest keeping time.

When the song ended Ramón dispersed the vaqueros with a sweep of his hand. They scattered in different directions and as I stood there I looked around and noticed that everyone had already left the rodeo ground. The herd was heading east toward the big ranch and Don Julián's wagon was trundling up the road across the creek.

Damián was the last man walking south and waving at me. I forgot that Father had told me not to wave my hand, and I waved back as he and his packhorse disappeared down the slope. Then I turned and walked Diamante across the little clearing. What change!, as my grandfather always said. The amusement park was now an empty desolate stretch of ground. "It is a continous change, *siempre un cambio.* ¡Ay! ¡Ay!"

A Surprise! A Surprise!

WE DROVE THE PARTIDA INTO THE HOME PASTURE and left it there, but we kept driving the packhorses that carried the bedrolls of Uncle Luis and Tom Ewell. As we neared the stable I could see Grandfather running from the house to open the corral gate. The five of us driving in and dismounting all at once caused quite a commotion. Father sat on the workbench and was kicking off his chaps and talking to Mateo at the same time when Grandfather came in and called to him, "A surprise, Agustín! A surprise for you!"

"Oh, Pa, save it for some other time. We're tired and in a hurry to unsaddle before it gets dark on us."

"Oh no, *hijo*, a surprise like this one can't wait."

Mateo was trying to get a drink of water at the faucet and Tom and Uncle Luis were getting the bedrolls down and stumbling in the already dark stable. Grandfather pushed his way between them to get to Father, saying, "*Tu mama vinó* (Your mother has come), Agustín; El Prieto Murrieta brought her in the little buggy this morning soon after you left."

"Mat," Father was saying, "that gelding can stay, *¿qué, qué?*—what, what?" Father suddenly boomed out in the middle of his unfinished sentence. He jumped from the bench and stood with his hands on his hips staring at Grandfather. Mateo spewed out the water and dropped the can. "What's the matter, Agustín, hombre? Looks like you have been struck by lightning."

"Your mamá, Agustín," Grandfather said again, a little short of breath. "She is here! She came in the stage, and then el Prieto brought her." Father stared at Grandfather, his gaze so intense I thought it would pin Grandfather to the ground. Not so. They stood like that until Grandfather somehow disappeared in the midst of all this activity. Father roused himself at last and asked, "Where did the old man go?"

"He went back to the house," said Mateo. "He really did surprise you. I'd even say he stunned you." Father seemed to have nothing to say.

"Come on Gus, aren't you happy to find your mother waiting for you?"

"Let's face it, Mat. We are earthy people and my mother doesn't fit here. She makes a nuisance of herself, and I never wanted her to come here. You'll see."

"Yes, we'll see, we'll see, Agustín."

"Let's go in, Mat. Come on, Eva."

I knew Father was very disturbed, because whenever we went anywhere riding or walking Father would always point out the trail and say to me, "Follow the trail, Eva. Come on, lead the way." If there was no trail he would point at some tree or rock and tell me, "Go straight to that tree, then turn to your right, then walk straight ahead." I would often lose the way or the trail and then Father would scold in his usual way, "Are you blind? Can't you see the trail? Don't you have any sense of direction?" But tonight he just took hold of my scrawny hand and led me out of the corral. This was the first time I had ever felt Father's big strong hand over mine, and I felt a great sense of security. I took long strides trying hard to keep up with him, lest he let go of my hand. As we arrived at the wall, Father and Mateo suddenly stopped. The kitchen was lit up with candles and lamps.

"Oh, yes!" said Mateo, peering in at my Grandmother Wilbur across the short distance. "That's the woman my ugk tells us about. He often describes her for us, and if you hadn't told me it was your mother, I would have known her anyway by my ugk's description. He tells us how she used to go with Dr. Wilbur on long trips searching for the Papago Indian children who were so often stolen and sold during the Apache Indian raids, how they would go far into Sonora and bring back the children to their parents. No wonder the Indians loved your parents, Agustín. It took a lot of nerve for such a woman to go through that hot desert country alone with her husband, miles from nowhere. My ugk told me she was just a young girl, Agustín. She had to be brave!"

"Come, Eva," said Father. "Let me put you up here so you can see what your grandmother looks like." He lifted me up to the wall and I sat staring. "She looks like the Noneña, Pa!"

"Mrs. Bernard, Eva," said Father, "not Noneña."

"I know, Pa, I know. But she looks like her. Doesn't she, Pa?"

"Yes, Eva—except my mother does not *ever* unbend."

I kept trying to talk to Father, but he didn't seem to hear me. He was talking to Mateo, so I watched the scene in the kitchen. Emilia Rosa was talking to Grandmother Wilbur who sat very straight with her hands on her lap. Her black hair was done up in a French roll with bangs dropping in curls over her pale, white forehead. Her white blouse had very wide cuffs with white buttons on the side.

At the Feast of the Holy Cross I heard John Bogan telling Dan Russel that when Grandfather Wilbur was living my grandmother had been the most beautiful woman in the Territory. I didn't think she was beautiful at all. She obviously didn't know how to dress. Someday when I grew up I would wear lots of lace and dainty things, never wide cuffs and big hairpins like she had.

My Grandmother Margarita and Aunt Rita were busy at the stove, and Mother sat across from Grandmother Wilbur holding William on her lap, looking almost like Wahyanita's Aunt Tula, the Papago woman—tired and awkward and none too clean. I felt sorry for her. There was Emilia Rosa, talking and entertaining Grandmother Wilbur and my own mother looking like an Indian! I would have to speak to her about all this. If she could just get rid of William she could have more time for herself. "Pa," I said, "why did Mother have to take William just because the doctor brought him here? Couldn't she tell him to take him away? He could give him to someone else, couldn't he?"

"Your little brother?" said Father, shocked. "Your little brother belongs here with you and Ruby. Do you understand me?"

"Yes, Pa." I fell silent, listening to Mateo talk about the sad stories he had heard from his father about my grandparents: how the doctor had struggled, how he fought for the Indians, how he took care of the sick without pay. "I never thought I would meet your mother, Agustín. I'll have to tell my ugk. He will like to know that your mother came back to visit the old home. And now I'm going to clean up a bit and I'll meet you later, Gus."

"All right, but don't be too long, Mat. We're going to have supper in a few minutes." Mateo jumped down from the wall and hurried toward the washroom.

"Eva," said Father, "you address your grandmother as 'Grandmother,' not 'Ma' like you do Grandmother Margarita. Will you remember that?"

"Yes, Pa, I promise."

We walked into the kitchen, Father still holding my hand.

"Hijo, hijo!" cried Grandmother Wilbur. Father picked her up, and after their warm greeting ended, he turned and introduced me. "My daughter, Eva." My grandmother took both my hands and told me that she heard I had been trampled by a cow.

"No, Grandmother," I said, "that's not true. I cut her face all to pieces and she ran right back to the *partida.*"

She laughed and wanted to know just how I had cut up a cow's face. "With your nails? or with what?"

"Of course not. You don't cut up a cow with your nails. You do that with a knife or something sharp. I cut her nose with the edge of a bucket and she ran back to the *partida* bleeding and squirting manure all over herself." There was a deathly silence. I looked around at all of them, puzzled, and suddenly everybody burst into hilarious laughter, except Father and my Grandmother Wilbur who said, "My, I didn't think I had such a rugged granddaughter."

"With a father like him," I said, touching my Father's arm, "you have to be tough."

"Come on, Mother." Father led the way to the sala as I followed, curious and inquisitive as I always was.

Grandmother sat in the big chair, Father at her feet on the ottoman. "Tell me, Mother, how is my sister, Mary?"

"She is fine, Agustín. She is now working for the railroad at Randolph's offices in downtown Tucson. She does very well and they like her work, but I wanted Mary to be a teacher, Agustín. There are always men around the offices, you know."

"Eva, go clean up for supper, Daughter."

"Yes, Papa." I ran back to the kitchen where Mother grabbed me with such force it startled me. "You be careful how you talk, Tonta. The idea, telling your grandmother that the cow squirted manure all over herself and bragging that you cut her up!"

"But I did, Ma."

"You did not. You threw up your hands and lucky for you and for us, you happened to hit her."

"I *didn't* throw my hands up! I let her have it!"

"Don't talk like that."

"What's the matter with you, Ma? You're tired, carrying that screechy baby. Why don't you give him away to Doña Tomaza or somebody and clean up. You look like Tula!"

I was lucky again. Mateo and Tom Ewell came in just then and Grandfather asked them to sit in the zaguán while Grandmother Margarita and Aunt Rita set the table. "We'd like to help, Pa," said Tom, so Grandfather had them bring in the chairs from the zaguán and told them where to place them and where they would sit at the table.

I slipped away unnoticed to the washroom, tired, hurt, and angry. First, Damián was gone. I had walked away from the rodeo ground with a lump in my throat big enough to choke a horse, all the time pretending that I didn't even notice he had left, because I knew that my father would be angry if I acted as if I cared. Then to come home and find a second Noneña here, and, worst of all, my mother angry at me because I had talked "like that." I had never talked any other way, and now all of a sudden I wasn't supposed to talk "like that." What the hell was it all about? I knew with absolute certainty that I was going to cry, and I knew I had better have something real to cry about, for Father would demand to know what I was crying for. I picked up the pretty pitcher with the violet flowers on it and looked at it. It matched the big washbasin. Too bad! I hit the floor with it, hard. I ran back to the kitchen, crying my heart out.

"What's the matter?" Grandfather and my mother asked both at the same time. Tom Ewell came to my rescue. "Everything is the matter. She is tired, worn out, and her nerves are all shot to hell. Even a fifty-year-old man doesn't work any harder than this five-year-old!"

"I agree with you, hijo," said Grandfather. "I agree. But you know her father!" By now Father was at my side, sure enough, demanding to know what had happened. "I broke Mother's pitcher," I cried.

"What did you break it for?" demanded Mother.

"I just dropped it!"

Father was exasperated. "You know you don't have to cry because you broke the pitcher! I don't care *what* you break as long as *you* don't break! You are not supposed to cry over nothing. You understand?"

"Yes, Pa." But I continued to cry, and finally Grandmother Wilbur told Father she thought that I must be suffering from shock. Father stopped scolding me and told me gently to go and sit next to Grandmother Wilbur. Barreplata had come to my side and I said, still sobbing, "But I want to sit next to Tata."

"You will sit where I tell you," he said in the stern voice that always frightened me. I moved, but Barreplata quickly changed places with Uncle Luis so as to be next to me also. "Rafaelita," he said to Grandmother Wilbur, "she has been taught to be self-willed by none other than her father."

"I can see," said Grandmother, "I can see."

"Well, you will have to put up with these *malcriadas,* my ill-bred little girls," said Father defensively.

"Don't worry, hijo," said Grandmother, "I am very grateful to have had the opportunity to come back to the old home that is so full of memories for me and to find you and your family so well."

"Your being here brings back memories for us also, Rafaelita," said Grandfather. He went on to tell Tom Ewell, who had just been introduced to Grandmother Wilbur, how she and the doctor used to cook big vats of rice to feed the Indians. From there the talk turned to Indians and to the many problems my Grandfather Wilbur had when he was Indian agent.

Grandfather reminisced, "Those were wonderful days when the doctor was here with us and Agustín was still riding his broomstick horse. Do you remember, Rafaelita, when you and the doctor went to Sonora in search of the Papago Indian children the Apaches had stolen and taken across the line?"

"How can I ever forget it, Don Francisco. It almost killed us. There were no roads, no water, no food, and the heat was terrific."

Barreplata interrupted. "I knew how bad it must have been when I saw the doctor getting down from the wagon when you got back. 'Don Francisco,' I said, 'I think the doctor is sick,' and he said, 'He's just worn out, Barra. That back country is a killer!'"

"That it is, Barreplata," said Grandmother. "It was a terrible trip, but I am glad I went. I would do it again if I could. We came back through the little town of El Saric, down to the Jarillas Ranch, then all the way down to Oro Blanco. There we met Don Pedro Acosta and he greeted us by saying, 'You are pretty lucky people! It must be fun to run all over the country and get paid for it, too!' Imagine, Tom!" said Grandmother to Tom Ewell, who had been fascinated and had kept asking her questions. "To think it was *fun* for us to go miles across those Apache-infested mountains in the heat of summer! Of course we were glad to be back with all of the children who had been stolen, except one. But certainly we didn't have 'fun,' and the doctor was not given transportation by the government to go anywhere. Fortunately, Cruz had agreed to go with us. He knew the country and the people, and that was half the battle."

"Did you go on horseback?" asked Tom.

"No, Tom, we had a wagon. My husband spent three days frantically looking for a wagon and not finding one. He finally remembered Cruz and thought he would let us have his small wagon. As luck would have it, the following day Cruz came by on his way to Arivaca to get the mail and he asked him. Cruz laughed and said, 'Yes, you can have the wagon and me, too, because you're going to need a lot of help.' The doctor told me that since Cruz was going I could stay at home, but I just wouldn't think of it. You know, Margarita," she said to my other grandmother, "I always had a terrible premonition that someday something would happen to my husband and that I wouldn't be there to help him."

"Did you, Rafaelita?"

"Yes, I always felt he wouldn't be long with us, so I insisted on going to Sonora with him. Once that was settled I cooked, and washed, and I packed food and bedding and clothing for all three of us, and the following morning we left at dawn. By noon we were across the line just below Sasabe. As soon as we got to a shady place Cruz pulled to the side of the road and unhitched the team. We had lunch there and stayed out of the heat of the day. But once we left the vicinity of Sasabe it was work every inch of the way. One man would drive and the other would walk ahead blazing a trail. Sometimes both of the men would work moving rocks, filling holes, leveling ditches, cutting down banks, and making slopes so the wagon could go up or down while I drove the team. And so we went at a snail's pace. We came to Jesús Manzanares' ranchito just before sundown.

"These people were very poor, but they were lovely. There were Jesús, a very young man, and his wife Panchita, who was expecting, and her mother, Doña Lolita, who had come to stay with her daughter to serve as midwife. They also had Nachito, a young man who helped with the chores.

"Cruz knew the Manzanares so they immediately began to give him directions, trying to tell him where we could find the children. The woman added plates to the table and made me feel at home. And Nachito took care of our horses so that all we had to do was clean up and then relax. For dinner we had corn on the cob and spare ribs, *calabacitas* (zucchinis), and tapioca pudding. And truly delightful talk. I was so happy for the doctor because it had been such a difficult day for him. After dinner Nachito carted in a barrel of water and sprinkled their patio, and in no time, all the beds were being hauled outside. I laughed to myself when I saw Doña Lolita walking around putting a fan on each bed. But it really was unbearably hot. I asked her if she wasn't afraid to sleep outside. 'Oh, no,' she said. 'The dogs are good watchdogs and it is very peaceful. It is not like in town. When we were in Guaymas it was so noisy! It took me a week to get used to the noise. But here in this country it is different—peaceful and quiet.'

"Agustín, hijo, no sooner did we go to bed than all the calves in the corral began to bawl, the dogs barked and coyotes howled, and at the corner of the corral there was a big hackberry tree where an owl had settled for the night, and it called and called, and another owl answered from the nearby hills. A burro brayed so close I thought he was in the patio. Your father whispered in my ear, 'So this is what Lolita calls peaceful and quiet!' However, he did finally get a few hours' sleep. I myself, I remember, was dropping off to sleep when the roosters began to crow. I never heard so many roosters. Some would stop crowing and others would begin. I heard Cruz laughing at the far end of the patio, so I knew he hadn't slept either. Finally, everything, even the roosters, had just gone quiet when Doña Lolita came tiptoeing to my bed and whispered 'Rafaelita, my daughter has been in labor all night.'

"'I'll wake up the doctor, Lolita. Don't you worry.' But she left my bed wringing her hands."

"What a lovely night," said Barreplata.

"It was a nightmare! But you remember the doctor, Barreplata. He never complained. He was patient and kind and by sunup both mother and child were resting easy."

By now I had relaxed, listening to Grandmother talk and to everybody laughing and sympathizing with her. I was beginning to think she was a human being with feelings like everybody else. She had been in Tres Bellotas. I knew where that was. When we had gone to the Cochis Ranch, Father pointed out to me the black mountain and had told me that the Tres Bellotas was at its base.

My grandmother continued her tale. "Immediately after breakfast I began to pack our belongings, but the doctor came in and stopped me. 'You know,' he said, looking at the bundles I had piled on the bed, 'we can't leave today. We have to see how the patient gets along.

It just doesn't look right to take off as if we didn't care.' So I pretended that I too didn't care when we left, when as a matter of fact I was fighting back my tears like a silly ten-year-old girl. Jesús came in and nailed up a sheet for a screen and then ordered both of us to bed.

"I slept at last, and when I woke up the doctor had already gone to help Jesús who was repairing their corral. Lolita was fixing something to eat for some Indians who were on their way to Pitiquito and had stopped to beg for food. They told the doctor that there were three Indian children at Sasabe and that they knew exactly where they were. One of them would go with Cruz, they said, and help bring back the children for one dollar.

"Cruz and the Indian man left on horseback leading one packhorse and going all the way back to Sasabe. Nachito had long since left, having gone to bring back another of the stolen children, an Indian boy that Jesús knew was at a ranch fifteen miles northwest of the Manzanares Ranch.

"The Indian woman and two boys made themselves at home under the hackberry tree, and Jesús took them some beans and cheese and a large pot for them to cook in. All these doings made me feel that we were not ever going to be able to leave early on the following day.

"Jesús was a proud and happy new father and he kept us laughing all the afternoon with his good humor and amusing stories.

"Nachito returned late in the afternoon, bringing with him a ten-year-old, Felipe Luna, an Indian boy who refused to talk. When spoken to, he would put his arms between his legs and his head between his arms and stay in that position. The doctor finally took him outside where the boy ate his supper. Then Jesús tied him loosely to a post in the patio where we could keep an eye on him. We slept on and off and listened for Cruz, but he did not come. The following day about nine o'clock the dogs startled us and we ran outside. They were coming single file with the children riding behind their saddles and one very small child tied to the Indian man's back. 'If that isn't worth a dollar!' said the doctor, laughing. 'We won't be going back empty-handed, Rafaelita!'

"We left the Manzanares Ranch loaded with six young roosters and plenty of roasted jerky and white rice and a bag of corn to feed the roosters on the way.

"That night we camped on the banks of the Saric Wash. The men unhitched the team for the night and again we tied poor Felipe, this time to the wagon wheel. He seemed to get more wild as time went on. The following day we picked up two more of the children: six children now to feed besides the three of us. We were running out of food and the children were beginning to beg for water. We arrived again at the outskirts of the town of Saric well after sunset. Cruz killed two of the roosters and warmed some beans and tortillas Lolita had packed for us. The children ate, stretched out on the ground, and went to sleep, and there was no waking them up. That was the biggest bed-wetting clutch of children I had ever seen, and we were the worst-smelling group that had ever walked up that wash.

"Life is so hard in that country! We saw three young men driving three burros loaded with wood. They had no shoes, no shirts, no hats, but each carried a long stick and now and then they would poke the burros and urge them, calling 'Burro, burro!' They disappeared down the bank, but we could still hear the gutteral sound for a long time, ''Urro, 'urro, 'urro.'

"We arrived at Saric hoping to buy some groceries, but they told us that we would have to put an order for the groceries we wanted. They would order them and we could call for them in ten days! So Cruz went a mile down the arroyo to a milpita, and there he managed to buy a sack of green corn. While he was gone, the doctor bought three large flour-sacks from a woman who was washing at the stream. We cut them up and made loincloths for the children, and that's the way we were able to wash their ragged little dresses. Cruz came back and boiled some corn on the cob for supper. Then he went to several different houses inquiring about more Indian children. He came back into camp leading three more hungry children and carrying some corn tortillas and a mess of ribs he had bought somewhere.

"We left Saric before sunup and arrived at the Tres Bellotas Ranch late in the afternoon. My serious-minded husband and sober old Cruz were both acting like children, capering and singing, 'We're home in the Territorio!' I waited with the children in the corral, watching the different animals milling about and bawling for water, pawing the ground and raising clouds of dust. Porfirio had been away and the water trough was empty. Three dogs came, barking viciously, but Cruz talked to them and I guess they recognized him, for they quieted down and followed him to the house. Cruz began digging a hole below the dirt floor and he soon caved his way in.

"'No, no, Cruz!' said the doctor, horrified at the break in.

"'Sí, sí,' said Cruz. 'There is coffee inside and mi compadre Porfirio always has plenty of tobacco.'

"We spread the tarp by the side of the house while Cruz built a fire and ground some coffee. He pounded jerky and slammed the oven door, and finally he came out carrying a small table and a couple of benches. We had a delicious dinner of cazuela, white rice, beans, stewed dried fruit, and the best biscuits I ever ate.

"We went to bed but stayed awake listening for Porfirio. The crescent moon was already going down over toward the Mexican border when we heard the wagon trundling down the hill toward the corral. We heard Cruz open the gate and greet Porfirio and we could hear them quitely visiting over a late snack. There was the murmur of voices and finally loud laughter. All was well! We slept so soundly that Cruz had to awaken us the next morning.

"Porfirio had a nice breakfast ready for us—twelve people for breakfast, Margarita!"

"I am sure that he didn't mind a bit, Rafaelita," said my Grandmother Margarita. "Porfirio is a good man and willing to help whenever he can."

"Yes, Margarita, he actually brought us home. Without his help we would have wrecked the wagon, and I am certain I would have perished."

"You would almost certainly have wrecked that wagon, Rafaelita," said Grandfather. "That is very rough country. You remember Don Antonio Aros? He had a herd of one thousand goats right there at the *pantano,* the swampy area right over there. He decided to take the herd up to the Cochis Ranch for the winter. They tried to take the camp up there on a buckboard and they turned it over just past the Jarillas Ranch on that high hill. That buckboard is still there."

"I believe it, Don Francisco. You know, that very hill you are talking about was the worst we had to climb.

"We left the Tres Bellotas Ranch riding in the wagon with Porfirio following us on his horse. Traveling was difficult all the way, even when we could travel normally. But climbing up that hill, Cruz and Porfirio actually had to hold up the wagon while the doctor drove it at a snail's pace. I'll never forget those steep sharp slopes with those enormous boulders that had to be moved from the path of the wagon, only to drive it up a few more feet to a ditch, or loose rocks, or some more boulders. And then *those* had to be moved!

"I watched those poor men struggling so hard while I brought up the rear with nine children howling like little coyotes. I had to carry the little ones and go back for others who were much to small to climb by themselves. Even the five-year-olds stumbled and fell and cried and yelled, all at the same time. Really, Mateo," said Grandmother Wilbur, turning toward Mateo, who had been all attention, he was so fascinated by this tale, "I feared for my sanity. The children were so hungry and thirsty and then they were all scratched and bruised, and most of them had been bone-tired even before we had found them.

"I was left at the bottom of the mountain with Porfirio's horse and we again had Felipe tied up under the shade of an old tree. I sat waiting for the rest of the children to get down, one at a time. I kept looking up at that wagon, skirting the slope of the mountain like a fly crawling on the side of a wall, and I began reciting my rosary. I was so afraid the wagon would fall on those men. I didn't even hear the children anymore. I just stood holding my breath and praying, 'Hail Mary full of grace, the Lord is with thee . . . Cecilia, stop! . . . Blessed art thou amongst the women . . . Felipe, leave that child alone! . . . and I finally finished my Hail Mary just as the wagon reached the path and stopped. I knew I was going to cry and I dropped the rosary beads in the cup of my hand and held onto them tightly. Well, I didn't actually sob, but my abominable tears burst out and there was nothing I could do about it. The poor children, upon seeing me crying, stopped their yelling at last and just stood looking at me. It was like a lull in the storm, and at the moment I remember thinking 'Someday we'll laugh at this,' but, you know, I haven't yet really found any humor in that experience!

"I saw Cruz and Porfirio coming down to help us up the rocky slope, and I quickly wiped away all signs of tears with my fingers. The children smiled happily, knowing we were going on, and were quick to forget, as children do. The doctor had stayed with the wagon and I was glad he didn't choose to come down. Cruz carried two little children and Porfirio took three of them on the horse, and I followed, actually crawling up that dangerous rock pile. As the men reached the rim of the mountain, going back down for the rest of the children, I saw my poor husband coming down to help me up the last few feet. 'That was great driving, my dear,' I said to the doctor, pretending that I had not once thought of any danger.

"'It will be easier traveling now and we'll soon be home, my brave one,' he said to me, holding my hand. I kept silent and never let him know how cowardly I had behaved.

"The trail down the arroyo, by contrast, was a *camino real,* a royal highway. We watered the horses at the Jarillas Ranch and fed the children some burritos that Porfirio had prepared for us. He planned on going back to Tres Bellotas from the ranch, but Cruz begged him to go with us as far as Oro Blanco because there were some more bad places ahead. So Porfirio again tied his horse to the tailgate and we plodded along, stopping often to remove rocks, cut brush, fill ditches, and many other things that we could not have foreseen. But our greatest difficulties were behind us.

"We finally arrived at Oro Blanco and were watering the team and looking like what we were—a group of bedraggled refugees—when Don Pedro Acosta came by. He stopped to tell us condescendingly how 'lucky' we were, gadding about and getting paid for it! I was furious! I turned away, ignoring him, and busied myself washing the children at the water trough until he left. The heat was scorching, and I let the children play in the cool water while the man walked up to the ranch house where the Bogans were butchering a young heifer. The doctor bought half the beef, and as they loaded the beef and the children in the wagon, Cruz and the doctor again talked Porfirio out of starting back to Tres Bellotas. 'Get your rest tonight with us, Porfirio, and you can go back early in the morning,' said the doctor. And so again Porfirio tied his bay to the tailgate and we started out on the home stretch.

"Our problem now was what to do with the children for the night. Should we keep them at the ranch or take them to the Guijas Village? But lucky for us we arrived to find Martin Mariano, your father, Mateo, waiting for us. He had been gone to Sonoita for a long time, and we didn't expect to find him here. And Martin was so good, Agustín. He hurried us into the house and just took over. He and Cruz and Porfirio went to work in the patio, and in no time we had a great dinner with all the trimmings, saguaro wine, saguaro jam, and some fresh pitayas that Mariano had brought."

"All right, girls," said Father, as Grandmother Wilbur finally sat silent, "Your grandmother will have more stories for you tomorrow, but now you must go to bed. Eva, you're very tired."

"I'm not tired, Pa."

"Go to bed, mijita," and I knew he meant it.

Aunt Rita took us to bed and when we entered the room I saw another bed there. "Where did that bed come from, Rita?"

"That's your grandmother's bed and never mind the questions. Tomorrow you can ask me and I'll tell you."

"And all that is hers too?" I asked, pointing at the small table covered with a white oilcloth and a mirror resting on its center and already nailed to the wall.

"Yes," said Aunt Rita, "and don't you dare touch anything. Just go to sleep and don't be getting up, mind you." Ruby went to sleep as soon as she put her head on the pillow, but I got down from my bed and went toward the alien table, tiptoeing, stopping between each step, always listening for someone coming. I finally stood before the table, examining every object. There was a glass bottle full of cotton balls, a pink bottle full of water, and a very small washbasin, like a toy. There were small boxes of powder and some jars of white salve. Lying on the foot of the new bed was a white nightgown with small blue ribbons and a small jacket of white lace. I picked it up and held it against my own body and I looked in the mirror. My heart pounded. Someday! Someday there would come a change. That's what Grandfather always said. "*¡En lo futuro un cambio por seguro!*" Right now I would like to know where that bed had come from. The only one I could ask right now was Ruby. She would know and this time Ruby would wake up—I would see to it. She didn't. I left off shaking her and went to look over some suitcases and a big box. I opened it and there was a large brown hat with red-brown roses scattered down the sloping brim, a brown ribbon, and some feathers and a brown veil. I wanted to try it on, but I heard steps coming and I hurried back to bed. Grandmother came in and I pretended I was asleep, but I peeked out as she undressed and dressed in her nightgown all at the same time, without my ever seeing her actually undressed. She sat at the table and poured some water in the toy washbasin, took a ball of cotton, dipped it in the water, and cleaned her face. Then with a very small towel she wiped her face dry and smeared some white salve all over it. She took out a brush and brushed her hair. She put the brush away and sat pinching her fingertips for awhile, then stood up, and put on the white lace jacket. It was very beautiful, not at all like the faded brown nightgown my mother wore all the time. Grandmother walked to the suitcases, and, picking up a little one, she took out of it a small pink pillow, threw a newspaper down by the side of the bed and dropped the pillow on top of it. She knelt down on the pillow holding her white rosary beads. I watched through slitted eyes. I finally slept, and woke up again, and the white figure was still on her knees. "Grand-mother," I said, "if you don't go to bed it will be time to get up."

"And what are you doing awake?"

"I was asleep but I woke up. I was awake before you went to pray, and I saw you pinching your fingertips. Nobody does that. Do they?"

"You go to sleep this minute, young lady."

I turned to the wall and slept.

We Visit the Punta de Agua

THE FOLLOWING TEN DAYS WERE PAINFULLY DIFFICULT for me. Every
word I spoke was vulgar, in bad taste, and if I kept silent, the
silence was offensive too. Grandmother told me that children were to
be seen and not heard, but that I was one who should be *neither* seen
nor heard—a monstrosity to be kept hidden.

In working with the animals we called a spade a spade. It had never
dawned on us that some words we knew were not to be used at all.
So how did we say things? Did we point? Use sign language, or what?
It was in using these forbidden words that I disgraced myself with
Grandmother Wilbur beyond forgiveness.

Because I had stayed awake until the early morning hours that first
night that Grandmother had shared our bedroom, I slept late. When
at last I woke up, the lateness startled me and I hurried to the kitchen
full of questions, but there was so much going on by then I had no
time to ask anything. In the kitchen, Grandfather and Tom Ewell were
still drinking coffee and smoking at the table. I heard Tom say, "*La
viuda!* This widow has a classic beauty that is stunning. Strange she
didn't marry again."

"They are very difficult people to get along with," answered Grandfather. "Proud people are no good, hijo. Just no good."

I walked into the kitchen. "Where is everybody, Grandfather?"

"Well, your father went to get the saddle horses to take your beautiful
grandmother for a ride down to the Punta de Agua." The Punta de
Agua was a small ranch that Cruz had long ago begun to homestead
for my Grandfather Wilbur.

"I guess I'll be going too, huh, Grandfather?"

"*Como no*, of course."

I left the kitchen in search of Mother and met Grandmother Wilbur coming in from her early morning walk. She was dressed in a long blue kimono that had a row of pink roses down the front. Her black hair looked beautiful against that particular blue. "Where do you think you are going dressed like that, Grandmother?"

"Does that mean 'good morning,' Eva?"

"Good morning, Grandmother," I said and I ran on toward the corral, where I had a head-on collision with Mateo who was going to the kitchen to get the milk pail to milk the goats. "How come you're going to milk the goats, Mat?" I asked him, rubbing my head.

"Barra is busy getting wood," he told me.

"I'll wait here for you," I said. He surprised me a moment later by returning with Grandmother Wilbur who wanted to see our goat herd. Mateo began by explaining to her which were the milk goats. "The Nubians," he said, "are very good milk goats."

"What about the Angoras, Mateo?"

"Their milk is not so rich. They are for wool only," and he pointed out some Angoras with such long coats that only their toes showed. A small *lepe*, a motherless kid, came begging to be fed and Mateo picked it up and continued to talk to Grandmother. Much of what he said went over my head, but I definitely heard him telling Grandmother that the Nubians had developed "two laps" and I had never heard that word before. Mateo had said "dewlaps" but I had heard "two laps." Ruby and I called the skin that hangs under their throats "little tits" and since no one had ever corrected us we thought that was the right name.

"The Angoras," Mateo went on, "don't have them."

"They do too have them, Mateo," I said. "All of them do. What's the matter with you, hombre?" I asked, sure that he was now talking about the reproductive organs of the males.

"No, they don't, Bonnie."

"Didn't we just castrate fifty little Angoras?"

"Eva!" said Grandmother. "Ladies don't talk like that, young lady!"

"Well, Grandmother," I said, "the Angoras do have two laps. They all do." Just then two Angora bucks locked horns and the younger buck pushed the older one back toward us. He stood there, braced, his two hind legs wide apart and his genitals exposed to full view.

Pointing at the spectacle I said, "There, Grandmother, there you have two laps." Grandmother took me by the throat with such a powerful grip I thought she would choke me to death. She pushed me against the corral fence and, holding me there, said with a fierce and frightening softness, "I would like to pull out your tongue and cut it in little pieces." She gave me one final shove against the fence and, picking up the front of her skirt, she went back toward the house, running lightly and jumping over rocks and sticks. I looked up at Mateo and his complexion had turned the leather-red that he seemed to don whenever he was choking with laughter. I buried my face in the spaces between the fence logs and cried.

"Come, Bonnie, don't cry. You know your father doesn't like for you to cry."

"But I don't know what to do, Mateo. My mother scolded me last night for talking "like that" and I don't know what she means. I always talked like that and it was all right and now it isn't. And this Noneña wants to pull my tongue out, Ruby doesn't speak to me except to call me *loca*, and my father, he's going to whip me with the reata, and that hurts, Mateo! It is like a cut with a knife every time he hits, and he hits and hits, and I get welts and my skin turns purple!"

Mateo pulled me away from the fence and finally said, "Bonnie, your father is not going to whip you." He picked up the hungry kid at his feet. "Look, Bonnie, see this skin that hangs under the throat of this little *lepe*? These are called 'dewlaps'."

"I see," I said, and I stood looking at Mateo and feeling embarrassed at having been so stupid. "I didn't know, Mateo. I can't help it, I just didn't know, but if my father whips me I am going to run away."

"Where will you go?"

"Up to the mountain. I have a house up there and I am not afraid to be alone. I talk to the animals. They are my friends."

"What kind of a house do you have up there and where exactly is it?"

"It is made out of rocks, you know, and it's at the Encino Spring. You can see it from here. I like it up there, me and the roadrunner and Cafecita, that goat there," I said, pointing to one standing only three feet from us, "and the skunk, Valentina—she comes too. And then I have Diamante, you know. The eagles, too. They come down to water at the spring and I watch them from the rock. I'm not afraid of them. I can kill an eagle. I'll just twist its neck and it'll be dead."

"No, Bonnie, an eagle can rip you with her talons and you can bleed to death, so don't ever try that. Do you hear me, Bonnie? And anyway, your father would find you and bring you back."

"No, he'll never find me. I can get right under that big rock. There is a big hole under it. I have to crawl in, but when I'm inside I can stand up. It's just like a little house."

Father drove the saddle horses up to the corral just then, and Mateo hurried to help him.

I followed at a distance. I stayed inside the barn, my ears glued to the corrugated iron wall. I could hear them talking, but I couldn't hear what they said. After what seemed a long time I heard my father laughing. I clapped my hands silently. He was not going to whip me? Mateo laughed, too, and then both of them were suddenly laughing. I ran out and down the bank. It would never do for my father to find me eavesdropping. I ran down the river and came up to the goats' corral from the south. Father and Mateo were coming up to the house now, and Father met me at the gate. "Did you have a fight with your grandmother, Eva?"

"No, Pa."

"Now you listen. She'll be going back very soon, so be patient and help me with her so I won't have to run her off, won't you?"

"Yes, Pa."

"You don't need to talk to her except when she asks you something, then you can answer 'yes, ma'am' or 'no ma'am,' but don't you talk to her, all right? So get your shoes on now and come on."

"Yes, Pa."

"Agustín, Agustín," Grandfather arrived, out of breath, from across the creek. "I have another surprise for you, hijo."

"No more surprises, Pa, please."

"Cipriano came yesterday, hijo, and he brought you Moraga's bed, clean and shining. We put it in the girl's room and your mother slept on it last night, and now you can tell her that she slept on her ancestor's bed. Cipriano was very glad that you got that job for Damián, you know."

"My mother'll love a surprise like that, Pa." We were in the kitchen now and Father went on to see Grandmother. I stayed to talk to Mother. Mateo and Mike began unloading the buckboard outside. "Where are they going, Ma?"

"They are going to get some agave so we can make *biguata* for your Grandmother."

"And, Ma, what's a *viuda?*"

"A woman whose husband has died."

"Last night she prayed all night, Ma, and she pinched her fingers for a long time."

"She was tapering her fingers so they'll look pointed and not square like a man's fingers," said Mother. After that, for a long time I would lie in the dark tapering my own fingers, but with all the hard work I had to do my fingers didn't seem to respond to tapering, and I finally gave up.

Father came out hurriedly. "Just a minute, Mat!" he called, and we heard him telling Mateo to stop at Jesús Moraga's and tell him that Grandmother Wilbur was here for a few days, and that if he cared to come over to see her he could. "And before you go, help me get out of here, Mat."

"Sure, Gus, sure."

"What's the matter with Father, Ma? What does he want that old goat to come over here for?"

"You be careful how you talk about that man. Your father and your grandmother think the world of him, and besides, he is a very nice man."

Don Jesús Moraga wore a heavy black beard that covered all of his face from his eyes down. A pinkish ball stuck out of the black hair in the center of his face—that was his nose. From under his bushy eyebrows, his piercing black eyes danced like beads of mercury. His forehead was very narrow and white, and everybody but me thought him a very dignified man. "Look," said Mike, "the *tatarabuelo* (great great-grandfather) of that man was sent here by the King of Spain as a conquistador."

"He still looks like a *petochi*," I said, "just like a devil!"

Father and Grandmother came out, ready to go. "Ready, Eva?" asked Father, and I nodded.

"Is she going with us, Agustín?"

"Of course, Mother."

"Well, I have to speak to you about that young lady. It is serious, Agustín!"

"Oh, yes?"

We started toward the corral, my grandmother on Ewell's arm, Father and Mateo leading the way, and me walking on the flank. Just before we got to the gate a Minorca rooster ran across our path, almost tripping Grandmother. She stopped suddenly, startled, and I tried to soothe her. "That's all right, Grandmother," I said. "He's just going to lay that hen, see?" And I pointed as the rooster caught the hen. Grandmother gave me a look that stopped me momentarily. Then she turned away and went on. I followed and when I got to the stable, Ewell was in the corral helping Grandmother onto the horse. Father was putting on his spurs and Mateo was standing nearby with his leather-red complexion on again.

"Didn't I tell you not to speak to your grandmother? Don't you know how to mind?"

"Yes, Pa." I stood looking up at the Encino Spring far up near the rim of the Cerro. I felt like a wild animal, trapped and longing for my retreat on the mountain.

"Come, Eva. Don't stand there gawking." In the corral Grandmother was already in the saddle, her piercing eyes on me, like an eagle getting ready to swoop down on some defenseless animal.

Father put me on Apache, a lazy bay horse that I didn't like, but I had to ride him because Grandmother was riding Diamante. I led the way down the river toward the Punta de Agua, Father and Grandmother following and talking all the time. I listened, but everything she said was disconnected, just a blurred sound. I heard, "It's a disgrace . . . you and her mother should be horsewhipped," and more blurred talking, talking, talking, and I couldn't hear. Suddenly, "Your father would turn in his grave" . . . and the mumbling sound of ummm, ummm . . . *Va a ser una cinicia.*" And I repeated the word *cinicia* to myself. I would be a *cinicia*, cynic in English, I knew, but what did it *mean?* "She sits almost under the stove with that terrible frown and never speaks!" Ah, she was talking about Ruby now. And more mumbling as my father's horse poked along silently beside her. "Mary and I will come in the spring, to stay," she said emphatically, "to teach them, and you. It's our duty . . . with the help of God . . . a shame . . . a disgrace . . . a terrible job . . . to fight the devil and you . . . Samaniego . . . Don Ignacio Pesqueira . . . Moraga . . . Charles Poston . . . Governor Safford . . . Father Suastigui . . . royal blood . . . and more royal blood" and we were at the door of the old house. "We're here, Pa." I said.

"Yes, hija. Thank God."

"Would you like to get down, Mother?" he asked her.

"Yes, that's what I came for," and she dropped her knee from round the saddlehorn and slipped down without waiting for Father's help. Father went past her and helped me down.

The vacant old house stood with all its windows open. A horned owl sat on a rickety shelf inside, but he left through the nearest window as soon as we walked in. Grandmother walked from room to room.

"Your poor father, Agustín, worked so hard to keep the two places. Cruz was homesteading this place for us, but he left when your father didn't return."

Father didn't have much to say, but Grandmother kept reminiscing, and looking in corners as if she expected to find something. "In the winter, hijo," she said, as she stood looking out the back door, "the sun would set over the very crest of that beautiful hill and it was then as it is now, covered with the blue mist of Indian summer." I was angry, but I still felt sorry even then for this bewildered, lonely old woman. Weighed down, as my mother was so often to say later, "with that strange heritage handed down to her from her Castilian ancestors."

We left the house and started back home. Hordes of Indians were ahead of us, going toward the Guijas Indian Village.

"I guess the poor Indians are getting ready for the winter, Agustín," said Grandmother, her eyes on the ragged Indians shuffling along ahead of us.

"No, Mother, they're getting ready to go to the reservation, to the strip. In fact, Mateo told me this morning that they are all leaving sometime next week."

"Really, hijo? Now that you mention it, Emilia Rosa was telling me something about this, but I didn't quite understand her."

"They are going any day now, Mother."

"I think I'll stay to see them leave, Agustín."

"Do that, Mother, why don't you?"

Back at the house Mike and Mateo were already preparing the agave and waiting for the flaming fire to settle into embers in the barbecue pit. Many Indians were now milling about the place. Tula and María Nieves with their friends were sitting on the east side of the wall, their ollas and baskets at their feet, and more Indians were struggling out of the thicket and footing it toward the house. A herd of horses had come down from the hill and was running across the clearing. Grand-mother reined Diamante to a stop. "What a familiar scene! Your father is the only one missing here, Agustín. I can just see him walking out with bowls of rice for the Indians." She rested her forehead on her knee which rose across the saddlehorn. Father stopped the Big Grey alongside Diamante, and I stopped too. We sat three abreast watching the Indians coming and going all in a hurry. "You came just in time to see them again," said Father. "A few more days and you would have found the place desolate, Mother."

"I am glad I came. I had been thinking about it and suddenly I couldn't put it off one more day. Mary was impatient with me as she wanted to come in the spring, you know. Two or three times I dreamed of your father, hurrying to the ranch as he always did. I think his spirit brought me back and I am glad I came." José-José came down the trail and stood leaning against the wall and looking toward the Baboquivari.

"Do you know him, Mother? This is your old friend, José-José."

"Amazing! He was an old man when I saw him last," said Grand-mother. "You know, Hijo, I would like to visit the villages before the Indians leave."

"You'd better not put it off too long. They'll be leaving any day. Your friend, Tom, will be glad to take you to the Guijas Village. It's right there just over the hill and he loves to visit the Indians."

"He's a fine man, Agustín."

"He should be. A Harvard man."

"Is he really, Agustín?"

"Ask Pa to tell you about him. You'll like the story, Mother. I'm go-ing to the Cochis with Mateo in the morning. I'm going to bring back some *potros* (wild horses) that I'd like to break now that he is here. He'll be going to the reservation in a few weeks. Tom could take you tomorrow. There are three or four villages that are very interesting."

"Will you ask him to take us, Hijo? Rita could go with us, too."

"You'd better ask Emilia Rosa, Mother. Rita and Margarita run that house and it is a big job as you can see."

"I'll ask Emilia Rosa and maybe we can go tomorrow. Agustín, I think we should give the Indians a dinner before they go."

"I'm already working on that project, Mother. That's what Mateo is working with over there. Barra is going to nail up some crude tables, anything to set the food on."

"I am so glad I came. I am sure it was the spirit of your father that brought me." Grandmother had tears in her eyes. She wiped them away with the tips of her fingers and went on telling Father that no one in Tucson had believed that she could make the long difficult trip.

"And least of all me, Mother. I didn't believe Pa when he told me that you were here. Come on, Mother. I have to give Mateo a hand now."

"I just can't believe that he's Martín Mariano's son. He is so well educated and so fine."

"Why not? He was raised by William White. He is actually White's adopted son," Father reminded her. At the stable Mike helped Grandmother Wilbur down and unsaddled Diamante. Grandmother walked toward the house and I followed at a distance.

"Did you have a nice ride?" asked Mother.

"Lovely ride and a lovely day. The country is enchanted, under a spell." Grandmother was again as haughty as ever as she went on to her room, but when she met Grandmother Margarita she broke down and cried, telling her that she was full of thoughts of her husband. The memories were so alive it seemed like only yesterday that he had left. She went on to tell her how all those years ago she had disapproved of Grandfather Wilbur's trip to such cold country when he didn't feel well, of the premonition she had had and the anguish it had caused her. "But when his health broke down, I finally agreed that it would be best for him to return to Plympton, Massachussetts, for medical treatment. But his letters from there were not encouraging. I could tell that he wasn't feeling any better than when he left. It was the middle of June when I received a large box of toys he had shipped back for the children and a letter saying that he expected to leave in a few days and to be home by the early part of July, but the days went by and I didn't hear from him again, Margarita.

"Then in early July I got a letter from Frank, his brother, telling me that my husband had been quite sick, again, but was much improved now, and that he would soon write and tell me when to expect him." She stopped, folding her hands and looking off into space for so long that she seemed to have forgotten Grandmother Margarita was there. Finally, though, she said, "And then . . . silence, Margarita. Only silence. And I spent the nights unable to sleep, walking about alone and wondering if he was really getting better. I wrote telling him not to hurry, but to stay until he was completely recovered. But I got no answer.

"Finally, one morning the doorbell rang, and I saw a Western Union messenger boy waiting outside. My heart threatened to come out my mouth. I just knew the letter didn't bring good news. I opened it quickly and a picture of a gravestone fell out on my lap. I didn't read the letter, Margarita. I sat there staring into space. My sister Engracía came in some time later and I remember handing her the letter and telling her to take care of the children, and then I dropped back on my bed and slept. When Engracía came back I remember that I could see her speak, but I couldn't hear what she said, and she sat on the rocking chair and cried. I turned my face to the wall and slept. I woke up the following day, my house full of people and Father sitting at the head of my bed. I tried to speak, but I couldn't find any words. When my sister offered me a bowl of soup I took it, drank the soup, and hurled the bowl across the room. It was this ugly act that brought me to my senses, so that I finally acknowledged the priest's presence and apologized to Engracía. The children were so frightened. We all sat in silence listening to Father Juán talk and pray. I just didn't think I would ever get over the shock, Margarita."

Grandmother Margarita patted her shoulder, but when she spoke it was only to invite Grandmother Wilbur to come have lunch at her house across the creek. After Grandmother Wilbur changed her riding habit they went across together. When she came back, we could all see that she was more at peace. She told Father how beautiful she thought my grandparents' little shanty was. "It is a *capillita*, a little chapel in the heart of that lonely hill. Inside of the *chozita* is a truly spiritual atmosphere, and I felt there as I feel when I walk in the cathedral. On the wall of their sala hangs a sign that reads, '*Esta es la casa de Dios, y nosotros somos sus siervos*—This is the house of the Lord and we are his servants.' How beautiful, Agustín, how beautiful. It brought me such great peace of mind. I feel restored. I feel like a different person."

All went well the rest of the day until we went to bed that evening. This time Grandmother brought Ruby and me to the bedroom, and while she was gathering her prayer books, rosary, and kimono and making herself ready for bed, Ruby and I got into our ugly, flour-sack nightgowns, jumped into bed, and covered up. Instantly, Grandmother was at my throat pulling off the covers. Since I didn't know what was the matter with her I slipped further down under the covers which she lifted up, leaving me uncovered and curled up at the foot of the bed. Taking hold of my arm, she lifted me out of the bed saying, "Get on your knees this very minute!" I didn't know how to kneel down or what she wanted me on my knees for. Prayer never crossed my mind. I squatted down. "On your knees, on your knees." Grandmother raised her voice and Ruby jumped out of the bed and ran out of the room in search of Mother. I heard her say, "I don't know what's the matter with Grandmother! She threw Bonnie on the floor!"

Father came in, leading Ruby by the hand. "What's going on, Mother?" asked Father, looking at me on the floor.

"What's going on, Mother?" mocked Grandmother. "As if you didn't know! Your daughter doesn't know how to kneel down; she doesn't even know how to cross herself. She jumped into bed like a savage without ever thinking that there is a God." Ah, she wanted me to pray! Ruby slipped her hand out of Father's and ran to Mother. "Come back here, Ruby," he said.

"No, Pa, she might hurt me."

"Come back here, Ruby," Father said firmly with the voice that always made us tremble. It affected Grandmother, too. She let go of me and stood looking at Father with something like fear in her eyes. She seemed to regain her wits and began lecturing Father in rapid excited tones, telling him of his uncle, Father Suastigui. And telling him that the whole household, with the exception of Don Francisco and Margarita, was a disgrace. She went on and on and on until she had Father and Mother and the two of us all on our knees following the prayers she was reciting. Finally, Father interrupted: "No, Mother, don't expect us to stay on our knees all night. If you want to recite the rosary, you do it. The girls are going to bed and so are we."

Grandmother finally stood up and said, "Maybe tomorrow you'll be able to pray a little longer."

"Yes, Mother, maybe tomorrow. You go to bed and get a good rest. Girls, get into bed."

"Yes, Pa." Grandmother kissed my parents good night, turned off the light, and dropped back on her knees.

Up at the Cima, Alone, Olé

I WAS AWAKENED EARLY BY A COMMOTION in the kitchen. Upon investigating, I found Father and Mateo eating their breakfast by candlelight. "Come here, Eva." I walked to the edge of the table. "Now listen, and listen good," said Father. "We are going to the Cochis to bring the *grullos* (buckskin horses). Your grandmother will be going to the villages and if she asks you to go with her, say 'Thank you, Grandmother, but Father told me to stay here and help with the chores.' And don't you go. Can you remember that?"

"Yes, Pa." When they finally left I followed them to the door where I stopped and saw the morning star in the east. I heard a coyote yapping across the creek and felt the crisp cold morning air of November. I hurried back to the warmth of the woodstove, and while I ate my breakfast I told Mother that I was going to go to the mountain. She said that I would have to wait until Grandmother Wilbur left. She would go about ten or eleven o'clock. "We must not let her see you go alone because she won't approve of it. Now finish your breakfast and go back to bed."

"I don't want to go in there, Ma."

"Lie down in my bed," said Mother. When I woke up again it was almost ten and I stood at the window watching Tom Ewell help both my grandmothers into a surrey that I had never seen before. "Where did that come from, Ma?"

"Your grandfather borrowed it from Don Miguel, and don't get funny ideas. Don Miguel said that it was for the use of Doña Rafaelita only."

As soon as the surrey left the yard I got on Diamante and raced down the river singing my favorite song, *mine* because I had invented it.

About two months before, as we rested after lunch, I told Father that I had made up a song and I wanted him to help me with it. "Bring it here," he said, and I handed him a piece of brown-sack covered with what looked like chicken scratches. Father looked it over and said, "Looks good! Very good. You read it for me now, and I'll listen carefully."

I recited:

> One, two, three, one, two, three
> Me and Diamante go galloping free
> One, two, three, two, three
> Me and Diamante, to the mountain we go.

"Why don't you say 'to the mountain we flee?'" asked Father. "Then it will rhyme."

"Well, Pa, I don't like fleas."

Father wrote in big block letters: "I see the sea," and explained in detail the difference between "see" and "sea," in spelling and meaning. He went on to explain "flea" and "flee." "So," said Father, "when you say 'to the mountain we flee,' you're not talking about a flea at all."

Father recited my song again, ending it with "flee." "And now," he told me, "you'd better say 'Diamante and I,' not 'me and Diamante.' Only babies talk like that."

In a couple of minutes he handed me back the sack paper with my song written in his pretty handwriting and asked, "Do you like it?"

"Yes, Pa."

"You did very well! It is a very pretty song." And he left the house.

A few days later I went to my mother: "Ma," I said, "I've invented another song because Pa, he ruined my first song. Will you write this song out for me now, Ma?"

"What's wrong with this one?" asked Mother, looking at the song Father corrected.

"I want to say 'me and Diamante'."

"It is wrong," said Mother.

"Ma, 'Diamante and I' means that Diamante is over there and I am way over here. 'Me and Diamante' means that we are close together, I am on his back, see? Write it the way I tell you, Ma, and don't tell me it's wrong."

Mother wrote what I dictated, but then she looked up at me 'L M O P, L M N O P, and L M N O' doesn't mean a thing. It is very silly! Even Ruby could do better than that."

"Sure, she could, Ma, but she doesn't do nothing. She just sits and pouts."

"You're very silly and stubborn and you'll never learn anything. You had better be spending your time learning to obey, or maybe you can tell me what 'L M N O' means."

"What do you care what it means, Ma? It's my song, not yours."

"Even the bird that called 'Toribio' makes more sense than that," said Uncle Mike, who had been listening to us argue. This comparison was too much and I got even angrier. Don Toribio was the man who came to shear the herd every spring. One day he was sitting half asleep at the foot of the willow tree and Mother had sent me to ask him for lunch. As Don Toribio followed me to the house he said to me, "I think I'll go back to my country."

"Why, Don Toribio? Don't you like it here?"

"Sure," he answered, yawning, "but don't you hear that bird calling me?"

Then I noticed the bird swinging on a branch of the hackberry tree and singing loudly, "Toribio, Toreebiooo."

After Don Toribio left the house I asked Mother why she hadn't told me about this wonderful bird. "I didn't think it was necessary," said Mother shortly. I was not happy with her answer, and I was even unhappier when Don Toribio went back to Mexico and the bird disappeared. Here was a fascinating, marvelous thing I wanted to know about. Why did this bird who said a man's name go away when the man went? I asked and asked, but no one would tell me anything.

Now I was very angry at Mike for telling me that even that bird made more sense than my song. "Shut up, Mike! I'm not talking to you!"

"*¡Malcriada!*" exclaimed Mother. "Don't talk to your uncle like that!"

"My uncle don't mind his business," I shouted, "and he better or I'm going to tell my father on him!" The three of us shouted some more and finally Mother took the song and shook the paper at me. "It is not *right!*"

"What if it isn't? *I* made it, not you!"

"Have it your way, *Zonza*," and Mother gave me the paper, the song written the way I wanted it. I hid it under my mattress so Father wouldn't find it, and then I forgot it.

But this morning after Tom Ewell had helped my two grandmothers into the surrey and driven away, I galloped Diamante along the ravine singing the final version at the top of my voice:

> L M N O P, L M N O P
> Me and Diamante go
> galloping free
> L M N O, L M N O-O
> Me and Diamante
> To the mountain
> We go-o.

I followed the trail up the hill and stopped at my tree, Old Gnarled. I dismounted Diamante and climbed up its dry branches. Looking out over the countryside I could see the Indians coming and going in all directions. They seemed to be in a big hurry. There were moving a lot faster than they usually did.

My two grandmothers had been talking about the Indians the night before. I heard them both say that it was "very sad." Grandmother Margarita had sighed and then they talked about other days when other Indians lived along the creek. I got down from my tree and, back on the saddle, I headed toward the Encino Spring. I dismounted again and let Diamante get a drink at the *aguaje* while I sat on the big rock and looked down the rocky slope. I was more than halfway up the mountain. If Diamante would take me up just a little higher, I would be at the picacho, this time alone, all by myself. "Olé! Come on, Diamante, let's go up." And so "me and Diamante" followed the trail up toward the peak.

When Father brought me up here the first time, he had come up on the south side of the Cerro. It had been rough and frightening—no trail and the terrain was bad all the way. This time I was going up on the north side. It was much easier climbing and before I knew it I was up on the path. From here I could see the tree where Father had left Diamante when we climbed afoot to the picacho. This time I left Diamante near a big cliff and made only the last few yards on my hands and knees. I stood up and again I saw that great blue distance stretching before me. There were the browns, the mauves, the dark blues, the light blues, and the farthest little blue mountains touching the sky! Right there was Tucson. Father had told me so. A great sense of confidence surged over me. I could do things the Noneña couldn't do. She would die on the way! But me and Diamante, we were a team, me and my horse! I walked around the *cima* (a new word I learned for "summit" or "picacho" when I heard Grandfather talking to Grandmother). I walked on top of my world alone for the first time. I loved the *cima*, and I loved to be alone. This would be my home!

When I had come with Father, it had been early June and everything looked bright and clear. It was before the rains, but there had been green things, eggs in the nests, and mockingbirds warbling everywhere. Today was different. Everything was cloaked in the thick blue mist of the Indian summer and the mountainside was quieter. Little birds were twittering softly in the high barren crags. The wind was humming softly through the rigid thorny branches of an ocotillo—shoooshooo, shooosh. Looking down the slope I saw an antelope standing beside a tall cliff. He ignored me and stood twitching an ear and shaking his head. The wind seemed to be going down the mountain for I could see the tall brown grass gradually laid low all the way down and then it would slowly come up and stand erect until it began to lie down at my feet. And so it went all the way to the foot of the mountain again.

The Indian summer was beautiful and peaceful. I could see it. I could feel it. It was real. Father had told me that it was the evening of the year when everything was going to sleep. It seemed to me that Father, too, like the wind and the birds, was more softspoken at this time of the year. The sunlight through the blue mist was soft and caressing. The herd went down the mountain, and I heard the goatbell's *tang talang talang tang.* Even the bell had a muffled sound. I would come up here often. "Goodbye, Cima, me and Diamante will come again," I said as I stood looking at the waves of golden grass coming up and going down.

Down on the foothills the Indians looked like crawling ants. They too, like the grass, were coming and going in different directions, seeming to move faster than they really did. I had always heard that they would go away someday, and now the day of their leaving was here. I wondered what the country would be like without them. They had always been good to me. There was the day I sat playing on the edge of the bank, not an Indian in sight, when I rolled down the slope into the water hole, grabbed a nearby mesquite root and screamed for help. In seconds the water hole was surrounded by Indians.

With the Indians gone I would really be alone. I would have to
depend on myself more. I sat down on a nearby rock below the point
of an old broken tree. The inside of the slivered point was covered
with a brown variegated fungus arranged in an intricate pattern. I
reached out toward it, then stopped. Some of the trees along the
riverbanks had streaks of golden brown fungus and Mother had told
me not to touch it, that it wasn't clean. So I turned back to observing
the Indians and thinking what it would be like to be left alone with
the animals. Of course there would be Ruby and Juana, and I would
always have Diamante. If things got bad down there I would come up
to the *cima*. Here were the animals—antelope, rabbits, squirrels, and
birds—and the plants, and the big upright slabs of stone, and the
passages between them. There were whole worlds for me to explore
up here. It was hard climbing up to the *cima* and hardly anyone ever
came up here, so I would be high above the world and alone, but
together with many things. Live things.

Looking down the foothills I saw the shadow of the mountain
growing long toward the east, and I decided to get down to the creek.
Father would be getting back from the Cochis with the *grullos* by now.
I took hold of the pointed log above me to help myself up, forgetting
the fungus. It felt soft, and as I pulled my hand away a brown cloud
of monarch butterflies lifted up. They made a golden lace pattern in
the sky weaving in and out. It was startling, delightful, and fascinating,
but it also reminded me that I had not learned to be alert, to *see* when
I looked, as Father had often told me to do. Only last year Mother
had scolded me when I had mistaken a lynx cat for a stump. And now
I had mistaken a cluster of butterflies for a streak of fungus. I had
actually put my hand on them! That "fungus" could have been a snake!

I stood watching the butterfly pattern getting bigger and bigger as
they flew in different directions. A banner of golden lace floating in
midair! It was breathtaking! It was what Grandfather had once called
a "gift of a moment."

One day Grandmother Margarita, Juana, Ruby, and I had come up
the bank carrying armloads of wood. Grandfather, who was in the
zaguán cutting jerky into long strips, had come out yelling, "Margarita,
Margarita!"

"Francisco, what's the trouble? You look like a crazy man!"

Grandfather yelled again, this time pointing up at the sky, "Look
up quick, Margarita! *¡Es obsequio de un momento!*" We stood looking
up at a foamy white cloud that a wind current had whipped into a

white rose, its petals edged by the pink light of the setting sun. It was truly beautiful—a gift of a memory for a lifetime! Grandfather, Mother, and Aunt Rita had joined us, as well as Father and Mike, who had come up from an opposite direction.

My grandparents, their eyes on the sky, had prayed separately, silently and reverently. Grandmother Margarita, unlike Grandmother Wilbur, often recited short little prayers, and then she had ended as she often did, whispering, "Jesus into thy keeping I commend my spirit." Much too quickly the wind tore off the rose petals and sent them into different directions. "There is the change, Margarita," said Grandfather. "Always the change!"

Suddenly, Mike let out a wild scream in the style of Carmelo Tosco. Grandfather had shaken him roughly, "You are a sacrilegious man, Mike, far worse than Carmelo. What does it take for you to see the work of God?"

"I don't know why I did that, Pa," Uncle Mike had said, chastened. "I just had to let something out, something that was choking me, and out came a scream."

And now, as I leaned on Diamante's shoulder watching the beautiful lace pattern growing bigger and bigger and disintegrating in space I too felt something choking me. I remembered Grandfather saying, "Always drink up and enjoy these little scenes, Margarita. They are the boosts we need. Sometimes things get tough, and these are the things that keep us sane—they are muscle-building and shock-absorbing, so watch them with a prayer, Margarita."

I had asked Grandmother what Grandfather meant by "muscle-building" and "shock-absorbing" and all those things he had said, and she explained that he meant such moments give us strength to bear blows, like an anvil.

My pattern was changing. Already the butterflies were going away. A few were clinging to Diamante's mane. I looked down at the log, hollow and empty. The brown, golden lace-float fading in the sky. Always a change! I put my hands palm to palm as Grandmother Margarita always did and said her words, "Jesus into thy keeping I commend my spirit."

I had reached the lower foothills and was scanning the high skyline and wondering just where the *atajo* (drove) of the *grullos* (buckskins) would show up when Mateo himself appeared unexpectedly beside me. "Bonnie, will you run and stand at the gap? And get Mike to help you. I am going to stand here and head off those horses," he said, pointing to the west side of the Cerro where I suddenly saw a herd of horses spilling over the rim and heading toward us.

"Where is Pa, Mateo?"

"He's following the *atajo.*" I headed toward the creek as fast as Diamante would go, arriving in time to get Mike to come stand at the gap with me.

I knew the grandmothers were back, as I could see the surrey standing at the kitchen door. "What did they bring from the villages, Mike?" I asked him.

"Ollas and baskets and a whole bunch of Indians—Lupita Boylan, Tomás José, your friend Wahyanita, la Chueca, y la Tuerta, and all the rest of the *Indiada,* you know. Your Grandmother Rafa" (Mike called Grandmother Wilbur that when Father and Grandfather were not listening), "she has been asking for you." Just then we saw her come out of the house toward the bank. She called, "You'd better get home, young lady! Right now this very minute!"

"You better go back in the house, Grandmother, or you'll scare the horses away and my father won't like it." Grandmother ignored this and came on down the slope to the very edge of the stream. We heard the splash of the water where the herd was crossing. "Go up the bank, Grandmother, the horses will run over you!" I yelled as loudly as I could. She stood there. We saw the atajo now, coming out of the river willows, a wall of horses heading for the gap. Mateo came up behind us and helped us fight them off. The whole herd stampeded to the side of the bank where Grandmother was standing. They ran down the river and Father fought them back. They ran in a circle. I looked back at Grandmother and saw her still standing above the bank looking shocked and disheveled. I left Mateo and Mike to guard the gap and, like a wild Indian, I splashed into the water. Criss-crossing the stream, I joined Father and helped bring the herd back to the corral. We got down and left our horses standing, pink foam dripping from their heaving flanks as they rocked back and forth fighting for breath.

I saw Ramón Ahumada's surrey standing at the edge of the willow thicket, so knew Ramón and Virginia must be visiting my grandparents. Now Ramón himself came across the creek to the corral and stood admiring the geldings.

"That Limoncilla is worth her weight in gold, Agustín," he said, pointing to a copper-sorrel mare. "I am sure Mateo is licking his chops."

"Yes, he likes her all right, but I gave him that palomino there," and he pointed to a regal animal that stood not far from us.

"I hate to see you part with a beautiful horse like that, hombre."

"Mateo is a big help to me when he's here, Ramón."

"I'd like that sorrel mare for my saddle, Pa," I said. I knew I would never forsake Diamante, but I feared that Father would give that beautiful mare away, too! But if I wanted her, maybe he wouldn't.

"I'll break her for your saddle," said Father, "but it will be a long time before you can ride her." Father called to Mateo who was already surrounded by a group of Indian women, and added, "Join us for a quick lunch, Ramón?"

"Gracias, Agustín. I have to gather my family and head for the big *charco*. You know what would happen if I wasn't there in time to inspect the work done and give the assignment for tomorrow. Your mother has invited us to the fiesta tomorrow and if it is all right with you, Agustín, I would like to invite None and his wife."

"Sure, Ramón, the more the merrier. Bring your friends." Ramón walked back to my grandparents' house and we rushed into the kitchen and gathered around the table where Mother and Emilia Rosa were serving. Grandmother Wilbur had been scared off to her bedroom. Emilia Rosa brought a large platter filled with fragrant *biguata* (roasted agave). "This is really good, Emilia Rosa," said Father when he had taken a bite. "Thank you, thank you."

"Yes," answered Emilia Rosa. "I good cook. I feed people good. I good teacher, too. Wilbur family learning to say, 'thank you'."

To Father's obvious embarrassment Mother and Mateo began to laugh and said they were glad Ramón wasn't present to hear this; he had such perfect manners.

We finished lunch and were leaving the house when Grandmother Wilbur called to Father. "I want to talk to you about Eva, Agustín."

"No, Mother, not now," said Father firmly, and we walked toward the corral where all the broncs stood, their ears pointed toward anything that moved, their muscles tense and twitching. Our arrival set them to running around the corral again.

The five *grullos* were roughly the same age, but varied in size and markings. The largest was a dark dun color with a black cross-stripe over his shoulders and down his spine. He had a skimpy black mane, a short tail, and a large head. He was muscular and strongly built, but not pretty.

The sorrel mare danced about on her small feet; with her grace and glossy coat she stole the show.

Father had decided to keep the mare, along with Mateo's palomino and the other *grullos*. The smaller colts would be branded and allowed to go back to the range. After building the fire and branding them, we put the sorrel mare whom Mateo had named Doradita, or Golden, in the stable with the five grullo geldings.

"That ugly grullo there we'll name Javelin. He's going to be the best of the lot. You'll see, Agustín," Mateo told us. "These buckskins are never very pretty, but they make the best workers. We have lots of them in Mexico. The old-timers tell me they are thinning out now. They are all looking for well-marked grullo stallions to keep the breed alive. I learned from history books that the Spanish could never have thrown the Moors out of their land without the help of the rock horses. Some say the grullos are descendants of the Tarpan, an old ugly breed. Their hooves are like iron and they survive where other horses die."

And I again remembered Don Toribio, the old man who came to help father with the shearing. One evening at sundown he arrived at the ranch from Mexico at the same time Father arrived from Tucson. Father handed him his horse and told him to unsaddle and leave him in the stable for the night. When Don Toribio returned to the house he told Father that riding an unshod horse for seventy miles was a criminal offense. "Well, you shoe him in the morning," said Father.

The first thing Don Toribio did the following day was lead the grullo to the working bench and begin to shoe him. After an hour of struggling without success he came to Father and asked, "What kind of hooves does that horse have, Agustín? The nails bend! Just won't go in."

"Iron hooves," Father told him. "They don't need shoes." And now Father was laughing as he too remembered. He went on to tell Mateo how confused Toribio had been at seeing the nails bend over.

"They are great on the rocks," said Mateo. "No other breed comes close to them. And now, Gus, why don't we start on Doradita if you want to break her. We can saddle a couple of horses before sundown if you want to."

"All right with me, Mat," answered Father. So the horses were saddled, and Mateo roped Doradita. While he struggled with the mare, I ran to Father and asked, "Pa, I want to go wrangling with the boys. Can I, Pa?"

"Yes, you can," Father tossed back as he ran to help Mateo. The mare was struggling against the rope and kicking the corral fence. She fought, she pulled against the rope and fell, and she got up and went through the same performance again.

The third time she fell Father told me to get on Diamante and ride up to her. He tied the rope around my saddlehorn so that when the mare pulled and struggled, my saddle tipped to the front. I felt the cantle hitting me on the back of my head as it always did when Father tied to the saddlehorn some large animal. Out of the corner of my eye I saw Grandmother Wilbur getting off the fence and walking toward me, but Grandfather stopped her and took her out of the corral.

Then Tomás José arrived and ran to help me. He held Diamante and when the mare was tied he led Diamante forward. When the mare was tied down Father called to me and I followed him to the house to get my hat and spurs on. Grandfather followed us. We saw Tom Ewell taking my two grandmothers to the edge of the riverbank to see Mateo mount the horse.

"Agustín," said Grandfather, "What will your mother think when she sees Eva run down the river with the Indians? I know they are good boys, but it doesn't look nice. What will your mother say, Hijo?"

"My mother doesn't have anything to say, Pa." Just then Tomás José came in. "Mateo say Eva go?" he asked.

"Yes," answered Father.

"You go take care of her?"

"No," answered Father. "Eva takes care of herself."

"She go, I no go," declared the Indian. "I go, she no go."

"You take care of yourself and the bronc, Tomás José," he ordered. "Eva will take care of herself."

"What for she go?" he protested. "She get hurt, we bad." Finally, the Indian agreed to let me follow him and Mateo as long as I rode a good distance behind them. I could see that he wasn't happy.

Grandfather insisted that Father go along to protect me.

"No," said Father. "I have other things to do."

"How can you let your five-year-old daughter run off wrangling with a couple of pagans miles away from home?" Grandfather demanded. Then he enlisted Mother's support and she, too, thought it was wrong to allow me to go alone with the boys. The argument got bigger and louder. My grandfather raised his voice and Father raised the roof.

Grandfather spoke of church and morality and the fiber of society. Father said angrily that I was the owner of my own soul, and that we didn't owe a damned thing to the *mundo cara panda*—the sway-backed world. "Anyone who comes judging us by Vatican standards can go to hell with their standards. Only when we go meddling with the hypocrites do they have a right to reject us. I want my daughter to learn that she is a free soul. This is where we live and survive, and we make our own moral standards. If Eva chooses to follow hypocrisy when she grows up, that will be her business. I won't interfere."

"You are making a libertine of her," countered Grandfather. "Just like yourself. She will grow up an ugly misfit and she will blame you, mark my word!"

Father suddenly dropped the argument, stood up, and said, "If you're going with the boys you'd better get yourself to the corral, Eva."

I grabbed my hat and said, "My shoes are on top of the workbench, Pa."

"All right. Go put them on."

On the way to the barn I stepped on a mesquite thorn and was walking on the ball of my foot when I reached the stable. Father was still angry and he was yelling at the Indians to get out of the corral when he saw me limping my way toward the workbench. "Take care of your sister, Mateo," he ordered in the voice that made everybody listen. Mateo picked me up and set me on the workbench. Before I could speak he pulled the thorn from my foot. I started to scream but Mateo placed a heavy hand across my mouth. "The thorn is gone, so save the scream for another time. Now put on your shoes before your father gets mad again. I can't stand anymore *gritos y sombrerasos*— yelling and hat-swatting."

Father came up and put his hand on Mateo's shoulder and both of them burst into hilarious laughter. Mateo was the one person with whom Father was in complete rapport, always. I used to sit at the peak and watch the eagles fly. If one turned west, both turned west in unison. Both would swoop down together. I used to think "two eagles with one head."

"What makes that, Ma?" I had asked Mother.

"Ask your father. He knows all about Indians and eagles and things like that." My father and Mateo together reminded me of the eagles.

They led Diamante to the riverbed where Mateo eared her while Tomás José hefted up her saddle. Every time Tomás José glanced toward me, an ugly expression crossed his face. It was a warning to me to keep out of the way. He didn't approve of me at all.

I sat on Diamante to the left side of the mare. Mateo was on her right. We were tense, waiting for action. My grandparents, my uncles, and several Indians were on the bank above, and Father was standing below listening to Grandmother Wilbur who was on the edge of the bank looking down at him as she spoke. I couldn't hear what she was saying, but by the tone of her voice I knew she wasn't happy.

Finally, Tomás José pulled the blind from Doradita's eyes. The horse reared up, then plunged forward and sped off at a dead run. Mateo and I were at her flanks, keeping her on a straight course. I rode pell-mell along the south bank of the creek, just managing to keep Diamante's shoulder close to the bronc's neck to keep her from escaping up the slope and running for the hills. Not until we were safely past the first slope did I look around and discover that Mateo was no longer with us. I had no time to worry about him; it was all I could do to guard Doradita at the next incline. Then as the slope spread out she reared back and took the incline before I could turn around. I raced on and managed to get ahead of her on the hill. I brought her back to the bank, but we missed the curve and ended up above the creek on the edge of a ten-foot drop. Swiftly, I ran Diamante between the bank and Doradita and headed her straight toward a big mesquite tree. A large low-hanging branch finally brought her to a halt. Tomás José quickly jerked the reins of her snaffle bit up and to one side, turning her head away from the riverbank. I slipped down from my saddle. There was a long pole on the ground left there by the last flood. I picked up one end of it and pushed it toward the fork of the tree. "You can't lift it, Eva," warned Tomás José. "It is too heavy for you."

He handed me a looped rope and told me to put it under the end of the pole. "I'll lift it while you push it through, Eva."

"You just hold it high, Tomás José, and I'll pull it through the fork." I tugged, pushed, and pulled until I had the end of the pole through the fork of the tree, staying wary every second of the bronc's striking hooves. When I had got it through I went around to the other side of the tree and tugged the pole on through the fork of another tree, until it finally rested against the horse's chest. There was little chance now for Doradita to duck sideways and fall down the high riverbank.

Tomás José looked down at me and smiled for the first time. "*¡Buen trabajo, Amigo!* Good work!" I could not help but notice that he had used the masculine form of the word friend, telling me that I had shown the skill of a man in coping with the problem at hand. And now I strutted, quietly gloating, around the curve of the bank, mounted my horse, and went to help Tomás José get Doradita from under the mesquite tree. I had won Tomás José to my side. He had accepted me!

In those days it was even more difficult than it is now to break down men's prejudices against a woman, of whatever age—to make them accept our competence. We started early, as I did, and went one step at a time, sometimes gaining ground, sometimes losing it.

At the turn of the century, especially in the West, this was not only a "man's world," but the fact was virtually undisputed. No woman dared to deal with a man in his work. If she so much as tried, she was immediately put in her place by both men and women; she was singled out as a "hussy," an undesirable to be shunned. In later years Father took care of this problem on our ranch by telling the hired men early that I was one of their bosses and that if I asked him to fire a man, that man was as good as fired. So those who needed work tried hard to please me. It was not difficult to do so. There were very few men that I didn't like. I admired their strength and the ease with which they did their work, and as long as they obeyed my orders they were secure in their jobs.

When I was only ten years old Father told me, "You hire them and you fire them, but I will hold you responsible for anything that goes wrong. Now when you fire your men, you figure out what they have earned, write them a chit, and let them go. When you hire them, tell them how much you will pay them and what you expect from them. If they agree, put them to work; if they don't agree, send them away. No giggling and no crying!"

This wasn't fun. It was too big a job, and I often had to engage the help of my mother, who didn't at all approve of my being at the head of a gang of working men. Nevertheless, people eventually got used to the idea that on our little spread the ten-year-old girl, who wore pants and a boy's haircut, was a full boss of the outfit. Many were envious and they did not hide their dislike of me. But what they didn't know was that their envy was misplaced; being a boss was a living hell. Being a boss on the Wilbur Ranch was not a desk job. I was working with livestock and livestock are unpredictable. Many incidents would surface and rise to the point where I could not cope with them.

There were times when I had to kiss the ground, lift myself up by my bootstraps, and lick my wounds in silence. I did not dare tell Father about my painful experiences, as it would only anger and antagonize him. "It serves you right," he would say. "That happened because you don't have things under control. Your horse, your men, and your work must be under complete control." And this sort of talk would go on and on. If I told my mother, she would worry herself sick and to no avail. So things were better unsaid. Some incidents are still vivid in my mind.

There was the time when Federico Lara and I were driving some cattle up to the Mora Pasture, which was east of the little town of Arivaca. When we went out of the home pasture I told Federico that we would drive the *partida* up the road.

"No," said Federico, "let's drive them up the creek; it's a lot easier."

"Up the road, Federico," I said. "You know there is always cattle along the creek and by the time we leave it we'll have more strays than $\frac{E}{W}$ s."

"No, Evita, if we drive them up the road they'll scatter on us and we'll have to fight all the way to keep them together." This became a heated argument, and soon we were yelling at one another.

"Your father is going to be furious if we don't get there pretty quick, as you very well know."

"I am driving this cattle, not my Father, and not you, either. I don't pay you to tell me what to do. I pay you to do what I tell you to do."

"I don't work for the money you pay me, Evita. I work for you to take care of you and your sister and your little brother, to see that some animal don't kill one of you."

"Then I don't need you, Federico. I can take care of myself, so please leave." And I dismissed Federico with arrogant and insolent words.

"All right, all right, Evita. We part friends," he said, and he left rolling a cigarette as he went. Immediately, I went to get off the horse to close the gate, and as I threw my right foot back over the saddle, Blue Del, the horse I was riding, swished his tail and caught the rowel of my spur. Blue Del was not the easiest horse to ride, but I was considered a good rider and I enjoyed riding him. Now he was more difficult than ever. He plunged forward and I rode standing on the stirrup on my left foot with my right hand holding on to the saddlehorn, and with my left hand I kept a tight rein, remembering well that a rider with a foot tied to a horse's tail was as good as dead.

Blue Del took the bit and went toward the thicket, kicking with both his hind feet. At the noise and commotion Federico looked back and, seeing Blue Del running for the thicket, ran and took hold of the reins and stopped him. He stood holding the horse that pawed, reared, and kicked. "Keep a tight rein, Evita, and don't faint. Be strong and courageous." I knew Federico had Grandfather's prayer in mind and I took it up. "Be strong and courageous. Do not be afraid or terrified because of him, for the Lord your God goes with you. He will never leave you nor forsake you." Blue Del was striking and kicking. The more he fought, the more I pulled his tail with my right foot which was actually tied to his tail, and the more frightened he became. I repeated the prayer three times. I don't think I felt stronger, but Blue Del suddenly stopped fighting and stood shaking. Federico managed to get his handkerchief out and tied it across the bridlehead, covering the horse's eyes. Quickly he tied a rope around the horse's neck and to the hindfoot. "Now, Evita, pat him and talk to him. See if I can take off the spur." I felt my shoe slip off. I was free! I moved my foot to the stirrup. I could now fall off, jump down, or do whatever I wanted. I was free! No longer in the death trap. I wanted to get down to see what Federico was having so much trouble with, but I didn't trust myself. I had to regain my composure. I had to show Federico that I was what he had always called me—*Vaquerita de hierro.* So I sat talking and patting the horse, and finally I felt that I could talk. I got down and went to see what was taking Federico so long to take the spur off the tail. I saw that the spur was so well wrapped with hair that the rowel was well hidden. Federico had to cut some of the hair to bare the rowel and untangle it from the hair. All this time I was feeling well and contained. As soon as Federico handed me the spur and the shoe I walked away to a log where I sat to put on my shoe when my heart began to pound like a sledge hammer. "I have to stay here, Fed."

"Oh no, Evita. You can't do that. You were so brave and everything. Come on now."

"I can't, Federico. My heart is not right and everything is getting dark." Federico dropped on his knees and began to rub my arms briskly while he kept on talking to me. I blacked out for one brief moment. When I opened my eyes again I saw him far away from me. I yelled at him.

"I am right here by you." I closed my eyes and when I opened them things looked normal, but I couldn't breathe and my arms were painful. Federico kept talking about different things and would now and then say, "Your color is better. Do you feel stronger now? You look like yourself again." And finally, I took a long breath and I stood up, still wobbly. I wasn't as weak as I pretended to be. I was now suffering from the humiliation of having had to call Federico for help after I told him that I didn't need him for a damned thing. Federico handed me the reins of Blue Del. I took them and I said, "Thank you, Fed. Maybe sometime I may be able to repay you for all this."

"You can repay me now. Let me help you drive the cattle up to the pasture. I know that they scattered everywhere."

"All right, Fed, you can help me, and if you want to we can go on from where we left off."

"*¿Como no?* After all, you're a great rider and a brave girl and best of all, you're my little sister. And let me tell you this. If you ever run me off again, I'll just follow you at a distance like a dog to see that no harm comes to you."

"Federico, I won't tell my father or my mother, either. I won't tell anybody. So don't you tell, either. Will you not, Fed?" Federico took the reins from my hand and reined Blue Del to a stop.

"Evita," he said, "you don't have to tell anybody if you don't want to, but I do. I have to explain. It is improper, inconsiderate, and not right for me not to explain."

I finally agreed with Federico and we hurried to locate the cattle that had scattered. And now I pause to pay tribute to those rugged vaqueros who were always nearby to help me control the Blue Dels and keep me from harm.

I Saw Plenty!

AT DINNER GRANDMOTHER WILBUR REMARKED that she had been very impressed with the country she had seen on her ride to the Indian village. She wanted to know if I had ever been to the Guijas Mountains.

"Sure, Grandmother," I said, "I've been all over that country."

"And what did you see there?"

"I saw plenty, Grandmother. I saw plenty!"

"Really! What did you see?"

"Agustín," warned Grandmother Margarita, alarmed. "I wouldn't let the niña tell Rafaelita about her experience up in that country."

"Well, Ma, if my daughter wants to talk about her gruesome experience and my mother wants to listen, why should I stop them?" he asked, turning back to his food. After a moment of silence as Grandmother Wilbur looked inquiringly at me, I decided I had permission and went on.

"You see, Grandmother, I went up to that high ridge," and I raised my arm across the table to indicate the height of the mountain, as I had seen cowboys do, "and when I reached the top I stopped and looked down. I saw a lot of buzzards flying around a mesquite tree, and I knew I had to go down and see what they were eating. Pa always told me not to start for home until I found out what the buzzards were eating, so I hurried down the slope to the arroyo and I galloped along a trail and went up the slope where the tree stood. The buzzards flapped their wings and made a loud noise taking off. I saw two white sacks hanging on the mesquite branches. So I reached up and broke one limb and the little sack fell to the ground, see? It was tied with baling wire, so I got down from my horse and undid the twisted wire, then I picked up the sack by two corners and emptied it." I put my elbow on the table and rested my face on the palm of my hand and sat looking at Grandmother Wilbur. "What do you think was inside the sack, Grandmother?"

"A piece of meat," said Grandmother.

"A baby. A dead baby, Grandmother, and there was another baby in the other sack that I left hanging on the tree."

Grandmother put her fork down and said, "*Hijo!* Agustín, what kind of a *yarn* is this?"

"It is the truth, Mother. Two babies were left in the sacks tied to the mesquite limbs, and Eva happened to be the one who found them."

"But what a *horrible* thing for a child to see, Agustín. That's why I absolutely don't approve of Eva running all over the country alone. This is *wrong*, hijo! Really, can't you see? What is the matter with you? You should have your head examined, Agustín."

"Well, Mother, this country is rugged. You never know what you're going to find, what you're going to see, or what you'll have to cope with, and this happens to be Eva's life. She will have to toughen up a bit and learn to cope with the unexpected. The country *is* rough, and it won't change just to accommodate Eva, you know."

"Hijo, hijo, the thing is that she doesn't have any business out there in that country. She belongs inside the house with her mother."

"I agree with you, Rafaelita," said Grandfather. "That child was sick for a week after she found those babies. She ran a temperature and couldn't hold anything in her stomach."

"That's what I mean when I say that she has to toughen up," said Father defensively.

"Mary and I will be here in the spring without fail," said Grandmother firmly, "to take care of these children and give them proper lessons."

"Eva will still have to do her work and the country will be as hard as it is today. Your being here won't change the country, Mother."

"I don't want to change the country. I want to change you and your terrible ideas of training children," she shot back at Father.

"Where did you go today, Eva?" asked Father, ignoring her as he tried to change the subject.

"I went up to the Picacho."

"By yourself?" asked Grandmother.

"Yes, by myself. I always go by myself. On Diamante, though."

"Did you go up there, Eva?" asked Father with a big smile on his face.

"Yes, Pa. Diamante and me, we went to the top of the Cerro."

"And what did you see up there?"

"I saw plenty, Pa."

"What do you mean by plenty? Plenty what?"

"Butterflies. Millions and millions. They took off from a log and they looked like lace in the sky."

"Eva, I am proud of you for having gone up by yourself, but don't tell me yarns. Remember, I'm not old man McTavish."

"But I *saw* them Pa. They got on Diamante's mane and on my hat. They did. They did, Pa."

"She did see them, Agustín," said Mateo. They're migrating. We see them in Mexico very often."

"Sure, you see them in Mexico, Mat, not here."

"Yes, here too, Agustín. They go north to Canada. She was lucky to see them. That is a beautiful sight, and when they're clustered on a tree people go miles just to see them."

"Yes, Mateo, they were on that dead tree that is on the Picacho," I said.

"Well," said Grandmother Wilbur, keeping her eye firmly on the point that concerned her, "I don't care how beautiful they are. Eva has no business up on the Cerro alone. You," she said to me with a very stern look on her face, "should stay home and learn to cook and to sew. Someday you'll grow up and get married and have your own home and your own family, you know."

"No, Grandmother, I will never get married," I told her.

"Why not? You would like to have your own family, wouldn't you?"

"No, Grandmother, because if I got married to a man who talks to me like my pa talks to my ma, I'd just feed him poison, you see, so I can't get married at all," I said with perfect infant logic.

I have often wondered since what I would do if I ever again found myself engulfed in a silence like the one that followed my statement that night. No one spoke. Father ignored me. Grandfather wiped his face with his large blue handkerchief and sat without a word. William, always so noisy, became silent and motionless except for the spoon swinging in his hand. Mateo sat with a sober face staring up at the picture on the calendar that hung on the wall across from him, a picture of a bull, a cow, and a little calf that was butting the bull on the chest. Mateo looked at the picture and then at me. I smiled, unaware that the silence was my doing, and his sober face turned leather red. I wonder what I would do now with such a total vacuum. Would I get up and leave, challenge someone to speak, ignore the cruel silence, or what? What does one do in a sea of silence? As a child then, I unconcernedly finished my dinner.

The Farewell Dinner

T HE BLOWS OF THE AX AT THE WOODPILE woke me up, and I slipped out of bed quietly. In the kitchen the first relay of breakfast was over and Mother and Rita were resetting the table. Juana had been peeling apples all morning and was now going after the cleaning equipment.

"Ma, I want my breakfast on the little table by the stove." Mother set before me a baked apple with cream and left hurriedly, returning with a blanket which she wrapped around me. She set my pants and shoes next to my chair. "Eat and dress quickly," she said.

"Yes, Ma."

Outside big piles of ashes showed where the bonfires had burned all night. Grandfather was loading the wood in a small cart.

"Where is everybody, Grandpa?"

"Mike, Mateo, and Barra are sleeping late. They worked all night. Pull that cart to the door of the *sala* for me." I pulled the load of wood and he followed with large chunks of fireplace wood. The *sala* felt cold and damp, but Grandfather soon had a roaring fire burning and crackling away. He rearranged the furniture and started to clean the windows. Juana came in with broom and dustpan. After she had swept, Grandfather took down the pictures from the wall and Juana began wiping them with a wet rag. Grandmother Wilbur came in carrying a bundle of ironing. She laid it down and began to help Juana, polishing each picture quickly as she handed it back to Grandfather to hang up. There was the picture of Grandfather Wilbur. Grandmother held it close to her for a moment and then handed it to Grandfather Vilducea. The picture of the Harvard Medical College was hung above that of the

Doctor. "That's the way he always had it in his office," said Grandmother, pleased. Then came my favorite—"The Return of the Grand
Army." I never forgot how disappointed I had been when I was told
that the man on the white horse in the picture was not my father.
Father himself had been upset when I insisted that he was the man
riding El Blanco. He was riding ahead of the other man, wasn't he?
Now Grandmother stood admiring the print as Father entered the *sala*.

"You know, Don Francisco," she said, "when Agustín was three
years old he used to cry when we told him that the man on the white
horse was not his father. And when Charles Poston came to see me,
Agustín told him, 'The man on the white horse is my father. My
mother says it isn't, but that's because she doesn't know any better!'"

Mother, who had just come in, remarked tartly, addressing my
father, "I'm glad to know that. It won't be long until William will be
saying that the man on the white horse is *his* father, and I don't want
to hear you scolding and chewing him up like you did the Star of your
Heaven!"

Everybody looked at me and laughed. "If you thought he was your
father, too, when you were a little boy, what did you scold me for,
Pa?" I asked.

"I want the Star of my Heaven to be smart, not dumb like me,"
Father told me.

Grandfather and Juana moved the long table near the fireplace and
Juana padded it with a folded blanket and laid a white sheet on top.
Here Grandmother Wilbur spread out her black dress to be ironed as
soon as the flatirons had heated up on the grill on the fireplace. While
Grandmother waited for them, she and my father and mother argued
about something that I did not understand. I tugged at Mother's skirt
to try to find out, but she ignored me and kept on saying to Grandmother Wilbur, "No. I will not. You invited them, you receive them.
This dinner is for the Indians, not for everybody."

"Hija, hija, we have to be attentive to the people," said Grandfather,
soothing.

"I have to be attentive to William and to Agustín and that's enough
to kill an elephant, and now you want me to be attentive to people.
No. Won't they be able to see that we'll have almost a thousand
Indians to feed? I will not be bothered!" And Mother stalked out.

"I'll be right out, Mat," Father called to Mateo who was waiting
for him to come out and handle the horses.

"Where are you going to receive these guests?" he asked Grand-mother.

"Wherever I can, but receive them we will. You and I. You under-stand?"

"Of course, of course," said Father, already on his way out. From that time on the turmoil grew bigger and bigger and more uncontrol-lable.

Tom Ewell came into the kitchen and said to Father that those who came to see the Indians should talk and mix with the Indians if they wanted to, but that they should not expect to be fed, too. "That's an imposition, Agustín."

"That's the way I feel about it, too," said Mother.

"They were invited," said Grandmother Wilbur, joining us in the kitchen.

"Surely they don't expect it, Mrs. Wilbur," said Tom.

"We'll see, Tom, we'll see," she told him ominously. She hurried back to the *sala* to straighten up and get things ready.

The men went to meet at the milkhouse to discuss the food problem. I held on to Father's hand and stood close while they talked. The milkhouse was cold and the men gave their opinions and suggestions hurriedly, but the available food supply remained the same and the number of Indians was growing steadily as small groups of them kept coming from the south and heading north to the Guijas Village.

"Only six months ago at the Fiesta de la Santa Cruz," said Celso Vargas, who had recently come with Uncle Mike, "you had a lot of people, Pa, and the food went around."

"Everybody contributed then, hijo," said Grandfather, "and then it was in the spring. We had lots of eggs and milk and cheese, and all the nopalitos we needed. Now, though, None Bernard has contributed one young steer and Agustín another, and the Soporeños have given us two sacks of apples, so we have the barbecue, apple turnovers, beans, and corn tortillas. We just don't have the food to feed all the Indians in southern Arizona."

"Pa," said Father, "why don't we ask Ramona what she thinks? She gets good ideas sometimes."

"Eva, go get your mother to come here, but be careful that Grand-mother Rafaela doesn't hear you."

"Hija," began Grandfather, when I came back with Mother, "it looks like we have more people than we can feed. The food is just not going to go around."

Mother took control of the situation even before she began to speak. "We do have enough food to feed the Indians, Pa, but we *don't* have enough to feed all the people of southern Arizona and northern Mexico. Agustín, you had just better send someone to the gate to stop everyone from coming in and to tell them that this dinner is for the Indians only. The non-Indians will not be served. Come on. Who wants to volunteer? We can't waste time because people are coming now. I just saw a buckboard coming around the hill."

"I will go," said Celso Vargas.

"All right, Celso, be very polite and nice but very firm. Will you?"

"Sí, Señora, and Celso got on his horse and galloped out to the gate.

"And, Agustín, you help your mother entertain her guests and keep her away from us. She can serve them in the sala and my mother and Juana will help her. That will give the rest of us the freedom we need to feed the Indians Indian-style without fear of her criticism!"

"Oh, we'll get that anyway, Ramona, no matter what we do," said Father resignedly.

"And now," Mother went on, "we have to have those who are going to dole the food out, and more important, we have to have someone who can move the Indians away as soon as they're handed their portion of food. Otherwise they'll circle and come back for more. Mateo, you and Pete and Carmelo with the help of some others can do that, don't you think?"

"Sí, Señora. I can do that," said Mateo.

"Now, the only problem is your mother, Agustín, and you can handle that!" Mother teased him though her voice was very firm and not at all yielding.

"But hijita, hijita," said Grandfather, "remember that some people might take offense."

"Ramona's is really the only way to handle the problem, Pa," said Tom Ewell, "and we'd better not waste time or we'll have everybody here. What do you think, Agustín?"

"I like the idea," said Father, "except this business of helping my mother with her guests. But I will do my damnedest to keep her away from here."

"Do that," said Mother. "That's a must and no one can do that better than you."

"Well, Pa," said Father, "you're the boss out here, then. Keep the goodwill and give everyone a word of good cheer. And you, Ramona, clean up your children and keep them under control." Father re-established his authority, pointing a finger sharply at me as he rapped out this order.

No sooner did we get out of the milkhouse than Don Julián drove his buckboard up to the door. He had come to buy a goat, and he wanted it properly slaughtered and dressed. So the goat herd was brought into the corral for him to make his choice. Mike and Mateo slaughtered and began dressing the goat while Father and Don Julián bartered and dickered over the price.

"Tell you what, Julián," said Father, "Have you any *tesguin* at your house?"

"I always have tesguin and mescal," answered Don Julián, and he went on to tell Father what he wanted for his end of the bargain. "The corrida is coming in the spring and I'll need some meat then when I go to feed the vaqueros, you know. So you can give me two young goats in the spring and this here goat now," he said, running his hand over the hindquarters of the goat that was being dressed, "and you can let me and Pepe eat some *barbacoa* now and I'll get you ten gallons of *tesguin,* and then I'll get in that kitchen and get everything ready for you for your feast today. I can cook and serve. I know how to organize and get things done. This is my work, after all, Agustín. I had a *fonda,* a restaurant in Santa Fe for years."

"Julián, that sounds great!" said Father. "But let me tell you exactly what I want you to do to get the three goats and dinner for the two of you. I want you to help the old man take the barbecue out of the pit and carry it to the kitchen to be carved and gotten ready. Then I want you to go in the sala and arrange the best way you can with a table to serve some of the people there in a civilized dinner, and we'll take care of the Indians out here."

"Who is coming to the sala, Agustín?"

"My mother is here and she has invited the Egurrolas, the Ahumadas, the Bogans, and the Bernards, and some other stragglers, maybe. They'll eat in the sala because the kitchen is always so crowded, you know, Julián."

"Well, show me the sala and the kitchen and the dishes I have to work with and I'll tell you whether I can help you or not. Let's go before they start coming in." And Don Julián turned and headed for the house.

I followed them in. "Ramona, Don Julián is going to do the serving, so he wants to acquaint himself with the house, the dishes, and the food."

"What a blessing!" said Mother. "Does my poor father know that?"
"We'll tell Don Francisco as soon as we get back. He'll be glad,"
said Don Julián, "I know."

Father took Don Julián through the house and introduced him to
Grandmother Wilbur. By the time Don Julián came back outside, the
Indians had begun to arrive. The young Indian girls were like bright
flowers in their greens, yellows, and reds. Lupita Boylan came wearing
a wide blue drawstring skirt that swept the ground and a white blouse
with a round neck which made her face look even more round than
it was. Her long hair, straight black and falling to her ankles, set her
apart from the other Indian women and made everyone look at her
twice. Her hair was not what we would call clean, but it was brushed
smooth and it clung together like a black cape, giving Lupita a cubic
figure. She was different. No other Indian looked like that—or non-Indian, for that matter. This large flock of Indian girls moved down to
the patio and stood looking like frightened birds that had fluttered
down in a strange place. All looked to Mateo for guidance and reassurance. Many of the older people sat along the wall or wandered about.
Our own most familiar Indian friends hurried to find my Grandmother
Margarita, so they ended up in the kitchen. María Nieves immediately
began to tell Grandmother how sad Lupita had been all week. "She
cry, she no eat," said María Nieves, "but today she better."

Tula, too, was very upset. "The creek our home many years," she
said. "I no like this going away from home."

While Mateo and Mike were dressing the goat for Don Julián, Father
took him to Grandfather, who was overjoyed that someone so efficient
was going to take charge of a job that had fanned out, growing to
embrace all sorts of other little problems besides that of feeding the
Indians.

There was the problem of serving my Grandmother Rafaelita's guests.
Grandfather knew them all, and it was embarrassing not to have ready
the nice things they were used to. Then there were my father and
mother: "Independent, aloof, unchristian," he said to himself, not
realizing I was listening. As he went down the slope I heard him asking
himself, "What's the matter with them? Where did they come from?
Dios mío, what made them like that?" And there were other people
who had found their way in and he had to ask Tom Ewell to make
excuses for his not receiving them. He couldn't do that himself. He
didn't know how and didn't want to know for he was a devout Catholic
and his very being was charity, love, and hospitality. Then, seeing the

familiar Indians going away, whom he had loved and agonized over, was frustrating and painful, too.

Amid all this bewildering confusion appeared Don Julián, ready to take charge of everything.

From the trunk on the back of his buckboard Don Julián produced a clean white apron and a tall white cap. Grandfather's melancholy seemed to fade away at last, and as he walked about helping Don Julián he had a spring in his step again, looked taller, and very straight.

"Now, Agustín," said Don Julián, "I'll be helping Pa here, and as soon as you want me to set the table up at the house you just bring Rafaelita's precious *monigotes* out here to be entertained and that will give me a chance to work at the house, you see?"

"All right," said Father, "when you see those elegant nobodies coming out, go right away. Don't wait for me to tell you."

"Understood! *¿Cómo no?*" said Don Julián.

The Bogans and the Bernards had just arrived so Father went on to greet them and I followed, as I always did. "That's old Phoebe, Pa!"

"Aunt Phoebe, Eva. I don't want to hear you talk like that again. Do you understand?" And we were at the side of the black buggy.

"Welcome to the *posta*, friends," said Father.

"Thank you, Agustín," said John Bogan. "We wouldn't have missed this for anything. We just came through the largest Indian gathering I have ever seen!"

"They are congregating to leave," said Father as he helped Phoebe down.

"Hello, cowgirl," she said briefly to me.

"Hello, Aunt Phoebe. My Grandmother Wilbur is here."

"So I heard, Eva. We are coming to see her before she goes back to Tucson." And Father led the way to the *sala* with me following close behind. Looking west of the house, I saw two women coming up the riverbank and recognized Marian McGuire and Helen Russel. Catching up with Father, I said, "Pa, here comes *la Lengona*." Father's look froze me to a standstill. I felt my heart galloping against my chest and my tongue going dry. Hadn't Father heard? Not too long ago I had heard Mother's Aunt Jesucita, wife of Tío Reinaldo, telling Mother that it was Marian McGuire's fault when Reinaldo tried to kill Father.

One day Father and I had gone to Arivaca to get the mail. On the way back, Reinaldo crossed the road on foot in front of our buggy. Father pulled up and asked him, "What are you doing afoot, Reinaldo? Where is your horse?"

"I come out to see you, Agustín," he said, pulling the gun out and walking up close to our buggy. "My niece, your wife, comes from fine people. Now I hear that she is wearing a parted skirt. Why, Agustín? You are going to account to me," he said, pointing his gun at Father.

"Oh," said Father, "you want to kill your best friend, Rey?"

At that Reinaldo relaxed his grip on the gun, shifted his eyes, and in that split second I heard the impact of Father's fist on Reinaldo's face. The gun arched above the road and fell in the brush. Reinaldo was struggling to sit up when Father jumped out of the buggy and struck him again. He then dragged him across the road and retrieved the gun. Father got back in the buggy, and we made a speedy trip home.

It was Marian McGuire who had been gossiping at the store, telling everyone that Father was raising me in pants, and now my mother, too, was wearing a disgraceful skirt, and that everybody agreed we were lost to the devil.

"Reinaldo was drinking and he got all excited, Ramóna," Tía Jesucita had told her, "but you are his favorite niece, Ramoncita, and if I were you I'd send him his gun back. I'll be glad to take it to him."

"No," Mother had answered her, "you ask Agustín for the gun. I don't have it."

Tía Jesucita had been horrified. "*No, el Americano es muy cabrón,* and I don't intend to be here when he comes, but I wanted you to know that *La Marian es una lengona*—a tongue wagger. She has the whole town in an uproar. She doesn't care what she says. Every man is a thief and every woman is a whore according to Marian."

And now here was Marian talking to Tom and pointing to the barbecue. Father had taken the Bogans and Bernards in the house, but he came out alone almost immediately, leaving Grandmother Wilbur with her guests. My heart threatened to come out of my mouth.

"Eva, if I ever hear you talk like that again I am going to give you the biggest thrashing you ever got." He wheeled away toward the corral in search of Mateo. Head down, I followed at a distance and when I got to the corral I stopped outside and looked in through the openings between the logs. Mateo and Tomás José were blowing up the goat bladder from the goat they had just dressed for Don Julián.

"What are you doing with that?" Father was saying, incredulously. "Don't tell me you fellows don't know that's a bladder!"

"Sure, Gus, we know," answered Mateo, "but I was telling the boys here what the Indians in northern Mexico use the fish bladder for," said Mateo.

"What *do* they use it for, Mat?" Father asked him.

"A condom," Mateo said.

I was always looking for a big word to throw at Phoebe, even after Mr. McTavish had told me not to do that. It was impolite, he said, and also, Phoebe was a very intelligent woman, and she would know that I was trying to put her down. But the temptation was too great this time. Condom! What was it? It sounded rolling and sonorous on my tongue.

I walked to the sala where Grandmother Wilbur was entertaining her guests. I stopped, got my breath, and then asked, "Aunt Phoebe, do you know what the Indians in northern Mexico use the fish bladder for?"

"No, little cowgirl, I don't."

"Eva!" exclaimed Dr. Ball who was sitting next to Phoebe. I ignored him and, backing away toward the door, said, "They use it for a condom!" The ladies dropped their jaws, opened their eyes wide, and furrowed their brows, almost as if they were one person. Grandfather, who had just come in, yanked me outside and actually dragged me around the house, calling me "*sin verguenza, malcriada, loca* (shameless, ill-bred crazy girl)!"

"Grandpa, you're going to pull my arm out," I cried.

"I'd like to pull your tongue out," snapped Grandfather. "You are truly *una lengona!*" He left me at the door by the wall to go in search of Father. I hid under some leaning boards that were stacked at the end of the wall and watched Grandfather flailing his arms as he talked. For the first time it dawned on me that some words scare people, just as the crack of my father's rifle scared the goat herd. Words could make people laugh, could make people cry, they could make them angry—they could actually *frighten* people, like the *monigotes* (rag dolls) in the sala who looked so frightened that they had frightened me. What had scared them so? I thought about it. I decided that the mention of the Indians must have frightened them. My mother used to actually jump at the mention of the Apaches, for my grandfather had told her about how he as a little boy had hidden inside an erosion hole on a bank. The Apaches had jumped over him, one by one, and run up the *cañada*, yelling and dragging the head of his father behind them. It had to be the idea of Indians that had scared the ladies.

I saw Father coming toward me and I trembled. "What did you do, Eva? What did you tell them?"

"I just told them about the Indians in northern Mexico, Papa."

"You go talk to the Indians, to Diamante, or to Hunga, but not to anybody else again tonight. Nobody. Do you understand?"

"Yes, Papa." And Father went back to the corral, got on a horse, and galloped toward the gate to find out why Marian and Helen had come up the river. It turned out that Marian had come to the gate and argued with Celso, who had delivered the message that the barbecue was for the Indians only. She told him that she didn't have to come through that certain gate and, apparently, she and Helen were approaching the house from the creek. They were almost here.

Don Julián now told Father that he had everything ready: *tesguin*, barbacoa, beans, and apple turnovers for Rafaelita's guests. "And I suggest that we feed the stiff-necks first and then the Indians. And we're going to need all the help we can get."

Helen and Marian arrived. "Agustín, we have come to taste the Indian fare," Helen said.

"Talk to Tom Ewell," said Father, throwing up his hands. He led the way to the serving table and Tom took two corn husks out and loaded them with barbecue. He handed them to the ladies and they stood aside, tasting the meat with pieces of tostada.

By now Ramón had taken the initiative and was bringing Grandmother Wilbur's guests out to show them the place. "Agustín," called Don Julián, "here come the *catrines* (dressed-up ones), so I am going to work at the house."

The "*catrines*" of that era didn't know how to be casual. Even here on a poor ranchito among poor peasants and nearly naked savages they were *Señores*, dressed up and formal every inch of the way.

"Oh here come *our* people, Marian," said Helen, and looking at Tom Ewell she asked, "May we join them?"

"If you were *invited*," answered Tom, who passionately disliked the Russels. Helen and Marian sniffed and looked embarrassed. They drifted over to talk to Prieto Murrieta who had just arrived with his violin and guitar.

Mateo and Tom began to cord off the serving area in order to control the Indians as they came to get their food. The guests stood on the slope above admiring the country and expressing their disgust with the milling hordes of Indians who were cluttering up that scenery at the moment. I noticed that my mother was with them, so I left Wahyanita, to whom I had been talking after joyfully spotting her among the Indians near the house. The ladies ignored me except for

Mrs. Bernard, who gave me one ferocious look. Grandmother Wilbur finally noticed me and said, "Ramona, I think Eva should go back and play with the Indians."

"No, Ma'am," said Mother, "Eva belongs here."

I stayed very quiet because John Bogan was talking to Dr. Ball about Grandfather Wilbur, and Dr. Ball and Mrs. Bernard were just saying that the whole thing was weird and atrocious. And how could Bishop Salpointe have accused his best friend of stealing two thousand dollars? Rowana and William Wright had lived near the Punta de Agua Ranch when my Grandfather Wilbur had been riding from one ranch to the other trying to keep up the two places. The Wrights were the closest neighbors, and Rowana and Grandmother Wilbur had become great friends. The Wrights arrived late that morning. I stood listening, trying to get things straightened out in my mind.

"Outrageous!" exclaimed Mrs. Bernard, but they continued to talk in undertones and I couldn't tell whether she meant the accusation was outrageous, the theft, the Bishop, or my grandfather.

"My husband and Bishop Salpointe," Grandmother was saying, "were the best of friends. They would work together and when the work was done they would ride horseback to the mission every day. I spent hours getting dinner for them and when they sat at the table for their evening meal I was the happiest woman on earth. All of a sudden, Rowana," said Grandmother, wiping her eyes as if to see things more clearly, "I began to hear ugly undertones and like a thunderhead they grew uglier by the minute. And the Bishop didn't come to our house anymore.

"One day I went to my sister, Engracía, and I asked her point-blank what was going on. 'Hasn't the doctor told you?' she asked me with a surprised look on her face. I told her that he had not, and that I didn't intend to ask him anything if he didn't volunteer to tell me about it. She had the most terrible look on her face and she said, 'Well, Rafaela, Bishop Salpointe says that the doctor stole two thousand dollars from the Obispario, and you know that the Bishop and the doctor are the only two people in the chancery who have access to the safety box.'"

Rowana's arms went around my grandmother's waist, for she was trembling as she told the story.

"I'll tell you, Rowana," said Grandmother, "I think I died for one brief moment. Everything went dark and silent, then I heard a loud ringing in my ears and I thought they would burst."

Dr. Ball went to Grandmother's side. "Only those who were envious of the doctor believe that, Rafaelita."

"That's right," said John Bogan. "Nobody can make me believe it. I never did!"

I saw tears in Rowana's eyes as she held Grandmother close to her. Grandmother herself stood like a statue, her simple black dress without frills, only the black lace sleeves that were so beautiful. The knuckles of her fingers showed white against the taut skin of her clenched fingers. She stood looking into the distance dry-eyed but obviously agonizing. I had been angry with her but now I felt sorry for her and I moved closer. I said, "And why couldn't the Bishop have taken it himself, Grandmother?"

"The Bishop?" asked Grandmother in horror. "Bishop Salpointe was a *holy* man, Eva."

"No, I have asked the same thing," said William Wright slowly. "And besides, I was once told that there never was two thousand dollars in that safety box." A murmur ran through Grandmother's guests, their voices rising and falling gently.

I stood, quiet for once, thinking about this old happening that we all knew so little about. Even my mother and father, I felt, knew little. I remember that my father had often been called to jury duty and when he returned home from this task he would talk to Mother about the details, the ordeals, and the amusing incidents that had occurred in the court battles of that day, so I had learned that a judge was a man who sat and listened to the arguments of the people who were "on trial." Trial was a battle in the courtroom fought by lawyers who used words instead of guns or fists.

Father's friend, Antonio Orfila, a great criminal lawyer of that day, had visited us often. He would talk about the necessity of warning his clients against making twitching movements and shifting their eyes, and he often said that a man was innocent until found guilty by a jury. So now, remembering all I had heard of this, I went to Phoebe and asked, "Did my grandfather have a trial?" No answer, just an impatient look.

"Well, if he didn't have a trial, how was he found guilty?" I said, louder now. They all stopped talking and stood looking at me. Had I scared them again? I turned to John Bogan and asked why my grandfather had not had a trial.

"I don't know, darling," answered John finally and he caressingly pulled my pigtails as he turned back to the group.

Mrs. Bernard smiled at me for the first time. She was very pretty when she smiled. "Eva," she asked, "What is a jury. Can you tell me?"

"A jury is twelve men who sit around and talk it over until they find out if the man on trial is telling the truth or lying." How strange, I thought. They no longer seemed to dislike me so. The whole group was now all smiles, all but Grandmother Wilbur.

"Eva, do you see where Che and Ruby are playing with your little brother William?" she asked.

"Yes, Grandmother."

"Why don't you go over there and play with them?"

"I don't like to play with them. Ruby pouts and William cries and Che just sits. If I want to play I'll go play with Wahyanita."

Mother threaded her way through the group and took my hand to lead me away, but Father, who had been looking for Mother to come and help Grandfather serve at the *sala*, had also come up and, seeing the amused smiles, he asked what had happened.

"Your daughter, Agustín, wants to know why her grandfather didn't have a trial in the affair of the chancery, and she also wants to know why Bishop Salpointe couldn't have taken that money himself."

"Good thinking, Daughter, good thinking!" exclaimed Father. "I always wondered myself."

"But what kind of talk is that, hijo? And how can a little child think like that? It just isn't right, Agustín," argued Grandmother.

"Come on, Mother, let's go see what you think of the barbecue." Taking Grandmother's arm, Father led the way to the *sala*. As we walked, one of the men wanted to know what method Father used to teach me such things. "She asks questions and demands answers and that's how she learned that a jury is not a cricket," Father answered. "You know, for a long time Eva thought that a jury was some kind of cricket and she once told old man McTavish that the juries went through the holes in the courthouse and that the judge had swatted every one of them. I guess I must have talked about the cricket invasion they had in that old courthouse and she got things mixed up."

"Cricket invasion! I never heard about such a thing," exclaimed Rowana, looking very confused.

"You remember the time the crickets were eating everything in the courthouse, don't you, John?" asked Father.

"How can I forget, Agustín? I was one of the things they went after!" Rowana and Virginia laughed. John Bogan had a great sense of humor and was always the life of a party. "You know," he went on, "one day I sat on a chair and put my feet on the desk there in the treasury department and a cricket ate a hole in my pants as big as a twenty-five cent piece and a twenty-five cent piece fell through the hole inside of my pants leg. Phoebe got mad at me for going to sleep on the job."

"But where did they come from, Beany?" asked Rowana. ("Beany" was John Bogan's nickname.)

"I think they came from the mesquite thicket that was right there only a few yards from the west wall, don't you think, Agustín?"

"Oh sure. Juán Elizardo used to sprinkle the ground between the courthouse and the treasury department and the coolness and dampness drew them. I saw old Judge Meyer swat crickets all through the Ortega trial. Remember, that, Ramón?"

"Yes," answered Ramón, "and Juán named him *El Mata Grillos*, the cricket killer."

"So, Rowana," Father continued, "the stucco inside of the courthouse fell off and there were holes between the adobes and the crickets used to come in through these holes."

"Really," said Mrs. Bernard, "that old courthouse is a disgrace! Did you know all that about that old courthouse, Eva?" she asked me.

"Yes, ma'am, I heard Pa telling my mother about the crickets and I thought a jury was a kind of cricket, but Pa told me what a jury really was."

"And does Ruby know these things too?" asked Phoebe.

"Of course not, Phoebe. When Ramona and I talk this one sits between us and listens and asks questions, but Ruby sleeps so she is not apt to know," answered Father.

"I don't understand why the other little girl is so withdrawn," said Phoebe.

"Some people are just like that, Phoebe," said John Bogan.

In the sala Don Julián, Grandfather, and Mother were serving now. Grandfather went around the table dropping *melcocha de granada* in the glasses. It looked like chunks of pink glass and the ladies admired it, asking what it was. "Caramel of pomegranate, just to color the drinks," said Grandfather.

"Smart!" exclaimed Phoebe, "and I want the recipe."

Don Julián poured the drinks and indicated everyone's place at the table. Prieto Murrieta came in with his instruments. Don Julián instructed him to keep the music in the background unless the guests asked him to do otherwise.

"Is that the portrait of your father, Agustín?" asked Mrs. Bernard. The guests briefly looked up at the portrait of Grandfather Wilbur and the talk again turned to the affair of the chancery.

"I just don't believe that anybody stole anything from anybody," said my father. "My father was a fine man from a fine school. He knew his values and I'm sure that he wasn't going to trade *oro por plata* by sticking his fingers in the till like some retarded *mendigo.*"

"You're right, Agustín!" said John Bogan. "Why trade gold for silver, as the saying goes. Besides he was already a firmly established man. I understand that this place was already bringing in quite a livelihood. Only last spring at the fiesta, Cruz was talking to me and he told me that this place had been a lively little money maker by then."

"That is certainly true, John," said Grandmother Wilbur. "This was a *posta* and people coming or going to Mexico stayed here overnight and paid well for their lodging. Besides that, the doctor was still the company physician for the Colorado Mining Company and the company paid him a regular salary for his services."

"Not only that," said Barreplata, who had brought in a wooden bowl loaded with barbecue, "Cruz and I delivered milk, cheese, butter, eggs, and half a beef to the mine every week. In the early seventies, Dr. Wilbur and Pedro Aguirre were the only two cattlemen in this area. You Bogans came later. The doctor had over two hundred head of cattle and Pedro had a small herd, so they were making good money from sales, too. And let me tell you, that Dr. Wilbur was a good man. He mixed with fine people. Governor Safford baptized his daughter, Mary. Didn't he, Rafaelita? Now, why," continued Barreplata without waiting for an answer from Grandmother, "didn't they have the man arrested if they really thought he did this thing?"

"That's what Eva wants to know," said Rowana, and everybody laughed. Barreplata left still mumbling and beckoning Father to follow him. But Father stayed on, talking to William Wright, who had just asked where the curly horses came from. Father explained to him that his father, the doctor, had brought the curly horses and some fine Morgans from Colorado. "And," said Father, "he also bought twenty-five brood mares from Juán Zepulveda, when Juán brought the 1,000-horse drive from Rancho Dolores in Mexico. Fine, tough little Spanish horses. They have been a godsend for us now in this era."

"So I hear, Agustín. Old man Moyza says that it takes five Morgans to do the work of just one of these little *criollos.* And your father was a good manager. He did an awful lot in the short time that he was here. And besides all that, he had the Indian agency, too."

"My husband knew how to do everything and he was a hard worker and a kind and honest man," said Grandmother.

"I heard that he fought hard to keep the Indian agency," said William Wright.

"Nothing could be further from the truth," said Grandmother Wilbur. "The truth is that he wanted to give that work up and establish himself as a practicing physician in Tucson so that the children could go to school when the time came for them to start school. The trips to San Carlos Reservation were a nightmare and his health was not holding up. He even wanted Cruz to take his place over so we could move to town."

"Yes, Rafaelita," said Ramón. "Cruz still talks about that. He certainly would have loved to move his family to this place."

Barreplata looked in at the door and said, "Please, Agustín, come give us a hand. The Indians are becoming impatient." Father left hurriedly and I jumped up and followed him to the outdoor kitchen where the Indians were now pushing against the rope that separated them from the serving area. Doña Tomaza had arrived and was excitedly looking for Father. "Agustín! Those Indians are going to mob those poor men and take the food!"

"Do you think so, Tomaza?" asked Father who appeared at a loss for a way to handle the situation. "What do you suggest, Tomaza?"

"Police it, hombre. A couple of men standing there with rifles will break the tension. Get that Indio to help you." So Father called Mateo, who came running up. "Mat, why did they divide like that?" he asked, pointing. All the men were along the riverbank and the women were on the slope of the hill next to the house.

"That's all right, Gus. They do that. The men go to their men friends and the women usually stay with the children and the other women. There are a hundred servings on the planks ready to be handed out." Just then one old Indian woman who had been away from the neighborhood for a long time followed the rope downslope until she stood opposite the loaded tables. "Put food. I take," and she held up four fingers.

"No, Viviana, we only give you food for you," Grandfather told her.

"Four daughters, me and man," and she raised her four fingers again. She called back to her girls and they stood up. The man she had called moved away from the line of men and joined his family. So Grandfather placed four servings on a large tray and Tom Ewell carried it for Viviana who led the way back up the slope where the four Indians suddenly sat on the ground and began to eat.

Other Indian women quickly followed Viviana's example and Grandfather, Barreplata, Tom, Tomaza, and Father were handing out food as fast as they could. Mother came out and she, Mateo, and Pete Boylan, with the help of some of the Indians, kept track of those who were being served. The need for rifles and policing had simply been eliminated, and the families all moved together to get their food, so the need for taking the food to them was also eliminated. Soon they were all moving in an orderly circle, picking up their rations and moving peacefully on to the sunny slope where they dropped to the ground and ate, their eyes on the distance. The hillside was soon covered with Indians all the way from the door of the house to the riverbanks. A few went to the corral fence and some sat along the wall as was their habit.

Marian and Helen appeared, finished with their food, and walked away toward the river. "They're going," I said, pointing them out to Doña Tomaza.

"Let them go," answered Doña Tomaza. "That Marian is a holy terror, a vicious gossip. Nobody lives according to Hoyle except Marian. She spatters on about society and nobody knows that sacred group except Marian. But nobody wants her around and she can't see it."

El Prieto Murrieta, who had been entertaining the guests in the *sala*, came out with his accordion. "That's a nice group in the *sala*, Agustín. They enjoyed the dinner. *Democraticos los Sajones*, Agustín, and your mother is in her glory. She took them into the bedroom to show them the bed of Moraga."

"¡Upale!" exclaimed Doña Tomaza, "*Está en sus verdes* (she must be in her greens—at her happiest), Agustín."

"Yes," said Father, "she must feel she is in her seventh heaven."

"But look at the Indiada, Agustín," whispered Prieto, suddenly pointing. "And all on the ground, Agustín. What does it mean?"

"I don't know exactly, Prieto. *Está acariciando su tierra antes de dejarla* (they are caressing their soil before leaving it)."

"That is it, Agustín, they are caressing their soil before leaving it."

"¡Ay Pobrecitos!" sighed Doña Tomaza. "They must feel bad and they were so good here, Agustín! They took the *bocado* (bite) that was offered them and moved away in peace. God bless them!"

"I'll find out if they want me to play something for them."

"Do that, Prieto." Father urged him, and we soon heard some of the *corridos* being played as some of the Indians and the men sang along with the guitar. There was a sad note in the voices of those who sang. The warm sunlight of that November day seemed to float in the air. The blue mist still cloaked the mountains and the peace and quiet of Indian summer lulled us as the Indians got closer to the ground, and Prieto stood somewhere in the center of the crowd, stretching his accordion to the left and back, to the left and back, again and again. I thought it was beautiful, but I heard Doña Tomaza whispering to Father, "It is all so very sad! The older people are heartbroken!"

"What can we do, Tomaza?"

"Bless them, Agustín, only bless them!" sighed Doña Tomaza.

The guests were coming out now, led by Ramón. Moving together they paused on the upper end of the slope. "Agustín," said Tomaza, "I will go sit in the buckboard so your mother won't be forced to speak to me. You know how she feels about me and so do I."

"You don't have to go anywhere, Tomaza. We are here together and I, for one, don't care who likes it or who doesn't. You just stay where you are."

The guests began to walk to the serving area where they talked a moment to Grandfather and Grandmother Margarita, to Mother, and to the boys who had served the barbecue, and then they came slowly on toward us. Tomaza walked away to the wall where she stopped to talk to María Nieves and Tula. None Bernard was first to arrive at Father's side, asking him what the Indians were doing on the ground.

"Sunning themselves, hombre," said Father.

Tom Ewell approached them and interrupted with a very serious look on his face and the question everybody was asking: Why did the Indians have to leave and who told them to leave?

"Their answer to that," said Father, "is that the government men drove them to the 'reserva' and they were told that they would be driven back again if they ever left it, so they want to go on their own. John Bogan and Phoebe approached the group and said that the government had never asked the Indians to leave. Barreplata stopped to say that he had seen the government men drive the Indians out of the Cieneguita Wash. Phoebe wanted to know just how Barreplata knew that the men he had seen were government men. "Well Doña Feebe," said Barreplata, "do you think the government men came dressed in suits of stars and stripes?" The Russels, Dr. Ball, and others came asking the same question. An argument ensued and finally Jesús Manzanares said that his father had told him that Mexican cattle interest had driven the Indians to the Indian homeland, which at that time was known as the "reserva" but in 1916 was officially registered as the Sells Reservation.

"And when was this?" asked Ewell.

"Maybe in 1850," answered Barreplata. Before the Gadsden Purchase! It sounded feasible. Everyone agreed that it could have been.

None proceeded to tell Father how he had enjoyed the dinner and the visit with Grandmother Wilbur. The rest of the group followed, all saying their thanks and their goodbyes. Soon their surreys and buggies were on the road and Grandmother Wilbur was left standing there by Father. She asked him something about "that *persona non grata.*" I could barely hear her and the words I heard I didn't understand. Father answered her in a firm voice and Grandmother walked away toward the house. Doña Tomaza came back to talk to Father. "Lupita Boylan just now told me that Jesús Moraga will come by early in the morning, Agustín. She tells me that he will bring his wagon and will take all the crippled Indians who can't walk. Your mother will probably enjoy a visit with Jesús, Agustín."

"Yes, Tomaza, she will. I don't think she has seen him for twenty-five years." My heart pounded again and I felt disturbed. I didn't like Jesús Moraga and yet Father always called him "Pariente."

We watched the Indians who were now moving away slowly in all different directions. Tomaza threw her arms around Father and thanked him.

"That's all right, Tomaza," he said. "If you want to come in the morning, don't hesitate."

"Grácias, Agustín. I must go see the old man now," and she went in search of Grandfather.

"Come, Eva." Father took my hand and we went in to the kitchen where he built a big fire and asked Mike to kill and clean a couple of young roosters. He then called out to some young Indian children and offered to pay them to pick up the cornhusks and other trash lying scattered in the yard. Tomaza passed by the door, taking long strides and waving at us as she left. "I might come in the morning, Agustín."

Mike came back then with two cleaned chickens and Father quickly fried them in the twenty-four-inch skillet. An hour later he went out carrying a big wooden bowl loaded with fried chicken. By now the yard was clean and empty. All the Indians had gone and the boys were smoking their cigarettes alongside the wall. The sun was hanging off the right shoulder of the Cerro, looking as if it sat there on the mountain.

"What are you going to feed us now, hombre?" asked Mateo.

"Not for you wolves," said Father, and he handed the bowl to Grandfather. "This is for your friends across the creek, Pa," he said of the victims of the white plague who Grandfather still cared for.

"Ay, hijo!" exclaimed Grandfather, "I already sent Margarita to the house to see what she could find for them. Those poor people, Agustín, they must think we have forgotten them. Come, Tom, go with me." Tom and Grandfather hurried off to feed his white plague patients for the night. I heard a child crying quietly.

"Are *they* over there, Pa?"

"They have been there all day, Eva," answered Father, and he took my hand and led me back into the house where we met Don Julián and his grandson coming out.

"Well, Agustín, everybody was fed and I dare say the *barbacoa* was the best. ¿*Cierto*?"

"*Cierto*, Julián. Everything was good and appropriate. I was very much pleased, and I appreciated your help very much, Julián."

"*Gracias*, Agustín, y *hasta luego*." And they left, the last to go.

It was now dark, cool, and quiet except for the usual yapping of the coyotes who came to the creek every night. I listened for the familiar noises of the Indians, but I heard none. This is the way the nights would be from now on. Silent!

Yours Is the Land

THE DAY AFTER TOMORROW WAS HERE, cool and blustery with strong gusts sweeping the ground clean and buffeting the chickens down the hill to the protected areas between the walls of the scattered one-room houses. Big clouds hiding the mountaintops signaled a storm was on its way.

"Come and have your breakfast quickly, Bonnie," called Mother as she set the customary bowl of white rice and milk before me.

"Who are those people out there, Ma?"

"Just the neighbors. They've come to see the Indiada leave."

"Did the *lengona* come too, Ma? She was just here last night."

"Bonnie, if you insist on talking like that your father is going to blister you. Do you understand me?"

"But that's what your Tía Jesucita called her, Ma."

"*Malcriada,* vulgar girl!" Mother threw at me, exasperated. "You will call people by their names and not by what Tía Jesucita calls them. I'll talk to you about this again, but not just now. I must wake up Ruby or she won't have time to eat her breakfast."

I sat eating, spooning up rice and watching Grandmother Wilbur going out and coming in, out and in, over and over. She appeared perfectly calm and serene, but even I could tell this was a pretense, and Mike confirmed my guess when I overheard him say to Aunt Rita, "Rafa must be worrying about the *persona non grata* coming back today. She just doesn't know that in this neck of the woods that lady is a 'grata.'"

I did not understand all Mike's words then, but somehow I knew just what he meant. In our cruel and rugged country one who would help others—who could even save lives—was a first-class citizen. Doña Tomaza was a *curandera*, a practical nurse and a good midwife. And she was always ready to come and help others as she had come to help us so many times. The mistakes she may have made in her own life were her own affair. The people in the valley were willing to forget all they had known or heard of her lurid past, because when trouble struck them now, Doña Tomaza was there. She had come this morning very early and positioned herself comfortably on the east side of the wall where most of the neighbors greeted her with respect and affection. She had deliberately stayed out there, half-hidden, so that she would be able to see the Indians leave without Grandmother Rafaelita's knowing she was anywhere near. But my grandmother apparently sensed something was in the air anyway, something she did not like, and she had not been able to sit still.

Mother helped Ruby and me to dress and told us that we could go out to the wall, but to be sure not to mention to Grandmother Wilbur that Doña Tomaza was out there, too. Around the corner of the wall we found Mateo and Tomás José talking to Doña Tomaza as they looked over their riding gear. At intervals they would look up toward the *llano* (a clearing) to see if the Indians had started gathering. The boys were planning to start their long ride ahead of the big horde.

"You're going, Mateo?" I asked him.

"Yes, Bonnie, but we'll come back. ¿*Cierto*, Tomás José?"

"*Cierto*, hombre, and I going to miss the good vaquerita who saved my life," said Tomás José. "You take good care of that Doradita, Eva. She be good saddle horse."

"You coming back too, Tomás José?"

"Yes, Eva. I want come back." He stopped talking and looked off at the *llano*. Finally, he went on. "Maybe long time, I come back. Remember I go on salt caravan in the spring. You pray for boys in caravan?"

"I will pray for you, Tomás José," I told him, "but when is spring?"

"When you hear *pitayeras* (whitewings) sing, it is spring, and then I will go. Then you pray. Will you pray?"

"Yes, I will, Tomás José, but don't go in the sea. Stay out of the water. And when you come back bring me some *conchitas*, will you?" He promised me to stay out of the sea and to bring me conchitas, but there was a very serious look on his face I did not understand. Tom Ewell was suddenly standing beside us. Grandfather wanted to give the boys his blessings before they left, so they followed Tom, talking and looking up anxiously at the clouds that were speeding over the mountains. I ran ahead and was in the *sala* before them.

Both my grandmothers were there and prayed with Grandfather. The prayers over, the boys went to the kitchen to say goodbye and shake hands with my uncles, Mother, and Aunt Rita. Then Ruby and I dogged their footsteps as they went to get their horses. Mateo was telling Father how he hated to leave him with so much work, but that he had to help his own father with the preparations for the *caravana.* "And then after the boys leave," he said, "I'll have to stay and help with the work there until they all get back from the salt pilgrimage. So when you come to the corrida, Gus, don't pass us by. I'll really be looking forward to seeing you by then."

"Sure thing, Mat, and you tell your father I wish him a good trip and tell him I wish I could go along."

"*¿Bueno, Agustín, hasta la otra vista, eh?*" Mateo and Father hugged each other and gave each other punches in the back, laughing. Father thanked Mateo very formally for all the help he had given him.

"It was fun, Gus." Mateo turned away and swung onto the saddle. Everyone on the wall stood up to wave as the boys rode away, and I ran along their flank yelling, "Remember, Tomás José, don't go in the water; don't go near the sea!" And the Indian called back to me, "I will not forget. You remember pray for me all the time when the *pitayeras* sing."

They disappeared around the curve of the *lomita* and I stood looking at the tracks of their horses going away. Soon the wind and the rain would come and wash them away. Then there would be only what Grandmother Margarita called *recuerdos* (memories).

Back at the wall Doña Tomaza was drinking a cup of coffee Grandfather had brought her. "I hear the wagon coming and your Pariente, old Moraga, yelling his head off, Agustín. He is bringing Manuel Manzo from the Sopori village. Manuel is over a hundred years old, you know. He could never walk all that way."

"I hope Ruta will take Brijida in the wagon, too," said Father. "You know how that poor old Indian is now. Carmelo told me that she lies bedridden on the ground all the time. And there are some other cripples that can't walk anymore. A good thing they could get Ruta to help them."

"Sí," said Tomaza, "but Carmelo Tosco offered him a wagonload of ollas and baskets, and I think Ruta can sell them and get a little money, so it won't be just out of the kindness of his heart he's doing it. It couldn't be, after all," she added, "not if he's related to the mestizos."

"No, Tomaza," Father said, "the mestizos are a lot like you—money hungry!" Doña Tomaza laughed and threw her arms around him. "Don't you worry, Agustín. Me and the mestizos may be money hungry, but there's a lot of love in our hearts, too, and we're ready to give a helping hand when it's needed, and that's more than some others I could name would do!"

As the old wagon came trundling over the ruts across the *llano* toward our house I pulled at Father's hand and led him away. "I want to tell you something, Papa, and I don't want them to hear me."

"Well, what, Eva?"

"Papa, please don't tell anybody that Ruta Moraga is your relative. Will you please don't do that, Papa?"

"Eva!" said Father, laughing. "And why not? We *are* related. Lieutenant Moraga was the very last conquistador to come to Arizona and he is one ancestor I'm very proud of."

"But did he *look* like Ruta, Pa?"

"Oh, Eva, he traveled with Juán Bautista de Anza and they had beautiful horses and good saddles and dressed according to their rank, and so I suppose he looked a lot better. What difference does it make? Poor Ruta has a very hard time making a living, but the Moraga blood runs in his veins and in ours, too."

"I don't care about blood, Papa. I just don't want you to say you're related to that *barbón*," and I pointed to where the bearded one was already tying his lines to the brake.

Father sighed. "Trust me, Eva. When you grow up you will understand better about people who choose to have hair on their faces and the people who don't and about blood and a lot of other things." And he called back to Ruta Moraga, "Buenos dias, Pariente, how is everything with you?"

"Fine, Agustín, fine. I came to bring Manuel Manzo and to pick up other crippled Indians as we go. And how are you, Chiquita?"

"Fine," I mumbled, digging the ground with my big toe.

"I guess the Indiada are leaving us, Agustín."

"Yes," said Father, "pulling out this morning. Mateo has already left."

"We're going to miss these devils, Agustín, mark my word. . . . I stopped to see your mother, Agustín."

"Sure," said Father, "she's expecting you, Jesús." And Father led Ruta and the old, old Manuel Manzo into the kitchen. Grandmother Wilbur came and Ruta took her in his arms. I was surprised that she didn't object, because I was very conscious of how his big, rough hands looked on my grandmother's spotless white blouse.

They sat for quite awhile over several cups of coffee, talking about old times. Manuel, an Indian who was *muy castellano* and spoke very fluent Spanish, told us that he had been born in San Miguel de Allende, way back in 1810. He was almost a hundred years old, he said proudly. He went on to say that his father had told him many stories of San Miguel de Allende in even earlier days, in his father's own time—of how in 1774, Juan Bautista de Anza with Alférez José Joaquín Moraga, the famous ancestor of Ruta, had left San Miguel together with their families, horses, cattle, chickens, and masses of equipment to go and explore the north.

"My father told me," said Manuel, "that the people of San Miguel had given the explorers 'peecky-neecky' (he meant a picnic) right at the foot of the Montezuma Mountain. He told me how different that festive day was from the day the expedition left for the Territorio, except it wasn't the Territorio then. He said to me that the dawn came with a funeral atmosphere, that everybody was silent, and even the chickens tiptoed across the yard. The people had a mass, and the bell tolled, and the ladies went to mass dressed in black with their black mantillas, and the white handkerchiefs stood out like white flags in their hands."

"Yes, Manuel," said Grandmother Wilbur. "Those who left and those who stayed knew well that they would never again see one another. The parents and the friends who stayed in San Miguel were mourning the loss of their dear ones. *Mi tío, el padre* (my uncle, the priest), has told me this same story about this day in San Miguel."

"And you know, Señora," the Indian continued, "in 1874 I went to San Miguel and everything was different. The town had grown great and the Spanish flag was gone, replaced by the Mexican flag. There were stairways winding up the slopes of the Montezuma. At the peak of that mountain is a spring—el Chorro they call it—and that was the only thing that had not changed. Its water was still plunging down the side of the mountain, beautiful as ever."

Mike was standing at the door looking out, his cup in his hand, as all the older ones reminisced, and now he called to them so excited he could hardly talk, "The Indians are coming to the *llano!*"

"¡*Vámanos*, Moraga, *vámanos!*" urged old Manuel.

"*Bueno un millon de gracias,*" said Ruta. "We must go and pick up old Brijida, poor thing. I'll stop to visit with you again, Rafaelita, on my way back. I am so glad you got the old bed back. If you ever want to sell it I'll buy it from you."

"Sí, Jesús, stop by here on your way back," answered Grandmother Wilbur.

They left and all of us but Grandmother Wilbur ran to the wall and craned our necks to see the Indians coming. They were coming out of the arroyos on the east side of the pasture. They were oozing out of the thickets and washes and climbing over the ridges of the nearby hills. All moved toward the center of the llano where some put their wares down and sat down to wait; some stood silent; others wandered about impatiently.

The gathering was growing ever greater as more Indians continued to join it from all different directions. Suddenly we saw our neighbors, the Indians from the Guijas village, emerging from the north thickets. They came tumbling out like a flash flood and joined those who were waiting in the llano, mixing and milling around like cattle. Finally, the masses quieted and stood waiting for what seemed to us a long time.

More Indians were coming from the south now, crossing the creek and going past us only twenty feet from the wall. Some waved to us. Some of the women were carrying large ollas on their heads and the children walking at their flanks laughed, stumbled about, fell, and rose again in mock pantomime. These Indians were carrying sacks of bellotas and some of the women stopped to trade the acorns for jerky or cheese.

There were Viviana and her husband, Sayas. "Sayas" was only a nickname, like so many of the others; his real name was Ricardo Rosario. I remembered a day when I was riding behind the saddle with Father and we met Ricardo Rosario with a big sack on his back and Father had said, "*¿Qué hubo, Sayas?*" The Indian had grunted in answer and Father had asked, "What have you in that sack, Sayas?"

"Sayas," the Indian had answered him and later Mother had told me that people called him Sayas because he was always up and down the hills hunting for the *sayas*, the tubers that were like wild carrots.

Viviana and Sayas came to the wall now and greeted Doña Tomaza. Then Sayas spoke to Father, telling him how very sad it was to leave the creek.

"*Muy triste*, very sad to go," he said, and I saw Viviana putting down her head and tears dropped on the back of her gnarled hand, running down her arm to the point of her elbow where they gathered and fell in larger drops onto the dry earth on top of the wall. They left a wet circle the size of a silver dollar.

I was jolted. For the first time, I think I realized that the Indians were leaving the country *forever.* I ran to Father who was getting some jerky for Viviana and pulled his jacket, "Pa, are the Indians going away for good?"

"Yes, Eva. For good."

"Is that why that whole bunch of Indians are at the *llano?* But Mateo said he was coming back, Pa!"

"Yes, Eva, but the Indians aren't going to be around here anymore, even if Mateo does come back to visit us."

"Won't they come back here at all? Won't they come back to their *jacales?*"

"No, Eva, there won't be any Indians here again."

"Just us? And the cattle and the horses and goats?"

"That's right, Eva. Mateo will come back to see us, though, in the fall next year."

I stood silent, looking at Viviana and Sayas hurrying off to catch up with their group, which was trudging on toward the *llano.*

"You know, I didn't realize there were so many Indians along our creek, Agustín," said Celso Vargas. "There must be more than five hundred at the *llano* now and more coming."

"At least. And more are leaving from San Luis, you know," said Father. "Some are coming from the Cerros Prietos, too. This is Indian country, Celso." Indian country. And now it would no longer be that. How could it be Indian country with no Indians, I thought, confused and frightened. I could not yet take it in.

In the *llano* now one man began walking westward and the others began following him, single-file. Soon all the Indians were moving like a massive slow flood. Father ran to get Grandmother Wilbur, but she called to him that she could watch from the door and did not want to come out to the wall.

"There they go," yelled Mike. "*Pobrecitos,* Agustín. It must be tough for them."

"Damned tough, Mike," said Father, and all of us on the wall fell silent. The only sound near us was the *tang-talang-talang* of the bellgoat as the herd moved toward the creek. The wind brought down a rain

of yellow cottonwood leaves and swept them across the ground past the wall toward the north.

The Indians were now coming toward us, straight south, silent, and looking straight ahead of them. We could see their faces glistening against the morning sun. Pete Boylan was leading them, walking with a deliberate step that said he was not only certain where he was going, but was assuming full responsibility for those he led.

"There's Ruta's wagon coming out of the thicket, and boy, is he loaded!" exclaimed Mike. The wagon kept going downhill ahead of the horde and Ruta and Manuel waved from their high seat as they finally disappeared down the road. "And there goes Lupita Boylan now," said Grandmother Margarita. Lupita stood out even in the distance with her abundant black hair.

The Indians wheeled and turned due west, passing some two hundred yards from us. María Nieves broke away and came running to my grandparents. Tula came following her and, one by one, the Indian women we knew pulled out of the group and came hurrying toward the wall. Its discipline broken, the whole horde swayed uncertainly and Pete Boylan seemed to be following his crowd instead of leading it. The very Indians who had so often annoyed us were the ones who broke our hearts now. La Chueca, Carmelo Tosco's sister, and Big Lola, who was Dreyah's mother, and who had been a very unfriendly Indian, now came toward us with baskets of saguaro jam and nuts. She gave one basket to Mother and one to Grandmother Margarita, telling them brokenly how much she would miss them. Her life was hard, said Lola, "No time for friends I love," she moaned, repeating it over and over. Belen and countless other nameless ones said goodbye and moved on in distress. Belen stood for a moment with one arm around Father and the other around her own daughters. "Come to see us, Agustín. You know we be heartsick and lonely in those awful sierras where we go," and Father promised to see them when he went to the corrida.

Wahyanita and Dreyah, Lupita Ríos, and Chepa Soltero, my Indian friends who were so often with me came, too, with some others who had usually been less friendly to tell me how much they would miss me. "We play with you in creek again someday," said Dreyah, crying. Chepa, Lupita, and Wahyanita had wrapped their arms around my legs, which hung down from the wall where I was sitting. "You come play with us," said Lupita Ríos. "I no stay—I come back," Wahyanita whispered to me and we both laughed.

I saw María Nieves reach my grandmother, throw her arms around her, and cry, "*No te olvides de mí* (don't forget me), Margarita."

"No, María," said Grandmother, "*no te olvidare nunca* (I will never forget you), and you remember all the happy hours we spent together." María wept uncontrollably.

Teresana, another Indian woman who had spent a great deal of time with my grandparents, came, too, to tell Grandmother how much she would miss her. She begged Grandmother to pray for all the Parientes. "All broken-hearted," said Teresana, "going don't know where. No need to stay. Gup'ment men will come and drive us away. They drive Pariente away before, many people died. People could not walk fast like horses and they hit people. Run down people. This our beautiful home. Now we leave before they come, Margarita."

"*Dios te bendiga, Teresana, y te de la fuerza que necesitas* (God bless you and give you the strength you need, Teresana)." And Grandmother wept as she said it again. "God bless you always, Teresana."

Pete Boylan, his horde broken and milling around, came in search of Grandfather. Pete was known to be a witch doctor who could put a curse on those he did not like or cast a spell and make them sick. Many rancheros thought him an evil man, but I knew that Pete had often come to the milpita and asked Grandfather to read from the book of God. I had seen him standing, nodding his head in approval while Grandfather sat at the trunk of the willow tree reading and explaining scriptures. Grandfather told us later that at the farewell dinner Pete Boylan had come to him and said, "Old man, read for us from God's book when we go." So Grandfather had copied some of the scriptures onto notepaper last night, so that if Grandmother Wilbur happened to see them she would not know that these things had come from the Protestant Bible, the forbidden book. He pulled these sheets of paper out now. But Pete would not have it this way. He wanted to *see* God's book. Now. It was important. "No, *not* paper," he said. "The *book.*"

So Grandfather went to the house and returned with his Bible hidden under his jacket. He stood beside the wall and began reading the scriptures that Pete knew best, ending with his own favorite: "Be strong and courageous. Do not be afraid or terrified because of them, for the Lord your God goes with you. He will never leave you nor forsake you."

Emilia Rosa, who had been looking at the book over Grandfather's shoulder, now tapped him on the hand that held the book, saying,

"It is good, like cool shower. I will come back. I no stay. I go where I want. God goes with me. *Cierto*, Pa?"

"*Muy cierto*, Emilia Rosa," he said, and Carmelo Tosco pushed through the crowd and said to all of them, "I in Poso Verde see black cloud *here*, and I, *there*, will say to myself 'it raining in home, Wilbur country,' and I come back all same as horse!" And he laughed boisterously.

"Good boy, Carmelo, you come back whenever you want," said Father. Carmelo shook hands with Father and hurried off, yelling back to the uncles that he would gather acorns with them again in the coming summer.

Pete had moved from Grandfather to Father. "Bueno, Agustín, all these people want me thank you for good dinner you gave us. We know you did not have to do this trouble for us, but you good brother. You hard man, but good brother, too, and now we part not just friends, but brothers." He solemnly shook hands, holding his left hand over Father's shoulder, saying, "Yours is the land and God is with you. We're happy to know you stay in our home. You take care our land." Then his voice trembled and he said, "*Quedate con Dios* (God be with you), Agustín."

"*Que Dios te bendiga y te ayude con tu gente* (God bless you and help you with your people), Pete." This was only the second time in my life that I had ever seen tears in my father's eyes.

José-José came next. He didn't speak well, like Pete, but he managed to make himself understood. "Many time hungry, many time you feed. I remember. You come corrida, you come see, in Poso Verde. God stay with you and all." He turned abruptly, and, going up to Belen, took her arms away from Grandmother Margarita. "Arriba!" he said. "We must go."

Pete Boylan again took his place at the head of the people, and, raising his hand high in a come-on motion, he began walking west. The young men followed him and slowly the crowd of Indians moved away from our wall to join them. They flowed over the slope of Pesqueira Hill, leaving a cloud of dust trailing over the mesquite thicket.

We stood silent a long time watching them move away. Grandfather followed them with his eyes, shading them with his hand long after there was nothing to see but the dust. His white beard quivered on his chest and he kept repeating, "*Vayan con Dios, vayan con Dios.*"

Epilogue

THE GREAT EXODUS HAD LEFT US STUNNED. We had known the Indians were going to the reservation, yes. But I think that most of us had expected them to leave one family at a time, day by day—and the *en masse* movement had exerted a powerful and unexpectedly frustrating impact on all of us.

That day, after the Indians had finally disappeared over the westward horizon, Grandfather led the way to the kitchen and sat at the "talking-it-over table." Opening and closing his Bible, he said, "We have seen the close of an era, *carisimos*. We are standing at the threshold of a new world, and we are not ready for it; but it is upon us. Things will be different for us from now on, so we must turn a page in our book and read on."

Already, this drastic, sudden change seemed to be invading our long-established way of life: Juana tiptoed from the stove to the table, Aunt Rita whispered, Ruby went about studying everyone's faces; and I, annoyed at myself, sat silent and bewildered in this odd vacuum, where everyone around me seemed to be looking for a way out. Suddenly, Father jumped up and put on his slicker, saying, "Going to get the mail. I'll be back right away."

"Being me a cigar, Hijo, to celebrate the newborn." Grandfather later told me he had meant the new way of life so suddenly thrust upon us, but Father had understood immediately, and had asked, "Is it a son, Pa?"

"Sí," answered Grandfather, "*es varón y muy macho.*"

"Don't forget I am leaving in the morning, Hijo," interrupted Grandmother Wilbur, unwittingly.

"I'll have you in Arivaca in plenty of time, Mother. The stage doesn't leave 'til eight o'clock." And Father walked off toward the stable.

Grandmother Margarita put her arms around Grandmother Wilbur and motioned for her to sit down again. "Juanita, please bring us some hot coffee." And as Juanita served them steaming cups of coffee with golden brown *buñuelos,* Grandfather tried to put everyone at ease again. "I just can't get over your coming at such an opportune time, Rafaelita, to see the poor Indians leave."

"I am glad, too, Don Francisco, even if it was such an emotional experience."

"Yes, it was in some ways a very sad occasion, Rafaelita, but at least you also got to see your son and your grandchildren. It was very good of you to come all this way."

"Yes," said Grandmother Wilbur, becoming a little more animated. "And, as for that"—looking sideways at me—"my daughter, María, and I will come again in the spring, to help with the children."

"It would be wonderful if you could come. Agustín and my daughter work very hard, and they don't have much time to teach the children. Margarita and I, we try to help them all we can. I manage to put a few fresh vegetables on the table; and I work hard to keep peace and harmony among the neighbors. All else is waste, Rafaelita. We try to live a Christian life, so that these children can see, and hear, and learn by our example."

"You are doing a wonderful job, Don Francisco. God will bless you both, and I must thank you again for inviting me to your little house— so full of a spiritual atmosphere. It is like a *capillita* (little chapel) on the side of the hill. That little visit with you was only a minute's retreat, but the healing way it had for me will last forever."

"Thank you, Rafaelita. *Dios te bendiga,* and don't forget to pray for us all. We will need your prayers." He was silent for a moment. "I have a premonition of tragedies ahead. I don't know why. I just don't know," said Grandfather, shaking his head from side to side. "But we are facing a great change. There is turmoil ahead, Rafaelita."

We moved aimlessly through a few chores, until Father returned with a stack of mail and a happier outlook, saying that the people in Arivaca were talking of national news. They had great hopes that President Taft, installed in office some months before, would do great things for the country. And Father had seen Federico Lara, who was on his way to Saric. Federico, who had worked for us off and on, had become a great friend of my grandparents.

"He was actually on his way to see you, Pa," said Father, "but with the storm coming, he decided to go straight across the Jarillas, you know."

"Yes, Hijo, yes, I understand." But Grandfather sighed as he took the letter Federico had sent him, and a package of cigarettes that Father had bought him instead of the cigar.

"I did mean to bring you a cigar, Pa, but they didn't have them in the store." Poor Grandfather, I thought. A letter instead of a friend. Cigarettes instead of his cigar. But he said, "This is great, Hijo. They are fine and thank you very much."

As evening came, the storm worsened, and Mother decided to have dinner early so that Grandfather and Grandmother could go home to their "capillita" and not be out late in the bad weather.

The talk over the evening meal was livelier, and when dinner was over, we all stepped outside to see my grandparents leave for the night. Mike led the way. He stood outside, listening to the muted noises of our deserted country, and he said, "The change is more chilling than the weather, Pa."

"Yes, Hijo, yes, it will be difficult. You will have to keep your hand on the plow and your eye on the furrow," sighed Grandfather. And my grandparents left for the night.

I remember so well from that night the eerie sound of the howling wind on the corner of the barn, the dark clouds speeding over the mountains, and the moon flying west. Many times in the years since 1909, they indeed seemed to me to have been forebodings of things that were to come.

Early the following morning, Grandmother Wilbur had her breakfast and went for a last walk along the riverbanks, up Pesqueira Hill, down the slope, around the corrals, and back to the house. She stood over the wood stove, warming her hands. "A bad storm is coming," she said, a catch in her voice. "I hope it doesn't last too long."

"The winters are always too long for us," said Mother, "but the spring will come."

Father brought Grandmother Wilbur's suitcases out, and Tom Ewell loaded them in the surrey. "On the way back, I'll stop at Miguel's and leave the surrey," he told Father, as they waited for the others to finish the leavetaking. My mother, my uncles, and grandparents—all seemed to have so much to say at the last minute. Praises, thanks, warnings, requests for prayers accompanied all the repeated goodbyes. Tom Ewell finally opened the big black umbrella and held it over Grandmother as he took her arm and led her to the surrey. Father put on his yellow slicker, turned up his collar, and mounted the Big Grey, wheeling him around so he could ride ahead of the surrey to see Grandmother Wilbur off.

Grandmother's departure was one more reminder that we were being left in a great space in a harsh land, now emptier than ever before of the Indian humanity that had peopled it for so long. There was a lonely, long winter ahead of us, and our whole ranchito began to seem more and more like an empty house. All that winter, we would find ourselves standing, looking up at the slopes of the neighboring hills, seeing Indians where there were none. As they had used to stand, staring westward toward the Baboquivari, home of their god I'itoi, now we stood, looking in the same direction for them.

The flow of news that we were so accustomed to suddenly stopped, as if its very source had dried, instead of its conduits, now lost to us. No more Indians arriving with bits of news from Yuma, Pinacate, or Magdalena, leaving to take *our* news with them to the next place. We were alone with the animals. By late the night after the exodus, the wind had died, and a heavy snow had begun to fall, so that the following morning the strangeness intensified, as we woke up to a weird, lonely, white world.

My grandparents' house leaked badly, so six days later, Mike, with the help of Dr. Ball, borrowed the Earle house for the winter, and the grandparents packed belongings into the buckboard and drove to the big house, two miles east of our ranch. Barreplata came in to stay in Don Ignacio's room, a one-room house away from the main house. He had finished fixing its roof ahead of time for this year, and he now spent his days shoveling snow off the roof, but the one-room house remained dry and warm for a time.

We stayed inside, mostly, listening to the beams and rafters creak. The third day after my grandparents had left, the rafters began to pop louder and more often, and Father became increasingly worried about the roofs of our part of the house on which the yearly repairs were still incomplete. The next morning, he loaded our cooking utensils and bedding in the buckboard, and we moved almost a mile away to the brick house, the storehouse of the Heintzelman Mill, long since burned and left abandoned. This house consisted of only one large room, so Father quickly put up partitions that gave us two bedrooms and a kitchen. It was a crude arrangement, but the brick house did have a gabled, slate roof that neither leaked nor popped, and so we were comfortable for the winter.

We would go back to the old house each morning to feed the chickens and goats and to milk the cows, returning to the brick house about noon. The blizzard finally stopped, but the snow continued to fall, fast and steady.

A few days after the blizzard winds had stopped howling, the roof of our sala at home caved in, and then the roofs of the other rooms followed quickly, burdened under more snow than we had ever seen before. We gathered the rest of our belongings and sadly made up our minds to spend the winter in the brick house. We missed the big house, and I missed my grandparents dreadfully.

They could not come to see us very often during that hard winter. Grandfather became bedridden. He had caught a bad cold early during that first blizzard and had not been able to get rid of it. His rheumatism, too, had worsened. We had gone to see them when we heard, and they had begged us to let Ruby stay with them. She stayed, and I rode back home with my parents and William. I felt helpless, stranded, and I missed the companionship of the Indian children. In my isolation that winter, even Carmelo Tosco would have been welcome.

I went around looking up at the trees for signs, and finally, one day, I heard the *pitayeras* (whitewing doves) sing and I knew it was spring, and I prayed for Tomás José, as I had promised him that I would. When we went again to visit my grandparents, Grandfather told me that he had dreamed of Tomás José. "I hope," said Grandfather wistfully, "that everything goes well with those poor Indian boys."

"Sure, Pa, they'll be coming back to see us soon," said Father; but he added quietly, "I hope."

With the way things were in early spring, Father just could not go to the corrida. He could not leave the ranch. Barreplata was hobbling around on crutches, and Father had to go over to get his breakfast nearly every day and see that he had enough wood to keep warm.

The corrida that year started at the Cerros Prietos, so the remuda had been driven by way of Las Guijas, and we didn't even get to see it. And, as if to make things worse for Father, Juán Zepulveda arrived one day, saddle-weary and hungry, from a long horse-drive to Kansas

City, where the stockyards were. He had seen a bunch of our horses watering at the Lakes in New Mexico, close to Stein's Path. "Are you sure they're W̲ horses, Juán?" asked Father.

"Agustín, Juán Zepulveda knows your horses when he sees them. Canelita is with them, Agustín, and she has two colts following her. But I'll tell you, Agustín, this problem of the horses roaming so far away will soon come to an end, because everybody is fencing now. Fencing, fencing everywhere. The open range will soon be a thing of the past."

Father threw up his hands and began to plan a trip to the Lakes to bring the strays home.

Nobody talked of having the Feast of the Holy Cross that year. My uncles and Aunt Rita and my mother worked in the milpita. Tom Ewell stayed close to my grandparents, helping them and doing errands for them. I knew Mateo wouldn't come. He would have to stay on the reservation and help with the work until the *caravana* came back.

I found myself longing for companionship as I had never done before, and since Diamante was the only companion I had, I spent whole days on his back. I went to the mountain as often as I could, hoping to see the butterflies as I had seen them that November day, when they had exploded and covered the whole mountainside, but I never saw them again. I rode to the mountain anyway, and finally, I fell in love with rocks.

First, I found a large, flint stone which I brought home. Father struck it with the edge of a horseshoe, and it sent out sparks of fire. The big boulder at the waterhole sent out a stream of water, and this small rock sent out sparks of fire. No wonder, I thought, that Barreplata was always saying rocks were precious. He worked and extracted a little gold, a little silver from them and made his living from the rocks.

I told Father another day that I had seen some rocks that had red roses and strands of green leaves all over them. "Lichen," said Father, "that's lichen."

"And does lichen know that roses are red and leaves are supposed to be green?"

"Well," said Father, "your mother's rosebush seems to know. I never see it with green roses and red leaves," missing my point, but making another of his own.

This was a tremendously intricate problem for me. How did the lichen know so well how to imitate the roses? I didn't talk to Father about it anymore, but I decided that there must be a God somewhere. My grandparents had always said so.

I explored the whole mountain, and I examined closely every rock I saw. There was a square rock with a flat top—a rock table. I climbed on it; and from there I climbed up a mesquite tree; and from its branches I stepped out onto a higher boulder. Looking down, I saw that this boulder had been split in the middle. No question about it—there was the other half right across from me. It had been pushed away about twelve to eighteen inches, and at the bottom, between the two halves, lay a black, round rock, about the size of a small watermelon and just as smooth-looking. I talked to Father about it one evening, and I asked him if he could get it for me. When he asked what I wanted the rock for, I could tell him only that I thought it was pretty, and very odd. "And," I said uncertainly, "it's like a different breed, Pa. It just doesn't belong to those big boulders. I think someone must have thrown it there." Father eventually did get it for me, and we brought the rock to the house. It became quite a conversation piece. Some thought it was a meteorite; others, that it was a volcanic rock thrown there when the volcano had erupted at the Cerro Colorado, some fifteen miles away, approximately a million years ago.

I began to hunt for arrowheads and tomahawks, and brought some home nearly every day.

The uncles, Mother, and Aunt Rita continued to work in the milpita; they raised green vegetables, watermelons, and some fruit, but when harvest time came, there seemed not to be very much to be harvested.

I knew by now that my grandparents were not coming back to their casita anymore. Tom Ewell came one day, driving Miguel's buckboard, and he loaded all the plants and took them to my Grandmother Margarita. Later in the summer, he came once again and brought my grandparents to visit us and to see the milpita. Both were very down-hearted, saying over and over how they missed the days when we were together, and the milpita was producing enough to feed all who came. "And I miss my *enfermos* (sick ones)," said Grandfather sadly. "I really do. And the Indiada! All gone from us!"

They ate lunch with us in the kitchen, among the shambles of the fallen roofs, and under a new, makeshift roof. They enjoyed it all and visited with us until suppertime. Father and Tom fried a chicken outside, and so we had fried chicken and corn on the cob for supper. Grandmother again made us her favorite drink, hot chocolate. Barreplata joined us for dinner, and we had a delightful time. "Just like old times, just like old times!" Grandfather kept repeating, joyfully.

Both my grandparents left that evening in good spirits, saying, "We'll come again, we'll come again!"—but they didn't. That was the last time we were all at the old house together.

Grandfather, Don Francisco Vilducea, died the next winter, and it has since seemed to me that much that was important in our lives died with him. A simple, but deeply feeling and intelligent man, he cared strongly for all people who came within his range. If he seemed to worry or disapprove of the barbarian he thought I was becoming, it was, nevertheless, not so much the family name he bemoaned as it was the effects my upbringing would have on my later life and the consequences for my immortal soul in which he devoutly believed.

He did not so much preach as *practice* the Christian code, striving to keep peace between factions, caring for the sick, and feeding the hungry wherever he found them, even in the face of insults and hatred. With his death also died in our valley the words *Hispanico, Anglo, Sajon;* and in their place, too quickly, came new, unpleasant epithets: *Mexican, greaser, spic.* And the Mexican Americans became to some an abomination, something to be annihilated from the face of the earth. And the Anglos became *gringos, topos, basura blanca,* looked down upon by many Hispanicos much as were the "Okies," later, during the influx from the middle west. Racial wars raged like wildfire in our valley for many years.

After I had suffered several ugly incidents at the hands of both hot-headed Anglos and Hispanicos, Father finally put a gun in my hands and said, "I don't ever want to hear or know that someone came inside this fence and hurt you again. This is your home. Defend yourself. If anyone comes in without permission, order him out, and if he doesn't leave, shoot him out." This was what we had come to. I was never again physically harmed, but I lived in constant horror of someday having to kill someone. Grandfather had once told me that if I ever deliberately hurt or killed someone, God would disown me. So, to be on the safe side, I learned to avoid people and to live by myself. I loved the land, the rocks, the plants, and the animals, for these things posed no cosmic problems.

When Grandfather died, Tom Ewell cut long, ribbonlike strips of paper on which he printed in large block letters: "KEEP THE PEACE, THE LOVE, AND THE HARMONY: ALL ELSE IS SAND." He had pinned these stringers on the wall just above where Grandfather was lying in state. Two large candles burned on each side of his coffin.

People came to pay their respects, saw the message on the stringers, and said, "That's like hearing him speak. We'll have to remember those words." But, of course, they did not.

In looking back, it has seemed to me that keeping "the peace, the love, and the harmony" had been Grandfather's life work. The devoutly Catholic Don Francisco Vilducea, with his practically memorized Protestant Bible, would spend days, sometimes weeks, helping to iron out the neighbors' problems, ever searching for some way to allay their anxieties and solve their difficulties.

Grandfather would spend hours defending the Anglos. I heard him saying to Miguel Egurrola one day, "The United States is in its cradle, Miguel. Don't be so thickheaded, hombre. They will not always believe that only a person with a very white skin can be an American."

"Are you so sure?" said Miguel. "The other day, I just asked Fred if he and his Anglo friends intended to camp at the Cochis, and he put up his fists and asked me, '*Quiere combate?*' In *Spanish*, he asked me that!" Miguel marveled.

Mother laughed, but Grandfather shook his head sorrowfully. Not too long ago, he said, he had been talking to a neighbor, a very well-known and wealthy man, whose name he would not mention when Mother asked, and Grandfather had said something about "Hispanicos." "And," said Grandfather, "he said to me, 'What are those animals?' How do you expect them to behave any better when they don't even know simple words?"

"I wrap up a whole year's work in the Feast of the Holy Cross," I once heard him telling Dr. Ball. "That's where I see our unfriendly people praying together, feasting together, and laughing together. The Fiesta is the time and the place where all can see for themselves what joy it is to live in harmony with our neighbors. Where peace and harmony are, there is prosperity, too. The discord and hatred always threatening us breed sickness, want, and such bitter unhappiness! But my Fiesta is the one time and place where people will listen. You have said to me, Doctor, that I suffer insults and threats. Yes, sometimes. But always, one day, they come looking for the old man, and ah! the battle is won. Their anger has been washed out of them, and they are ready to learn love."

Grandfather prayed constantly that his milpita would produce enough to feed all who came to him hungry; and while he lived, the milpita seemed truly a horn of plenty. When his trees along the river-banks were so heavy with produce their branches would break, when his *pizca* was so abundant he had trouble storing it, my grandfather was truly a happy man. He had gained the love and respect of all who knew him, but he found his own greatest fulfillment when his Anglos, his Hispanicos, and his Indiada came together to feast and worship in peaceful mutual understanding.

Not until the late seventies did I hear again these more dignified words, lost for decades, that seem to acknowledge peaceful difference: Hispanico and Anglo, just as Grandfather said it would be someday. To me, they sounded like musical notes in the throat of a songster in early spring, after a long, silent winter.

¡Glorificado Sea!

About the Author

EVA ANTONIA WILBUR-CRUCE has lived most of her life in Arizona. She bought her family's ranch some time in 1934 and has owned it ever since. She and her husband, Marshall, live in Tucson where the author now spends most of her time writing.